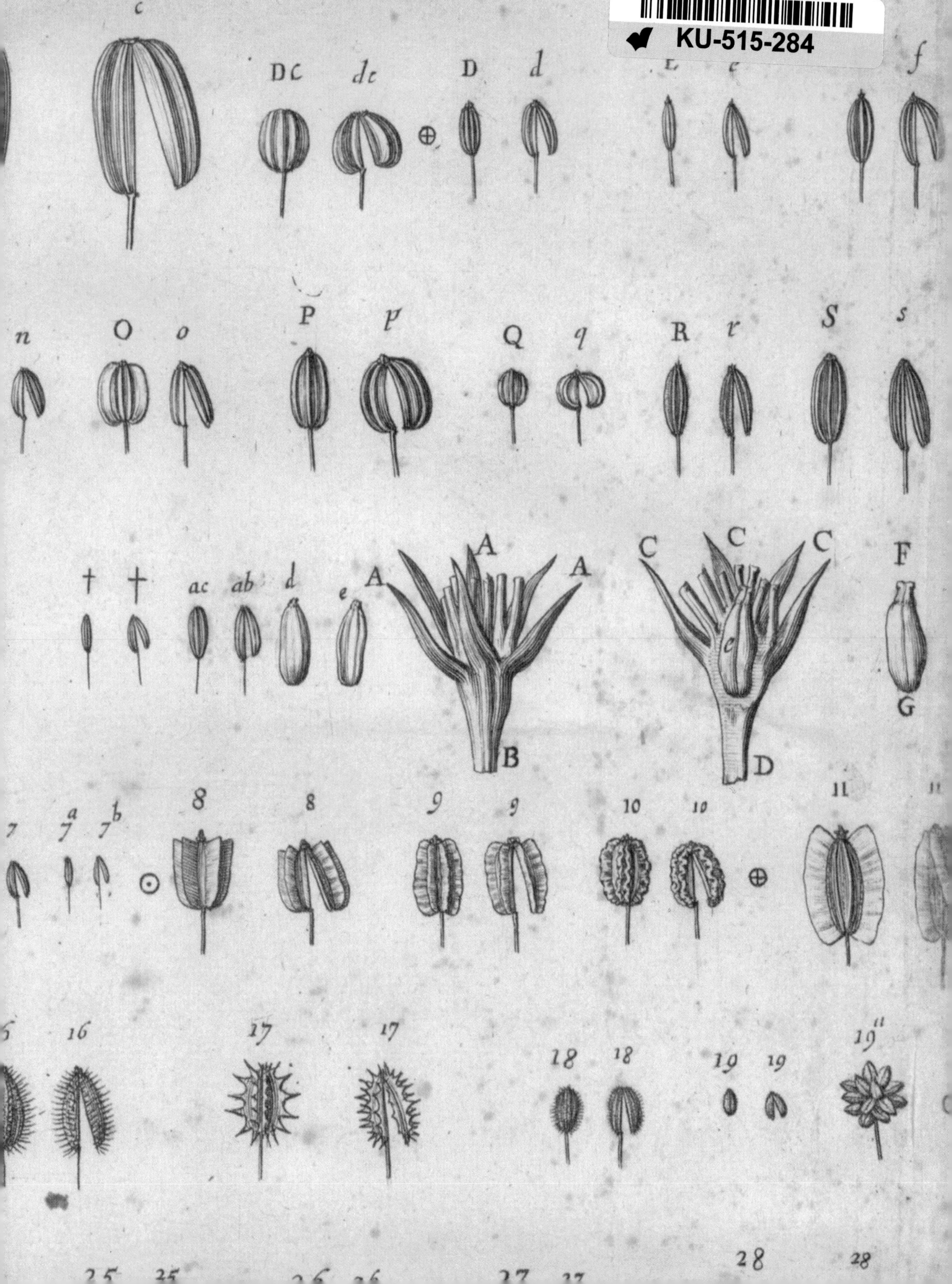
c
DC
dc
D
d
e
f
n
O
o
P
p
Q
q
R
r
S
s
†
†
ac
ab
d
e
A
A
A
A
B
C
C
C
e
D
F
G
7
7a
7b
8
8
9
9
10
10
11
11
16
17
17
18
18
19
19
19
28
28

THE NAMING OF NAMES

BY THE SAME AUTHOR

THE FLOWERING YEAR

GARDENING COMPANION

THE BORDER BOOK

THE NEW KITCHEN GARDEN

THE TULIP

PLANT PARTNERS

THE NAMING OF NAMES

THE SEARCH FOR ORDER IN THE WORLD OF PLANTS

ANNA PAVORD

BLOOMSBURY

Title page: A waterlily, here called by its ancient name,
'Nenufare'. This woodcut appeared in The grete herball
of 1529, the English translation of a book that had
been published in France in 1486
© *Royal Horticultural Society, Lindley Library*

Endpapers: Seed tables from Robert Morison's Plantarum
umbelliferarum distribution nova (Oxford, 1672)
© *The Natural History Museum, London*

First published in Great Britain in 2005

Bloomsbury Publishing Plc, 36 Soho Square, London W1D 3QY

A CIP catalogue record for this book is available from the British Library

ISBN 0 7475 7952 0
ISBN-13 9780747579526

10 9 8 7 6 5 4 3 2 1

Typeset by Palimpsest Book Production Limited, Polmont, Stirlingshire in Berling and Serlio

Printed and bound in Italy by Graphicom

CONTENTS

To Colin Hamilton and Kulgin Duval,
who were there at the beginning.

INTRODUCTION

HIDDEN DEEP IN the viscous gloom of Guyana's tropical rainforest are two monster waterfalls: Kaiteur on the Potaro river and Orinduik on the Ireng. No maps show the faint, foot-narrow trails that connect them. They are known only to the Patamona Indians who live here, and a few miners – Portuguese in origin – who set up solitary camps deep in the bush to pan for gold and dig for diamonds. Kaiteur, almost five times higher than Niagara, I'd first seen from the co-pilot's seat of a twin-engined Islander plane, flying with a prospector up to his camp on the Venezuelan border. We'd been following the Potaro river, which from the air cuts a series of wide, lazy, muddy loops through the dense canopy of trees. The green stretches from horizon to wild horizon, broken only occasionally by shocking red, where a vast tree explodes into bloom. On a whim, the pilot had brought the plane down low over the great arc of the Kaiteur fall, and landed it on a makeshift strip that he sometimes used, cleared from the bush. Beating our way through scrub, the noise of the fall dumbing any possibility of thought, we'd emerged by the wide, flat river at the very point where it throws itself off the edge of the world to land 820 feet below, in a narrow, rocky chasm of aweful savagery. Rainbows made and remade themselves in the spray that hung in the valley beneath the lip of the fall. Swifts darted behind the pounding curtains of water to the nests they had built on the rock face behind. Bromeliads and orchids shivered in the turbulence created when the torpid bulk of the river suddenly broke on the rim of the escarpment. Free of its bulk, it became air and prisms. Liberated, it flew. Here I learned of Guyana's second great waterfall, Orinduik, and of the trail that was said to connect it with

Kaieteur. The pilot did not know of anybody who had walked it, but a week, he thought, would do it, if we could find Amerindian guides to take us.

So that is why, six months later, I am stumbling, disorientated, through the filtered gloom under the canopy of this same rainforest. In front of me, a snake in a perfect camouflage jacket stretches out over the trail, motionless, disregarding. Without the warning from our Patamona guides, I would not have seen it. What sort of snake is it? I don't know, but they are indicating I need to treat it with the careful respect that they have shown. I know nothing here. I depend on the guides entirely. There are no roads, no signposts, no indicators. I don't know where we are, which way we are facing, how far we have travelled, how much further we will be going before our two companions decide to set up camp for the night. To 'How far?' or 'How long?' questions, they give the same elegant, liquid wave of the arm. That way. In time. So we continue to slither, and climb, and slip, and creep, and wade, and swim, and trip, and fall, and curse, and swing, and jump our way through this outlandish territory. Though so evidently familiar to our Amerindian guides, it is a world as strange as Mars to me.

Our route seems to be following the Potaro river upstream, perhaps to a point where it meets the Kopinang. The river is usually hidden by impenetrable curtains of growth, but I can sometimes hear it, crashing over rapids or surging through a narrow chasm of rock. If it was navigable, we'd be navigating it, in the narrow dug-out canoes that the Patamonas excel in making. Water is easier to travel over than land. When there is no river noise, the forest is oddly quiet; few birds, the two guides moving in absolute silence through this world of theirs. Only once do they shout, when a group of jaguars cross the track in front of us with the self-contained, intent look of hunters on a mission. Early one morning, though, a strange sound passes through the forest, high, as though caught in the web of the treetops. The noise swells and falls away, swells and falls away, like some great animal gasping for breath. It is pitched low and in a minor key, and it wraps all around us, ghostly and insubstantial, ebbing and flowing. But what can be making such an unearthly sound? Howler monkeys? Baboons? I can't see them moving through the canopy. If I could, at least one question would be answered and I would feel less adrift in this world that I can't interpret or understand.

Occasionally we meet a hunter in the forest with bow and quiver of poison-tipped arrows. Sometimes an entire family passes by: babies, cooking pots, hunting dogs, bags of farine. I watch a child, three years old at most, running barefoot over a river on a fallen tree, the only bridges that exist here. It is set high over a boiling torrent of water, impossible to swim across, and the damp, mossy log has no rope sides to it, no handholds. It is like a tightrope. These log crossings terrify me more

Plate 1: A man cutting the cure-all betony (our Stachys officinalis), *shown wildly out of scale in a manuscript made in the early thirteenth century*

than anything ever has in the whole of my life. We do perhaps a dozen a day. I have nightmares about them; I wake up kicking and screaming. I do not have the physical skills I need to survive here, but I'm disorientated in a mental sense too. Born and brought up in a temperate country, I'm lost here in the tropics where no living thing in this complex, interwoven understorey has a name that I know.

I reach out to pick a leaf, which is about the size of a hazel leaf, though more leathery and tough. I think it is the one that soothes the bite of a cabouri fly. But is it though? Or is it the leaf that I was warned never to touch, even fleetingly, for fear that my heart would stop, right there on the track, because of the poison it contains? What are the distinguishing, the essential, differences between the two plants? Someone, somewhere has worked these out, set them down, commissioned drawings, published descriptions, assigned each plant a place in a particular family, christened them with a two-part name that shows its botanical genus and its species. The taxonomist, the namer of names, will have described the plant's characteristics, explained its kinship with other plants in the same family, shown how, through some minute distinction, perhaps veining on the leaf, hairs on the stem, habit of growth, it is not the useful, medicinal leaf I thought it might have been, but the powerful drug. This work has transmuted local knowledge of plants, critical to the survival of indigenous people anywhere, into a comprehensive system of naming, of ordering and classifying, which now embraces every known plant in the world. But I am here without access to this knowledge, able only to define plants as they were defined in the Middle Ages in Europe – by their usefulness, their potential for food, medicine or magic. If I lived here, I too would learn to pick out the particular saplings that the Amerindians use to make their overnight shelters. I would also recognise the tree that produces the invaluable gum which our companions use as firelighters. In the pouring rain, as darkness falls, with a pile of wet sticks for a cooking fire, a small ball of this gum provides an infallible flame. Salvation. But nobody else, not even the Macushi or the Wai Wai, Amerindian neighbours, would recognise the name that the Patamona people use to describe it.

We do the final leg of the journey to Orinduik by boat, down the Ireng river. The canoe shoots through the rapids, while with wild cries the two oarsmen stem the current either side and the bowman, with a long pole like a quant, tries to keep the bow of the boat pointing in the right direction. Sometimes he loses it and the boat spins round and round like a leaf in the current, until the river spits us out of the rapids into calmer water. At Orinduik, the river fractures into different branches, pouring over steps of jasper and pure crystal. That night there is a storm somewhere over the mountains. We had arrived with a full moon and now sit with the waterfall thundering in our ears, watching that great glimmering disc haul itself up over the mountains into a hemisphere thick with stars. Opposite the vast moon, sheets of lightning throw into relief the jagged rims of the Pakaraima mountains.

In a tiny chartered plane, we leave the great Orinduik and fly out again over the canopy of trees. Sitting in the co-pilot's seat, looking down on this mass of green, I finally regain some sense of my relationship to the natural world. Following a ravine and the river as it tumbles over the rocks, we fly towards the sun, drifting over a landscape of huge flat-topped mountains that loom like islands from the sea of the forest. We have spun a thread between the two waterfalls. Gazing out from the Piper as it winds its way through this Conan Doyle *Lost World* landscape, I am as happy as I have ever been in my life.

On the morning of 13 July 1629, Thomas Johnson (*c*.1600–1644), newly qualified apothecary, is waiting in the churchyard of St Paul's in the City of London. He is twenty-eight years old, has left his shop, just recently set up in Snow Hill at the sign of the Red Lion, and is about to embark on a journey into Kent with some carefully chosen companions from the Society of Apothecaries. The purpose of the expedition is to make a list of the plants that grow in that county, the first step in preparing a complete account and description of British plants, a British flora, which does not yet exist. Various herbals have been published in Latin and English, including Gerard's notoriously unreliable work of 1597, but they have all been translations, amalgamations of Italian and Flemish plant books. Though some of these European plants are to be found in Britain too, English plantsmen struggle to match the descriptions printed in the bowdlerised herbals with the plants they gather from quite different habitats in Britain. The apothecaries have a particular need to sort, name and categorise indigenous plants. Medicine is their business and plants the raw material from which they brew, distil and decoct their elixirs and tonics. Licensed by their Society, they are the only people allowed to prepare and sell medicine, but they themselves are dependent on the herb-women who collect and sell the raw materials. Are they being duped? Are they being fobbed off with cotyledon when they think they are buying umbilicus? Johnson believes they are. 'Almost every day in the herb market', he writes,

> one or other of the druggists, to the great peril of their patients, lays himself open to the mockery of the women who deal in roots. These women know only too well the unskilled and thrust upon them brazenly what they please for what you will . . . Is not the fate of patients who rely upon the help of such doctors and druggists pitiable? For the doctor relies on the druggist and the druggist on a greedy and dirty old woman

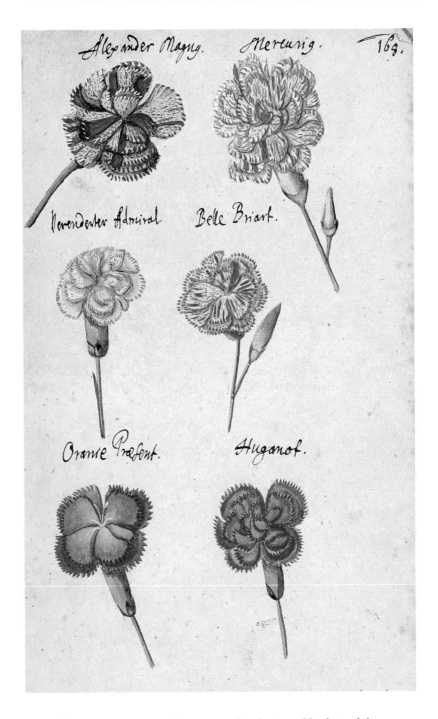

*Plate 2: Various named varieties of pinks (possibly derived from
Dianthus caryophyllus) from German drawings of the seventeenth century collected by Christian Wenzel van Nostitz-Reineck*

with the audacity and the capacity to impose anything on him. So it often happens that the patients' safety depends on the herbal knowledge of an ignorant and crafty woman.[1]

So here is Johnson, after an eight-year apprenticeship in his profession, setting out with some fellow apothecaries on the first of a series of journeys to familiarise himself with the country's native plants. The party hopes to get as far as Rochester and Gillingham, returning by way of Dartford. They have no map (the first large-scale guide to the area will not be published until the eighteenth century) though Philip Symonson had made a rudimentary plan of Kent in 1596, an aid to navigators on the river and round the coast, marking the position of various parish churches and showing whether they had steeples or towers. There are few roads for travellers to take, no signposts and a great deal of mud. The fastest highway into Kent lies along the River Thames and that is how Johnson and his party plan to get themselves as far as Gravesend, on the south bank of the river. At this point the Thames begins to swell into the wider estuary that eventually brings it into the North Sea.

'Hurrying to the river's bank', as Johnson writes, the party hires two boats for the first part of the journey. But, 'battered by the violence of the weather', the boat carrying Johnson's friends, Buckner, Buggs, Weale and Larking, has to turn aside to Greenwich to ride out the storm. Johnson and the other half of the party land safely at Gravesend and continue on by road to Rochester, crossing the fine stone bridge built 'with the spoils of France' by John Cobham and Robert Knowles in 1387. At the Bull Inn in Rochester, Buckner, Buggs and company finally catch up with them. When the storm had passed over, they had set sail again from Greenwich, but the tide was falling and their progress slow, so they left the boat at Erith and, picking up horses at Gravesend, rode fast for Rochester. 'We were all happy', writes Johnson, 'and had supper together.' Afterwards they make lists of the plants they find growing in the garden of the inn: tobacco, rosemary, day lily, lungwort, sage and wallflower.

Next morning, they make their way to Chatham, where the British fleet is lying at anchor, 'the best appointed fleet that ever the Sun saw' as the historian William Camden described it in *Britannia* (1586). They get permission to go aboard the *Prince Royal*, which at 1,200 tons is by far the biggest naval vessel in England. She is still quite a new ship and Johnson is impressed. 'Sixty-six bronze cannon of the larger size,' he records after his visit. 'It is so notable in its build, its size and magnificence, and it so surpasses all expectation that I dare not describe it.'[2] After dining at Gillingham and plant-hunting in the cemetery, Johnson and his party cross the river and install themselves in two inns at Queenborough on the Isle of Sheppey. Their arrival (they were a relatively large party) is noted with suspicion by the mayor, who sends for them and asks them their business. Self-importantly, the mayor proclaims the 'great and far reaching privileges' granted to him, the better to protect the Sheppey islanders from injury. It is his duty, he insists, to discover the cause of their journey. Smuggling and piracy is rife. And then there are the oysters, the chief source of Queenborough's wealth. Is the party perhaps planning an illicit raid on the Queenborough oyster beds?

John Buggs, who a few years later would be thrown into prison for practising, without a licence, as a doctor, explains that, as apothecaries, the group is 'devoted to the study of the science and material resources of medicine'. They have come, he continues, to see for themselves the rare plants that they have heard grow on the island of Sheppey. Jonas Styles tries a different approach. They have come, he says, because it gives travellers such as themselves an unrivalled opportunity to meet with a man of such merit as the mayor, a captain of the Royal Fleet, well versed in seamanship. Without a trace of shame he tells the mayor how 'especially gratifying' it is to him to become acquainted with 'so eminent' a man. 'By these and suchlike words', records Johnson, 'the Mayor was entirely satisfied.' He offers them beer, drinks their health, discusses medical and naval matters with them. With his blessing, the party moves on to Queenborough Castle, collecting wall rue (*Asplenium ruta-muraria*) from its crumbling walls. On the shore at Sheerness they find horned poppies, grey-leaved *Crambe maritima*. They collect starfish and the flat white carcasses of cuttlefish.

From Sheppey, the furthest point of their journey, Johnson and his friends hire a barge to take them across the Medway river to the Isle of Grain opposite. Flat, windswept and featureless, the rounded promontory of the almost-island separates the Medway from the Thames to the north. It is a low point in the Kentish adventure. 'After leaving the little ship,' Johnson writes, 'we walked five or six miles without seeing a single thing that could give us any pleasure. The road ran along the water's edge. In the heat of the day we were tormented like Tantalus with a misery of thirst. We were in the midst of waters, but they were brackish. We were equally afflicted with hunger in that inhuman wilderness, where there was no town within reach, no smoke to be seen, no barking of dogs to be heard, none of the usual sights of habitation by which we could arouse our fainting spirits to any breath of hope.' There were not even any plants of interest.

Exhausted, they arrive finally at the little village of Stoke. When dinner has been set and served, the whole company (with the exception of Styles and Johnson) boards a brewer's dray to hitch a ride to Rochester. Leaving their comrades 'lolling among the barrels in the wagon', entrusted to the care of the drivers, Johnson and his friend strike out west through the hamlet of High Halstow, past Cooling Castle, and spend the night in an inn at Cliffe. It is a productive foray, for they collect

A.M. 3267.ᵉ '56.

V. A. M.

Plate 3: Daffodil with Red Admiral, *watercolour by Jacques le Moyne de Morgues (c.1530–1588), c.1568*

many new plants (including cannabis), a high proportion of them never before noted as British natives.[3] On the steep hillsides around Cliffe itself, though, they find nothing that they have not previously seen, so they alter their course and move down to the saltings east of Gravesend. There they find hollyhock and the straw-berry-headed clover, named *Trifolium fragiferum* by the great French botanist, Clusius.

Passing through fields of rape, harvested with sickles, Johnson and Styles arrive again at Gravesend, where they wait for news of their 'waggoner comrades'. While they are eating dinner, Thomas Wallis arrives on a horse he has hired at Rochester. Leonard Buckner and Job Weale are only a little way behind him, he explains. As for the others, he does not know. But the tide is ebbing. No boats will be sailing that evening for the port of London. Instead, the small party hires horses and hurries along the king's highway to the Bull at Dartford. There, they set off directly for Chalkdale, 'a place packed with many rare plants, because stones had once been quarried here for making quick lime. We found it now decked with grass and many beautiful plants,' writes Johnson. Lady's bedstraw, clustered bellflower, rich mahogany fly orchids, and lesser bugloss are added to their now rather impressive list of plants discovered in the county of Kent.

That night they dine with Richard Wallis, 'preacher of divine grace', who refreshes them with a lavish supper and takes them plant-hunting in his paddock. The next morning, the reduced party sets out by way of the public footpath to Erith, where they hire a boat to take them upriver to London. On the way, they pass three ships, recently returned from the East Indies. They are invited on board, and Leonard Buckner, who later will become Master of the Society of Apothecaries, is presented with 'a big Indian nut, a piece of sugar cane and an Indian bamboo'. After that, writes Johnson, 'We left the ship and crossed the most famous bridge in the British world; then we were told that our Fellows had got back and where they now were.' The waggon party, they learn, had travelled in great style through Hoo to Rochester, where Anthony Allen, the first Mayor of Rochester under its new charter granted that same year, had provided a 'sumptuous repast'. They had eaten lamb prepared in a new fashion and caroused merrily with John Larkin, prebendary of Rochester Cathedral. A most satisfactory trip, agree the reunited fellows. They have found about 270 plants that have never previously been recorded in Kent. Nearly half of these are first records for Britain. So they plan a further outing: a journey in August by horseback to the wilds of Hampstead Heath.

I am riding with Kazakh horsemen through the Tien Shan mountains of Central Asia. It is late April and a storm has passed briefly through the snowy peaks. Now the sun is shining again and a rainbow hangs out over the great flat plain below us. The plain, littered with failed enterprises of the Soviet era – broken irrigation channels, fractured gas pipes, ruined factories – stretches from the foothills of the Tien Shan northwards to the beginnings of the next great range of mountains, the Karatau, which we can see, spiky and stark against banks of white cloud. Steam is rising from the narrow flanks of the grey-spotted horse in front of me and from the rough canvas saddlebags slung over its rump. My saddle is a bright velvet cushion, packed on top of a boat-shaped metal frame. The rein is a plaited braid and red rags are tied either side of the horse's head on the rope cheek-straps of its bridle. Passing over the flat, grassy plain between the village and the foothills, the horses have moved briskly, jumping with an odd rocking-horse motion over the narrow streams that run through the pasture. Now the going is steep and rough, not a track that I can see, so I concentrate on the way the horse in front of me is weaving in and out of low mounds of evergreen juniper, skirting vast boulders, slithering down muddy banks to cross yet more streams, swollen now by the rain. Occasionally the horses disturb red-legged chukar partridges; like mechanical, wind-up tin toys, they whirr up over the junipers on fast, noisy wings.

Water drips from the rim of the Kazakh horseman's hat, built like a fisherman's sou'wester, curved up in front, with a brim that sweeps down low over the nape of his neck at the back. It is made from thick pads of felt, the same kind of felt that covered the shepherd's yurt we've passed, pitched ready for summer on the slopes of the mountain. Rounding a bluff, we emerge on a plateau where, crammed over the ground, more tightly than the stitches of a Kazakh carpet, are mahogany-coloured fritillaries, blue iris, crocus the blue-white colour of icebergs, yellow junos, sheets of tulips with snakeskin-mottled leaves, low bushes of pink flowering cherry, alliums, patches of violet, spears of eremurus emerging like red-hot pokers from elegant sheaves of leaf, brilliant explosions of giant fennel spun from thread as fine as green silk, purplish-magenta vetches, corydalis, arching plumes of Solomon's seal, arrow-shaped arums. I know all these plants and can give them names because there is scarcely a plant lover in the Western world who has not tried to grow them, tried to persuade them that a bed of damp clay and a summer of cloud and drizzle is a fair exchange for life out here on the shale-strewn slopes of the great Tien Shan mountains where summers are hot enough to burst a thermometer. These plants are flamboyant, irresistible superstars of the plant world, destined since man first set eyes on them for a stage far wider than the corner of Central Asia that Nature chose for them. After the fall of Constantinople in 1453, and the appearance of European embassies in the capital of the new Ottoman empire, the way was clear for these Eastern plants to be introduced into Europe, which they were, in increasingly large

*Plate 4: Dioscorides and an assistant collecting herbs, from a
manuscript made in Baghdad* AD *1224*

numbers. In the hundred years between the mid-fifteenth and the mid-sixteenth centuries, twenty times as many plants entered Europe from the East as had arrived in the previous 2,000 years together. Moving along the Silk Road, the long-established route by which merchants transported valuable goods from Eastern producers to Western consumers, lilies, fritillaries, hyacinths, anemones, turban ranunculus, crocuses, iris and tulips from these same mountains had travelled with bales of silk through Tashkent, Samarkand, Bukhara, Turkmenistan, then on to Baku and Jerevan before arriving at Constantinople, the springboard for entry into the countries of Western Europe.

While my horse grazes with finicky care between the gageas and the wild roses, I'm thinking of those baggage trains, the saddlebags, the hand-made harnesses, the yurts put up and dismantled, the fires built against bears and wolves, and the practicalities of carrying plants, intact, so far from their natural habitats. They survived, of course, because the best of the plants, the most desirable and dazzling flowers, were bulbs. Once they had flowered, they rapidly gathered their resources back into themselves and rested underground for the summer, protected from the heat by the stony soil lying over them. During these months of dormancy, bulbs could be carried long distances without any harm, perfectly packaged, growth suspended. Like the silk that gave its name to this great trade route, they were high-value, low-volume goods, worth a merchant's trouble.

Alexander, the horseman, has been gathering mushrooms, field blewits, that bulge up like pale creamy stones between the flowers. Shouting, he points now to an impressive mound of fresh dung piled up by a clump of wild tarragon. Bear, he says, a bear that has breakfasted on juniper berries and lunched on rhubarb. He thinks it must have spent the winter in the cave above us, a dark hole framed by a sweep of *Fritillaria sewerzowii*, now in full bloom. This flower, which European gardeners find one of the most rare and strange and difficult of its family to grow, is here filling a bear's front garden. It is spread as thickly as nettles, throwing up stems of whorled glaucous leaves studded with bells of a bizarre and intensely desirable yellowish khaki.

My horse is moving to join Alexander's through a big patch of yellow Juno iris, squashing them under its unshod hooves. 'Sorry,' I say to the flowers, as they lie crushed in their sheaves of wide, white-rimmed leaves, 'I'm so sorry.' I've seen this iris only once before, at the Royal Botanic Gardens, Kew, a single bloom held reverently in front of me in a clay long tom pot, cultivated by the one man in England who has the skill to persuade it to flower. 'Iris,' I say to Alexander, who speaks Kazakh with a bit of Russian on the side. '*Ukrop*,' he replies, '*Ukrop*.' It's the flower's local name. '*Iris orchioides*,' I say, more to myself than him, for that is its botanical name and surname, its passport out of Kazakhstan. With this tag round its neck, assigned by the French taxonomist Ebie-Abel Carrière in 1880 (he'd seen it growing in a nurseryman's collection and published the first description of it in the *Revue Horticole*), it can pass through the hands of Spaniards, Belgians, Americans, Australians, Brazilians and Japanese, who will all recognise it as one particular species, with special characteristics that separate it from other Central Asian irises such as *I. tien-shanica* and *I. bucharica*. From medieval times onward in Western Europe, Latin was the language of the written word, understood equally well in France, Italy, England or the Netherlands. The Latin names applied to plants in the first written herbals were gradually honed over the next 300 years into a special botanical language, a kind of Latin Esperanto, understood by anyone, anywhere in the world, who is interested in plants. The tag, of course, is meaningless to the plant itself, which, as for millions of years past, responds only to external stimuli: light, darkness, warmth, cold, moisture, drought, horses' hooves. It's not of much interest to Alexander either; he's spent his whole life so far in Dzhabagly, the village on the plain below and is likely to spend the rest of it in the same place. The common names by which he knows at least 80 per cent of the plants in the mountains are the most useful in this community. My pear is their *grusha*. My nettle is their *krapiva*. My tulip is their *kyskaldak*. The mushrooms he has been collecting are *sinenozhka* and that local name is all he needs to signify that these fungi are not poisonous and that, being delicacies in the area, he will be able to sell them for a good price to his neighbours.

But what was the process by which all these fabulous plants found new, universally understood names after they had arrived in foreign lands, far from home? Passed from merchants to ships' captains, from travellers to nurserymen, from diplomats to noblemen, from missionaries to monks, moving from Central Asia to Pisa, Padua, Provence, Paris, Leiden, London they will have lost their common names, their local identities. And yet they must have names, if only for practical reasons. Many plants were brought into Europe for medicine, to increase the range and effectiveness of the druggist's pharmacopoeia. Most medicines came from herbs ('simples' they were called) and new ingredients promised the hope of new cures, provided the ingredients were true to name. A plant's pharmaceutical value depended on the plant-hunter's ability to distinguish one botanical species from another; its economic value would increase in equal measure.

But apothecaries worried that they were often duped with substitutes, plants that were more easily obtained than the real thing, which is why Thomas Johnson and his friends undertook their plant-hunting journey into Kent. It was the first of a series of expeditions they planned into different areas of the country, collecting the wild plants they saw, noting their characteristics and known uses and trying, for the

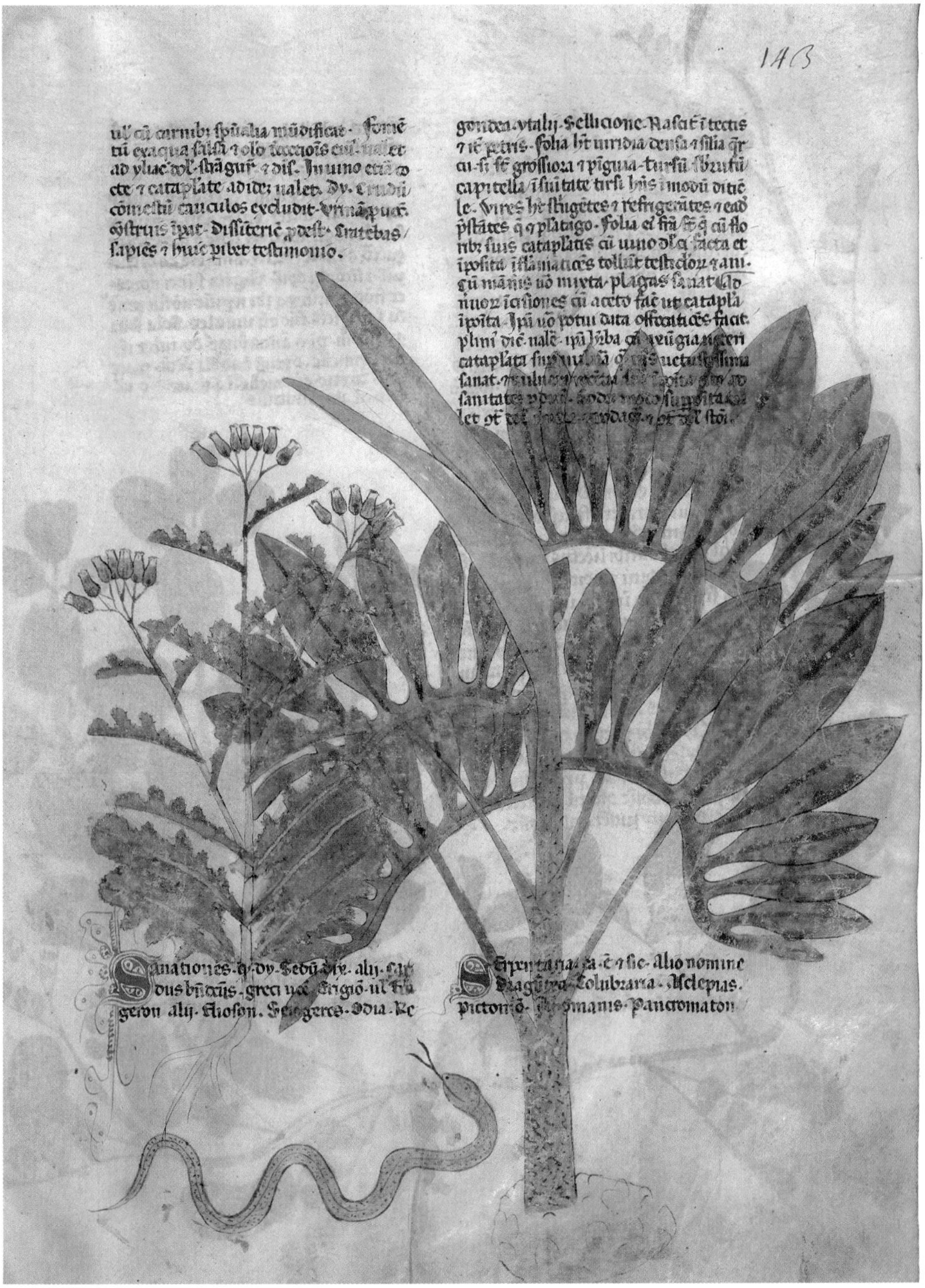

Plate 5: 'Senationes' (possibly our groundsel, Senecio
vulgaris) and the dramatic 'Serpentaria' (our dragon
arum, Dracunculus vulgaris) in a manuscript made
between AD 1330 and 1340. Is the snake suggesting
that these plants are good antidotes to snake bite?

first time, to establish some kind of agreement as to what plants grew in Britain and what they should be called.

This naming of names was a process that had been going on in Italy and France for some time before it happened in England; Johnson's journey and the motive behind it had been inspired by the young Italian botanist Ulysse Aldrovandi's expedition to the Sibylline mountains in 1557, the first journey ever undertaken in Europe with the aim of recording the plants of a specific area, creating, in effect, a local flora. Aldrovandi, of course, would not have called himself a botanist. The word did not appear in print until more than a century after his Sibylline adventure. The study of plants was, however, intimately connected with the study of medicine. A sixteenth-century apothecary, surgeon or doctor had necessarily to be a plantsman. Aldrovandi, who had studied at Bologna under the great teacher, Luca Ghini, was part of a pan-European network, an information exchange, a sixteenth-century internet that connected all those interested in a better understanding of the natural world. By introducing a system of nomenclature, they tried to bring order to that world, setting alongside the common names a set of Latin names, agreed by gradual consensus, advanced by contact with other enquirers in other countries, a system that could be universally understood. Already, in his early thirties, Aldrovandi was in touch with an influential Spanish pharmacist, Bergaso; he exchanged information with Bishop Rossano, the papal envoy to Philip II in Madrid, and with Micon de Viez, a doctor in Barcelona. He started a seed exchange with Philip Brancion, director of the botanic garden at Malines in France. In 1578 he sent Grand Duke Francesco I de' Medici, who had a famous garden at Pratolino, a drawing of a dramatic orange crown imperial (*Fritillaria imperialis*) which had only just arrived in Europe from the East. The development of a logical system by which the natural world could be organised was intimately linked to this European network of scholars and their patrons, the noblemen and landowners, all of whom communicated in a common language, Latin.

But alongside this practical, pharmaceutical reason for wanting to pin the right labels on things was another wider imperative: the desire to make sense of the natural world that was one of the defining characteristics of the Renaissance. Gradually, the active, the secular, gained precedence over the religious, contemplative mode that had defined the Middle Ages in Europe. The spirit and culture of this new age encouraged classical scholarship, scientific discovery, geographical exploration, a sense of the potential of the human mind. Art escaped from its religious straitjacket. As a more rational, scientific mode of thought developed, the study and classification of the natural world became a driving force in, and an essential part of, the early Renaissance. The hardships of the fourteenth century – harsh winters, food shortages, a series of plagues – were subsumed in a movement towards empirical research, characteristic of the first half of the fifteenth century; it marked a new dimension in man's relationship with nature. Fruitful links developed between botanists, herbalists, landowners, farmers and diplomats travelling in Europe and Asia. The Venetian ambassador, Andrea Navagero, travelling on horseback between Barcelona and Seville, made detailed notes on the crops being grown there by Arab farmers. The patrician Pietro Antonio Michiel, born in Venice in 1510, cultivated a fine garden on the island of San Trovaso in Venice. He received plants from Venetian ambassadors serving in Constantinople and Alexandria. He had contacts in Dalmatia, Crete and the Levant. He was in touch with merchants from France, Germany and Flanders whose business brought them to Venice. As so much European trade passed through Italian ports, it was not surprising that Italy should dominate the first phases of the search for order in the plant world; soon, though, information began to flow freely from scholars based round the Mediterranean to those of Northern Europe, linking Venice, Florence, Provence with Paris, Leiden and London.

Of course, printing, when it was invented (the first text to be produced by the new process was the indulgence printed at Mainz in 1454), had a cataclysmic effect on the spread of knowledge. Up till that point, information was a personal asset or property, passed at its owner's discretion from hand to hand, by word of mouth or by letter. Each person in possession of information could add or subtract from it before passing it on. The printed book changed the way information was received. It sent the same message to all. It was not necessarily the right one, but it set an agenda; it was a fixed point from which the fight for elucidation could continue.

The earliest printed plant book, a German herbal, appeared within thirty years of Gutenberg's great invention, but the first bestseller, the first new printed herbal to be read throughout Europe, was written in 1530 by Otto Brunfels, a Carthusian monk turned Lutheran schoolmaster (and also the town doctor of Berne). The key to the book's success was not the words, mostly cobbled together from the classical texts of Theophrastus and Dioscorides, but the woodcuts contributed by Hans Weiditz, draughtsman and engraver. Unlike Brunfels, he was not a copyist. He drew the plants in the herbal direct from life. He created the first printed images, of water lily, nettle, plantain, liverwort, vervain, lesser celandine, borage, wood anemone, pasque flower, that could be unequivocally recognised throughout Europe. Artists, not writers, paved the way for the botanical Renaissance in Europe.

Weiditz's model and tutor was the master of the German Renaissance, Albrecht Dürer. 'Be guided by nature,' his mentor had written. 'Do not depart from it, thinking that you can do better yourself. You will be misguided, for truly art is hidden in nature and he who can draw it out possesses it.' Dürer's flower studies are aston-ishingly realistic snapshots of the natural world, taken straight from the field, the

Plate 6: An iris (Iris germanica) captured in watercolour, almost life-size, by Albrecht Dürer c.1503

plants botanically accurate in every detail – the corrugated leaf of a primrose, the small horned spurs of an aquilegia – but different in their natural groupings from the botanical specimens captured by Weiditz. In Italy, Leonardo da Vinci had already been experimenting with physiotypes, which were like woodcuts made without either wood or cutting. Coating leaves with the soot produced by a candle flame, he pressed them on sheets of paper to make carbon copies showing the intricate system of veins and ribs supporting the leaves. The sixth part of his *Treatise on Painting* is a study of plants, the structure of their roots, branches, bark, flowers, leaves.

So, aided by artists, the botanists and naturalists of the Renaissance set out along the long road towards consensus in the naming of names. Botanic gardens were established at Pisa, Padua and Bologna. Disaffected Protestants, barred from studying at the University in Paris, swept out of Antwerp by Philip II of Spain and his Catholic crusades, finding themselves suddenly on the wrong side of the religious fence in England, gathered at the famous medical school at Montpellier in the south of France, exchanged information, dispersed, and later established new centres of excellence in Northern Europe. Two hundred thousand Huguenots, who in Flanders had established themselves as particularly knowledgeable and gifted growers and nurserymen, left France to settle in Switzerland, Germany, England and the Netherlands. Out of this persecution came progress, as the floods of immigrants swirling through Europe brought with them fresh information about plants and created webs of knowledge. Entrepreneurs such as the French nurseryman Pierre Belon brought news from outside Europe; between 1546 and 1548 he was in the Levant and the account he published of his journey and the things he had seen increased the desire of European gardeners to own for themselves the fabulous plants, many of them bulbs, that he described. But with each new wave of introductions from abroad, the pressure to sort, describe, and organise plants into a rational system of nomenclature increased. When plants began to pour in from the newly settled lands of America, the task became even more urgent. The Spaniard Nicolas Monardes was the first to describe the cornucopia of hitherto unknown plants that grew in this unchartered territory and already by 1577 his book, which included reports of novelties such as sunflower and tobacco, had been translated into English as *Joyfull newes out of the newe founde worlde*. The business of naming plant names, which had begun in a desultory fashion with the Greek philosopher Theophrastus in the third century BC, occupied the best minds in Europe. This is their story.

I

IN THE BEGINNING
370 BC—290 BC

THEOPHRASTUS IS THE first in the long list of men who fought to find the order they believed must exist in the dizzying variety of the natural world. He lays out the puzzle, nudges together a few pieces that he thinks might fit. Fitfully, over the next 2,000 years, the puzzle is taken up by a series of philosophers, doctors, apothecaries, each of whom adds to the picture, links a few more pieces together, until finally, by the end of the seventeenth century, the whole picture begins to make sense. We now have written descriptions of 422,000 plant species. Theophrastus knew about 500, half of which had already appeared in Greek poetry, plays, essays (Homer mentions sixty). But Theophrastus was the first person to devote serious attention to the business of naming plant names. He was the first person to gather information about plants, and to ask the big questions: 'What have we got?' 'How do we differentiate between these things?' He was the first person to discuss plants in relationship to each other, not just in terms of their usefulness to man. Magic and medicine both provided powerful practical incentives to know more about plants, but Theophrastus wanted to know them in a different way, just for the sake of knowing. From that knowledge, connections between plants gradually emerged which helped to make sense of the natural world and its terrors. The Greeks believed passionately in order.

On the north side of Syntagma Square in Athens, there is a boundary stone, of old unpolished marble, incised with the remnants of an inscription. It is only about two feet tall, but it is set on a much newer swagged column, which makes it almost as tall as the kiosk close by selling fizzy drinks and ice creams. The stone marks the boundary of the Lyceum, the school where Theophrastus taught in 320 BC. Forget the traffic hurtling with suicidal speed round the dusty circuit of Syntagma Square. Forget the hoardings, the looming presence of the Hotel Grand Bretagne, the Greek guards in their crazy bobble shoes. See instead Theophrastus, pacing up and down in front of his audience (more than 2,000 people came to hear his morning lectures at the Lyceum).[1] In one hand, he has a leaf from the plane tree that shades the stream running through the Lyceum grounds, in the other, a vine leaf. The leaves are roughly the same size, roughly the same three-cornered shape. Can this mean that there is some kinship between them? But the vine produces an edible fruit. The plane tree does not. Does this rule out the possibility of any relationship between the two plants? And the plane grows tall, in our measurements, thirty feet or more. The vine is a shrubby kind of plant, never attaining the stature of a tree.

Is the difference in height, in general habit of growth, a useful, valid way of distinguishing between things, of grouping them? Theophrastus thought it was and explained to his pupils why he favoured separating plants into four different categories: trees, shrubs, sub-shrubs and herbs. That does not sound much of a breakthrough to us. But we have to unknow such a vast amount of knowledge to get back to Theophrastus and the world he was trying to understand. There had been no Darwin. No *Origin of Species*. No conception of evolution. The early Greeks saw cultivated types of grape, plum, peach, apple as gifts from the Gods, in benign mood after a particularly good day on Mount Olympus. The Ionian philosopher Hippon had already suggested that cultivated plants may perhaps derive from wild ones, but it was a wildly radical thought to absorb. Theophrastus noted it as an interesting proposition, but still suggested a division between wild plants and cultivated ones as a primary mode of classification. He knew nothing about the mechanics of pollination and yet, in writing about date palms, noted that 'it is helpful to bring the male to the female; for it is the male which causes the fruit to persist and ripen, and this process some call, by analogy "the use of the wild fruit". The process is thus performed: when the male palm is in flower, they at once cut off the spathe on which the flower is, just as it is, and shake the bloom with the flower and the dust over the fruit of the female, and, if this is done to it, it retains the fruit and does not shed it.' This is where the biggest chasm looms between our mind-set and his. How could he so accurately describe the process of pollination without going on to ask himself why this particular trick worked? He understood the concept of a male and a female plant.[2] He understood that a good fruit set depended on the female flowers being visited by the males, but he never puzzled out the concept of pollination. Seeds and fruits came, but the how of it was a mystery.

He tells us what other authorities have to say on the matter: the Greek philosopher Anaxagoras (c.500–428 BC) believed that all things were made from minute particles arranged by a supernatural intelligence. To him, the air contained seeds of all things, and these, washed down by rain, produced all the plants on earth. The Athenian historian Kleidemos believed that plants were made of the same elements as animals, but that they fell short of being animals because their composition was less pure and they were colder. The Greek poet Hesiod said that the oak produced not only acorns, but also honey and bees. So instruments of pollination, such as the catkins of the hazel tree, seemed to him to have absolutely no purpose. Theophrastus described them minutely:

> The filbert after casting its fruit produces its clustering growth, which is as large as a good-sized grub: several of these grow from one stalk, and some call them catkins. Each of these is made up of small processes arranged like scales, and resembles the cone of the fir, so that its appearance is not unlike that of a young green fir-cone, except that it is longer and almost of the same thickness throughout. This grows through the winter (when spring comes, the scale-like processes open and turn yellow); it grows to the length of three fingers, but, when in spring the leaves are shooting, it falls off, and the cup-like fruit-cases of the nut are formed, closed all down the stalk and corresponding in number to the flowers; and in each of these is a single nut.[3]

He described only what he could see with his own eyes. Spectacles had not yet been invented. Nor had the magnifying glass or the microscope. He could see the veins in a leaf, but not the stomata, the tiny pores that control the passage of oxygen and carbon dioxide in and out of the plant. But of course he did not know anything about oxygen or carbon dioxide or the way leaves breathe.

His mentor and master, Aristotle, led the way with animals, and in his treatment of plants Theophrastus started with a concept of the plant as an animal with its feet in the air and its mouth in the ground. In some ways, he could make the analogy work: like animals, plants could be described in terms of their veins, nerves and flesh. And he worked most often by analogy: this leaf is bigger, smaller, hairier, lighter in colour than that one, a method which relied on his audience (or readers) having a clear image of the 'that'. So, looking out at the *Trachelospermum jasminoides* twining round the supports of the loggia outside, I could describe it as like bay in that its leaves are elliptical and evergreen but smaller. The flowers come later than the bay's and are sweetly scented. Theophrastus observed that the leaf is very varied in form, but reasonably constant within a species, and so therefore provided a good basis for making distinctions. In his lectures, he could hold the one and the other in front of his students. He could make his analogies immediate. Most lanceolate leaves he described as being like laurel. Oblong leaves were compared to the foliage of the olive. For rounded leaves, almost as broad as they were long, the standard was the pear. Hornbeam he described as having leaves 'in shape like a pear's, except that they are much longer, come to a sharp point, are larger, and have many fibres, which branch out like ribs from a large straight one in the middle, and are thick; also the leaves are wrinkled along the fibres and have a finely serrated edge.'[4] It is a brilliantly vivid description. Was the leaf lying on his desk in front of him as he was writing it? But leaves could not always be depended on as indicators because they were not always the same on the same plant. Ivy confounded him. So did the castor oil plant.

His work, like a series of lecture notes prepared for his classes at the Lyceum, survives in two collected volumes, the *Historia plantarum* and the *De causis plantarum*. They set down the extent of plant knowledge in 300 BC. This is what was known. The quest for order starts here. But unfortunately for Theophrastus, his work was shamelessly plagiarised and regurgitated by the later Roman writer Pliny and it was Pliny's work *Historia naturalis* that was handed down to future generations. As Pliny was quoted and requoted, Theophrastus was forgotten. Knowledge can only be built up from what is known, and tricks of fate – wars, deaths, fires, shifts of power and language – prevented Theophrastus's pre-eminence from emerging until Teodoro of Gaza (*c*.1398–*c*.1478) finally turned into Latin the body of knowledge Theophrastus had so painstakingly amassed.

This great gatherer together of knowledge was born at Eresos on Lesbos (Mitylene) in about 372 BC. His father, Melanthus, worked in the cloth trade as a fuller. Theophrastus left Lesbos for Athens to study under Plato at the Academy, one of the greatest of the Athenian philosophical schools. Aristotle was a pupil there too, and when, after Plato's death in 347 BC, Aristotle set up the Peripatetic School at the Lyceum, Theophrastus joined him there. There were only fifteen years between them, but the influence of the older man on the younger showed in everything he wrote. When Aristotle died (he was sixty-three), he left Theophrastus his library, said to be the best that had ever been put together. It included manuscripts of his own works and those of his master, Plato. It provided a solid matrix for Theophrastus's work. Aristotle had already started on his *Historia animalium* before Theophrastus began his similar enquiry into plants. Both were influenced by Plato's theory of ideas, which made an important distinction between the things we see (trees, shrubs, birds, animals, fishes) and the universal forms of which they are an expression. Both Aristotle and Theophrastus were mocked by their contemporaries for spending time and thought on living things. Theophrastus could (and did) write on politics, ethics, rhetoric, mathematics, astronomy. Why waste your brain on palm trees? And catkins?

Philosophy, though, underpinned his enquiries into plants just as solidly as it did his other work. Theophrastus wasn't writing an encyclopaedia of plants, ranged alphabetically from almond to vine, the essential characteristics neatly annotated to aid identification. He was asking questions about plants. How do you define a plant? Which parts are most useful in choosing a way to classify them? Many difficulties were caused by the assumption that plants corresponded at every level with animals. Could you call the flower or fruit of a plant a part of it? The plant, as it were, gives birth to the flower and the fruit, but you would not call the young of an animal a part of it. And where was the seat of the soul in a plant? It had to have one – inconceivable that it should not – but if a plant could grow from roots, stems, leaves, or seeds (taking cuttings and layering plants were both techniques known to the Greeks), then it would seem that the soul of the plant, its essential beingness, was everywhere in it. But that couldn't be possible. Arguing carefully through various propositions, Theophrastus finally concluded that the soul of a plant lay at the junction of its root and its stem, though that in itself was rather a shady area.[5] Frequently, he signals the need for more research, as he does in writing about the water chestnut of Egypt. Some said it was an annual, others that the root persists for a long time, new stalks growing from old roots. Theophrastus notes the divergence of opinion: 'This then is matter for enquiry.'

His two works provide a synthesis of the information about plants that was available at the time. Some things he has seen with his own eyes, such as the ability of pine to shoot again from the root after a forest fire. 'This happened in Lesbos [his birthplace], when the pine forest of Pyrrha was burnt.' He notes the knots that often grow on the trunks of apple trees 'like the faces of wild animals'. He writes of the plane tree growing by the watercourse in the Lyceum; while the tree was still young, 'it sent out its roots a distance of thirty-three cubits, having both room and nourishment.' On the other hand, the planes 'which King Dionysius the Elder planted at Rhegium in the park, and which are now in the grounds of the wrestling school and are thought much of, have not been able to attain any size'. Other information (sometimes conflicting) is reported from Mount Ida and Macedonia, Arcadia and Crete. Northern Europe is almost unknown to him. He notes only that iris grow well in Illyria on the shores of the Adriatic and that the people of Panticapaeum in the Pontus find it very difficult to grow the bay and myrtle they need for their religious ceremonies. The winters are too cold. Conversely, the plants of Egypt and Libya get special attention, and Theophrastus gives the first account of cotton, pepper, cinnamon, myrrh, frankincense and the banyan tree, curiosities reported by Alexander's officers as they made their way through India. He paints a vivid picture of a mangrove swamp, the description brought back by men sailing in Alexander's expedition to the East. They were 'great trees as big as planes or the tallest poplars'. When the tide came up, 'while the other things were entirely buried, the branches of the biggest trees projected and they fastened the stern cables to them, and then when the tide ebbed again, fastened them to the roots'.[6] He notes the confusion caused by different names being used in different regions to describe the same plant. Sometimes life itself may depend on getting the name right: 'Of the various plants called *strykhnos*,' he writes, 'one is edible and like a cultivated plant, having a berry-like fruit, and there are two others: one induces sleep, the other causes madness . . . The kind which produces madness has a white hollow root about a cubit long. Of this three-twentieths of an ounce in weight is given if the patient is to become merely sportive and to think himself a fine fellow; twice this dose if he is to go mad outright and have delusions; thrice the dose if he is to be permanently insane . . . four times the dose is given if the man is to be killed.' He treats with respect the art of the poisoner.

Stitched through the text is the influence of Plato's belief that by grouping things in their 'natural kinds', philosophers could arrive at an idea of the 'ideal forms' of the natural world. Inherent in this belief was the principle of classification. But you cannot classify until you know what exists. The more examples you have in front of you, the easier it is to see likenesses and differences. Working with too few examples is like playing Pelmanism with too few cards. Nothing matches up. The principle of classification may have come from Plato or Aristotle, but no one before Theophrastus had applied that principle to plants. 'What are the characteristic features that distinguish this plant from others?' he asks. 'What is its essential nature?'

His first difficulty lies in defining the essential parts of a plant, given the prevalent notion that plants corresponded in some way to animals. Nobody had ever done this before. Nobody had grappled with the problem that the parts of a plant are not necessarily permanent, as they are in animals. The transience of blossom, fruit, foliage created a philosophical difficulty. Which parts, he asked himself, belong to all plants alike and which are peculiar to one kind? The differences, he felt, could be separated out into three sorts: one plant may possess parts that another will not; those parts will probably be unlike each other in terms of appearance and size; the parts may be differently arranged (he noted, for instance, how the branches of the silver fir, one of the most important timber trees of ancient Greece, were always arranged opposite each other).

The seminal parts of a plant, he suggested, were the root, stem, branch and twig. Nowhere does he ascribe any importance to the flower. Nor did anyone else working in the field over the next 2,000 years. Mushrooms and truffles troubled him since they had none of these important parts, but since they couldn't be animals, they must necessarily be considered part of the plant kingdom. 'Your plant is a thing various and manifold, and so it is difficult to describe in general terms,' he concluded. There weren't universal characteristics, in the way that a mouth and a stomach were universal to animals. Why did vines have tendrils? Why did oaks have galls? How could these oddities, characteristic of these particular plants, be accommodated in a satisfactory and universal system? And yet he remained convinced that by seeking analogies with the animal kingdom, man could arrive at a better understanding of plants. 'It is by the help of the better known that we must pursue the unknown, and better known are the things which are larger and plainer to our senses.'

Carefully, he proposes dividing plants into four different classes: trees, shrubs, sub-shrubs and herbs. Trees (he gives olive and fig as examples) are distinguished by having a single stem and several branches. They cannot easily be uprooted. Conversely, a shrub, such as Christ's thorn, grows up from the root with many branches. Sub-shrubs such as savory or rue have multiple stems with smaller branches breaking from them. Herbs grow directly from the root with leafy stems. Throughout his work on plants, the first attempt to beat out a way of grouping them into a coherent system, you see Theophrastus testing his propositions to see if they can be universally applied. They rarely can. We still use the four divisions he first proposed, but he immediately recognised a difficulty, for example, with cultivated apples and pomegranates. These were often pruned and trained to grow with several trunks rather than one. They were surely still trees, but they no longer conformed to the most important characteristic that he had laid down to set them apart from shrubs.

So was it possible to classify plants by their size, their comparative robustness or their longevity? Or should distinctions be made between wild and cultivated plants, those that bore fruit and those that didn't, those that had flowers and those that had none? Perhaps a line could be drawn between evergreen plants and those that drop their leaves in autumn. It's a distinction we accept quite easily – yew evergreen, ash deciduous – but Theophrastus, who never ducked from difficulties, knew that in some areas, 'neither vines nor figs lose their leaves'. And he'd heard that in Crete, around Gortyna, there was a plane tree by a spring (it was the tree under which Zeus lay with Europa) that never lost its leaves. Where did these things fit in the *catalogue raisonné*? He was happier with the idea of a natural division between plants that grew on dry land and those that grew in water, perhaps because a similar distinction had already been made between aquatic and land-based

Plate 7: The cedar of Lebanon (Cedrus libani) in an
illustration prepared for Fuchs's unpublished encyclopaedia
of plants. The tree that Theophrastus called cedar ('kedron')
is more likely to have been a juniper

animals. Even here though, he foresaw problems. Plants such as tamarisk, willow and alder seemed to him almost amphibious, not particularly concerned whether their roots wandered in earth or in water.

And then, of course, as he pointed out, there were many different kinds of wetness: marsh, lake, river, sea. Theophrastus talked ecology before the word was ever invented.[7] From the beginning he understood the importance of habitat to plants 'because they are united to the ground and not free from it like animals'. Plants 'peculiar to particular places' must be considered separately. He noted that some mountains produced a special kind of vegetation: the cypress of the Ida hills in Crete; the cedars of Syria and Cilicia; the parts of Syria where the terebinth grew. He understood, even then, that differences in soil and situation give a special character to the plants that grow there. He describes a place called Krane in Arcadia,

> a low lying district sheltered from wind, into which they say that the sun never strikes; and in this district the silver firs excel greatly in height and stoutness, though they have not such close grain nor such comely wood . . . Wherefore men do not use these for expensive work, such as doors or other choice articles, but rather for ship building and house building. For excellent rafters, beams and yard arms are made from these, and also masts of great length which are not, however, equally strong; while masts made of trees grown in a sunny place are necessarily short but of closer grain and stronger than the others.[8]

But also, by announcing that he intended to treat plants 'peculiar to particular places' in separate sections of his thesis, he avoided the impossible task of trying to relate the strange, new plants reported from Libya, Persia and India to the better known pantheon of plants in his native Greece. He did not have to struggle to establish the similarities and differences between them.

Trees dominate Theophrastus's *Enquiry into Plants*. Perhaps, given their size and longevity, he considered them more worthy of attention than more ephemeral, lowly plants. And he was deeply interested in function, as it related to form. Those who worked with wood had already accumulated a vast amount of knowledge based on use and experience. For shipbuilding, silver fir, fir and Syrian cedar were the preferred choices. Triremes and longships were made of silver fir because it was light, though the keel of a trireme would be made of oak 'that it may stand the hauling'; lime was chosen for the deck planks of longships. The timbers cut for Demetrius Poliorcetes's ship of eleven banks of oars were thirteen fathoms long. Merchant ships were more usually constructed of fir because it did not decay. In house-building, silver fir was the most useful wood. Lime provided the best wood for boxes and the manufacture of measures. Kermes oak was preferred for the axles of wheelbar-rows and the crossbars of lyres and psalteries. Elm was turned into doors and weasel traps; because it was least likely to warp, elm was also used for hinges, with wood from the root making the cylindrical pivot above and branch wood used for the supporting socket. Holly and Judas tree provided walking sticks; wild olive was the choice for hammers and gimlets. Religious images were most often fashioned from palm wood, which was light, easily worked and soft, but less brittle than cork oak. The best charcoal came from close-grained wood such as holm oak, oak or arbutus. This was the charcoal that was used in the silver mines for the first smelting of the ore. But ordinary blacksmiths generally needed charcoal of fir rather than oak: it was not so strong, but blew up better into a flame and was less inclined to smoulder. All this information, acquired over centuries by builders and carpenters, shipbuilders and foresters, depended on an intimate knowledge of plants. The use to which the various trees were put depended on essential characteristics, the fact that its wood split straight (like silver fir), had a close grain (like boxwood), or could be easily bent (like limewood). But utility alone could not provide a satisfactory way of sorting and organising the plant world (though it later became the standard way of cate-gorising plants among those who were primarily interested in their medical proper-ties). Notwithstanding his deep interest in the various uses to which plants could be put, Theophrastus, rightly, was looking for a way of grouping plants that depended on essential characteristics, not mere function.

He looked at the differences in bark: thin on bay, thick on oak, cracked on vine, almost fleshy on the cork oak. He considered differences in root: long in the plane tree, few in the apple, single in the silver fir, stout in the bay and olive, slender in the vine, absent altogether in the truffle, fragrant in orris, much used in the perfume industry. He considered the form of leaves: broad in the vine and the fig, narrow in olive and myrtle, spiny in fir, fleshy in the houseleek. He noted that some seeds such as the date, the filbert and the almond were packed immediately inside a containing envelope (he was wrong about the almond). In some fruit, such as olive and plum, juicy flesh lay between the outer envelope and the seed. Some seeds (Judas tree, carob) were enclosed in pods. Others such as wheat and millet were wrapped round in husks. Poppy seeds were held in a vessel like a pepper pot. Of flowers, he has very little to say at all. But all these separate parts – roots, leaves, fruit – presented possible ways of sorting and grouping plants. When, after a hiatus of 1,800 years, Theophrastus's work returned to the mainstream, each of these elements was tried out again, now by a succession of plantsmen struggling to find, as Theophrastus had done, a universal system that would fit and codify the multi-farious elements of the universe.

After Book I of his *Enquiry*, Theophrastus moves away from the philosophical problems posed by the parts and general character of plants to consider more practical matters. He looks at habits of growth, methods of propagation, noting as all gardeners still note, that 'while all of the trees which are propagated by some kind of slip seem to be alike in their fruits to the original tree, those raised from the fruit, where this method of growing is also possible, are nearly all inferior'. He doesn't know it, but he's talking about clones. Where he is given contradictory evidence, he impartially reports it all, without prejudice. The Arcadians say that the black poplar never bears fruit. The Cretans disagree, citing a number that do, including a specimen growing at the mouth of a cave on Mount Ida 'in which the dedicatory offerings are hung'. In their reports of plants, and in the names they call them, the Arcadians often seem to be at odds with the people of Mount Ida and indeed everybody else. Theophrastus explains the difference between pines and firs as he understands it: 'The fir has many leaves, which are glossy massed together and pendent, while in the pine . . . the leaves are few and drier and stiffer; though in both the leaves are hair-like.' It seems clear enough but 'The Arcadians dispute altogether the nomenclature.' The wood of silver fir is soft and light, that of fir more resinous, heavy, fleshy, more knotted. The ordinary form is much used for painters' boards and writing tablets. But once again, 'The Arcadians appear to differ as to the names which they give.' Painstakingly, Theophrastus picks his way through this muddle of names, collecting synonyms, calmly laying out the facts, highlighting the areas where further enquiry is needed. In the mountains a certain maple is called *zygia*. In the plains, it is *gleinos*. Is this the same tree, under different names, or two different kinds of maple? Local, common names were important (still are) but already, Theophrastus could see an advantage in plants having tags that everybody – Macedonians, Arcadians, Aeolians, Libyans, Cretans – could agree on. Research could then progress on a firm footing.

In his descriptions of plants, Theophrastus uses a wide range of indicators: habit of growth, bark, leaf, the type of wood produced, fruit, root system. He also includes notes on distribution – 'about Mt Ida', 'plentiful in Macedonia' – and habitat. Bird cherry grows where there are rivers and damp places. Elder also grows chiefly by water and in shady places. Box grows most abundantly in cold, rough places such as Cytora, though 'the largest and fairest' are to be found in Corsica, where the tree grows taller and stouter than anywhere else. Sometimes, he makes a family group of plants: three kinds of *mespile* (our medlar, which he throws together with two kinds of thorn), the five oaks recognised by the people of Mount Ida (though others say there are only four . . .). The various kinds of wheat take their names from the places where they grow: Libyan, Pontic, Thracian,

Assyrian, Egyptian, Sicilian. The differences between them are in colour, size, form and their value as food. Varieties may be early or late in cropping, vigorous or weak in growth. The grain may have many coats or few. Some mature more quickly than others.

'The Sicilian', he says, 'is heavier than most of those imported into Hellas, but heavier still than this is the Boeotian; in proof of which it is said that the athletes in Boeotia consume scarcely three pints, while, when they come to Athens, they easily manage five . . . in the country called that of the Pissatoi it is so strong that, if a man eats too much of it, he bursts, which was actually the fate of many of the Macedonians.'[9] Theophrastus, an enquiring kind of man, accepts that as the truth. There are no qualifying phrases, as there so often are when he includes snippets of folklore. He remarks, for instance, that hornbeam (his *ostrya*) 'is said to be unlucky to bring into a house, since, wherever it is, it is supposed to cause a painful death or painful labour in giving birth'. Though he is respectful towards the rituals associated with religion (the juice of elderberries, he says, 'is like wine in appearance, and in it men bathe their hands and heads when they are being initiated into the mysteries') he is generally scathing about the superstitions that surround various plants, such as cinnamon. 'They say that it grows in deep glens, and that in these there are numerous snakes which have a deadly bite; against these they protect their hands and feet before they go down into the glens, and then, when they have brought up the cinnamon, they divide it into three parts and draw lots for it with the sun; and whatever portion falls to the lot of the sun they leave behind; and they say that, as soon as they leave the spot, they see this take fire. Now this is sheer fable.'[10] He is judicious about customs associated with cutting various herbs – 'That one should be bidden to pray while cutting is not perhaps unreasonable' – but the additions he finds absurd. When cutting allheal, for instance, 'It is said that one should put in the ground in its place an offering made of all kinds of fruits and a cake; and that, when one is cutting gladwyn, one should put in its place to pay for it cakes of meal from spring-sown wheat, and that one should cut it with a two-edged sword, first making a circle round it three times, and that the piece first cut must be held up in the air while the rest is being cut.'[11] The inference, perhaps, is that the primary purpose of these rites is to scare away amateur herb-gatherers from plants that the professionals considered their own, lucrative preserve. Allheal, as its name suggests, had powerful properties. The fruit was used to cure disorders of the bladder. The juice healed sprains and strengthened the voice. The root was used by midwives in childbirth, and provided an antidote to flatulence in beasts of burden. It had power against snake bites, and provided a guard against epilepsy. But there were three different plants, the Syrian, the Chaeronean and the Asclepian, which all bore that same common name. You needed to know you had got the right sort. Another lucrative herb was cyclamen, widely used by women in ancient Greece as a diaphragm-like contraceptive; its Greek name, *kyklaminos*, is still the one we use today.

Poisons were of great interest to Theophrastus, as they perhaps needed to be for any prominent Greek. He favoured hemlock, which gave 'an easier and speedier death', over other similar poisons. It was the poison that Socrates had used for his suicidal draught in 399 BC. The plant grows in many places in Europe, including Britain, where it was perhaps introduced by the Romans. With us it favours damp ditches and Theophrastus says that this was where the best plants grew in Greece too. He calls it *koneion* (our *Conium maculatum*), and credits Thrasyas of Mantineia with its discovery. It was he who first

> used the juices of hemlock, poppy and other such herbs, so compounded as to make a dose of conveniently small size, weighing only somewhat less than quarter of an ounce. For the effects of this compound there is absolutely no cure, and it will keep any length of time without losing its virtue at all. He used to gather his hemlock, not just anywhere, but at Susa [in Arcadia] or some other cold and shady spot; and so too with the other ingredients; he also used to compound many other poisons, using many ingredients. His pupil Alexias was also clever and no less skilful than his master, being also versed in the science of medicine generally.[12]

In Theophrastus's opinion, the art of poisoning had progressed greatly in modern times. People had learned how repeated use diminished the efficacy of drugs. They now understood that not all poisons would have the same effect on all people. Much more care was given to the preparation of the various different poisons. The people of Ceos, he pointed out, had once just shredded up hemlock, as did most other people. 'Now', he says, 'not one of them would think of shredding it, but they first strip off the outside and take off the husk, since this is what causes the difficulty, as it is not easily assimilated; then they bruise it in the mortar, and, after putting it through a fine sieve, sprinkle it on water and so drink it; and then death is made swift and easy.'[13]

He knew about *nepenthes*, the famous drug said to cure sorrow and passion, inducing forgetfulness and indifference to ills. He had heard that in Ethiopia there was a deadly root with which the Somalis tipped their arrows. And, of course, he was familiar with wolfsbane, his *akoniton*, our *Aconitum anthora*, which grew plentifully in Crete and Zakynthos, but was at its best at Herakleia in Pontus:

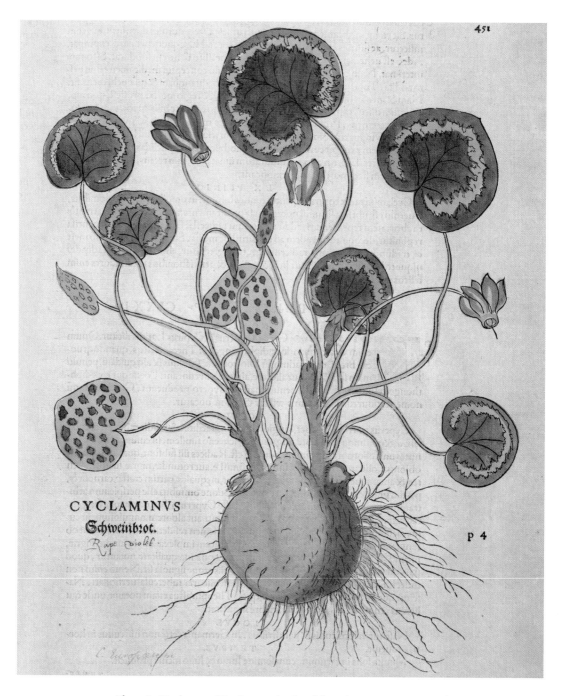

Plate 8: Cyclamen (Cyclamen hederifolium) in Cap CLXX of Leonhart Fuchs's De historia stirpium (1542). 'Of cyclamen the root is used for suppurating boils,' wrote Theophrastus, 'also as a pessary for women and, mixed with honey, for dressing wounds.'

It has a leaf like chicory, a root like in shape and colour to a prawn, and in this root resides its deadly property, whereas they say that the leaf and the fruit produce no effects . . . it can be so compounded as to prove fatal at a certain moment which may be in two, three or six months, or in a year, or even in two years; and that the longer the time the more painful the death, since the body then wastes away, while, if it acts at once, death is quite painless. And it is said that no antidote which can counteract it has been discovered, like the natural antidotes to other poisonous herbs of which we are told: though the country folk can sometimes save a man with honey and wine and such like things, only, however, occasionally and with difficulty. Wolfsbane . . . is useless to those who do not understand it; in fact it is said that it is not lawful even to have it in one's possession, under pain of death; also that the length of time which it takes to produce its effects depends on the time when it is gathered; for that the time which it takes to kill is equal to that which has elapsed since it was gathered.[14]

Writing in about AD 77, the Greek doctor Dioscorides reckoned the best remedy was to swallow a mouse whole. Theophrastus recommends the Medean apple (citron), newly imported from Asia, as a useful antidote. Mixed with wine, it induced nausea and brought up the poison. He explained how it was sown, like date palms, in pots with a hole in the bottom. The object was to produce plants that could more conveniently be exported on long sea journeys.

Theophrastus was intrigued, of course, by the plants that came into Greece as trade opened up with lands to the east and south. He devoted special sections of his *Enquiry* to the plants of Egypt, Libya and the parts of Asia that Alexander's army had conquered. He noted too how 'particular' these plants were to their countries of origin. Often nothing even remotely like these newcomers was known on the Greek mainland. The greater part of Theophrastus's work on plants is concerned with things that grew in his own country and even with these, he struggled to find classes and categories. The more plants that arrived on the scene, the more compelling the task became. European scholars felt the same urgency when confronted with the avalanche of superb plants, many of them bulbs, that came into Europe when trade with Turkey opened up in the sixteenth century. Egypt, whose civilisation was acknowledged to be much more ancient than Greece's own (Mesopotamian art showed cultivated date palms, vines and cereals 3,000 years before Theophrastus began his work in Athens), was of particular interest. The Greeks already had an established trading colony at Naucratis in the Nile Delta by the seventh century BC. From Egypt came the carob and the doum palm, whose fruit produced a very large, very hard stone. Egyptian craftsmen turned them into wooden rings to hold their embroidered bed hangings.

In great detail Theophrastus describes the lotus, the beautiful Nile water lily which he has never seen for himself. He also gives a long account of papyrus, which he knew as a product, but not as a plant. It grew, he explained,

> not in deep water, but only in a depth of about two cubits, and sometimes shallower. The thickness of the root is that of the wrist of a stalwart man, and the length above four cubits; it grows above the ground itself, throwing down slender matted roots into the mud, and producing above the stalks which give it its name 'papyrus'; these are three-cornered and about ten cubits long, having a plume which is useless and weak, and no fruit whatever; and these stalks the plant sends up at many points. They use the roots instead of wood, not only for burning, but also for making a great variety of articles; for the wood is abundant and good. The 'papyrus' itself is useful for many purposes; for they make boats from it, and from the rind they weave sails, mats, a kind of raiment, coverlets, ropes and many other things. Most familiar to foreigners are the papyrus-rolls made of it; but above all the plant also is of very great use in the way of food. For all the natives chew the papyrus both raw, boiled and roasted; they swallow the juice and spit out the quid. Such is the papyrus and such its uses.[15]

Papyrus (and date palm) appear on the frescoes at the King's Palace in Knossos (c.1900 BC) and were well known among the Greeks long before Alexander's expedition to Egypt in 331 BC.

This great work of Theophrastus's must have evolved over a long period. Speaking, for example, of frankincense and myrrh, he notes that 'these are about all the facts that have come to our notice at present'. His thesis is to be refined and extended as new information comes to him. He has contacts in Corsica, the Lipari islands, Crete, Boeotia. Most often quoted are the people of Macedonia, Arcadia and Mount Ida. Aristotle had set up the new Peripatetic School at the Lyceum in 335 BC. Theophrastus quickly joined him there and was head of the school by 322 BC. Aristotle's work had a great influence on Theophrastus's *Enquiry*. They had been fellow students at Plato's Academy. When they left the Academy in 347 BC, they travelled together, spending some time in Lesbos, where Theophrastus had been born. Some of Aristotle's earliest observations on marine biology were made on Lesbos, so it is highly likely that Theophrastus was already at work on his own *Enquiry* at this time. A few more clues come from incidents he mentions in the text. Talking about the special reed used for the mouthpiece of the pan pipe (the original pipe

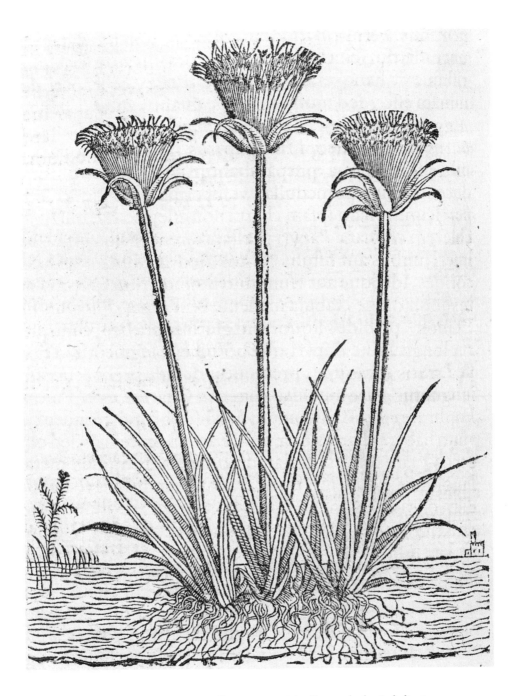

Plate 9: Papyrus, in an illustration originally made for Lobelius's
Adversaria *(1570) and re-used for a 1644 edition of*
Theophrastus's Enquiry into Plants

had a single vibrating reed like a modern clarinet), he notes that the best reeds were cut when the Lake of Orchomenos flooded. 'This is specially remembered to have happened in recent times at the time of the battle of Chaeronea.' That was fought in 338 BC, so the *Enquiry* has to come after the battle. Another pointer comes in his comments about the pomegranates that grow around Soli in Cilicia near the River Pinaris, 'where the battle with Darius was fought'. Darius died in 330 BC. Then, speaking of the trees and shrubs special to Libya, he describes the lotus with fruits as large as a bean. They grow, he says, like myrtle berries, close together on the shoots. 'To eat, that which grows among the people called the Lotus-eaters is sweet, pleasant and harmless, and even good for the stomach . . . The tree is abundant and produces much fruit; thus the army of Ophellas when it was marching in Carthage was fed, they say, on this alone for several days, when the provisions ran short. It is abundant also in the island called the island of the Lotus-eaters; this lies off the mainland at no great distance.'[16] Ophellas was a ruler of Cyrene, the ancient Greek city near the coast in Cyrenaica, North Africa. Some time around 308 BC he invaded Carthaginian territory (near present-day Tunis) with the Sicilian tyrant Agathocles. The date, the latest mentioned in the text, suggests that Theophrastus's work must still have been in progress at that time. By then he was sixty-five, but still had twenty years of work ahead of him.

Then there are the reports of the strange and outlandish plants that Alexander's men had seen in the East. Alexander had set out for India in the summer of 327 BC; by the spring of 326 BC, his admiral, Nearchus, was leading the fleet from the mouth of the Indus (near modern Karachi) along the Beluchistan coast to Hormuz at the entrance to the Persian Gulf. A separate expedition under Androsthenes explored Bahrain on the eastern side of the Gulf. Accounts of the voyage, with detailed descriptions of the new plants of these places, previously unknown in the West, were regularly sent back to Athens. What were these puzzling things to be called? How could they be portrayed? The banyan was initially described to Theophrastus as a kind of fig tree, but a very weird one 'which drops its roots from its branches every year . . . these take hold of the earth and make, as it were, a fence about the tree, so that it becomes like a tent, in which men sometimes even live . . . They say that it extends its shade for as much as two furlongs; and the thickness of the stem is in some instances more than sixty paces.' He heard for the first time of 'a cereal called rice' and a tree [we know it as the jackfruit], very large and bearing wonderfully sweet fruit 'used for food by the sages of India who wear no clothes'. Reports came back of another tree 'whose leaf is oblong in shape, like the feathers of the ostrich; this they fasten on to their helmets, and it is about two cubits long'. Is this the first description of a banana palm? He speaks of the plant from which the Indians make their clothes: it has 'a leaf like the mulberry, but the whole tree resembles the wild rose. They plant them in the plains in rows, wherefore, when seen from a distance, they look like vines.' He is talking about cotton, which, like the banana and the banyan, were then completely unknown in the West. He can only describe them by using more familiar, Greek plants as analogies. The first European settlers in America adopted the same strategy. Any tree that bore acorn-like fruit they describe as an oak. Any plant with a trumpet-like flower is reckoned a lily. Rarely does a plant's own native name travel back with it alongside its description. Theophrastus acknowledges that there are, in India, many plants 'which are different to those found among the Hellenes', but, he says, 'they have no names. There is nothing surprising in the fact that these trees have so special a character; indeed, as some say, there is hardly a single tree or shrub or herbaceous plant . . . like those in Hellas.' Among these newly discovered plants of Arabia, Syria and India, he considered the wide range of aromatics the most exceptional, the most distinct from the plants he already knew.

Theophrastus is hindered by the fact that he does not have the right terms to describe plants in detail. They haven't yet been coined. He separates out some of the most obvious parts – root, stem, branch, leaf. He notes elements such as thorns and tendrils that belong to some plants but not others. He tries out various devices for classifying plants, including a split between flowering and flowerless plants. And yet he does not have the necessary words to describe a flower itself. The petal he considers to be a kind of leaf. Where a flower has prominent stamens, as the rose and lily do, he talks of it as 'twofold', in the sense that one flower (made up of the stamens) sits inside the other. The trumpet flower of bindweed he decribes as having only a single 'leaf'. Compared with roots, bark and leaves, the flower was little used in medicine. Since function dictated to such a great extent the amount of attention that was paid to any one plant, nobody showed much regard for those dominated by their flowers. The rose is the only bloom that gets more than a cursory mention. Even by Theophrastus's time, there were many different kinds, differing he says 'in the number of petals, in roughness, in beauty of colour and in sweetness of scent'.[17] Philippi is especially noted for its roses, because the local people gathered them from Mount Pangaeus, where they grew abundantly, and planted them in their gardens.

In one sense, his lack of a technical vocabulary is an advantage. It means that his language is never too specialised, never excludes. And, as with Gerard, 2,000 years later, it encourages the use of colourful simile, as when he likens the dome-like outline of the silver fir to a Boeotian peasant's hat. Part of his problem was that so few plants had been given serious consideration. 'Most of the wild kinds have no names,' he says. 'Few know about them, while most of the cultivated kinds have received names and they are more commonly observed; I mean such plants as vine, fig, pomegranate, apple, pear, bay, myrtle and so forth; for, as many people make use of them, they are led also to study the differences.'[18] The fig was such an important source of nourishment that slaves' rations of bread were reduced by a fifth when ripe figs were available instead.[19] Of the 500 plants Theophrastus includes in his *Enquiry*, 80 per cent are cultivated.

Analogy was Theophrastus's way. Find the similarities. Observe the differences. But an analogy is not a description. It was certainly within his powers to describe, vividly and to the point. He gives a graphic portrait of the fleshy houseleek cushioned on the tiled roofs of Greek houses. 'Possibly one might mention many other eccentricities,' he says, but then immediately reins himself in again, for 'as has been repeatedly said, we must only observe the peculiarities and differences which one plant has as compared with others'. But analogy can take him only so far. In the end, there had to be more detail in the descriptions before the true analogies could be made.

Theophrastus also had to grapple with the prevailing notion that plants could change from one kind to another. Our system of naming names depends on the idea that a species is a fixed, constant thing. Wheat is wheat. Barley is barley, *Ruta graveolens* is always *Ruta graveolens*. But Theophrastus knew that tadpoles were not always tadpoles. They turned into frogs. Caterpillars went through a similar alchemical process, emerging finally as butterflies. If transmutation was so obviously part of the animal kingdom, it could be true of plants as well. People say, he writes (he often used that phrase, 'people say', or 'some say', when he was reporting matters on which he himself reserved judgment), that both wheat and barley could change into worthless darnel, a weed of cultivated ground, common in cornfields. The farmers of ancient Greece noted that this was most likely to happen in wet weather and in the muddiest parts of their fields. But, like Theophrastus considering the date palm, they did not take this observation in the direction that to us seems logical. They did not assume that the wet weather had rotted their seed corn and that the seed of this unwanted weed had germinated instead. The leaves of darnel, and its way of holding its seeds in clusters either side of the stem, were sufficiently like corn for them to suppose that the one must have degenerated into the other. Some observers thought flax did the same thing. A system, a plan, a structure, a scheme, an order depended on each plant having its own specific tag and not swapping it with another. Theophrastus, uncertain on the matter of darnel, was, though, absolutely sure that wheat did not turn into barley, or barley into wheat, as some people thought. 'These accounts should be taken as fabulous,' he says firmly. 'Anyhow, those things which do change in this manner do so spontaneously, and the alteration is due to a change of position . . . and not to any particular method of cultivation.'[20] In this Theophrastus was way ahead of his time. The assumption that plant species were inherently unstable was common right through until the end of the seventeenth century.

In the context of his time, his achievements are extraordinary. In the first sentence of his *Enquiry into Plants*, he writes: 'In considering the distinctive characters of plants and their nature generally one must take into account their parts, their qualities, the ways in which their life originates, and the course which it follows in each case.' Nobody before Theophrastus had even conceived an enquiry of such breadth, let alone produced it. Some of his most seminal thinking centred on the different parts of plants and how they might be defined. We suppose, for instance, that the root of a plant is the bit that is underground. He saw that wasn't true. Plants such as ivy had aerial roots. And, when it is growing, a large part of an onion is underground, but it is not all root. His four basic groups of plants – trees, shrubs, subshrubs, herbs (he has to use everyday words, because there are no others – his term for sub-shrub is *phruganon*, meaning firewood or kindling) – provided a useful start, but Theophrastus saw that these could never be rigid categories.

He laid out other distinctions too, not going so far as to suggest them as classifications, merely observing them, letting them lie there. There was a difference not only between plants that grew in water and those that didn't, and between cultivated and wild forms of plants (especially fruit trees), but between deciduous and evergreen trees. Many important cultivated trees were evergreen: olive, palm, sweet bay, myrtle, cypress. Many eyes watched them grow. Habit of growth, leaf fall among evergreen trees, all these things were noted, then recorded in Theophrastus's work. Among deciduous trees, he knows that some, such as almond, leaf up earlier than others, but the first into leaf are not necessarily the first to shed them.

He is the first to recognise, in the 500 plants that he includes in his *Enquiry*, many of the characteristics which eventually helped to determine how plants were to be classified. He notes that some plants are annual, completing the whole of their cycle of growth in a single year; others are perennial, springing up each year from the same rootstock, and dying down to the ground in winter. He sees how some plants seem to fall into natural groups or families, especially those plants which have tiny white flowers arranged in wide flat heads on top of hollow stems. Later, when a more specialised language began to emerge to serve this demanding new discipline, flowerheads of this kind became known as umbels. The term was then used to label all plants that had this characteristic flat head of flowers – the *Umbelliferae*: angelica, carrot, celery, dill, fennel, parsley, parsnip, cow parsley, hogweed, Queen Anne's lace, sweet cicely, alexanders, ground elder. And the deadly poisonous hemlock.

There was a clear and pressing incentive to understand the difference between this plant and its similar wild cousins.

Theophrastus uses the popular names of plants, where they have them, because there weren't any others. Many wild plants, he writes, have no names at all; he is the first person to suggest that, as these things are all part of man's landscape, they should be recognised and described. In treating animals, Aristotle, after all, had said, 'We will not leave out any of them, be it never so mean.'[21] Plants deserved the same close attention, the same embracing strategy. Theophrastus often uses the popular name to label the plant he thinks most typical of its kind. Then he adds describing words to distinguish other similar kinds of that particular plant. In speaking of oaks, he describes one that is broad-leaved, another that is straight-barked, a third called the Turkey oak and also the gall oak, which produces the growths that tanners used to prepare their leather hides. We use popular names in the same way to distinguish between different kinds of the same, basic prototype: spreading hedge-parsley, knotted hedge-parsley, upright hedge-parsley. The system works reasonably well while the whole business of plant names remains a parochial affair. Problems arise when one man's hedge-parsley becomes another man's hogweed. Even Theophrastus noted that the way the Arcadians distinguished between plants, for instance, was not a way that Macedonians or Aeolians understood. The confusion over popular names increased dramatically as later, in the Renaissance, knowledge began to travel between Italy and France, Germany and England.

When Theophrastus died, in 287 BC, he bequeathed his garden, its walks, and the adjoining houses to his friends, Callio, Callisthenes, Clearchus, Demotimus, Hipparchus, Neleus, Strato, 'and to those that will spend their time with them in learning and philosophy'. There were conditions attached: nobody should claim as their own any part of the houses or their grounds, or 'alienate them from their proper use'. The place should be enjoyed in common by them all; they should look upon it as somewhere they 'may familiarly visit one another and discourse together like good friends'. Theophrastus asked to be buried in his garden, wherever his friends thought most suitable. He did not want them to spend extravagant amounts either on his funeral or on his tombstone. He asked that his overseer, Pomphylus, should continue to live in the house, and take care of everything, including the slaves who worked in Theophrastus's garden. He called them his 'boys'[22] and asked that after his death, three of them, Molo, Cymo and Parmeno, should be set free. 'As for Manes and Callias,' he says, 'I will not have them given their freedom until they shall have laboured four years longer in the garden, so that there be no fault found with their labour and diligence.' After that, they too were to have their freedom. He mentions two other slaves: one, Cano, was to be given to Theophrastus's friend,

Demotimus; the other, Donax, was to go to Neleus.[23] In a life that lasted for eighty-five years, Theophrastus's great work on plants represents only 5 per cent of his output. At the end, in a sentence perhaps too neatly epigrammatic to be real, he said, 'We die just when we are beginning to live.' But you search Athens in vain for a memorial to this great man. At the spanking new Natural History Museum in Kifissia – nothing. Amongst the statues that crowd squares and piazzas – nothing. The botanical museum in Athens's Central Park, the National Garden, is firmly closed. Weeds grow in the pantiled roof and around the fine marble columns. There is an abandoned rill edged with stone. A few scraggy roses surrounded by chickweed and dandelion grow under the tall pines that throw their shadows on the diagonal pantiles of the museum's façade. Wild barley grass waves in the wind under an old Judas tree smothered in ivy. 'I'm looking for Theophrastus,' I say to a gardener close by, who is sporadically sweeping leaves to the accompaniment of Abba's 'Dancing Queen' on his radio. 'Is it a shop?' he asks. So think of him when you look at the bronze, thrusting shoots of paeony breaking through the ground in spring. His name *paeonia* is the one we still use. He is with you too as you bend to catch the spicy scent of narcissus, or *narkissos*, as he wrote it. *Aspharagos, elleboros, skilla, anemone, iris, krokos* are all in his book. Remember him.

Plate 10: The date palm, as shown in Descriptions of Some Indian Plants *(1600–1625)*

II

ALL MEN BY NATURE DESIRE TO KNOW

600 BC–60 BC

THEOPHRASTUS IS IMPORTANT because he provides us with the first written body of work on plants, the first naming of names, gathered in from farmers, herdsmen, market gardeners, carpenters, dyers, fullers and men of medicine and magic, all of whose occupations necessarily involved a relationship with plants. But the work at the Peripatetic School in Athens was itself the culmination of a long process of enquiry. Ten thousand years before Theophrastus started to teach in the Lyceum, there had already been attempts to cultivate plants in Western Asia. Seven thousand years before he started his *Enquiry*, pumpkins and squashes were being selected and cultivated in Mexico. Three thousand years before Theophrastus was even born, date palms, vines and cereals appeared in Mesopotamian frescoes. As civilisation advanced, people wanted plants because they were beautiful, not just because they were useful. Frescoes at Knossos, made around 1900 BC, show the lily, narcissus, rose and myrtle as well as barley, olive, fig, wheat and saffron crocus.

Trade was a powerful catalyst in promoting knowledge of plants, as previously unknown timbers, spices and foods began to arrive in Greek ports. Many of them came in from Egypt where, 2,000 years before Theophrastus began his *Enquiry*, cedar, cypress, juniper, ebony had already been imported from the East. In the eighteenth dynasty (*c*.1500 BC) King Thothmes III had sent an expedition to Syria which returned with gourds, irises and arums, all unknown then in Egypt. The King ordered images of the plants to be carved round the walls at Karnak, a kind of stone herbal, and an inscription underneath records the arrival of these marvels: 'As I live, all these

44

plants exist in very truth; there is not a line of falsehood among them.' Plants moved, too, with conquerors and tyrants. Theophrastus provides the first descriptions of plants growing in the Indus valley, from information handed down by the men of Alexander's invading navy. But already *c*.1100 BC, the ambitious King Tiglath-Pileser I of Assyria, conquerer of Babylonia, had recorded the cedars and box that he had carried off from the lands he had conquered, 'trees that none of my forefathers have possessed'.

The ancient Egyptians were particularly famed for their knowledge of medicinal plants and written on a papyrus of about 1500 BC found in a tomb at Thebes are prescriptions for ague and fever, bellyache and sickness, all arranged under the condition to be treated. Even in this document, which to us seems so ineffably ancient, references are made to other 'old writings'.[1] On tablets excavated from the library of King Asshurbani-pal (669–626 BC) in Nineveh, early scribes complain that the plant lists, extracted from earlier works, are not arranged in any logical way; they have difficulty in explaining some of the names. The lists divide plants into sixteen categories, based mostly on use: food plants, plants used in washing, dye plants, narcotics, plants for textiles, resinous plants. The Nineveh scribes make one of the earliest ever attempts to clarify and synthesise plant names; the old texts have been written in Sumerian script and they need to equate the old Sumerian names with the contemporary Akkadian ones.[2] Theophrastus had the same difficulty trying to find the right parallels between Arcadian names and those used around Mount Ida.

Much of the ancient culture of the Babylonians and the Egyptians had been assimilated in Greece by the time that Theophrastus began his *Enquiry*. New words, new plant names were quickly absorbed into the rich, flexible Greek language. *Hyacinthos, terebinthos, minte*, are all pre-Hellenic. *Anemone* and *hyssopos* came from the Semites. *Mandragora*, a vital ancient source of anaesthetics and painkillers, is an adulterated version of the Assyrians' name for the plant: *nam ta ira*, 'the strong drug of the plague god Namtar'. A fortunate blend of geography and history had turned the ports and trading cities of Ionia, the western corner of Asia Minor colonised by the Greeks *c*.1100 BC, into an important cultural centre. At a time when it was so much simpler to travel by sea rather than overland, a whole network of vital trade routes converged on the Ionian cities. Greek merchants and scholars were stimulated by the technical advances made in Egypt and Babylon, and they were not thwarted by a powerful, highly organised priesthood. Influential schools of medicine were established at Cos and Cnidos. A new rational spirit of enquiry began to coexist with a much older, more primitive tradition of medicine, dominated by ideas of demonology and possession, exorcism, ritual, magical spells and charms. The old root-gatherers, the *rhizotomi* (Sophocles wrote a play about them), were intensely superstitious:

ذكر زيابنون

لنوكسنطنى ومن الناس من سمه دياسون ومنهم
من سمه ارسرطابون هونائك له ورق شبه ورق
الباذرج مائل الزرقة لبنات المسى القسى الآله اصغر

Plate 11: 'Kirtim flower' (its Islamic name), from a Dioscorides
manuscript made and illustrated in the Islamic style in the
middle of the thirteenth century

some would work only by night (a good way of keeping secret the locations of plants that were much in demand). Paeony roots had to be dug in the dark because if the root-collector saw a woodpecker, he believed, he would go blind. Many of these superstitions found their way into Theophrastus's book: when gathering the powerful mandrake or the hellebore, he wrote, 'one should draw three circles round [the] mandrake with a sword, and cut it with one's face towards the west; and at the cutting of the second piece one should dance round the plant . . . One should also, it is said, draw a circle round the black hellebore and cut it standing towards the east and saying prayers, and one should look out for an eagle both on the right and on the left; for that there is danger to those that cut, if your eagle should come near, that they may die within the year.'[3] The force of such rituals enhanced belief in the potency of the plants. Plants could be full of terrors for the uninitiated. But the earliest enquirers into the natural world sought them out; they needed intimate knowledge of the plants themselves before they could construct any theory about them.

All this accumulated knowledge, whether real or spurious, lay behind Theophrastus when he began his *Enquiry*. He was sceptical of much of the superstition that surrounded plants, but respectful of the work done by those who had gone before him. He acknowledges the pharmacological skills of the Chian druggist, Eudemos, and those of Thrasyas of Mantineia and his pupil Alexias, all root-gatherers and expert distillers of poisons. He takes information from the first known Greek herbal, made by Diocles of Carystos in Euboea around the fourth century BC. That book is now lost, but was much quoted by those who, like Theophrastus, came after. In preparing his own herbal, essentially a book of medicine, Diocles had already gathered information on more than 300 plants, their habitats and uses.

'All men by nature desire to know,' wrote Aristotle in the famous sentence at the beginning of his *Metaphysics*. Knowledge comes from enquiry; enquiry means asking and trying to answer certain questions. In his *Historia animalium* and his *De generatione animalium*, the models for Theophrastus's *Historia plantarum* and *De causis plantarum*, Aristotle's purpose was 'first, to grasp the *differentiae* and attributes that belong to all animals; then to discover their causes'.[4] The creatures he writes about are not so much described as differentiated. 'Among things that fly, some have wings of feathers (for example, the eagle and hawk), some have wings of membrane (as do the bee and the cockchafer), and some have wings of skin (like the flying fox and the bat).'[5] We look back on his work through Darwin, through the theory of evolution. Aristotle, though, had no concept of a continuum. He thought in terms of fixed types, that differed only in proportion or relative size, or as he put it in 'excess and defect'.[6]

This idea of 'the more and the less' was a technical notion much favoured by those who had trained in Plato's Academy. As a way of distinguishing between kinds, Aristotle uses it constantly. Differences in degree are what he searches for: whether a bone is thicker or thinner, whether a body lighter or heavier, the beak longer or shorter, the feet webbed or clawed. 'Certain of the birds are long-legged. And a cause of this is that the life of such birds is marsh-bound; and nature makes organs relative to their function, not the function relative to the organ.'[7] Plato had set up the Academy in Athens in 387 BC; Aristotle joined it when he was seventeen and stayed there for twenty years. Then he became tutor to the young Alexander, whose conquering armies later swept through to the Indus. Returning to Athens in 335 BC, he founded the Lyceum; Macedonia had conquered Greece and the Lyceum's function would be to train the future leaders of this brave new world. The school, one of four major philosophy schools in Athens at that time, was established in a public sanctuary and gymnasium just outside the ancient city wall in what is now Syntagma Square. The sanctuary that Aristotle chose as the headquarters of the new school was dedicated to Apollo Lyceius. The school took its name from the god, though Lyceum students were generally known as the Peripatetics because of the covered walkway at the Lyceum, the cloister or *peripatos*, where most of the teaching took place.

Contemporary reports describe the teaching space furnished with a table, wooden sofas, a bronze statue and a globe; Theophrastus also wrote of a fine plane tree that grew in the garden. Because the Lyceum had been set up in public buildings, anyone could join in the debates. There was a museum and an excellent library, built up by Aristotle. Students were encouraged to research specific subjects: Theophrastus concentrated on plants, Eudemos on mathematics, Menon on the history of medicine.[8] Aristotle's purpose, realised through his own work as well as that of his brilliant pupils, was to survey whole fields of knowledge in a strictly methodical way. Members of Aristotle's school were voracious in their appetite for facts: they collected details of plays performed in Athens, collated the constitutions of different states, made lists of the victors at the Pythian games. Those were relatively simple tasks compared with the vast amount of information that Theophrastus sifted for his *Enquiry into Plants*. Constantly, Aristotle stressed the need for method, for systems; teachers regularly revised their lecture notes (*pragmateiai*) to keep up with new discoveries. At the Lyceum there was more instruction, less discussion than at the Academy. The spoken word was transposed to the written page. Markers were set down; for the first time, scholars could say: 'This is where we are. This is what we know.' Then they had to face the more problematical business of determining what the facts seemed to suggest. The whole gradual building up of material depended on peace and security. Neither Aristotle nor Theophrastus were Athenians, which made it difficult for them to own property in the city. But they were pro-Macedonia and when the Macedonians gained control of Athens, the new dictator, Demetrios of Phaleron, a former member of the Peripatetic School, gave Theophrastus a garden. That provided a secure place to keep the library and space to grow plants to study.

The historian Diogenes Laertius described Aristotle as a man with 'thin legs and small eyes; he wore fashionable clothes, and rings on his fingers – and he shaved'. The thin legs, the small eyes, do not suggest a man of much physical charisma. But the charisma must have been there, perhaps in his movements, his energy, his quickness of mind, certainly in his originality. Aristotle was the first teacher in the Western world to convince his students that a knowledge of plants or of animals was every bit as important as metaphysics or astronomy. Of all Aristotle's pupils, Theophrastus grasped most clearly what his mentor was trying to do. So when Aristotle died in 322 BC, it was not perhaps surprising that he nominated Theophrastus as the new head of the school. Diogenes, the William Hickey of his time, knew all the details of Aristotle's will. Antipater, the Macedonian governor of Athens, was to be the chief executor, but until Nicanor, Aristotle's adopted son, arrived back home, Aristomenes, Timarchus, Hipparchus, Dioteles and Theophrastus 'if he is willing and able' were to take care of Herpyllis, Aristotle's second wife, his children and his estate. When Aristotle's daughter came of age, his executors were to 'marry her to Nicanor'. If anything were to happen to Nicanor before this, then 'If Theophrastus wishes to live with my daughter, let the same provisions stand as with Nicanor.'[9]

Theophrastus took the school but not the daughter and headed it for thirty-five years until his death in 287 BC. In his will, Theophrastus bequeathed money for statues in the garden to be repaired, and left the school's library to Neleus of Skepsis. Neleus took the books away from Athens to his home and the loss of the library, so critical to the working methods of the Lyceum, contributed greatly to the decline of the Peripatetic School. By the time Theophrastus's successor, Strato, died eighteen years later, the active life of the Lyceum was effectively finished.

Perhaps it was inevitable that such a hothouse should cool down, as the most brilliant students left to set up their own schools elsewhere, or were lured into service by the rulers of newly founded cities and states. Or were the subjects to which Aristotle and Theophrastus had devoted so much energy, seen, once again, as unworthy of a scholar's time? Cicero evidently looked on Theophrastus's successor Strato with disdain, because he had abandoned 'higher' subjects, such as values and ethics, to concentrate his studies on the natural world.[10] Was there a kind of intellectual snobbery at work after the two great pioneers had gone that considered plants and animals too lowly a subject of study, suitable for doctors perhaps, but not worth a philosopher's time? 'For those who were attracted by comprehensive and dogmatic philosophical systems,' writes Bob Sharples, 'the Lyceum had nothing to offer that could compete with Epicureanism or the Stoa.'[11]

Unsettled times in Athens took their toll on the Peripatetics too. The Lyceum, outside the city walls, was vulnerable to attack. The method of teaching there depended on stability. Early in the third century BC, Alexandria and Rhodes, untroubled by war, began to rival Athens as centres of education. Elaborate research programmes, on a scale that only the Athenian Peripatos had previously embarked on, were set up at the Alexandrian Museum, munificently endowed with facilities and funds by an ambitious line of Egyptian kings. In a much-diluted form, the Lyceum, along with Plato's Academy and the other philosophical schools in Athens, staggered on for another 800 years until Emperor Justinian (his reign lasted from AD 527 to 566) shut them down in AD 529.[12] 'The light of science could not indeed be confined within the walls of Athens,' thundered Edward Gibbon in *The History of the Decline and Fall of the Roman Empire*. 'The living masters emigrated to Italy and Asia . . . The Gothic arms were less fatal to the schools of Athens than the establishment of a new religion, whose ministers superseded the exercise of reason, resolved every question by an article of faith and condemned the infidel or sceptic to eternal flames.' In the same year that Justinian brought to an end the Athenian philosophic tradition, St Benedict founded the first Christian monastery at Monte Cassino in Italy.

But what happened to the books that Aristotle had left to Theophrastus and which Theophrastus, in his will, had passed on to Neleus? The library, so carefully amassed, was the best in Athens. The manuscripts, covering a vast number of subjects, contained most of what was known about the natural world. Laboriously comparing and contrasting, Aristotle and Theophrastus had begun the search for the great idea, the logic that underpinned relationships between living things. But they were like people working on a vast puzzle with no idea of what the final picture should be. And quite a few of the pieces were missing. In this library was the seed of a system, a procedure for naming names in a meaningful way, which subsequent researchers could build on and amplify. But they didn't. For nearly 1,200 years, nothing happened. No progress was made until Albertus Magnus (Thomas Aquinas's mentor) brought out *De animalibus* in the thirteenth century AD. Why? The historian Strabo (*c.*63 BC – *c.* AD 23), who had studied Peripatetic philosophy in Rome, tells the story like this:

> Neleus took the library to Skepsis and left it in the hands of his heirs, ordinary men who kept the books locked up and not even carefully stored. And when they heard

363

Plate 12: Common poppy (our Papaver rhoeas)
*carefully arranged to show all the details necessary for
identification in Benedetto Rinio's herbal, the* Liber
de Simplicibus *made in 1419*

of the campaign by the Attalid kings, who controlled their city, to search out books and improve the library at Pergamum, they hid the collection underground in a pit. Sometime later, when the books had been damaged by dampness and moths, their descendants sold the library of Aristotle and Theophrastus to Apellikon of Teos for a large sum of money. Apellikon was a bibliophile rather than a philosopher; as a result, in seeking to restore the parts that had been eaten through, to make new copies, he altered the text with poor supplements and published the books filled with errors . . .

Immediately after Apellikon's death, Sulla, having captured Athens, removed the library to Rome. Here the grammarian Tyrannion, a lover of Aristotle, got his hands on it by insinuating himself into the good graces of the librarian, as did certain booksellers, who employed poor copyists and did not check their versions against the original.[13]

But how biased was Strabo? Was he, a Greek, in principle against the idea of Romans taking charge of Aristotle, the great Greek thinker? He is very keen to point out that errors were made by ROMAN copyists, that faulty editions were hawked around by acquisitive ROMAN booksellers. The erudite Greek grammarian, Athenaeus, has a different story. He reports that Neleus (or his family) sold a complete set of the works of Aristotle and Theophrastus to the Egyptian ruler, Ptolemy II Philadelphus, who was intent on making the new Alexandrian Library the best in the world.[14] So which story is true? Where did the books go?

In the last years of Theophrastus's time at the Lyceum, serious differences, personal as well as doctrinal, had arisen between the various senior members of the Peripatos. Theophrastus and Eudemos represented the orthodox tradition. Aristoxenus and Dicaearchus were more radical. Theophrastus wanted Neleus of Skepsis (a mediocre teacher, but a safe pair of hands) to be his successor and bequeathed him his library. But the elders of the Lyceum foiled Theophrastus's plan and elected Strato of Lampsacus instead. Shortly after Theophrastus's death, Neleus, as Strabo relates, moved back to his native Rhodes, taking the library with him. By the terms of Theophrastus's will, the books, which Theophrastus himself had inherited from Aristotle, became Neleus's personal property. The disagreements among the elders may have arisen because some of them, including Strato, were in favour of concentrating on scientific investigations at the expense of purely philosophical ones. Unlike the Academics and the Stoics, the Peripatetics had no strict dogma to guide them. They had a kind of constitution, which laid down that the head of the school was to be selected by an electoral committee. But Strato had directly appointed Lycon as his successor, saying meaningfully that 'it would be well if the others were to cooperate with him'. Lycon had his critics too. Antigonus of Carystos said he was far too fond of luxury and sport to be the head of a serious teaching establishment. Strato probably did not like Lycon either, but appointed him his direct successor because he saw that this was the only way to revive the school's fortunes. Students were leaving the Lyceum in great numbers. He guessed Lycon would put philosophical teachings back on the agenda and he was right. The natural sciences drifted over the sea to more fertile territory on the shores of northern Africa.

When Theophrastus died, Neleus was himself already an old man. As we are told, he left the precious books to family heirs. They were uneducated. They didn't know what to do with them. Perhaps they took advice. Perhaps, knowing that the Attalid Kings of Pergamum wanted to build a library to rival the Alexandrian one, burying the books seemed to be the best way of protecting them. They dug the pit. They carried out the books. The earth gently settled between the rolls and scrolls. The worms digested words, concepts, theories, and the beginning of a new science. Then c.100 BC, when nearly 150 years separated them from the imperatives of their ancestor Neleus, his family sold the books to Apellikon of Teos. It must have seemed like a good idea at the time. Apellikon was rich and paid a huge sum of money for the library; he was a powerful man, leader of the Mithradatic (anti-Roman) party in Athens during the early part of the first century BC. He was also known to be a great bibliophile. He took the library back to Athens with the intention of publishing a definitive edition of the Peripatetics' works. But he didn't understand philosophy and his copyists didn't care enough how they patched up the worm holes. The edition was full of mistakes.

Then in 86 BC Cornelius Sulla took Athens by force, and carried off Apellikon's library to Rome. After Sulla's death in 78 BC, the books came into the possession of his heir, Faustus Sulla, who shortly after 55 BC sold them at auction to pay off his gambling debts. Strabo says some Roman booksellers including the grammarian Tyrannion of Amisos, Cicero's friend and an avid book collector, got hold of the manuscripts at the auction of Sulla's library with a view to selling copies. But like Apellikon, they employed incompetent copyists (perhaps there never were enough good people available for such boring work), and would not cooperate to collate the various versions of Aristotle and Theophrastus's texts. The booksellers were interested in sales, not scholarship. But although it had not germinated, at least that seed – the beginning of a science – was still viable, still alive, capable of growing if only someone with the right skills could nourish it.

Tyrannion was not that man, though he was usefully placed to be. He had close links with Faustus Sulla's librarian, which put him in a good position when the Theophrastian library in Sulla's possession came up for auction. Tyrannion also had what newspapers now might describe as a 'close relationship' with Pomponius Atticus, a friend of Cicero's. Atticus had a huge private library, as well as being a well known book dealer and publisher. Some time around 60 BC Tyrannion became a partner in Atticus's publishing business. It was the object, rather than the ideas in it, that he responded to. The Roman philosopher Andronicus of Rhodes wasn't the man either. He was a better editor than either Apellikon or Tyrannion; he consolidated the corpus, perhaps made its survival less of a fragile accident than it had seemed before. Yet with Andronicus rests the Roman thread that connects us with Aristotle and Theophrastus.

There is another strand that takes us across the Mediterranean to Alexandria, with the story told by Athenaeus. He said that Neleus (or his heirs) sold the library to Ptolemy II Philadelphus, King of Egypt and founder of the famous Alexandrian Library. Certainly there was a great deal of Aristoteliean writing in Alexandria from the third to the second century BC. But both threads lead away from Athens. The city is finished now as a place where the things I'm interested in happen, though it will always be important as the place where it all began. Other places will emerge on this journey. Some I know about: Pisa, Padua, Florence, Montpellier, Frankfurt, London (though England was slow in producing people who could help find the right pieces to make the great puzzle of the natural world shine out clear). Slowly, slowly, with beautiful logic, the grand plan will emerge, to reveal all living things standing in their cohorts over the entire face of the earth: families, genera, species, varieties. Aristotle is finished too. He was never primarily a plantsman, but without him, Theophrastus is unlikely to have embarked on his *Enquiry into Plants*. This great project was the first attempt to look for kinship between plants, to understand their similarities and differences. Under Aristotle, Theophrastus learned how to organise information and was shown the benefits of an open, inquisitive mind. He raised the profile of the natural sciences, not permanently among the aesthete Athenians, but long enough for the first vital steps to be taken. Now the trail leads to Alexandria.

III

THE ALEXANDRIAN
LIBRARY

300 BC—40 BC

A FRAGMENTARY PIECE of papyrus of the second to third century AD describes the city of Alexandria as 'a universal nurse', harbouring soldiers from Macedonia, settlers from mainland Greece, Arabs, Babylonians, Assyrians, Medes, Persians, Carthaginians, Italians, Gauls, Iberians and a large and cultured Jewish population. Protected as it was by the island of Pharos lying offshore, the site had many natural advantages. When Alexander the Great sailed past it on 20 January 331 BC, he immediately recognised its potential and ordered Dinocrates, the architect accompanying him on his Egyptian adventure, to lay out a grand new city there. Alexander, who died in 323 BC, a year before Aristotle, never saw his namesake; in the distribution of empire that followed Alexander's death, his half-brother, Ptolemy Soter (see plate 13) got Egypt. But Dinocrates laid out a power-fully triumphant city: two great intersecting avenues divided it into four unequal parts; shady colonnades of marble lined the streets; the stone houses were built over vaulted cellars to keep cool the underground cisterns filled with fresh water; huge docks and warehouses rose along the harbour front. In *The Thirty-Second Discourse*, Dio Chrysostom marvelled at the grandeur and power of the new metropolis: 'Not only have you a monopoly of the shipping of the entire Mediterranean by reason of the beauty of your harbours, the magnitude of your fleet, and the abundance and the marketing of the products of every land, but also the outer waters that lie beyond are in your grasp, both the Red Sea and the Indian Ocean whose name was rarely heard in former days.'[1] The Macedonian, Ptolemy Soter, ruled supreme in the former

Plate 13: Ptolemy Soter, who founded the great library at Alexandria and was the first of a dynasty of Macedonian emperors who ruled in Egypt from 323 BC

ancient empire of the Pharaohs. He too inspired a renaissance – nothing to equal the Royal Museum or the Alexandrian Library had ever been seen in the ancient world. The Museum, part of the royal palace in the Greek quarter of the city, had a public walk, a curved exedra with marble seats, a common room and a refectory. It was connected to the Library by a covered marble colonnade; inside the Library were ten great halls, lined with shelves and cupboards, all numbered and titled, housing a vast collection of manuscripts. Another, smaller, library was built near the Temple of Serapis in the Rhakotis, the Egyptian quarter.

Each of the Library's halls was dedicated to a separate subject. Where is my man Theophrastus in this huge place, I am wondering? Who is reaching to pull *Enquiry into Plants* down from its numbered shelf? Aristotle's death marked the end of the great classic period in Greek literature but just as he and the great tradition of which he was part perished, a new age began in Alexandria. When Aristotle had first started to collect books for the Lyceum's library, he was considered a pioneer, an innovator. Now Ptolemy Soter began to put together something far more ambitious, employing perhaps a hundred scholars to seek out and translate texts for its shelves. He gathered together poets, philosophers, scientists, mathematicians (Euclid was one of them), as well as men of letters to build a new civilisation here in Alexandria, inspired by Hellenic ideals. But though the city he brought into being was new, the country in which it stood had seen a culture very much more advanced than the Hellenic civilisation that Ptolemy now imposed on it. At the time of the Pharaohs, long before Theophrastus embarked on his great work, the Egyptians had already created hieroglyphics for 202 different plants including opium poppy, fennel, acacia and reed.[2] They had learned how to make paper from papyrus as Theophrastus describes in his *Enquiry into Plants*;[3] they knew how to embalm bodies using plant extracts. Knowledge in ancient Egypt, though, was largely bound up with the priesthood, not secular as it had been at the Lyceum and the Academy in Athens.

Among those who went to Alexandria was Demetrios of Phaleron. It was he who first suggested that Alexandria should have a museum and a library and he who gathered in the first manuscripts for Ptolemy Soter's collection. Exiled from Athens, he wanted to make Alexandria into an Athens across the sea. An orator and a statesman as well as a philosopher, Demetrios was a follower of Aristotle, a pupil and friend of Theophrastus. So it seems quite likely that Athanaeus was right and that at least some of the Peripatetics' books came to Alexandria. Demetrios would have been the perfect intermediary. But, with a patron as cultured as Ptolemy to please, he would also have wanted only the best. So perhaps he acquired the most original of the manuscripts, leaving the rest with Neleus and his heirs to be consigned later to the pit, the moths and the worms. Both accounts could be true. The Library was most probably founded soon after Demetrios's arrival in Alexandria around 307 BC, when he secured large grants of public money to augment the collection. Contemporary accounts suggest that in the first ten or twelve years, he could have brought in as many as 200,000 separate works, transcribed on rolls of papyrus. Like the American collectors, Pierpont Morgan, Huntington and Paul Getty, all of whom gathered cocoons of old culture around them in a new country, Ptolemy Soter cast his net wide. When he ran out of Greek texts to collect, he brought in foreign ones, particularly those of the two great empires of the ancient Eastern world – Assyria in the east and Egypt in the south.

Demetrios of Phaleron was the first of a long list of distinguished librarians: Zenodotus of Ephesus (282–*c*.260 BC), Callimachus of Cyrene (*c*.260–*c*.240 BC), Apollonius of Rhodes (*c*.240–*c*.230 BC), Eratosthenes of Cyrene (*c*.230–195 BC), Aristophanes of Byzantium (195–180 BC), Apollonius the Eidograph (180–*c*.160 BC), Aristarchus of Samothrace (*c*.160–131 BC). Unfortunately, when Ptolemy's son took over the city, Demetrios fell out with him (overspending? Or just yesterday's man?) and was banished to Busiris in Upper Egypt. He died in 282 BC, bitten by an asp; some said he had been murdered. With his death, the direct link with Theophrastus came to an end.

The Ptolemys' empire lasted for 300 years, the city more than twice as long. It was a treasury of learning and science, preserving all the hard-won knowledge of the Greeks, as well as a great deal of learning from the empires that Alexander had conquered. There was a strict embargo on imported books. All vessels coming into the port were searched and if any books were found aboard, they were confiscated. Copies of the confiscated volumes were made for their owners, while the originals were kept for the Alexandrian Library.

The second Ptolemy also commissioned the most ancient translation of the Old Testament. He brought in seventy-two Jewish translators and kept them cooped up on the island of Pharos until they had finished the job. The Preface to the King James Bible (1611) acknowledges his primacy: 'It pleased the Lord to stirre up the spirit of a Greeke Prince (Greeke for dicent and language), even of Ptoleme Philadelph, King of Egypt, to procure the translating of the Booke of God out of Hebrew into Greeke . . . Therefore the word of God, being set foorth in Greeke, becometh hereby like a candle set upon a candlesticke, which giveth light to all that are in the house . . .' Dragged regularly as a child to the small thirteenth-century church that crouches at Llanddewi Rhydderch in Wales, I sometimes read that passage during tedious sermons. As a word, Philadelph took my fancy, as sop-or-if-ic did in Beatrix Potter's tale of Peter Rabbit. Then, in my first garden, I met the man again as a shrub, the syringa or mock orange (*Philadelphus coronarius*), sweet-smelling, white-flowered, and introduced from Turkey into Europe by the Flemish ambassador Ogier Ghiselin de Busbecq, in 1562. But syringa (it comes from the Greek word *syrinx* or pan pipe) was also the common name given to lilac because both shrubs have wood that is hollow and pithy and both were used by the Turks to make musical pipes. It was a muddle, having two completely different shrubs sharing the same common name. The French botanist Jean Bauhin resolved it in 1623 by giving the king's name, Philadelphus, to Gerard's 'white pipe tree'.

Philadelphus the king died in 246 BC so did not witness the cataclysmic destruction of his city, sacked by the Roman dictator Caesar in 47 BC. By then more than half a million rolls and scrolls were piled upon the labelled shelves of the ten great halls. Some (the greatest treasures) had already been given to Caesar by Cleopatra. Some were destroyed when the citizens of Alexandria, under a military commander called Achillas, rose up against Caesar and marched on the city. Caesar deliberately set fire to the Egyptian fleet in Alexandria's harbour, but the wind, blowing onshore, set alight the buildings of the waterfront too. Did the Library burn? No, not then. Later, religion accomplished what war had left alone. The gaps on the Library shelves left by Clepatra's 'gift' to Caesar, were conveniently filled by Antony, who gave Cleopatra 200,000 rolls from the library sacked at Pergamum. Tough skins joined Egypt's brittle, frail paper. Knowledge fragmented came together again. And was Theophrastus still there in that great repository? No catalogue survives. It can't be known for sure. But the work he produced was the kind of work in which the Library specialised. Unlike the Athenian schools, the Alexandrian Museum and Library were not places of philosophical controversy; they were academies of technical knowledge, especially that relating to medicine and the natural sciences. The work that Theophrastus started in Athens was central to what mattered in Alexandria, though they did not build on what he had done. While the Peripatetics had written as natural scientists, the Alexandrian scholars wrote as encyclopaedists, one step removed from the actual subject matter. Commentary was their forte. They explained the classical texts but did not, in Theophrastus's field at least, initiate new work. In human anatomy and physiology it was different.[4]

'I shall not recapitulate the disasters of the Alexandrian Library,' wrote Edward Gibbon, 'the involuntary flame that was kindled by Caesar in his own defence, or the mischievous bigotry of the Christians who studied to destroy the monuments of idolatry.'[5] But the survival of knowledge, the thread that connects us, now, with them, then, was jeopardised by enemies more insidious than fire and war, less dramatic perhaps but just as threatening. Water trickles through the roof of the Library, damp pervades the parchment and papyrus, mould slowly spreads over the seminal words, mice scrabble among the scrolls, shredding the soft paper for their babies' nests,

Plate 14: 'Astragalus' (commonly known as goat's thorn or milk vetch) from a Dioscorides manuscript made and illustrated in the Islamic style in the middle of the thirteenth century

moths lay their eggs between the undisturbed layers of skin. Nearly 700 years, the space between us and the medieval scribes of the fourteenth century, stretches between Theophrastus's death and the destruction in AD 391 of the Temple of Serapis at Alexandria by the Christian emperor Theodosius I. What state was the Library in then? Theodosius was the last ruler to govern an undivided Roman Empire and during the twenty years (AD 375–395) of his reign, the new Christian Church sent out tough edicts. Paganism, in all its forms, must be destroyed. The temple dedicated to the Egyptian divinity Serapis, god of healing, was rebuilt as a Christian church and monastery. Did the small library, built at the portals of the old temple, survive this radical metamorphosis? If it did, it was not for long. After Theodosius came the Saracens. They attacked the city in the seventh century AD, and it was said that when the first camel entered the gates of Medina, bringing the spoils of war from Alexandria, the last, in an unbroken line, had not yet left Egyptian soil. Omar, the Saracens' leader, was a fanatic convert to the cause of Islam. 'No other book but the book of God,' was his edict. Writing c.1227 in his *Histoire des Savants*, Ibn al Kiftī describes the fate of the books. The Arab scholar Yahya al Nahawi tells Amr ibn al-As, the conquering Arab general of Egypt, about the extraordinary treasures contained in the Alexandrian Library. The soldier, who has never heard of the books, says he can do nothing until he has received instructions from the caliph Omar. He sends a message to Omar, telling him about the books and asking what he is to do about them. With cool fundamentalist logic, Omar replies, 'If the books contain any thing which conforms to the Book of God (the Koran), the Book of God permits us to eradicate them. If they contain any thing which is contrary, they are useless. Proceed then to destroy them.' Amr ibn al-As piled the books up in carts and distributed them among the 400 public baths of Alexandria. There, they were burned in the furnaces that heated the warming rooms. There were said to be enough of them to keep the fires going for six whole months.[6]

The Alexandrian Library was the first great library. And the first to be destroyed, though many were after that great bonfire of ideas in Alexandria. When, ten years later, Hulako conquered Baghdad, he ordered all the books of learning to be thrown into the River Tigris. The libraries of that unfortunate, cultured city were again destroyed by Mongols in the thirteenth century and by Tamerlane 200 years later. When European invaders conquered Tripoli in Syria during the Wars of the Crusades, Count Bertram Saint Jeal ordered its libraries to be burned; an estimated three million books disappeared in that purging. The Spaniards did the same with the ancient libraries of Andalusia when they reclaimed the region from the Arabs in the latter part of the fifteenth century. It seemed almost a prerequisite to establishing a new order. But somehow, the ideas survived. And grew in importance.

IV

PLINY THE PLAGIARIST
AD 20—AD 80

FOR THEOPHRASTUS, HERBALISM – the medical uses to which plants could be put – was just one strand in a wide-ranging investigation of plants. That kind of practical, applied knowledge had developed over thousands of years in civilisations much more ancient than the Greeks'. In his own enquiry, Theophrastus had added something new, a philosophical overview. This embraced all plants known at that time, not just the ones from which drugs could be distilled. He started the debate about the correct names for plants. He was interested in the similarities and differences between them, and this led on to suggestions about ways in which they could be grouped. Though hampered by the lack of any precise terms, any specialised vocabulary, he managed nevertheless to describe plants in a concise, succinct fashion. He was interested in their distribution and ecology. He was the first to dealt with fundamental questions, such as the difference between root and shoot, leaf and petal. He asked the first important questions. And was answered by a deafening silence. Almost 2,000 years passed before writers in the Renaissance, with similarly enquiring minds, rediscovered Theophrastus and realised that most of what had happened in between had been a waste of time. Islamic scholars always understood his importance and stayed faithful to his original text. Soon after Alexander's time, Greek schools had been founded in Syria where scholars translated the work of Aristotle and Theophrastus into the Syrian language. Gradually, the teachings of the Peripatetics spread into Persia and Arabia. The Syrian versions of the texts were translated into Arabic. Arab physicians and philosophers kept

Theophrastus alive while Europe was groping through its long Dark Age. It was a long time before these Arab translations were turned back into Latin and Greek and European scholars were in a position to rediscover Theophrastus's complex, quizzical take on the natural world.

In Europe, the Roman lawyer Pliny (AD 23–79) and the Greek doctor Dioscorides (AD 40–?) became the models, the dubious founts of plant knowledge. Both of them produced compendiums of plants around the same time (AD 77). But neither Pliny nor Dioscorides asked questions. Neither pushed on in any way the complex process of naming plant names. They were copiers, compilers, not thinkers. Dioscorides was a medicine man first, a plantsman second; the medical properties of plants were his chief interest. The lawyer Pliny, whose *Natural History* was one of the prime source-books on plants from AD 50 to the early sixteenth century, was a Roman Gradgrind. Facts, facts, facts were what he consumed and regurgitated in vast quantities, but without making much of them. He didn't join them up to come to any conclusions. He showed little discrimination between things that were likely to be true and those that could only be fable.[1] Between them, Dioscorides and Pliny could have expanded the two disciplines, the philosophical and the practical, that Theophrastus so cleverly combined in his work. Instead they reduced the study of plants to its lowest form, of interest only when servicing the needs of man. The two strands, instead of multiplying, were reduced again to one – the herbal.

Writing after Pliny's death, his nephew, Pliny the Younger, describes his uncle's voracious appetite for information:

In the winter, he was accustomed to work until between one or two o'clock in the morning or at the shortest until midnight. He could fall asleep at once, no matter at what hour; sometimes even at work he would fall asleep for a few moments and awake again. Before the break of day he would go to the Emperor Vespasian – for he too used to work at night – to receive his orders or to fulfil some commission. Returning home he would study until breakfast time. After a light breakfast, if it was summer, and he had a little leisure, he would lie down in the sun and have a book read to him, taking notes and extracts; for he read nothing without making some excerpts, being accustomed to say that no book was so bad as not to contain something useful. After that, as if another day had dawned, he studied again until dinner time. Even at this principal meal a book was read, and comments written, and this without interrupting the reading. I remember that once upon a time one of his friends present checked the reader, who had given a wrong inflection, and had him read the line over again. 'But you understood the meaning at the first reading, did you not?' my uncle asked. The other nodded assent. 'Why then did you call for the repetition?' He was so greedy for time. He rose from the dinner table, whether while it was yet daylight in summer, or when in winter it was after dark, always with the same promptness, as if compelled by law. This was his manner of life amid the business and turmoil of the city. In the country the only respite he allowed himself was a daily bath; and when I say that I mean the actual time of the bath; for while the drying and dressing was going on he was either listening or dictating. On his journeyings, as if putting out of mind all business cares, he did nothing else but that; keeping always close beside him a rapid penman, a book, and a writing tablet . . . For the same purpose even in Rome he had himself carried from place to place in a sedan. I remember well how once in meeting me when I was walking he said: 'You ought not to lose these hours,' for he reckoned all time lost that was not given to study. It was by such exertions as these that he brought all those volumes to completion.[2]

Those volumes included a book on the correct way for a cavalryman to hurl a lance, written while he himself was in command of a cavalry company. His leadership, notes his nephew, 'was marked equally by courage and prudence'. He managed to contain the life of his friend, Pomponius Secundus, in two books but filled twenty with an epic history of the Roman wars against the Germans, which he compiled while on military service in Germany. He said the subject suggested itself to him in a dream. Even his sleeping time could not be wasted. Three books were devoted to 'The Student', a comprehensive guide to oratory from cradle to Senate. While lying low on his estate during the dangerous years of Nero's reign, he produced eight books on 'Hesitancies in Public Address'. Imagine, given his own relentless agenda, how wildly irritating he must have found any such vacillation. The waste of it. The squandering of time. Then in AD 77, he completed the *Natural History*, a vast encyclopaedia of the natural world: cosmology, astronomy, geography, zoology, minerals, metallurgy. And plants.

Uncritical to a fault, Pliny packed in facts in dizzying variety, but at the same time added little new to the existing debate. In his Preface to the *Natural History* he names a hundred writers whose work he has plundered for his own. That's a lot of talking books, hours of reading aloud for his poor *lector*, days of scribbling for his 'rapid penman'. In fact, he quotes 473 sources, 146 of them Roman, 327 Greek. He borrows more from Aristotle (on animals) and Theophrastus (on plants) than from any other writer. 'It is impossible,' he says, 'sufficiently to admire the pains and care of the ancients, who explored everything and left nothing untried.'[3] In the Preface too, he says he has assembled 20,000 facts. Whose ghastly job was it to come up with that figure? It's a suspiciously round one, but no one since AD 77 has

*Plate 15: A Roman fountain niche from Baiae in Italy,
made of mosaic in the first century* AD

had the will to check it. In all, he describes about 800 plants, dividing them by use: plants for wines and cordials, plants for food, for medicine, for garlands, for bees.

Three books (Books IV–VI) are concerned with plants for gardens. There is almost nothing of that in Theophrastus, writing more than 300 years earlier. Just once, in Book VI of his *Enquiry into Plants*, Theophrastus mentions the roses growing on Mount Pangaeus near Philippi which the local people dig up to plant in their gardens. But Pliny was very fond of his garden at Laurentum, the villa he describes as

> planted round with ivy-clad plane trees, green with their own leaves above, and below with the ivy which climbs over trunk and branch and links tree to tree as it spreads across them. Box shrubs grow between the plane trees and outside there is a ring of laurel bushes which add their shade to that of the planes . . . Between the grass lawns here and there are box shrubs clipped into innumerable shapes, some being letters which spell the gardener's name or his master's; small obelisks of box alternate with fruit trees, and then suddenly in the midst of this ornamental scene is what looks like a piece of rural country planted there. The open space in the middle is set off by low plane trees planted on each side; farther off are acanthuses with their flexible glossy leaves, then more box figures and names.[4]

The villa has a circular driveway sweeping round in front of it. In the middle is an island bed, planted with mulberry and fig trees and bordered by a hedge of rosemary and box. In the centre is a vine-covered pergola. This was the beginning of a garden style re-created over and over again through the centuries that followed. On the Italian Riviera, the Edwardian garden designer Harold Peto planted gardens for rich American clients that in style and content could have been lifted straight from Laurentum. The vine-covered pergola has become the hallmark of the kind of property most likely to find its way on to the glossy pages of *House and Garden* magazine. In Pliny's garden, an *olitor* looked after the vegetables; an *arborator* looked after the trees; a *vinitor* cared for the vines; an *aquarius* watered the plants (that was considered a low-grade job, but Ovid in exile said that he wouldn't mind being one if it meant he could return home). A *topiarius* clipped the topiary that became wildly fashionable in Roman gardens during the reign of Augustus. Pliny talks of cypress being cut 'to provide representations of . . . hunting scenes or fleets of ships'.[5] The concept of a garden as a place of fancy and of plants grown purely for pleasure does not emerge in Theophrastus. The typical Greek garden of his time is described in an inscription made at Thasos early in the third century BC, on a building used to display official notices in public. It lays down the conditions of a lease for a garden under the general supervision of a priest of the cult of Asclepius. The lease sets out the rent due, but stipulates other conditions too. Periodically, the tenant must provide a bull for sacrifice, keep the walls and latrine in good repair, and cultivate only speci-fied plants: fig trees, myrtle and hazelnuts. In return he can help himself to the wild plants of the field and, at certain hours of the day, have access to public water for irrigation.[6]

The plane tree, still a novelty in Theophrastus's time, was as highly regarded as a shade tree by the Romans as it had been by the Greeks. Like the Greeks, the Romans brought in plants chiefly from the East, rather than the West. Among the plants that Pliny describes (and which were unknown to Theophrastus) is the cherry, first discovered growing round about Pontus on the southern shores of the Black Sea. It was taken to Rome by Lucullus around 60 BC and quickly spread with the Roman invaders to Germany and Belgium. It was in Britain by AD 46, only three years after the first Roman landings. Romans imported apricots from Armenia, damsons from Damascus in Syria, peaches from Persia. He describes the garlands and swags of foliage and flowers – narcissus, roses, lilies, larkspur – strung on feast days between the pillars of the villa porticos. Garlands and chaplets were put on altars to honour the gods, the *lares* public and private, the tombs and spirits of the dead.[7] Theophrastus favoured the roses from Philippi. By Pliny's time, the most popular roses were said to come from Praeneste and the most sweetly scented from Cyrene in Libya.

Yet though Pliny introduces a new concept – plants to grow for pleasure rather than for food or medicine – and although indefatigable in gathering information, he remains a credulous compiler, not an original thinker. He's not even a serious researcher; little of what he writes has been gained from first-hand experience (though he does include information about plants he has seen in Germany, an area almost unknown to Theophrastus). He complains about a general ignorance of plants: 'The reason why more herbs are not familiar is because they are only known to illiterate country people who live among them . . . The most disgraceful reason for this lack of knowledge is that even those who know refuse to pass on their knowledge, as if they would lose what they impart to others.'[8] But at the same time, he himself is content to regurgitate information at second-hand. Over the next thousand years, that tendency got worse. Scholars stopped looking at plants, and saw them only through others' eyes. Personal knowledge of plants faded as derivative knowledge multiplied.

But that second-hand knowledge could at least have been derived from a good primary source. Why were Pliny and Dioscorides, rather than Theophrastus, the models for a later age? In short, because they were there. The direct link that scholars in Western Europe had with Theophrastus came to an end with the burning of the books in Alexandria. He lived on with the Arabs and was finally reintroduced to European scholars of the fifteenth century in a translation made back into Latin from an Arab manuscript discovered in the Vatican Library in Rome. Pliny never got lost and he wrote in a language, Latin, that was ubiquitous in the Middle Ages. Anyone that could read, could read Latin as easily as their own native language. In monasteries and chapterhouses in France, Italy, Germany, England, Pliny's *Natural History* was copied, copied and copied again. At least 200 transcripts were made during the Middle Ages and each new copy made the survival of Pliny's work more secure. Copying was such an immense and expensive labour (there were thirty-seven books of it after all) that the manuscript copies were looked after extremely well. The advent of printing made his survival even more certain. By the fifteenth century, only shortly after the famous bible emerged from the Gutenberg press, Joanes Spira had issued the first printed edition of Pliny's book in Venice (1469). Long before Christopher Columbus ever sailed to America, twenty-three separate editions of Pliny had been printed. Italian printers quickly followed Spira's lead and brought out their own editions in Brescia, Milan, Parma, Rome, Treviso and Verona. Over the next fifty years, printers in Paris, Basel, Lyons, Frankfurt, Cologne, London, Heidelberg, Strasbourg, Frankfurt, Geneva, Leiden and Vienna followed suit. These were all Latin editions, but Pliny was translated into Italian by 1476. Versions in French, Dutch and German quickly followed. For a thousand benighted years, all that European scholars knew of Theophrastus were those passages of his *Enquiry* bowdlerised by Pliny.

Pliny began his professional career in Germany, where, at the age of twenty-three, he joined the Roman army of occupation. He ended it in the Bay of Naples where, as commander of a naval fleet, he had been sent to suppress piracy. In the summer of AD 79 the fleet was at anchor in the Tyrrhene sea, sheltering behind what is now known as the Punta di Miseno, close to Vesuvius. On 22 August, at about noon, a cloud in the shape of a huge Italian pine, with a straight trunk and horizontal branches, is seen to rise from the crater of the volcano. Pliny commandeers a small, light sailing boat and sets out to get a closer view of the strange phenomenon. Then comes the earthquake and the volcano's frightful eruption. Molten lava and red-hot ashes pour from the volcano's mouth. Pliny sees immediately that the eruption has put in danger the lives of everyone living under the mountain. As they have no way of escaping except by sea, he orders the fleet to sail to the rescue. Showers of burning stones and ash fall on his ship. His sailors are terrified, but their commander quietly continues to dictate to his amanuensis his own observations on the volcano and its effects. Pliny goes ashore at a point where a friend of his has a country estate. He finds the local villagers already provided with boats, but a strong, onshore wind

رودا وهو الورد
الورد الطرى بارد وياضر والبابس منه
اشد وضا وبسع اروجذ الطرى و
بقبض منه اطراف السر بيفراح و
.در والباو منه وبعض و بساط
عصارته والظل الوارنحر اوبنقل
مرنخر وبعالجه فيا دطلى له العن
ودلخفف الورد والظل وخرك
كثرا بلا دلكح وعصاره الورد
اداطح بطلا كار صالحالوجم الراس
والعر والارا اداطلىت واللنة
ادامصصته والمعده والامعا
السفلى والرجم اداحمل واردوورقه
مرعر اربصر وصمد به مراو البطر الدرعرضه ورم حار نقعه وبسع مرلةالمعدة
ومر الحره ووربقع البابس داحلاط القح والدرا بروادوبه الحراحات والمعبوبات
ورخرو لت بعمل والاخال المنبه لهلب العن فقاح الورد
هرادا الصو باللنان وطع البله وارا حر مرصابه قلو وبنر بيع مرهن اللم
وعقلا لبطر ى الورىلرس وهو بنر الورد واما البرر الدرع
بسط الورد فانه ادارُوهو بابسر على اللنه انى بصت البها الصو كار صالحا
لها واما اتماع الورد فانها اداشربن وطعت الاسهال وهت اللم واما
الاوراص الوجال لها دود سرفانها بحا حدر حدمر الورد الطرى مالمبصه الما
وقدصمر ورر ابعر مرمثقال ومر البار در البهدر حمه مساه ر وامر سنه مافل
ودملابه اوراص وكل وصه بلنا انبلونبّانا وانبلوبس بلمه قاربط وحفه والظل
وحزر ع انامر حجار لسر مفر وبسل رأسه وعر البار مرزبد دسبه هره لازامر
مرالبسط ورود درجم وهو مقال وم السوسر البس ارسا الدرمر ابلورده وجدبون
الكل بالوسل والسرا ب الرحار ودب بعل هره الاوراص للبسا داوضع عر فقاح الرم
لوطع الرح الى بكور مر ا لعو وبرد ستعمل بارو وبنر على بنبر بقلا سنيا امر
فاذا حب بستل بما بارد وهر بعلر مبنها محاسو وعطه وبعلها بر زبا بعر

Plate 16: A rose, economically shown with three different
kinds of flower springing from the same bush, in a
manuscript made in northern Islam AD 1083

prevents them getting away. Meanwhile, the dangers of remaining on land increase with every hour. When night falls, Pliny, as if to inspire courage in others, takes his customary bath. He eats dinner and goes to bed as usual. Towards morning the falls of stone and ash increase violently. The earthquake shocks become much more frequent. Pliny's servants wake him up, fearing that the porch on which he has made his bed will get buried under the falling ash. It seems inevitable that all the buildings around will be demolished as the stones spewed out from the volcano fall thickly around. For protection, people bind cushions and pillows about their heads and rush down to the beach. Unfortunately the waves are still high and the winds unfavourable. It is not possible for anyone to get on board the ships waiting offshore. Although it is now daytime, everything at land and sea is still as dark as night, the sun obscured by the ash of the volcano. The blackness is pierced only by vivid flashes of lightning and flames that burst out with sudden ferocity from the great cracks opening up in the earth. The inhabitants rush backwards and forwards in a frenzy of despair. Pliny, helped by two slaves, rises from his couch and, overcome by sulphur fumes, falls dead. The great cities of Herculaneum and Pompeii are completely buried by ash and lava.[9] Almost 2,000 years later, researchers analysing pollen grains trapped in the ash find that while Vesuvius was venting its terrible load, southernwood, myrtle, asters, pinks, mallow, campanula, lychnis, cerastium and plantain were blooming in the garden of the House of the Chaste Lovers at Pompeii.

V

THE MEDICINE MEN

AD 40—AD 400

THEOPHRASTUS'S WORK ON plants survived among scholars in the East. Pliny endured in the West. But the book *De materia medica*, produced around AD 77 by a young Greek doctor, Pedanios Dioscorides (see plate 17), was for the next 1,500 years revered as the ultimate authority on plants equally in both East and West. A little less reverence would perhaps have resulted in a little more progress. Dioscorides only wanted to produce a decent field guide to plants useful in medicine. He had no interest in the larger aim of sorting and ordering nature into some viable system. He criticised his predecessors for their lack of method, but method to Dioscorides did not imply a search for some grand design. He just wanted a way of retrieving easily the kind of information he required to treat his patients. He needed a simple guide that would help him identify medicinal plants, along with a summary of the complaints and problems that each plant might cure.

The book he produced gives much less space to descriptions of plants than to ways in which they can be used. The author (though delivered to us with the gloss of many other hands upon him) comes across as a brisk, rational man, sceptical of superstition, but a man of his time in his acceptance of the power of plants to heal in ways that we now find extremely bizarre. In writing of asparagus, for instance, he says that it springs up from smashed rams' horns and that a stem of it, hung round the neck as an amulet, makes both men and women barren, 'not fit for generation'. Born *c.* AD 40 at Anazarbus in Cilicia (SE Asia Minor), Dioscorides studied in Alexandria and Tarsus, before joining the Roman army as a physician. He travelled

Plate 17: Dioscorides in Eastern dress,
from a manuscript made in AD *1229*

extensively with them, particularly in the Eastern Mediterranean (the command structure provided a doctor, a *medicus legionis* for every twenty-five to thirty legions – about 6,500 to 7,000 men). Plants for medicine had to be gathered and prepared in the field, spring, summer and autumn, and in each season a plant might show itself in a different guise. Dioscorides was one of the first people to point out that, 'Anyone wanting experience in these matters must encounter the plants as shoots newly emerged from the earth, plants in their prime, and plants in their decline. For someone who has come across the shoot alone cannot know the mature plant, nor if he has seen only the opened plants can he recognise the young shoot as well.'[1]

In compiling his own treatise, Dioscorides drew on local knowledge and traditions, previous authors (though he mentions Theophrastus only twice), and his own experience – he was well placed to correlate traditions of both East and West. Writing in provincial Greek, he arranged the material he had gathered into different groups and then divided the information into five books. First, he looks at oily, gummy, resinous plants, useful for making aromatic salves and ointments. He groups together trees and shrubs that produce raw materials useful in medicine. He considers cereals, pot herbs, and sharp, aromatic herbs. He writes about the importance of roots and the juices to be extracted from them. He lists the seeds that have medicinal properties and makes an inventory of the various wines and cordials he has found useful in treating patients. Very occasionally he groups plants of a similar form: plants with many-petalled flowers like daisies, plants with big flat umbrella-shaped flower heads. He catalogues thirty-five medicines that come from animals and includes prescriptions that depend on esoteric ingredients such as *rupos* (grime) from baths. But most of his medicines derive from plants and he includes nearly 600 of them, slightly more than Theophrastus, though fewer than Pliny, whose focus was not primarily on plants for medicine. Though his descriptions of plants are not as good as Theophrastus's, he gives more information on likely habitats and the geographical spread of plants, useful information for other herb-gatherers scattered through the ever expanding Roman Empire. He did no pioneering work on plant names and the way that they were used, but he collected them, codified them, and organised the resulting information in a clear, precise and commendably brief way. 'Kalamagrostis (reed grass) is greater in every respect than Gramen (agrostis), but being eaten it is a killer of labouring beasts, and especially that which grows in Babylon by the wayside.' Even a summary as short as that gives a name, a comparative reference ('greater in every respect than Gramen'), an idea of the plant's medical properties, its habitat and location. This is why his work became a standard reference. It was snappy and gave the impression of being authoritative. Men, far cleverer than Dioscorides himself, went on regarding him as a mentor and his book the *sine qua non* of plant knowledge. He mesmerised future generations and achieved such iconic status that nobody thought to question his work.

If Pier Andrea Mattioli, for instance, had had the courage to publish his own observations independently of Dioscorides, the *De materia medica* would surely have become obsolete earlier than it did. Instead, in 1544, Mattioli published an admiring commentary on the work of the man even he regarded as his master. It was the first of a long series of attempts by different authors in different countries to relate the plants that Dioscorides wrote about to the plants that they themselves knew. The sixteenth-century Spanish physician Nicolas Monardes said Dioscorides's work was 'so celebrated in all the worlde, wherby he gate the glory and fame, whiche we see he hath, and there hath remained more fame of hym, by writing them, then although he had gotten many Cities with his warlike actes.' Even as late as 1633, dear Thomas Johnson, the first man ever to try to compile a list of plants growing in England, wrote that *De materia medica* 'is as it were the foundation and grounde-worke of all that hath been since delivered in this nature'. Between 1652 and 1655, the fine English scholar John Goodyer made himself an interlinear translation of Dioscorides (Latin to English) to help in the important research he was himself engaged in at the time (by then, even more synonyms had to be accommodated and Goodyer includes them in parentheses).

> *Iris* [Somme call it Iris Illyrica, somme Theklpida, somme Urania, somme Catharon, somme Thaumastos, the Romanes call it Radix Marica, somme Gladiolus, somme Opertritis, somme Consecratix, the Egyptians call it Nar] is soe named from the resemblance of the rainbow in heaven, but it beares leaves like unto a little sword but greater & broader & fatter [or thicker]: the flowers on the stalke, are bended in, one over against another, & divers, for they are either soon white or pale or black or purple or azure. Whence for the varietie of colours it is likened to the heavenly rainebow. The roots under are knotty, strong [or sound], of a sweet savour, which after the cutting ought to be dryed in the shade, & soe (with a linnen thread put through them) to be layd up.[2]

Iris (or orris) root was good for coughs, and for purging 'thick humours'. It helped insomniacs sleep, would 'heale the torments of ye belly'. It was an antidote to snake bites, eased sciatica, filled up ulcers and cleansed them. It was good for headache and sunburn, in short, a paragon among herbs.

Writing 400 years earlier, Theophrastus had already found that, even within Greece, the same plant did not necessarily carry the same name. The Macedonians used one term, the Ionians another. As travel, trade and the intermingling of cultures increased, so did this problem of synonymity. Dioscorides wrote in his native Greek tongue and used local Greek names for his plants, correlated with Latin synonyms. But already, being a well travelled man, he was adding many extra labels: names in Egyptian, Persian, Syrian, African, Iberian, Etruscan. But had he tied the right foreign label to the right native plant? The situation got even more complicated later, when researchers in France, Italy, Germany, Switzerland and Spain all tried to add their own equivalent tags. Dioscorides mentions countries as widespread as Spain and India, where, after Alexander's initial foray, Greek traders had been settled since the first century AD.

Then, just when it seemed that the struggle to identify plants in a way that everyone could understand was going to sink under a great tangled knot of competing synonyms, a new device emerged: the plant portrait. Plants had been painted before of course – myrtle and roses on the walls of villas at Pompeii and Herculaneum, saffron crocus, iris, madonna lilies on frescoes at Knossos – but finally someone, somewhere, had the idea of using illustrations alongside text descriptions of plants, so that they could be more easily identified. It seems to have been a Greek idea rather than a Roman one. Texts such as Cato's *De re rustica* and Virgil's poetry show that the Roman landowner could be a marvellous observer of the natural world, but less interested perhaps than the Greeks of the Peripatetic School in debate about the essential nature of things. The earliest reference to illustrations comes in Pliny, who says the practice was 'less popular with our countrymen than it should have been'. Greek herbalists were quicker to realise the potential power of a picture to help identify plants. Pliny says that three Greeks, Crataeus, Dionysius and Metrodorus, were among the first to adopt this

> most attractive method, though one which makes clear little else except the difficulty
> of employing it. For they painted likenesses of the plants and then wrote under them
> their properties. But not only is a picture misleading when the colours are so many,
> particularly as the aim is to copy Nature, but besides this, much imperfection arises
> from the manifold hazards in the accuracy of copyists. In addition, it is not enough for
> each plant to be painted at one period only of its life, since it alters its appearance with
> the fourfold changes of the years.[3]

Bombarded with images, as we are now, it seems odd that it took so long to attach a picture to a piece of text, and so marry one way of absorbing information with another. But around the beginning of the second century AD, a technical change in the way paper was made provided the opportunity to do things differently. Up until the first century AD, most texts were written on long papyrus scrolls, like narrow rolls of wallpaper. If you wanted to read a text you used both hands, unrolling with one, rolling up with the other, so that you had in front of you just one or two lines of text at a time. This system worked with words but pictures were more difficult to accommodate. You needed to unroll much more of the scroll to take in the whole illustration. As different people were responsible for words and pictures, it was both onerous and perplexing to work out where gaps should be left in the text. But then, in a new development around AD 100, papyrus was produced in sheets rather than rolls. The sheets were gathered together and bound in manuscript volumes, books as we know them. It marked an important change in the way information was presented. It now became much less impractical to illustrate text. The whole page was laid open at once; words and pictures could work together. There was much more space to lay out information (Pliny said that the very best grade of paper, called the Augustus, was the equivalent of thirty-three centimetres wide). If an illustration was to be helpful, it needed to be of a certain size. If it was too small, it could not contain the kind of detail necessary to tell one kind of plant from the next.

A modern plant illustrator, such as the brilliant Stella Ross-Craig, communicates a vast amount of information in a plant portrait. All the parts of the plant are shown in a single image: root, stem, leaf, flower, seed. There's a clear idea of the scale of the illustration – life-size, half life-size, twice life-size. As Pliny pointed out, it was difficult to represent a plant in a single image when the plant itself changed all the time. Mrs Ross-Craig adopts what is now normal practice. She shows the plant in its entirety, in flower (if it is that kind of plant), but then packs in around the central, anchoring representation perhaps ten extra details to help in its identification. She might show the plant as a seedling. She will certainly show seed and seed pod, usually magnified in scale. She will indicate the number of stems a plant is likely to have and the way they divide. She might display a section of stem demonstrating whether it is hollow or not, whether it is hairy or smooth. The leaves of the plant will be shown in great detail, the shape, the way the edges are finished off, and the way they are arranged on the stem. There will be intricate representations of petals, stamens and other parts of the flower that are now recognised as crucial indicators in assigning plants to their correct places in the great design, the great scheme that men always thought must exist, if only they could work it out. But 2,000 years of understanding lies between Mrs Ross-Craig and the very first illustrators of manuscript plant books. Their pictures are single snapshots, the plant in its prime with roots, stem, leaves and flower all present. They were particularly keen on showing roots, which were regarded as the most essential, therefore, by inference, the most efficacious part of the plant. Many of the medicines of the time

Plate 18: Chinese lantern (Physalis alkekengi) *from Juliana's book, a manuscript derived from Dioscorides, given to her by the townspeople of Honorata* C. AD *512*

were prepared from roots, rather than leaves or seeds. But, as Pliny pointed out, there was nothing in the typical illustration which would help a herb-gatherer recognise a plant as it first comes through the ground, or when it has withered and set its seed. And the images are stylised, almost like blocks to be used to print on fabric or stencil on a wall. The smaller the illustration, the more schematic it became.

Occasionally, some very particular feature stands out clearly, as the bright orange heart-shaped seed vessels of Chinese lantern do in the Greek *Codex Neapolitanus* made in the seventh century (see plate 18).[4] Then, there is no problem in identifying the plant. Nothing else has fruits made in that distinctive way. But it is not usually that easy. Look at the round, blue-grey outline of one of the plants painted on the Johnson Papyrus made around AD 400.[5] In the literature on this earliest of all surviving illustrated herbals, the plant is firmly labelled Symphyton, our comfrey (*Symphytum officinale*) (see plate 19), an important drug plant, especially for bone-setters. But comfrey has a massive woody root. This illustration, schematic in the extreme, shows a straggle of rather inferior roots supporting the globe of blue-grey leaves above. In Mediterranean countries there are many plants that have bluish or glaucous foliage, an evolutionary trick which helps them survive through the long, rainless summers of the region. But comfrey has thick, coarse green leaves, not unlike those of the foxglove. In this case, if it is correctly named, the illustration does nothing to help us identify the plant. So, although it should have been a massive breakthrough, in those early days it wasn't.

Perhaps the very first illustrators made their pictures from live plants sitting in front of them. But the copyists didn't. As each copy was made, the image drifted further away from the original, the Chinese whisper of the real thing degenerating into a token, an emblem of the real plant. Pliny was right to talk of the 'manifold hazards' of copying and to doubt whether illustrators were using colours equal to the task. The palette was limited: usually one kind of green, a blue, a thick coffee-coloured brown for the roots, various ochre-based yellows and oranges for the flowers. And there remained the central problem of showing in a single image all the different stages of a growing plant. This difficulty was not resolved until *c.*1300 when a completely new treatise appeared, the *Tractatus de herbis*, written by Albertus Magnus, Bishop of Regensburg. This was not a copy but fresh work, and Magnus's words were illuminated by new illustrations evidently made by an artist who looked at plants clear and straight, without the veil of classical antiquity interposing itself between him and the world about him.

There was another innovation too, in the way that information was presented on the page. It had started in a small way with Pamphilos, a Greek physician practising in Rome in the first century AD, but was popularised by the Greek physician Galen

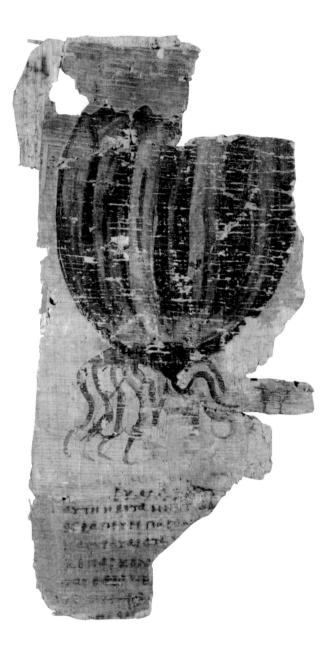

*Plate 19: The earliest known illustration of a plant:
symphytum (comfrey) from a fragment known as the
Johnson Papyrus, made c. AD 400*

(*c.* AD 130–200), who was the first man writing on plants to present his material arranged in alphabetical order. On the face of it, this seemed to be a good move. Material could be accessed more quickly. It introduced a kind of clarity, a kind of order to a mass of diverse material. Dioscorides, though, had been against the idea. An alphabetical arrangement, he wrote, separates 'both the kinds and the operations of things that are closely related, so that thereby they come to be harder to remember'. The system did not allow for connections to be made between plants. It was both systematic and arbitrary at the same time. But Galen made drugs, not plants, his starting points, so the alphabetical order related to medicines, not the ingredients from which they were made. Though he copied Pamphilos's system of arranging material, Galen was scathing about the man himself. Of all the quacks writing about medicine he was the one most to be avoided for 'He never saw, even in dreams, the plants which he undertakes to describe.'

Galen saw a great deal. He was born at Pergamos, and for ten years he travelled in Egypt (Alexandria), Bithynia, Palestine, Thrace, Macedonia, Italy, Crete, Cyprus and Lemnos, before going to war as physician to the Roman Emperor Marcus Aurelius in his campaign against the Quadi and Marcomanni. Plague broke out among the troops and the expedition was a failure. Almost 500 years separates Galen's book on plants from Theophrastus's. But here is Galen, still railing at the general lack of standards, deploring the ignorance of those who should know plants best:

> In as far as possible the physician ought to know all plants, and if not all, the greater proportion, and those most useful . . . He who knows the different kinds in all their states from young and small to fully grown, and can so distinguish between them, will in many places find certain useful plants, as I have done in various parts of Italy, where he who knows them only in the dead and dry, would never recognise them whether in the young state or the mature. There is no quacksalver who does not readily iden-tify the herbs that are imported from Crete by their fruits; but that some of these self-same things might be gathered on the outskirts of Rome they do not know, because the season of their herborisings does not correspond to that of the maturity of these plants. But that time is well known to me, and I go in quest of Chamaepitys, Chamaedrys, Centaurium, Hypericum, Polium, and others of that kind, at just the right time, and gather them in their perfect maturity, neither waiting until they are past that, and are sunburnt, nor going too early, that is, before the fruit is well formed.[6]

Galen's is the earliest alphabetical herbal to have survived; the alphabetical arrange-ment he favoured was adopted by other collators and copiers of the age, and in the fourth century even the *De materia medica* by Dioscorides, who had been so against it, was rearranged according to the new system. And in the process, the possibilities for mistakes in translation were vastly increased. Instead of simple word for word exchanges, material had to be shifted about, according to the letters of each different alphabet. Entries were lost, misplaced, bowdlerised. After Galen, there was a 'silting up of the channels by which the human mind could be refreshed'.[7] The dominance of the 'spoilt darlings of history' was over and the creative period of Greek science at an end. But in 1934 the plantsman Sir Arthur Hill was in Greece, collecting plants on Mount Athos with two botanists from Kew. In the hills close to the monastery, they came across a Greek Orthodox priest in a tall black hat collecting henbane (*Hyoscyamus niger*), which from classical times has been used as a powerful sedative; Dioscorides had described how hyoscyamus could be mixed with mandragora to induce a 'twilight sleep'. Carefully wrapped in a bag on his back, the apothecary-priest carried four handwritten folios of Dioscorides' herbal.

VI

JULIANA'S BOOK

AD 500—AD 600

DIOSCORIDES'S ORIGINAL TREATISE appeared in the middle of the first century AD. But his words were soon swamped by others', desperately trying to match the plants he talked about with their own native flora. Disease was universal and there was a general expectation that Dioscorides's plants would be too. To the original Greek/Latin names, were added hopeful synonyms in various other languages. Armenians, Boeotians, Cappadocians, Egyptians, Ethiopians, Gauls, Spaniards, Tuscans all contributed their own interpretations. Because Theophrastus was lost in the West, Dioscorides became the universal arbiter. His text was rearranged in Galen's alphabetical order. Extracts were chosen from it and illustrations added, possibly copied from an earlier herbal written by the root-gatherer Crataeus, physician to the powerful King Mithridates VI Eupator of Pontus (120–63 BC). Mithridates was himself a herbalist, with a particular interest and facility with poisons. Then, around AD 512, the townspeople of Honorata, a district of Constantinople, presented a grand gathering of this knowledge about plants to their imperial patron, Juliana Anicia (see plate 20).[1] Juliana was a pukka princess, descended from Theodosius the Great, emperor of the Romans' Eastern Empire. Her father was the consul Flavius Anicius Olybrius, and her husband was a consul too. The book[2] was a thank-you present to the deeply devout Juliana, who had given the townspeople a Christian church, dedicated to the Virgin Mary and built c. AD 512. The date of the church is taken to be roughly the date that the book was made (one illustration shows the grateful citizens presenting the book to Juliana). This

Plate 20: The dedication page from Juliana's book, a manuscript derived from Dioscorides, given to her by the townspeople of Honorata c. AD 512

exquisite compendium, with information on catching birds and fishes as well as medicinal plants (a sixth-century Mrs Beeton), includes superb illustrations of the 383 plants 'taken from' from Dioscorides. The illustrations may have been the *raison d'être* of the book, with the text chosen to match the pictures, rather than the other way around. The Dioscorides material mostly comes from the second, third and fourth books of his original treatise, in which he talks of cereals, roots, herbs and seeds.

It remains not only the earliest surviving, but also one of most magnificent plant books ever produced: 491 pages of fine parchment, almost three-quarters of them devoted to Dioscorides's healing plants. After the preliminaries, the title appears boldly on the tenth page: 'This is [the treatise of] Pedanios Dioscorides Anazarbus concerning herbs and roots and juices and seeds with leaves and medicines. We will start therefore from the [letter] A.' A is for Aristolochia 'a help against asthma, hiccup, shivers, spleen, abscesses and convulsions. Drunk in water it drives out thorns and splinters, beaten into a plaster it removes fragments of bones, dries up putre-fying sores and cleanses foul wounds. It is a good wash for the teeth and for wounds.'

The pages are big, which allows the artists to produce bold plant portraits, up to 33 cm tall x 20 cm wide. At the beginning of the volume there is a group portrait (the school picture) of five distinguished physicians, a useful indicator of contem-porary opinion. The citizens of Constantinople evidently rated Pamphilos of Alexandria more highly than Galen did, for he is in the picture and his plant glos-sary (compiled between the first and second centuries AD) is the source of the synonyms listed in the Index to Juliana's herbal. He is chaperoned by Xenocrates of Aphrodisias (*c*.50 BC–AD 50) who wrote on pharmacology, Quintus Sextius Niger (*c*.25 BC) who studied at Prusa in Bithynia (Dioscorides quoted him often), Heracleides of Tarentum (*c*.75 BC), one of the greatest physicians of the Empiricist school, and the pharmacologist Mantias (second century BC). Over these five great figures of classical antiquity (Theophrastus, you should be there) presides the figure of Chiron, the wise, kind centaur – half-man, half-horse – to whom Zeus had given the power of healing through plants. Another group on the following page brings the pantheon up to date: Galen sits in the centre with Crataeus on his right and Dioscorides on his left. Galen has his head turned towards Dioscorides, as though he is listening to him, the supreme authority. Underneath the presiding trio are grouped four lesser men: the poet Nicander of Colophon, born at Claros, Ionia, in the second century BC, whose *Alexipharmica*, discussing twenty-one different poisons and their antidotes, was paraphrased in Juliana's book; Rufus of Ephesus, who lived in Alexandria during the first century AD; Andreas of Carystos, personal physician to Ptolemy IV Philopator, murdered in 217 BC by assassins who mistook him for their real target; and Apollonius Mys of Alexandria, judged by Galen to be one of the greatest pharmacologists that had ever lived. Dioscorides thought the same about Andreas of Carystos. But there might have been another, political reason for including these particular people. All of them wrote in Greek and all were based in towns in the Eastern part of the Roman Empire. As Minta Collins points out,[3] this was visual propaganda. Greeks rule OK – especially the ones of the Eastern Empire. Other illustrations show Dioscorides with Heuresis, the personification of discovery and invention, and Dioscorides (again) with Epinoia, the personification of intelligence and the power of thought. Epinoia is holding out a root of the powerful mandrake for Dioscorides, shown in profile, to describe in his book, while on the left, an artist paints a picture of it.

The plant illustrations vary greatly in quality. Some, such as the mandrake, were obviously fanciful, others completely spurious. More than a third, including the onion (folio 185v), the asphodel (folio 26v; see plate 21), the rose (folio 282) and the spurge (folio 349r) are really good visual aids to identification. A bramble is shown with wonderfully wild vitality (see plate 22) and the painting of the autumn-flowering cyclamen demonstrates with great precision how the flowering stems rise from the upper surface of the rounded corm. The rest of the plant paintings – probably those not copied from a Hellenistic original – are schematic in the extreme; Byzantine artists themselves had little regard for naturalism. When illustrations first began to appear, the amount of text describing the physical characteristics of a plant began to shrink. Who needed words, when there was a picture instead? But when the picture itself began to degenerate from the truth of the original, the lack of a detailed written description made the whole business of identifying plants more difficult than ever. Pliny's reservations were valid.

Juliana's book stays in Constantinople for at least a thousand years. In 1350, the text is transcribed by a monk called Neophytos at the monastery of St John Prodromos in Petra, Constantinople.[4] In 1406 the codex is fully restored and rebound by the notary John Chortasmenos at the request of Nathaniel, who was also a monk at St John Prodromos.[5] Perhaps it is he who numbers the illustrations of the plants in the book and transcribes the plant names into Greek minuscule from the original uncial script. Synonyms are added in Arabic and Hebrew, perhaps by the Moseh ben Moseh whose name is written on the first and second folios. The book remains at the monastery until about 1423. After the fall of Constantinople in 1453, it comes into the possession of Hamon, physician to Sulaymān the Magnificent. The ambassador of the Holy Roman Empire, Ogier Ghiselin de Busbecq (1521–1592), travelling in Turkey with the physician Willem Quackelbeen (1527–1561), certainly knows about the princess's book, by then a precious relic, although a battered one. Writing in 1562, he says,

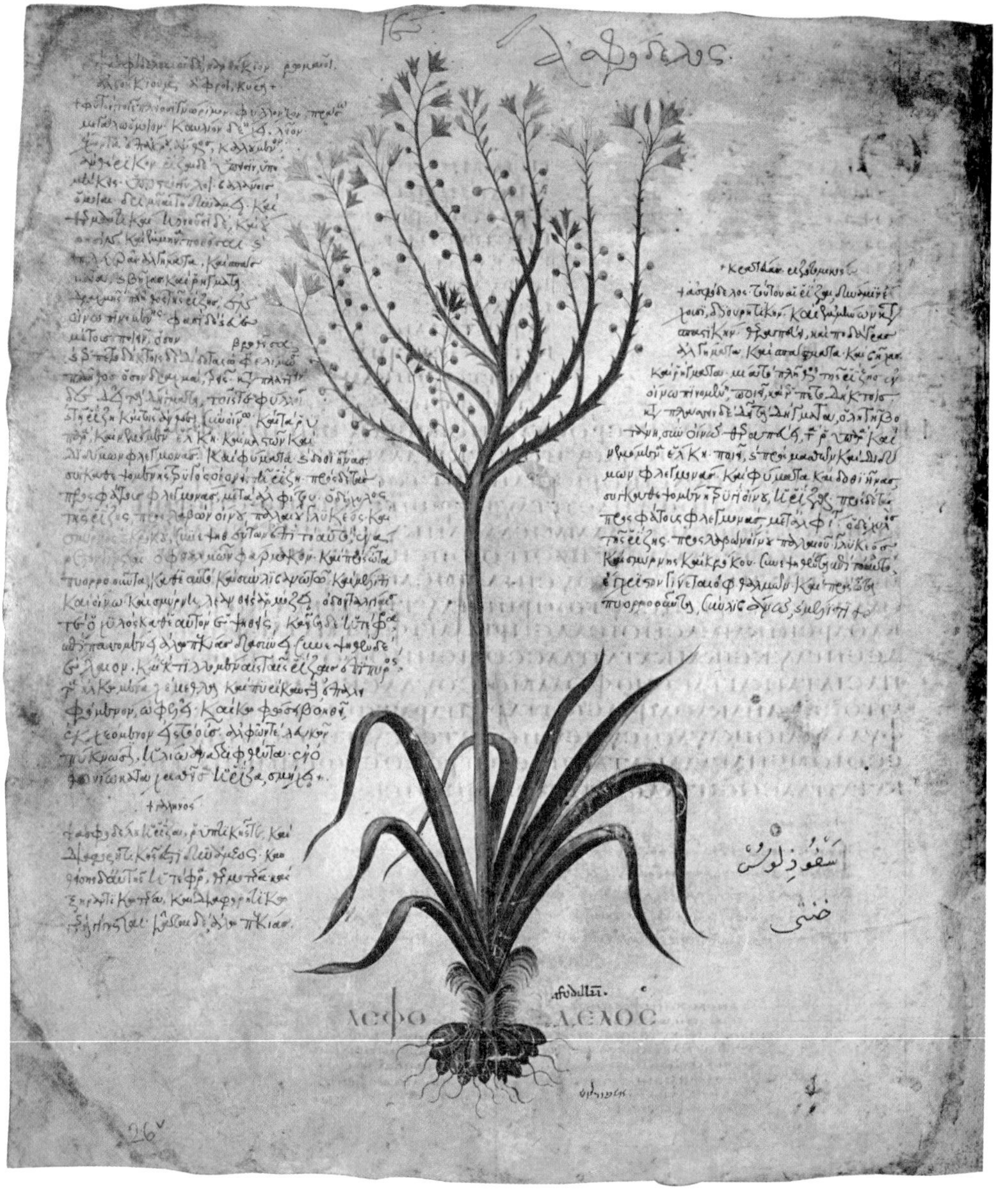

Plate 21: 'Asphodelos' (Asphodelus aestivus) from Juliana's
book, a manuscript derived from Dioscorides, given to her by the
townspeople of Honorata c. AD 512

Plate 22: *A bramble* (Rubus fruticosus) *from Juliana's book, a manuscript derived from Dioscorides, given to her by the townspeople of Honorata* c. AD 512

One treasure I left behind in Constantinople, a manuscript of Dioscorides, extremely ancient and written in majuscules, with drawings of the plants and containing also, if I am not mistaken, some fragments of Cratevas . . . It belongs to a Jew, the son of Hamon, who, while he was still alive, was physician to Soleiman. I should like to have bought it, but the price frightened me; for a hundred ducats was named, a sum which would suit the Emperor's purse better than mine. I shall not cease to urge the Emperor to ransom so noble an author from such slavery. The manuscript, owing to its age, is in a bad state, being externally so worm-eaten that scarcely any one, if he saw it lying in the road, would bother to pick it up.[6]

Seven years later the codex finds its way to the Imperial Library in Vienna, purchased either by the Emperor, Maximilian II, or by Busbecq himself, a voracious collector who loved rare things. It was he who, a few years before he saw the famous codex, had brought the first tulip bulb into Western Europe.

The codex provides then a direct link between sixteenth-century Europe and the court of the arch poisoner Mithridates VI of Pontus from 120 to 63 BC, the king who fought Pompey in battle and, when defeated, committed suicide. The link with Mithridates comes through the Greek herbalist, Crataeus, his court doctor. Crataeus is the putative author of a botanical pharmacology (now lost), one of the earliest works to set out plants in alphabetical order. Pompey introduces Crataeus to a Roman audience, in a translation prepared by Lenaeus Gramaticus. A painter is found to copy the illustrations which were the great innovation in Crataeus's original work. Crataeus's book is the main source for a later herbal made by Sextius Niger, which in turn is plundered by Pliny and Dioscorides. Dioscorides is the main source of the plant information then reproduced in Juliana's book. These fragile parchment pages carry a body of knowledge, a state of mind, through the vast ebb and flow of armies through Europe and Asia, through the birth and death of religions, through the rise and fall of cities and centres of learning. Vast empires are created and crumble while this corpus of plant knowledge survives and marches on, important to all men, whether Greeks, Romans, Turks, Arabs or Goths.

The style of Juliana's book, with illustrations closely allied to text, becomes the model for all that follow. It fixes the content and form of future work on plants for a long time. Too long, for although it is an extraordinarily pretty thing, it forges even more strongly the association between plants and medicine. Pharmacology mattered. But when plants were seen as nothing more than ingredients in a medicine chest, the larger questions of their kinships, their similarities and differences, *qua* plants, became more difficult to frame. The big picture, the altruistic, intellectual search for the key to the order of the universe, fractured into a series of quotidian concerns. Rhubarb: 'good for all manner of grief, convulsions, spleneticall, Hepaticall, Nephtriticall, torminaticall, & ye griefs about ye bladder'. Anethon (our dill): good for women 'troubled with womb-griefs'. Melisophullon (our balm): a help to those 'which are strangled of mushrooms'. Akoniton: 'kills both Panthers and Sowes, and Wolves, & all wild beasts, being put into gobbets of flesh, & given to them'. The translations are from the seventeenth-century English scholar John Goodyer's laboriously hand-copied script of the whole of Dioscorides with the meaning 'englished' underneath. By Goodyer's time Dioscorides has been translated into other European languages, but no English edition yet existed. His work covers 4,540 quarto pages of manuscript, neatly annotated with the date and time that he finishes each section of the original. It takes him three years to complete the whole work.[7]

Somewhere in a Greek-dominated area of Italy, possibly Ravenna, another compilation is made, the last expression of the Hellenistic culture of Constantinople, still dominant in a few Italian centres. It draws on the same source material as Juliana's book; she, however, was a cultured patron, a refined bibliophile, and the book made for her reflects that status. The Italian one is a little less sumptuous, made for a scholarly professional, made to be used. The colours are muddier, the illustrations smaller and cruder, generally laid out two or three to a page, with titles in red ink (possibly done with a brush not a pen) and the text in black ink laid out in columns under the pictures (see plate 23). These are similar enough to the ones in Juliana's book to indicate that they both had the same starting point, but there are enough differences both in text and pictures to rule out any possibility that the one was a direct copy of the other. This *Codex Neapolitanus*[8] is written in a script known as biblical capital, which helps date it to the late sixth or early seventh century. Later in the seventh century, script became less chunky, more artificial, more graphic. Dioscorides' original text has been cut drastically, reduced to a dry summary. A few synonyms, a few new medical prescriptions have been added. It's a later book than Juliana's and slightly smaller, the parchment pages measuring 29.5 cm x 25.5 cm. The illustrations, more than 400 of them, dominate each page. The text is subservient, makes no connections, sets forward no proposals or ideas. The words are reduced to captions, supporting the pictures. It's a book made for an age which prefers summaries and digests to the complexity of the real thing, an age that responds to pictures rather than words. It's a handbook for a busy man, a harassed physician perhaps, looking for ways to reduce the queues in the consulting room. As in Juliana's book, there is no indication of the relative size or scale of the plants illustrated on the

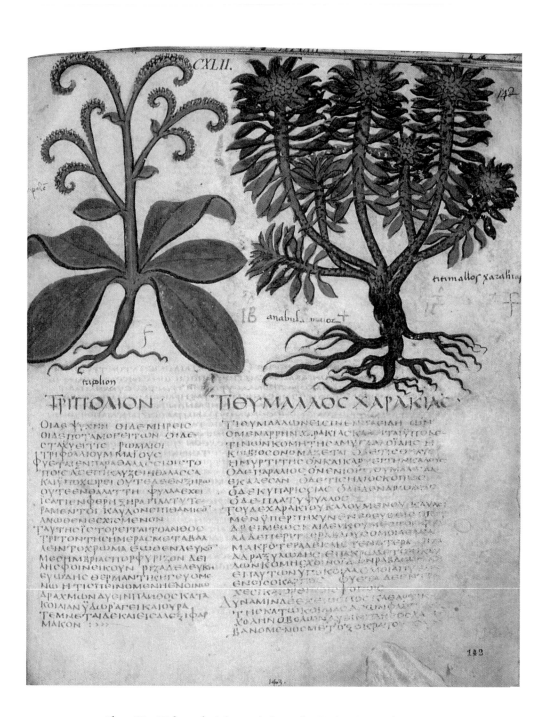

Plate 23: 'Tithymalos' (spurge) from the Codex Neapolitanus, a
Dioscorides manuscript written in Greek script probably at the
beginning of the seventh century AD

Plate 24: Adianton from the Codex Neapolitanus, *a Dioscorides manuscript written in Greek script probably at the beginning of the seventh century* AD

page. The amaranth ('bliton') and the blackberry bush ('batos'), set next to each other on the page because they both begin with b, are both the same height. Occasionally plants of the same family are brought together, as with the orchids on folio 133, but this seems to be dictated by alphabetical constraints, not scientific enquiry. Usually the plant is shown full frontal, the roots sometimes squashed into a horizontal matrix to accommodate the text underneath. Occasionally the view-point shifts. Adianton (our fern, *Adiantum*) is shown from on top, the fronds splayed out like the arms of a demented starfish (see plate 24). Occasionally, the illustrator makes an attempt to show the habitat of a particular plant: a caper bush growing from a crack in stone steps, maidenhair fern ('kallitrixon') rising from a pool of blue water. Sometimes the illustrations are weirdly fanciful, as with the rootball of hypneion (folio 78) which has been turned into a Gorgon's head. Fidelity to nature is replaced by a simplification, an abstraction of the original subject matter. Leaves are arranged with mirrored symmetry, sinuous stems are straightened, the irregular complexity of plants is reduced to graphic representation.

So begins the process of transformation which leads to the abstracted 'delirium' of the herbals of the early Middle Ages. The censoring tendency of Christian leaders did not foster a spirit of independent enquiry. 'You have ordered me,' wrote Pope Agatho to Emperor Constantine IV in AD 680, 'to send you a few bishops known for their purity of life and for their knowledge of the sciences of the Holy Scriptures.' In presenting the few he added, 'If they meet the first requirement, they meet the second only if science means the knowledge of true piety and is not intended as profane science (*eloquentia saecularis*).' When the two missionaries, Theodore and Hadrian, were sent to England by Pope Gregory the Great (AD *c.*540–604) they were primarily charged with correcting the Irish method of calculating Easter. But as part of their cultural baggage, they brought with them a style of illumination that spread like smallpox in the monastic houses of England. It simplified even further, it codified, it excluded almost all interest in naturalistic detail.

Scribbled on folio 172 of the *Codex Neapolitanus* is a note – *Antonii Seripandii ex Hieronymi Carbonis d[om]inici optimo munere* – showing that during the first decades of the sixteenth century, it was given by Girolamo Carbone to Antonio Seripando, man of letters, collector of manuscripts of ancient authors and brother of Cardinal Girolamo Seripando. When he dies in 1531, he bequeaths his books to his brother, the cardinal, who adds them to the library of the convent of San Giovanni at Carbonara. And there it stays until November 1718, when by order of the prefect of Emperor Charles VI's Imperial Library, the Neapolitan Alessandro Riccardi, it is transferred to Vienna to join Juliana's book.

VII

THE ARAB INFLUENCE

AD 600–1200

JULIANA'S BOOK IS the earliest and most beautiful of Greek herbals. Although it was made at the beginning of the sixth century, nothing better emerged in Western Europe for almost a thousand years. But as learning plunged into an ever deeper black hole in Europe, there was a renewal of intellectual life in the East, centred at first in Edessa, Syria. Originally founded as a Macedonian colony, Edessa was well placed on the northern edge of the Syrian plateau both for those travelling on the north–south trade route and the east–west route, the Silk Road to China. Its position at the limit of the Roman Empire fostered an unusual degree of independence and prosperity. Syrian merchants travelled widely in Europe and North Africa; via the Red Sea, they also financed trade to South-West Arabia, India and Ceylon. The city's position at the centre of a vast trade crossroads favoured the growth of an established group of cultured merchants, who by nature were against the domination of Rome and so *for* the Greeks (and their scholarship). There had been a medical school at Edessa since the fourth century. When, in 489, the Emperor Zeno declared it a hotbed of heretics and closed it down, the school's Nestorian teachers moved to Nisibis, and then on to Djundīshāpūr in Persia, 500 miles to the south. Djundīshāpūr had also welcomed the neo-Platonists expelled from Athens in 529, and the method and content of their teaching had a powerful influence on Islamic philosophy. Nestorian doctors came to control the famous medical school at Djundīshāpūr; cultures converged as Greek, Jewish, Persian and Hindu thinkers all met and exchanged ideas through the common language, Syriac.[1]

With the enthusiastic support of the Persian Emperor, a hospital and a medical school headed by Abu Zakarīyā Yūhanā ibn-Māsawaih (777–857), the son of an apothecary, were established in the city. It flourished for 300 years, until the Arabs conquered Persia and Baghdad became the principal centre of learning.

The Nestorian scholars[2] are important because they translated Greek scientific works which might otherwise have remained in oblivion in Byzantine libraries. They had first fled east to Syria when the Roman Emperor Constantine conquered Byzantium and from their Syriac treatises translations were made into Arabic and Persian. The work begun in Edessa continued in Djundīshāpūr, but came to a peak in Baghdad in the ninth century when Abu Yusuf Yaqub ibn-Ishaq al-Kindi (c.800–866) was head of the city's medical school. Between 819 and 825, many books, especially medical texts, were taken from Constantinople to Baghdad, which meant that Islam had complete (and accurate) versions of original texts (including Theophrastus), already lost to the West. The delegation sent by Abbasid Caliph al-Ma'mūn to Constantinople reported that the Byzantine Emperor had absolutely no knowledge of or interest in the fate of the ancient manuscripts; he did not even know where they were kept. But a scholarly monk did, and, perhaps feeling that they were likely to have a more secure future in Baghdad than Constantinople, revealed their hiding place. In AD 832, the Caliph set up a library and meeting place for scholars in Baghdad called the *Bayt al-Ḥikma*, the House of Wisdom, where the scholar-physician Ḥunayn ibn Isḥāk was head of a department wholly devoted to collating and translating foreign texts.

So, around 854, the first Arabic version of Dioscorides was produced by one of Ḥunayn's translators, Stephanos, a Christian living in Baghdad. Stephanos translated as many Greek plant names as he could but when he didn't know them, simply turned the Greek characters into Arabic ones, saying 'God will raise up someone who might translate them.' Stephanos's translation from Greek to Arabic was widely circulated in Arabic countries until 948. Ḥunayn himself, an Arab Christian whose father was a pharmacist, also made translations from Greek into Arabic. He was equally fluent in Arabic and Syriac and before settling in Baghdad had spent two years travelling, perfecting his Greek and collecting books. Writing in 987, the Cordoban physician, Ibn Djuldjul, said that without Ḥunayn the Greek Dioscorides texts would never have reached the Arabs in Baghdad. Of the dozen or so illustrated medieval manuscripts that still exist of the Arabic version of Dioscorides, five use the words of Ḥunayn's and Stephanos's translation, picked over in the House of Wisdom in Baghdad.

In 948, the Byzantine Emperor Romanos II[3] sent the Caliph of Cordoba, 'Abd al-Raḥmān III (912–961), a present: a Greek manuscript of Dioscorides, superbly

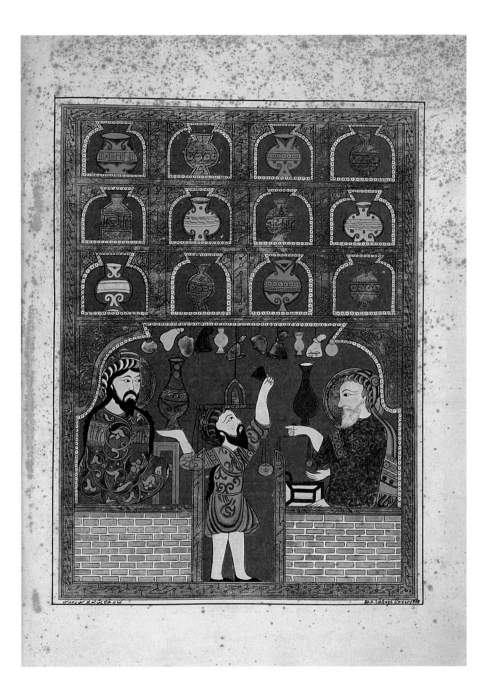

*Plate 25: An Arabian pharmacy from a manuscript
made in Baghdad* AD *1224*

illustrated with Byzantine pictures. In his letter to the Caliph, Romanos said that the book, though itself a great treasure, could only be useful if the Greek was translated into Arabic by someone who knew about plants and the medicines made from them. By that stage, none of the Christians of Cordoba[4] could read Ancient Greek, so for three years, the beautiful book lay in the Caliph's library, unread. Then the Caliph asked Romanos if he could provide an interpreter. A Byzantine monk, Nicolas, was sent to Spain to join the team of scholars assembled in Cordoba. With the help of a Jewish doctor, Ḥasdāy b. S̲h̲aprūt, and a Sicilian who spoke Greek and knew about medicinal plants, Nicolas gathered in another bunch of Dioscoridean plants, correlating them, not always successfully, with the flowers and shrubs that grew in Moorish Spain.[5]

Despite the magnificent cross-culturalism of Arab scholarship (and in terms of the body of knowledge I'm interested in, the Arabs are the only people that matter at this time in the Western world), the central problem remained. It was easier to translate a text about a plant than it was to understand what the plant itself might be. Every country, every region of every country, had a different common name for the plants that they used for magic and medicine. Folio 98r of Juliana's book shows a plant with dramatic arrow-shaped leaves, the plant we know as wild arum. Its official name is *Arum maculatum*, a name – thanks to the International Code of Nomenclature – now recognised in Europe as easily as in America, Japan, Australia or India. But when Dioscorides first wrote about this plant[6] it may have been called 'aron', 'aris', 'eparis', 'ephialton', 'kynozolon', 'onokephalon', 'parnopogonon' or 'phoinikeon'. If you were Egyptian, you'd have called it 'ebron'; the Romans knew it as 'beta leporina', the Etruscans as 'gigarum', the Daker as 'kurionnekum', the North Africans as 'ateirnochlam', the Syrians as 'lupha'. If you could not be absolutely sure that this Greek plant was that Spanish (or Italian, or French, or Czech, or Polish or German or English) plant, none of the directions for preparing it or using it to quell fevers, heal wounds, knit bones, ward off monsters, was of the slightest use. A good proportion of those plants did not grow any further west than Greece, the limit of their natural habitat. Conversely, many of Dioscorides's examples could also be found growing in countries further east than Greece. So Arabic scholars, though they struggled to equate the native flora of southern Spain with Dioscorides's Eastern Mediterranean plants, did not have to struggle quite so frantically as those who emerged later in northern Europe.

The way that Dioscorides chose to describe plants also increased the difficulties. Like Theophrastus, Dioscorides often used analogy: this plant was like that plant but with bigger leaves, smaller flowers. While Theophrastus used a limited number of exemplars as his 'standards' – bay, laurel, pear – Dioscorides used many more.

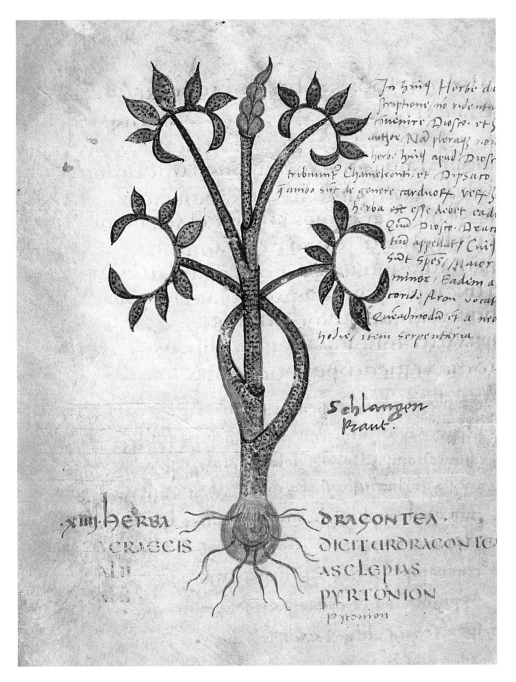

Plate 26: ‘Dracontea’ (our dragon arum, Dracunculus vulgaris)
in a manuscript made in the second half of the sixth century.
The artist has shown the plant in berry rather than with its
spooky dark spathe and has captured with great exactness the
semi-circular arc of the leaflets that make up each leaf

The probability of error was compounded. If you could not correctly translate the name of the standard plant used as a basis for comparison, you were even more unlikely to identify correctly the plant to which it was being likened. The body of plant knowledge embedded in the translations so carefully made from Greek into Arabic and Syriac by Ḥunayn and Stephanos remained tantalisingly obscure.

From the seventh century onwards, Arab conquests had fostered a revival of scientific learning throughout Islam, which contrasted vividly with the general stagnation in Christian Europe. Arabs controlled the main trade routes; prosperity created room for learning. By 976, the university at Cordoba, enlarged and endowed by Al-Ḥakim, was the best in Europe, the best in the whole of the Islamic Empire. In Baghdad the building of 'Adud ad-Dawla's teaching hospital, the al-Bimaristan al-'Adudi, was finished by 978 and the two dozen doctors who worked there set up a medical faculty, the first in the world. Islamic rulers supported scholarship and, at this time at least, showed an enlightened tolerance of other creeds, which compared rather favourably with the heresy-hunters of Christendom. 'Read in the name of Allah,' said the Koran. That was interpreted as a call to knowledge as well as a call to prayer. Study was a form of worship, and provided that scholarship could be shown to benefit humanity, few restraints were placed upon it. The Arabs excelled in the exact sciences – things that could be measured, research that was empirical rather than theoretical. Through the pursuit of knowledge lay salvation. Ḥunayn's work was gradually revised and refined, culminating in the eleventh century in a text written in neat naskhī script on 228 paper pages, the oldest surviving Arabic herbal in the world.[7] More than 600 illustrations decorate the pages, painted mainly in discreet shades of green, brown, orange and red, with much rarer touches of blue and yellow.[8] The plants are those familiar to Dioscorides: rose, water lily, balsam (shown with two dramatic daggers plunged into the trunk to open up the supply of sap), orchids, the forked rooted mandrake. They are neat, but fairly crude drawings. You can recognise them, but only if you already know the plant. The water lily (five of them actually, three white, two red, elegantly interwined; see plate 27) is shown rising from a blue rippled sheet of water. Economically, the rose shows a selection of different blooms – red, white and a dark-rimmed pink – all flowering on the same bush. But you would be hard pressed to identify an orchid in the field from the sketchy, two-dimensional image on folio 32. The image of sap being bled from the balsam tree does not re-appear until the *Tractatus de herbis* made in the early fourteenth century, by which time there had been an important shift in the type of images being made. Instead of copying, almost superstitiously, the images

في السكل أو كالحنتأسه و د اخله نمره سود أ إلى العرض و الكدا أه ماهو و
مراصه لزجه و ساقه أملس كبير و لس نعنط أسود سبه دنأ و فقور بون
و هو الفلفا سر الدر دعال له الناقلا المصري و أصله أسود حشر شبه حمود أو
حرز و يقلع ف نصل الحريف و مي سرد الأصل سرأ يمع مركا سهال البرم
و وجعه الأ معا و جللز ويم الطرال و بيمامنه ضماد لوجع المعده و وجع المثانه
و إذا خلط بالما و صر عل البهو نفاه و إذا خلط بالروت و صر على النقله
إبراه و قد سر هر أصر هر الكنره لأ حالام تمنعه و إذا الدسر شربه أصعه الكرى و
نزره أضا نفعا و النحار الأصر ف كل ما قلنا و سم العر و سر لانه يرئ الما الد يكون
فيه و كنيرا ما كلوي نهر يدعى سوطا و بالسرى نهر أ العبر و عند يا دطن نار
و جيلار ثمى و كدنك بالهزر برا و أهليا و محله لا لوأ رمنه و ردى اللوز و
بزرهر أ و أصله أ وا دشربا دنزاف أسود يمع مر سلار الطمت

نياوفر

carried down from antiquity (as if by changing them you might diminish the effect of their magical properties), artists began to draw plants as if they had them there in front of their eyes. Perhaps they did. However, it was the knowledge contained in Dioscorides that was further diffused by later Arab scholars such as Abū Alī al-Ḥusayn b. ʿAbd Allāh b. Sīnā (980–1037). Avicenna, as he was known in Western Europe, was born at Afshana near Bukhara and became personal physician to many rulers in the East, travelling over huge areas. His *Qanun*, translated into Latin by Gerard of Cremona in the twelfth century, remained a standard medical textbook for the next 500 years. It was a huge medical encyclopaedia, with details of 650 plants used in recipes for preparing 758 different medicines. Later, the celebrated Baghdad physician, ʿAbd al Latif (1160–1231) travelled throughout the East specifically to meet the greatest scholars of his generation. He taught both philosophy and medicine at Damascus and Cairo. That versatility, that curiosity was typical of this age of Arab scholars.

Though ideas travelled, became widely dispersed and understood, plant names did not. The Arab scholars, doctors and pharmacists intent on recapturing and preserving the plant knowledge of that Greek army doctor of the first century AD, relied to a great extent for their ingredients on herb-gatherers who only needed to recognise particular 'simples' which they knew to be in demand for particular prescriptions. It was not their business to be able to name that herb in any other language but their own. Though this conundrum remained, and was only slowly unpicked, Dioscorides's treatise remained a prime source for Arab authors. Arab writers preferred to sort and order the material they gathered in the alphabetical order Dioscorides deplored; although, as a source, they treated him with great deference, reverence even, they did not agree that Dioscorides's own way of arranging his material was the most practical one. And gradually, under the influence of these Arab scholars, Persian, Indian, and Arab plants completely unknown to Dioscorides were brought into the pharmacopoeia.

Though Islam encouraged scientific study – great progress was made in both medicine and agriculture – the making of realistic images was forbidden. Books on plants were beautifully illustrated, but the illustrations are stylised, flattened, almost as though they have been prepared as motifs for wallpaper or fabric (see plate 28). In the Süleymaniye Mosque Library at Ayasofia in Istanbul is an extravagantly illustrated Arabian version of Dioscorides.[9] Using the original translation made by Ḥunayn's assistant Stephanos, it was created in 1224, probably in Baghdad, then under the enlightened patronage of the Caliph Al-Nāṣir. Under his rule, Arab culture in the city reached a zenith, crushed and fractured only thirty-four years later when it was conquered by Mongol invaders. But even this manuscript, produced when

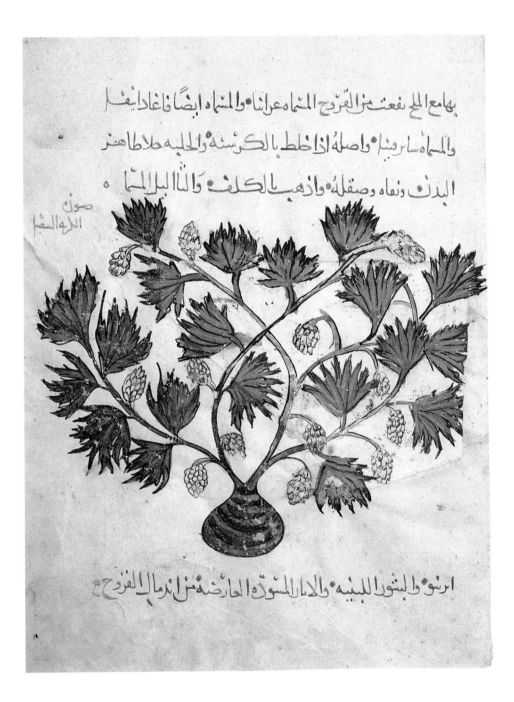

Plate 28: A vine, springing from a curiously bulbous root,
from a manuscript made in Baghdad AD 1224

Arab scholarship was at its peak, provides pictures of plants that are as fanciful as any in Edward Lear's *Nonsense Botany*. Momentarily, the picture on folio 21 intrigues me (see plate 29). Shown alongside the central image (supposedly representing the plant the Arabs called bantafullun – our cinquefoil) are two details, as schematic as the central portrait. To the left of the main image is a shape like a cupped flower with seven small bobble-headed stems sticking out of it. On the right is a similar image that at first looks like a stylised bloom (three pointed petals), with the same bobbly lollipops sticking up from it. Stamens, I think. This man is actually trying to show stamens. Someone has finally grasped what a vital role they play in the life of a flowering plant. He's giving us a detail, a close-up, to draw our attention to them. This is a breakthrough. And then I get out my magnifying glass and the theory crumbles almost as soon as it is born. Enlarged, the bobbles I've interpreted as stamens turn into miniature red and blue flowers, each with four petals. We are still hundreds of years away from any knowledge of the stamens and ovaries which will eventually play such a seminal part in the final naming of names.

The civilised, intellectually advanced Arab scholars of the twelfth and thirteenth centuries developed and elaborated the study of medicine far beyond the point where their Greek mentors had left it. They travelled widely, they drew on their own observations as Theophrastus had done, they organised expeditions specifically to look at and identify plants (in the early thirteenth century, the Muslim scholar Ibn al-Suri went plant-hunting in the Lebanon; it was a long time before any European botanist set out on a similar mission). But though they criticised, corrected, and added to the ancient Dioscorides text, they never abandoned it, never developed an entirely new cycle of treatises fuelled entirely from their own wisdom and experience. Why? This is what I wonder, as I sit in the poundingly silent rare book room at the University Library, Cambridge, looking at a fine Arab manuscript, probably made in the sixteenth century.[10] The collection of plant drawings, brought to England from Smyrna in 1682, is now bound in a fat book, covered with heavy, dark, stamped leather. I want to sniff the leather like a dog (but I daren't – the invigilator on his raised dais is a daunting figure) to catch a whiff of the manuscript's past life. Who created it? Who owned it? Where has it travelled? Each of the 372 folios shows a single plant: sempervivum, artemisia, camomile, pimpernel, many beautiful umbellifers, elder, cranesbills, a turnip. An elegantly drawn teasel shows the prickly stems and the big boat-shaped bracts from which the flowering stems emerge, the whole coloured in a dull olive green overpainted with ochre-yellow highlights. There's horsetail, iris, madonna lily, cyclamen, euphorbia (labelled with its old Greek name – 'tithymalos'), and lesser celandine with distinctive long seed pods. At the back is a whimsical image of coral, shown growing in two horns out of the head of a Neptune figure,

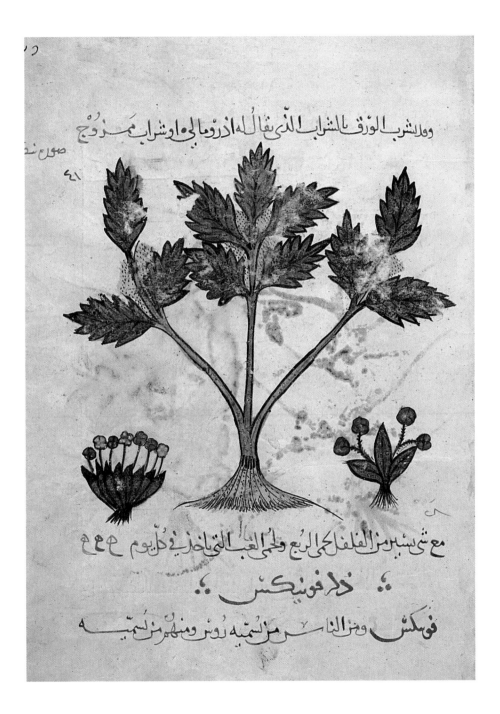

Plate 29: 'Bantafullun' (supposedly our cinquefoil, Potentilla reptans) from a manuscript made in Baghdad AD 1224

who sits on the seabed with fishes swimming around him and a serpent coiled uncomfortably in his lap.

Occasionally, on the reverse of one of the pages is a block of Arabic text, but this is chiefly a picture book. On the top right-hand corner of each page is a gathering of different names for the plant shown below. The University Library's *Handlist of Muhammadan MSS.* (Cambridge, 1900) notes that these inscriptions are in Hebrew, Greek, Arabic and in some cases Turkish. Later research suggests that the Hebrew is written in a sixteenth-century Sephardi hand. Although the handlist doesn't say so, the manuscript at some stage must also have belonged to an Italian, who added his own synonyms 'geranio picolo', 'regolizi', 'eleboro'. I'm looking at the crazed tunnellings that bookworms have made across the pages, remembering that pit, dug before Christ was born, where Theophrastus's great and original work on plants was buried and nearly perished. The pictures in the Cambridge manuscript are familiar, for the pages have been copied from Juliana's book. Here is her absinth, though the plumes of red berries, so elegant in the original Greek manuscript, are lumpier here, not drawn out so gracefully, and the foliage is not so airy. Here is her asphodel, though the Cambridge manuscript does not show the turn of the leaf so well, nor is the flower head so well placed and balanced. Dioscorides first wrote about absinth in the second book of his *De materia medica*. Five hundred years later, he was the main source for the material in Juliana's book. Another thousand years passes before this manuscript is made. Why, I'm wondering, were men still gazing at images of plants first made in the sixth century, still struggling to correlate names, still juggling synonyms? Why didn't those clever Arabs push the story on further? Why didn't they abandon the Greek script and write one of their own, more closely involving the cast of their own plant characters? Perhaps the gradual, but constant retailoring of Dioscorides was a sufficient shift in perspective for them. Perhaps, given their deep interest in medicine, they were content to extend the practical applications of the ancient text by continuing to tease out the likely identities of Dioscorides's plants. Nowhere did they show any interest in engaging in the debate started by Theophrastus. Where are the relationships between these plants? What are the similarities, the differences between them? Where could the key be found to unlock the gate, to reveal why things were as they were, to see for the first time plants not dotted randomly around the pages of a herbal, subservient to the needs of medicine, but arranged according to a huge, beautiful and orderly system, answerable only to its own internal logic? But a mind, however highly refined, can only move to the unknown from the known. Theophrastus had asked the questions. The answers could emerge only when a great deal more was known about the plants themselves. Arranging a system remained the key difficulty. And there, Dioscorides did not help. He was more interested in the medicinal possibilities of a plant than in the plant itself. So plants remained yoked to a drug list, and weren't examined in a wider perspective.

Compared, though, to the stagnation in Europe, the burst of intellectual activity in Western Islam between the tenth and the thirteenth centuries is a miracle. Christianity had not had a liberating effect on the medieval mind in Europe. St Augustine taught that knowledge (which included, of course, all the sciences) was the reflection of the divine mind in human intelligence. It encouraged a kind of passivity. Illumination, clarification, could only be brought about by divine authority, either direct or interpreted by the intermediary of the church. Nature was 'an empty vessel' as Charles Raven calls it,[11] a vacuum which the church filled with its own ideas. It did not foster or encourage individual observation and experiment. In the Middle Ages in Europe, interpreting the natural world was not so much a matter of teasing out the truth, as littering it with superstition, signs and portents. When the Arabs had completely assimilated all the knowledge that Western texts had to teach them, they re-exported that knowledge back into Europe. Through Arab infiltration, European scholars became acquainted again with the roots of their own culture. And learned a great deal else which had a profound effect on the way they subsequently viewed the world around them.

As slowly as Islam itself had assimilated the knowledge of the ancient Greeks, the fruits of Arab scholarship percolated to the West, often through Jewish intermediaries. They were scholarly, able to communicate in Greek and Arabic as well as Hebrew, multicultural before the word was even invented, men such as Sabbatai ben Abraham ben Joel (913–82), better known as Donnolo. He was a Jew of Otranto; when he was only twelve, he and his family were captured by Saracen raiders and taken to Palermo. By the time the family was ransomed by relatives in Italy, ben Joel was fluent in Arabic, which he had learned from his Saracen captors. He studied medicine and practised at Rossano in southern Italy. Like Constantine the African, who came after him, he claimed in his *Book of Creation* (*c*.946) to have studied 'the sciences of the Greeks, Arabs, Babylonians and Indians'. He travelled all over Italy in search of fresh knowledge, spreading Arabic erudition as he went. Constantine the African (*c*.1020–1087) was a native of Carthage, an Arabic-speaking Muslim who had travelled for many years in India and Persia. About 1065, he came via Sicily to Salerno, on the south-west coast of Italy. There, he learned both Latin and Greek, entered the monastery at Montecassino and spent the rest of his life translating Greek and Arabic works on medicine and plants into Latin. Single-handedly, he drew attention to this Greek/Arab body of knowledge a hundred years before translations began en masse.

For the most part, European scholars had to depend on these intermediaries to

نر اطائفی سومن النبات السائفؤ كونه فی دلمنسنة وله ورق

٦ شبینه بورق الحماص البری الا انه اشدسواد امنه وعلیه زغب

فقبض اللسان وله ساق لیس بعظیم واصل دقیق فصیر وفیه

عصاره ورزن هذا النبات وکفنی فی الثمر الکثار وله

*Plate 30: A bird and a grasshopper investigating
the leaves of a plant which may be* Rumex aquaticus.
*The artist has clearly shown how the plant propagates
itself, with 'pups' growing from the rootstock*

bring them the fruits of Arab scholarship. Arabic was too impenetrable a language, even for the great polymath Roger Bacon to decipher. He had no problems in teaching himself Greek and Hebrew but the only way to learn Arabic was to live in a country where the language was spoken. A few outstanding scholars such as Adelard of Bath (*c*.1080–1145) and Gerard of Cremona (1114–87) went to Spain and prepared their own translations of Arabic treatises – when Western science first began to draw from Islam, Spain was an important point of contact. After 1085, when El Cid stormed Toledo with Alphonso VI of Leon, the city became an important meeting point for East and West. I see the body of knowledge I'm interested in swirling across continents, as if on a vast map of the world displayed in a Second World War operations room. First, the action is in Byzantium, then Edessa, then Djundīshāpūr, then Baghdad. When the first medical school of medieval Europe is established in 985 at Salerno by four doctors – a Greek, a Jew, a Saracen and a local Salerno man – that becomes the focus of intellectual activity. I don't want my plants still to be yoked to the medical men, but without them, I've got nothing. In this whole vast period from Dioscorides to the Middle Ages, nobody seems to be looking at plants with a dispassionate eye. Medicine is skewing the plot. There is so much more out there that nobody is drawing or describing, because they yield no medicine, no food, no magic. Dioscorides is still regarded as the master, but of the 4,300 wild plants that grow naturally in Greece, he mentions only a fraction.

So I have to go to that medical school at Salerno, closely connected with the Benedictine monastery at Monte Cassino, where the best texts about Greek plants and medicine are available. Why was the school set up at Salerno? For the same reason that, in the eighteenth century, physicians flocked to Bath. Salerno, on the coast south of Naples, was where wealthy people went to take the waters. In the seventh century BC, just forty kilometres to the south on the fertile coastal plain, the Greeks had founded the flourishing city of Poseidonia, later taken over by the Romans who called it Paestum. It was a part of Italy where the former Greek colonies still preserved Greek traditions. It was close to Sicily where, at Palermo, the island's Saracen conquerors had set up a medical school a hundred years earlier. Gradually, the Salerno medical school established a reputation for producing the most reliable, the most practical treatises of the Middle Ages. Much of that was due to the influence of the Arabs and their knowledge. Sooner than any other seat of learning in Europe, the medical school at Salerno absorbed what Islam had to teach. But in 1224, Emperor Frederick II endowed a university at Naples which drew many of the best people away from the old school. By the time Napoleon closed the Salerno school down in 1811, it had become a place of bogus degrees.

نوع العليق

ما طين وهو العليق هذا نبات معروف وهو قابض مجفف واغصانه
اذا طبخت مع الورق صبغ طبخها الشعر واذا اشرب عقل البطن وقطع
سيلان الرطوبات المزمنة من الرحم ويوافق نشر الدماء التي تقال

العليق

لها قسطس واذا مضغ الورق شد اللثة وابرا القلاع واذا انضمد بالورق

Plate 31: An unlikely looking bramble (Rubus fruticosus)
from a manuscript made in Baghdad AD 1224. The rootstock
has been shown as a kind of bulb and a weird growth like a
wolf's tail rises from the centre of the plant

VIII

OUT OF THE BLACK HOLE
1100–1300

I N EUROPE, ADELARD of Bath was ahead of his time in stressing the need
to look for natural causes of natural phenomena before attributing them to the
supernatural. Theoretical problems associated with plants filled the first six chapters of his book *Quaestiones naturales*, written between 1130 and 1140. Nobody had
asked these kinds of questions since Theophrastus. Like Theophrastus, Adelard was
a philosopher by training. Supported while abroad by Henry I of England, he studied
at Chartres and then travelled to Syria, Greece and Sicily in search of Arab scholars
and scholarship, before settling at Toledo, by then one of the most prosperous and
technically advanced cities in Spain. Adelard restored the idea that plants were worth
studying as plants, not just as potential prescriptions.

At Toledo and in Salerno, both of them half West, half East, there was the possibility that plants could be liberated from the restrictions on image-making that had
accompanied them through the Arab herbals. The plants shown in the Ayasofia codex
*c.*1224,[1] are rarely recognisable from the image alone. Although it was produced
nearly 700 years after Juliana's book, the unmistakeable curling bramble in Juliana's
book, glistening with dark berries, is reduced here to a weird make-believe plant
with a bulb for a root and a strange hairy wolf's tail rising from it (see plate 31).[2]
The plant identified as Chinese lantern[3] could be any plant with a vaguely bladder-
like seed pod, here shown as pale yellow, shuttle-shaped objects. Juliana's book shows
the distinctive seed pods exactly the right colour – a brilliant burning orange-red –
and exactly the right shape, curving from a rounded top to a sharply pointed bottom.

Plate 32: A bulbous plant, optimistically identified as Gladiolus segetum, *from a manuscript made in Baghdad* AD *1224*

None of the Baghdad illustrations shows a clearly defined, instantly recognisable feature of a plant, though it does make a distinction between bulbous plants and those with roots. The plant identified as *Gladiolus segetum* (see plate 32) is very clearly growing from a bulb, though nothing about its foliage or flower suggests a gladiolus. The charm of the illustrations lies in the incidental details: the serpent that coils its way into the foliage of the so-called gladiolus (perhaps it was used as an antidote to snake-bite), the bird and the insect that might possibly be a scorpion, hovering round the implausible *Rumex aquaticus* on folio 3v, the attempts at a land-scape setting as with the blue-rippled watery background to *Cynodon dactylon* complete with stripy hills behind. But often even the settings are unconvincing, as with the unlikely corn poppy shown growing by water, the last kind of habitat it would actually choose. Even the colours show no advance on the palette employed by the painter of Juliana's book: a dull grey-green for foliage, an orangey-brown for trunks, stems, roots, a pinkish-red, occasionally a yellow for flowers. The birds fare better, flashing through the pages in rich turquoise plumage.

Compare this with a herbal made in Salerno at roughly the same time, which includes, among other medical works, a copy of a pharmacological treatise generally called the *Circa instans* (its opening words) that was written *c.*1150 by Matthaeus Platearius and described 273 drugs, 229 of them based on plants. The Salerno manu-script, the earliest surviving of a group of herbals known as the *Tractatus de herbis*, was made between 1280 and 1300 and its practical text was not a novelty. But the pictures that illustrate it are a revelation (see plate 33).[4] A gorgeous crocus (labelled *Croci oriental*) bursts out of a fat bulb, with narrow grassy foliage and vase-shaped flowers, the prominent stamens well displayed. A fat meaty sheaf of marigold leaves underpins the chorus line of many-petalled flowers ranged above. The cyclamen flowers are just the right shuttlecock shape. Wild bryony winds its distinctive heart-shaped leaves round the medieval text. The unmistakeable small seed pods of shep-herd's purse stand out in bold silhouette against the blotched parchment. The pinnate leaves of a summer jasmine are exactly observed, as are the long necks of the white flowers, widely grown for their scent throughout Southern Europe (see plate 34). Swollen nodes are faithfully recorded on the roots of filipendula. Fennel flowers rise from wispily thin threads of foliage, even finer in line than that of the gorgeous love-in-a-mist that takes up most of a page with its fat seed pods and blue five-petalled flowers. We are more used to semi-double flowers in a nigella. Here it is in its first, wild, unimproved incarnation (folio 68v). Something extraordinary has happened. Someone has been brave enough to make a new start.

In our terms, the pictures of the *Tractatus de herbis* are not yet naturalistic images: they look like plants pressed in a flower album, flat, two-dimensional. But they are not deliberately stylised. They dare approximate to nature's own offerings. At last. At last, at last, at last. It is not surprising that this manuscript should have been produced in southern Italy; by the time it was made the region was under Norman rule, but still imbued with Arab science. The physicians of the medical school at Salerno, the teachers at Frederick II's new university at Naples, needed practical textbooks. New legislation laid down by Frederick II in his *Liber Augustalis* of 1231 imposed tighter controls on pharmacists and the medicines they sold. From now on, there was a limit on the number of pharmacists allowed to practise; medicines had to be made up by two pharmacists working together under the supervision of a master of medicine. Doctors could no longer sell medicine themselves, and had to denounce any cheating pharmacists they came across. The pharmacists, of course, were still at the mercy of the herb-women who supplied whatever raw materials they were able to gather, knowing that few pharmacists would be able to tell whether these were the plants they had asked for or not. The text of the *Tractatus de herbis*, responding perhaps to Frederick II's new legislation, pays particular attention to substitutes and counterfeits, explaining how to distinguish between the real product and the dud.

But it's the illustrations, not the words, that make the *Tractatus de herbis* a great shining beacon. Writing as an art historian, Otto Pächt remarks that the illustrators of this herbal

> began to correct the transmitted plant pictures by consulting nature whenever possible and that meant in the first place that one started to make full use of the local flora . . . A new critical spirit becomes manifest in their work and a new courage to explore the visual world and to find out things for themselves. The . . . pictures cannot yet be counted as portraits in the full sense of the word; they are not based on studies drawn exclusively from life, but are rather the result of a careful comparison between painted models (of classical origin) and life models.[5]

The illustrations are done in pen and wash, 406 of them, simplified, yes, but including vital and characteristic details of flowers, seeds, and the way that each is arranged on the stem. They are particularly clear on differences in types of foliage – the pinnate leaves of elder, the hand-shaped ones of lupin. A clear delineation of the way that different parts of a plant relate to each other was perhaps the greatest gift the illustrator of the *Tractatus* passed on to those still fighting their way through a quagmire of synonyms. The illustrator didn't catch the dynamism that is such a feature of the plants painted in Juliana's book. Those move; they flow. You feel they are living. But in, as it were, ironing out the creases in living plants, he highlighted

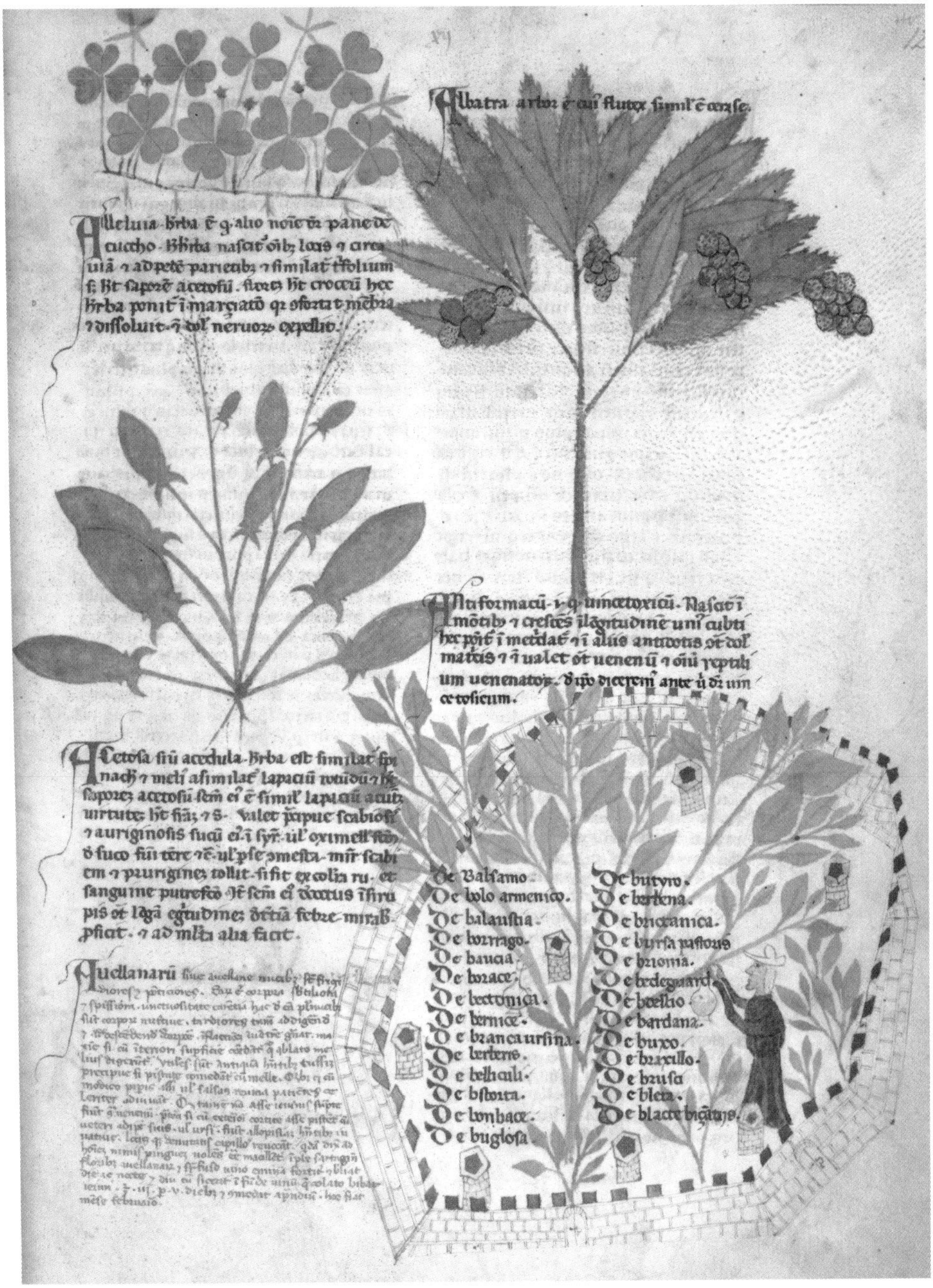

Plate 33: The distinctive leaves of 'Alleluia' (our wood sorrel, Oxalis acetosella), 'Acetosa' (our sheep's sorrel, Rumex acetosa) and, on the right, 'Albatra' (our strawberry tree, Arbutus unedo) with its bright red fruit, and 'Balsamo' (possibly our balsam poplar, Populus balsamifera), from a manuscript made in Salerno between AD 1280 and 1310

*Plate 34: 'Spargula' (possibly our lovage, Levisticum
officinale) and 'Silfu' (our common jasmine, Jasminum
officinale) elegantly filling a page from a manuscript made
in Salerno between AD 1280 and 1310*

their particularity and made pages of great, curiously informal beauty, the plants overlapping each other, the text wandering round and about them.

In the *Tractatus*, there is little of the magic, the superstition that imbued the herbals of Western Europe (though not those produced in the Arabic tradition). Even the mandrake (folio 61) looks like a plant rather than a puppet. Up to this point, it was always shown chained to an unfortunate dog, whose job was to haul the plant from the earth so that no human had to touch it. The herbal had to become credible again and the creators of the new *Tractatus* had two options: 'the return to uncorrupted classical sources of herbal illustrations or the recourse to nature. It seems that both cures were applied.'[6] Whether the *Tractatus* was a return to (as Pächt says) or a revival of classical sources is an argument for art historians. For me, the end result is the same. We are beginning to make progress.

Although Arab interest in plants was at a high point during the twelfth and thirteenth centuries, the illustrations in those Arabic manuscripts that survive are not inspired by direct observation of nature. Image-making was forbidden by the Koran, so the illustrator, for instance, of the Ayasofia herbal created decorative images, that could only in the very loosest way be considered interpretations of the plants that were being described. Though Sultan al-Malik al-Kāmil employed the botanist Ibn al-Bayṭār as Chief of his Herbalists, though Ibn al-Bayṭār went plant-hunting in the country around Damascus, and must have known that the images in the herbals bore no relation to the plants he saw in the wild, the style of image-making did not change. But Sultan al-Kāmil had close diplomatic relations with Frederick II's court. This was the interface. Arab initiatives were in tune with the general spirit of enquiry that was a feature of Frederick's reign. Invention, innovation had an effect on agriculture as well as on medicine and pharmacology. Scholars began to reject the anecdotal in favour of the rational. Under the influence of the Arabs, the text of early herbals had gradually been refined. Now with the *Tractatus*, the illustrations, too, started to sing a recognisable tune. Who commissioned it? A rich and learned patron of the sciences, who consulted it in the privacy of his own library, showing it occasionally to fellow scholars? Or a senior figure at the university or medical school, desperate for a teaching aid that would haul the study of medicine out of the doldrums? Whoever he was, he recognised the truth of Frederick II's *diktat*: 'One should accept as truth only that which is proved by the force of reason and by nature.'

The *Tractatus* was all the more astonishing because of what had gone before it in Europe. While the Arabs had progressed, the material available to scholars in the West had become less and less anchored in reality. In *De civitate Dei*, St Augustine (AD 354–430) had preached that the secular world was entirely corrupt and worthless. In the medieval mind, this world, the world of living things, was nothing but a symbol and instrument of another, higher world. The natural world could be studied and interpreted, but not for its own sake; the only point of such study would be to gain a better understanding of the heavenly world to come. So I won't find the kind of enlightenment I'm looking for in the bulky encyclopaedias gathered together in the thirteenth century by the Augustinian cleric Alexander of Neckham (1157–1217) or the Dominican Vincent de Beauvais (*c.*1190–1264). Neither does the Franciscan friar, Bartholomew of England (*c.*1260), have much to offer, though his magnum opus *De proprietatibus rerum* was still regarded, even in Shakespeare's time, as the standard authority on natural history. Like Neckham's work, the nineteen books of Bartholomew's encyclopaedia were mostly concerned with God and His angels; plants creep in right at the end. Most are there because they are useful: ginger, vine, mulberry and 'Sugre called Zucarum and Sucara also. And is made and yssueth out of certen Canes and Redes which groweth in lakes and pondes faste by a Ryver that is in Egypte called Nilus. And the Juys that yssueth oute of those canes or redes is called Canna mellis and of that juys is Sugre made by sethynge [boiling], as salte is made of water.'[7]

Obsessed as it was with the idea of the world as transitory, frail, destructible, there was little motive in medieval Europe for detailed, practical *research* into its mysteries. The situation was compounded by the fact that chance had saddled the scholars of Western Europe with a rotten role model. Instead of inheriting, early on, the brisk, practical treatises retained by the Arabs from Dioscorides, they muddled through the Dark Ages and the first part of the Middle Ages with a much murkier exemplar, the *Apuleius Platonicus*, imbued with magic, superstition and Anglo-Saxon nonsense about elf-shot, the doctrine of the nines and flying venom: 'For flying venom, smite four strokes towards the four quarters with an oaken brand, make the brand bloody, throw away and sing this three times.'[8]

The original *Apuleius* herbal may have been compiled in Latin *c.* AD 400, though the earliest version dates from the second half of the sixth century,[9] and even then it was full of synonyms from languages – Punic, Dacian – that had long been extinct. This futile activity, the copying of a herbal with unrecognisable illustrations and an often incomprehensible text, continued for hundreds and hundreds of years, though one sensible monk copying an *Apuleius* text at Bobbio in the ninth century left out all the plants he didn't know and substituted instead the medicinal 'simples' that were familiar on his own patch. The *Apuleius* compilation, with illustrations (see plate 35) that do not seem to have come from the same source as Juliana's book, includes bits of Pliny, bits of Dioscorides, tailored to fit a less practical cast of mind than was common among Arab scholars, and a treatise on 'vettonica', our betony

h enne belle·

Plate 35: 'Henne belle' (could it possibly be some kind of artemisia?) from an Apuleius Platonicus *herbal written in Anglo-Saxon* c. AD *1050*

(*Stachys officinalis*). Betony was one of the most important cure-alls in the medieval canon. The *Apuleius* compendium recommends it for healing eyes and ears, for curing toothache, as an antidote against drunkeness, snake bites or attacks by mad dogs:

> This wort, which is named betony, is produced in meadows, and on clean downlands, and in shady places; it is good whether for the man's soul or for his body: it shields him against monstrous nocturnal visitors and against frightful visions and dreams; and the wort is very wholesome, and this is how thou shalt gather it, in the month of August without [use of] iron: and when thou have gathered it, shake the mold, till nought of it cleave therein, and then dry it in the shade very thoroughly, and with its roots altogether reduce it to dust; then use it, and taste of it when thou needest. If a man's head be broken, take the same wort betony, scrape it and rub it very small to dust, then take by two drachms weight, and swallow it in hot beer, then the head heleth very quickly after the drink.[10]

The description of betony (or rather, of its uses, for the *Apuleius* herbal contains practically nothing that would help you identify the plants themselves) comes from a version known as the Cotton manuscript, Vitellius C III, translated into Anglo-Saxon between AD 1000 and 1066. It is not surprising to find the mandrake 'mickle and illustrious of aspect', wreathed around with magic and mumbo-jumbo. 'Thou shalt in this manner take it', advises the Anglo-Saxon copyist.

> When thou comest to it, then thou understandest it by this, that it shineth at night altogether like a lamp. When first thou seest its head, then inscribe thou it instantly with iron, lest it fly from thee; its virtue is so mickle and so famous, that it will immediately flee from an unclean man, when he cometh to it; hence as we before said, do thou inscribe it with iron, and so shalt thou delve about it, as that thou touch it not with the iron, but thou shalt earnestly with an ivory staff delve the earth. And when thou seest its hands and its feet, then tie thou it up. Then take the other end and tie it to a dog's neck, so that the hound be hungry; next cast meat before him, so that he may not reach it, except he jerk up the wort with him. Of this wort it is said, that it hath so mickle might, that what thing soever tuggeth it up, that it shall soon in the same manner be deceived. Therefore, as soon as thou see that it be jerked up, and have possession of it, take it immediately in hand, and twist it, and wring the ooze out of its leaves into a glass ampulla.[11]

I'll allow the medieval scholars their superstitious fear of this root that screamed as it was drawn from the earth, as I allow myself the equivalent lunacy of crossing my

Plate 36: Mugwort (our Artemisia vulgaris) *in an Anglo-Saxon herbal of about 1050. The pigments used have eaten away the parchment on which the plant was painted*

fingers as I walk under a ladder, or saluting magpies when they sail over a hedge. You could say, I suppose, that I am a worse case than that eleventh-century copyist. With another thousand years of research and discovery behind me there is every reason for me to be logical, sensible, reasonable. And yet, and yet. Just in case. Perhaps that copyist felt the same. Better stick to the ritual. Just in case. Even so, it's irritating, the blindness of these medieval scribes. Turning over the pages of the Cotton manuscript, Vitellius C III, in the British Library,[12] picking my way through the florid Anglo-Saxon sitting on its carefully ruled lines, noting how a virulent pigment has in places completely eaten away the vellum (see plate 36), it seems perverse that Ionian Greeks of the sixth century BC could conceive of the universe as a rational system working by ascertainable laws, but these people couldn't. Charles Singer talks of the medieval mind as 'saturated with superstition and deluded by hope'.[13] In Western Europe, knowledge becomes perverted, corrupted, ancient science collapses into a swamp of magic, the mysticism of *The Wanderer*, the impenetrability of *Deor*. And yet the Bayeux tapestry, made in 1080, at about the same time as the Anglo-Saxon *Apuleius*, shows that there were eyes that could see telling detail. And the fruit, foliage and flowers coaxed out of the stone of the Southwell Chapter House a hundred years later indicate that the beauty of the natural world was not unappreciated. The great Domesday survey that William ordered in 1085 signifies a society that had the capacity to organise and bring together a vast quantity of practical information. But here is an Anglo-Saxon herbal earnestly recommending mugwort, the herb we know as *Artemisia vulgaris*, for anyone planning a journey:

> Let him take to him in hand this wort artemisia, and let him have it with him, then he will not feel much toil in his journey. And it also puts to flight devil sickness [possession by demons]; and in the house in which he hath it within, it forbiddeth evil leechcrafts, and also it turneth away the evil eyes of evil men.

Here it is, promising impossible delights to the possessor of periwinkle:

> This wort . . . is of good advantage for many purposes, that is to say, first against devil sicknesses and against snakes, and against wild beasts, and against poisons, and for various wishes, and for envy, and for terror, and that thou may have grace, and if thou hast this wort with thee, thou shalt be prosperous, and very acceptable.

If either of these were rare or expensive 'simples' you could understand why such extravagant claims were made for them. But mugwort is a thug, a perennial weed widely distributed on verges and wasteland throughout Britain. Periwinkle, as any

Plate 37: A schematic 'Affodille' (our wild daffodil or Lent lily, Narcissus pseudonarcissus) *and an anguished centaur holding aloft his* Centaurea *or knapweed from a manuscript made* C. AD *1200*

gardener knows, can cover vast areas of ground, rooting wherever one of its tough stems lies down on earth. The propositions of the *Apuleius* herbal could easily have been tested. That is, if you could be sure that you had the right herb in the first place. The Anglo-Saxon *Apuleius* gives no descriptions, though it often gives an indication of habitat. Mugwort, for instance, is to be found 'in stony places and in sandy ones'. The lack of description would not matter if you could depend on the illustration for a lead. But you can't. The mugwort, with its stylised foliage, half blue, half green, could equally well be henbane or a host of other herbs. The foliage is cut and jagged, a reasonable approximation of the real thing, and the blue colour (as in the similar illustration of henbane, the artist has shown the blue on the underside of the leaves to the right of the main stem, but on the upper side of those to the left) may be his way of suggesting the silvery veneer on the undersides of the foliage. But the flowers are wildly misleading. In reality, they are remarkable only for their dinginess, plumes of a greyish-greenish-creamish colour. The artist of the Anglo-Saxon *Apuleius* has painted them carefully in a rich glowing red.[14]

In a technical sense, the arrival of the Normans brought about an improvement in English herbals: the standard of execution is better, the way the material is laid out on the page more orderly. The illustrations themselves become bolder, outlined in dark brown or black so that they stand out more clearly from the text, which now appears with extravagantly decorated initial letters (see plate 37).[15] But these advances, these refinements add nothing to the sum of knowledge about the plants themselves, the raison d'être of the herbals. The more beautifully designed the images, the less relationship they bear to the plants they are supposed to represent. The artemisias shown, for instance, in an *Apuleius* herbal made at the beginning of the thirteenth century[16] have become gorgeous flat brooches, pinned inside frames sumptuously decorated with silver and gold leaf (see plate 38). The roots drift elegantly out of frame, the flower heads are geometric, stylised triangles, the junctions of the stem are rendered as golden clasps. Then, just at the point when it seems as if the Norman herbal is about to implode on its own uselessness, the medium having entirely overtaken the message, the blessed age of Arab infiltration begins. Their influence had a profound effect on medicine, and therefore on the way plants were written about and illustrated. The elaborate, decorative but ultimately useless images of the Anglo-Norman painters, separated as though by a series of muslin screens from the actual plants of the actual world, are supplanted by those of the vigorous illustrators of Salerno, the makers of the *Tractatus de herbis*. The knowledge and scholarship surging across that map of Europe and the Near East that I have in my mind has completed a vast circle: Greek treatises have been translated into Arabic (often by Hebrew-speaking intermediaries) and those Arab treatises are now being

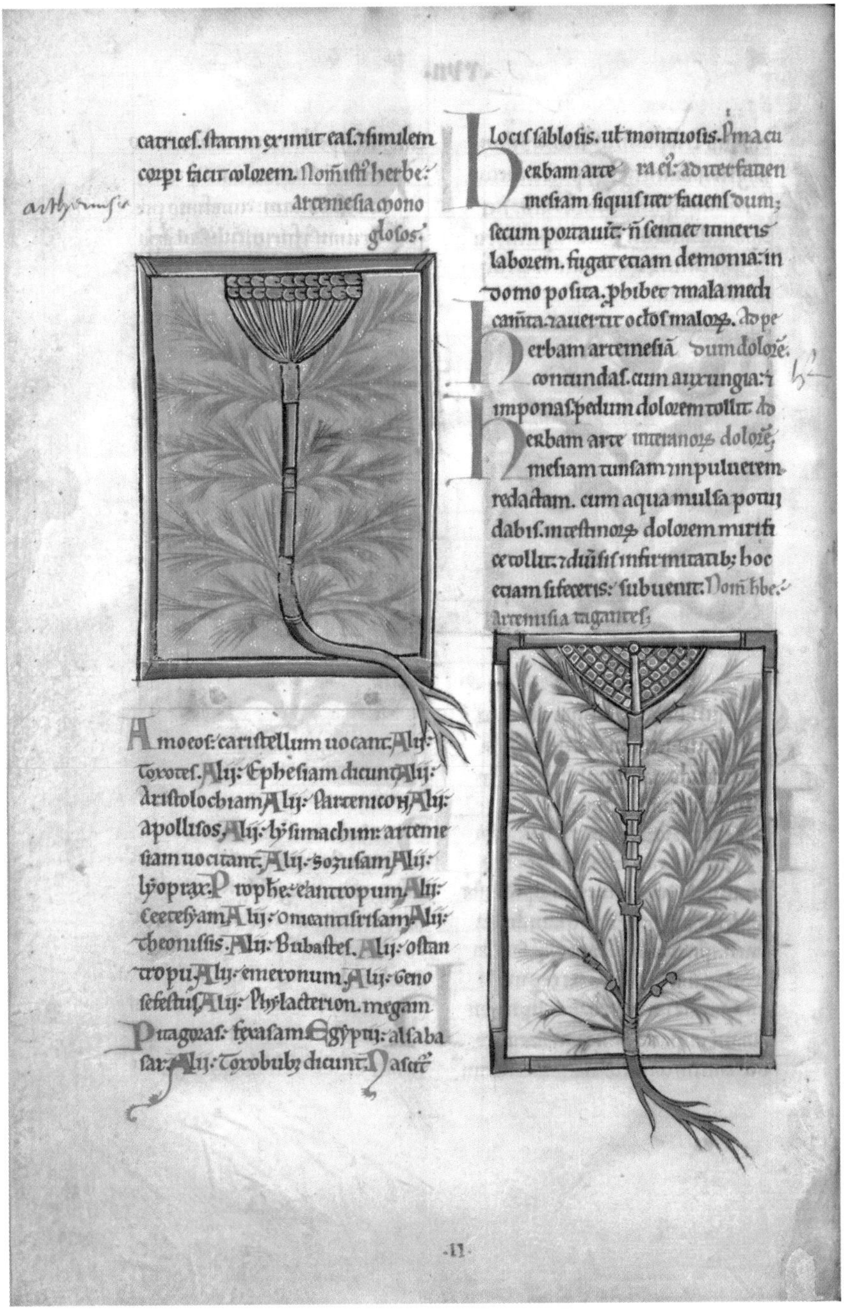

Plate 38: Highly stylised artemisias in an Apuleius Platonicus *herbal made in England* c. AD *1200*

translated into Latin, the *lingua franca* of the Western world, and reintroduced to the West. Mongol invaders are shattering the ancient civilisations of China and Persia; they are sweeping through Afghanistan, India, Russia. By 10 February 1258, they are in Baghdad, led by Genghis Khan's grandson, Hulako. The House of Wisdom and the magnificent library, so carefully built up by generations of Islamic scholars are destroyed. But Arab learning has now been annexed and disseminated in the West. Once again, the books have been burned, but the knowledge endures.

IX

THE IMAGE MAKERS
1300–1500

'HERE STAND I,' wrote the fourteenth-century Italian poet Petrarch, 'as though on a frontier that divides two people, looking both to the past and to the future.'[1] Behind him were centuries of superstitious dogma. Around him was a country paralysed by the plague in which a third of Italy's population had died. Ahead of him lay the Renaissance, the rebirth of a culture that had already been born once, the rediscovery of the glory that had been Greece and Rome (especially Greece). But humanists such as Petrarch also had a strong desire to build on the past. They were galvanised by the classical canon, not passively nostalgic about it. To them, human ingenuity mattered and could be harnessed to make better sense of the natural world. War and politics severed the old links between East and West; medieval scholars had been inspired and invigorated by Islamic culture but Petrarch was looking forward into an era when the clever Moorish and Jewish scholars of southern Spain would be silenced by the invading armies of Aragon and Castile. Byzantium was destroyed. The overland route to China, exploited so brilliantly by the Venetian merchant Marco Polo (1254–1324), was closed off.

From the East, though, came two inventions, one a product, the other a process, which had a revolutionary effect on European culture. Printing was the process, but without paper, which gradually replaced the parchment and vellum of the medieval scribes, the printing press would have remained a hungry monster.[2] When, around the middle of the fifteenth century, Johannes Gutenberg printed his famous Bible, it seemed as though the word would now race ahead of the image as the agent of

Plate 39: A beautiful Madonna lily (our Lilium candidum*),
complete with scaly bulb in a manuscript made between
AD 1370 and 1380*

communication. But until there were words worth reading, the fact that they could be mechanically printed on paper rather than scratched out by hand on vellum made no difference. Information could be spread about more quickly and more widely, but at the beginning it was material that was nowhere near as innovative as the machine that printed it. Until the body of knowledge about plants improved radically (and that didn't happen for another hundred years), Gutenberg's unwieldy beast could not demonstrate its power as an agent of change. There was change, important, revolutionary change, but it was brought about by painters, not wordsmiths.

The process had begun just before Petrarch was born when the unknown artist who decorated the pages of a herbal made (probably in Salerno) between 1280 and 1300, produced for the first time portraits of plants (see pages 111–115) that danced and sang and could tell you their names. In the pages of the *Tractatus de herbis* held in the British Library (MS Egerton 747), the artist throws away the old, debased patternbook and gives us real maidenhair fern (the stalks laid diagonally in a bold pattern across the page); real broad beans with fat juicy pods; the unmistakeable dappled leaves of lungwort. He even tried an elephant, though he ended up with something more like a pig with a stretched-out nose. But now, the illustrations of plants in these hand-lettered manuscripts mattered very much more than anything that was written about them (see plate 34). Between 1330 and 1340, Manfredus de Monte Imperiale, a scholar well versed in medicine, produced another version of the *Tractatus*[3] which in some ways was even better. He copied his illustrations from the earlier version, but paid even more attention to the colours he used and to the exact form of the flowers. Minta Collins deduces that by *c.*1370–80 an unknown artist in northern Italy, possibly Padua, was copying Manfredus himself and, like Manfredus, producing images even lovelier than his mentor's.[4] While no botanically inclined writer had yet emerged who could describe the scaly bulb of the madonna lily, its bright green foliage, the prominent stamens with their boat-shaped, pollen-loaded anthers, the groove down the centre of each of the flower's white petals, this artist has it all (see plate 39). He has grasped its essential nature rather better than Fra Filippo Lippi (*c.*1406–1469), who put a madonna lily in the left hand of his famous annunciatory angel.

This extraordinary sequence of soft explosions, each manifestation carrying a little further the artist's purpose in representing plants exactly as they appeared before his own eyes, culminated in the astonishing Carrara Herbal[5] made in Padua around 1390–1400. The text was prepared by a Paduan monk, Jacopo Filippino for Francesco Carrara, the last lord of independent Padua, who was deposed in 1403 and strangled in a Venetian prison three years later. It's an Italian translation of a treatise on medical botany, first written *c.*800 by the Arab physician Serapion the Younger. So

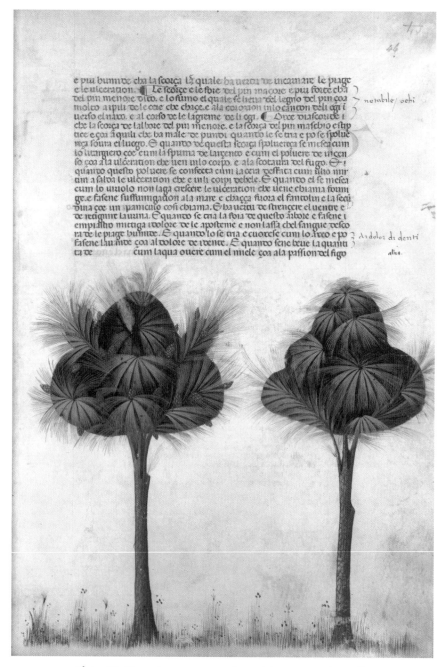

e piu buinvre eba la scorça le quale ha uertu de incainate le piaghe
e le ulceration. ¶ Le scorçe e le foie del pin maçore e piu forte cha
del pin menore vico. e lo fumo el quale se tiena del legno del pin coa
molto a ipili vele cose che chaçe. e ala coloraon inlo cancon deli ogi e
uerso el naso. e al corso de le lagrieme de li ogi. ¶ Dice Diascoride
che la scorça de tal bore del pin menore. e la scorça del pin mascho e stip
tice e çoa aquili che ha male de punoi quando le se tria e po se spolue
rça soura el luego. ¶ quando de questa scorça spoluerçia se mesea cum
lo litarugiero çoe cum la spuma de larçento e cum el poluere de incen
so çoa a la ulceration che uen inlo corpo. e ala scotauna del fugo. ¶ i
quando questo poluere se confecta cum la cera ţeffica cum olio mir
um a salva le ulceration che e inli corpi vebele. ¶ quando el se mesea
cum lo uuiolo non laça cresere le ulceration che uene chiama soum
gre.e fasene suffumigaçion ala mare e chaçça fuora el fantolin e la seca
vina çoe un paniculo cosi chiama. ¶ ha uertui de strençere el uentre e
de reſtrinţir la urina. ¶ quando se tria la foia de questo arbore e fasene i
empiaftro mitiga il dolore de le aposteme e non laffa chel sangue vesco
ra ve le piaghe buinue. ¶ quando lo se tria e cuoreſe cum lo aceo e po
fasene lauande çoa al dolore de voente. ¶ quando sene treue la quanti
ta de _____ cum laqua ouere cum el mele çoa ala passion del figo

Plate 40: Two pine trees, complete with cones and needle-
thin foliage on a page of Serapion the Younger's herbal.
It's known as the Carrara Herbal and was made in
Padua between AD *1390 and 1400*

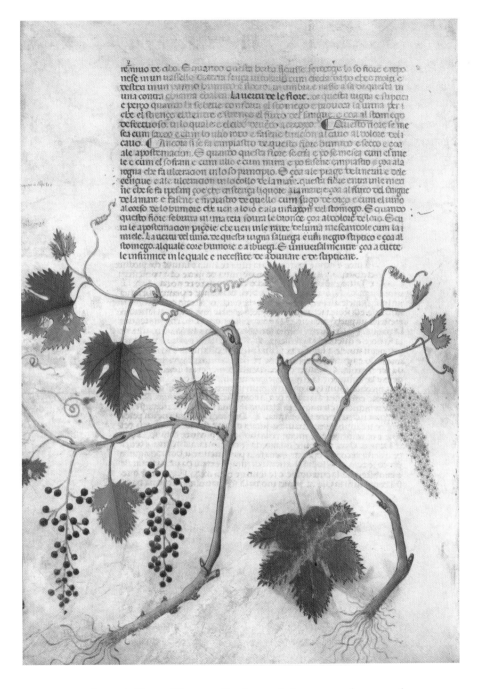

Plate 41: Vines (Vitis vinifera) *wandering across the page of Serapion the Younger's herbal. It's known as the Carrara Herbal and was made in Padua between* AD *1390 and 1400*

nothing new and revolutionary can be expected from the words. But the illustrations, painted in gouache on vellum, are mesmerising: privet, red clover, barley, asparagus, white convolvulus, camomile, grapes, pine trees (see plate 40), an enchanting clump of violets, several kinds of gourd. Space was left in the manuscript for a good many of these illustrations, but only about fifty were ever finished. 'Why?', I'm wondering, in the ultra-modern surroundings of the British Library's manuscript room, looking at these swirling, living images made more than 600 years ago. As much time separates me from this extraordinary creation as separated the unknown artist who illustrated it from the Arab who first wrote it. What governed his choice of subjects? Was it availability of living plants? (Many of the chosen subjects would have come to fruition in late summer.) Was it an artistic inclination to paint first those things (gourds, vines; see plate 41) that would make most impact on the page? Was he (or his patron) more interested in food plants than flowers or the medicinal herbs which Serapion discussed? Beans, barley, various stone fruits, different cucurbits dominate the pages. Four ears of barley are arranged almost heraldically in four parallel lines on the page with the enclosing sheath-leaf of the one on the left curling under the others like an enclosing banner. The plants are superbly drawn, but at the same time formal, patterned, self-conscious. Did the anonymous artist die before he could finish the commission? Or did his patron's violent end make it difficult, impossible even, for him to continue? As a painter, though, he was a brave man, the best of these fourteenth-century pioneers confident enough to abandon the old paradigms, bold enough 'to look nature straight in the face'.[6]

Many copies were made of the illustrations in the Carrara Herbal, including at least twenty of the images that shortly after appeared in the *Liber de simplicibus*,[7] made in the Veneto between 1445 and 1448. It was commissioned by a doctor, Nicolò Roccabonella of Conegliano (1415–1458), with paintings by Andrea Amadio. Some of the plants, such as deadly nightshade (*Atropa belladonna*), *Hepatica triloba* and dyer's greenweed (*Genista tinctoria*), had never been painted before. This was their first appearance.[8] Whereas the Carrara Herbal (and all others of its kind) had been made of sheets of parchment, Amadio painted his plants in gouache on the new medium now available – white paper. The first paper mill in Europe had been set up at Fabriano in Italy in 1340.

In Dr Roccabonella's herbal, plants were named in Latin, Greek and Arabic but not Italian. The German and Serbo-Croat synonyms were probably added when he practised in Zara and treated Slav and German patients. The book was used in the Testa d'Oro pharmacy at Rialto until the second half of the sixteenth century, when it belonged to a Venetian doctor, Benedetto Rinio. On his death, Rinio left the herbal

Plate 42: An apprehensive patient, covered in spots, waits to be treated by a doctor preparing medicine in which pig's dung is evidently a vital ingredient. The unidentifiable herb on the page is called 'Botracion statice' and may be a kind of wild celery

to his son Alberto, advising him never to part from this 'book of simples, painted from life and worth a small fortune'. But Alberto had no children and when he died in 1604, he left it to the monks of SS Giovanni e Paolo at San Domenico. They were told that they must guard the book carefully, secure it with chains and only allow it to be looked at in the presence of two monk-guards. Perhaps it was a monkish scribe who added yet more synonyms to the collection. This is how plant knowledge gradually developed: personal experience, personal observation slowly building on what had gone before.

By the time Dr Roccabonella commissioned his herbal, the focus of learning and exchange had shifted north from Salerno and Naples to Padua and the Veneto. Padua, with its university and medical school, and Venice, with its constant stream of travellers, were natural centres for this revolution. In the new herbals, the puppet human figures disappear. The plants are full-blown stars, demanding attention. They grow into the margins of the text, they spread exploratory tendrils and petals outside the rigidly ruled columns of the page. The illustrators working in the new natural style had a much clearer idea of scale. The illustrator who had painted *Apium* (parsley) in a *Tacuinum sanitatis* made in Lombardy *c.*1380–90[9] showed it as a tree-like plant, rearing with its feathery foliage way above the man and the woman standing in the flowery mead under it. But around 1400, it appears en masse in another *Tacuinum sanitatis* also made in Lombardy[10] as a low herbaceous plant, looking very much more like itself. The new interpreters produced images that could be more easily (and more correctly) 'read'.[11] In a short time, a huge shift had taken place.

In the process of stripping the plant from its *mise-en-scène*, presenting it alone against a plain background, spot-lit, as it were, a few things were lost. In early herbals, artists had sometimes tried to indicate the habitats where plants were most likely to be found – a sempervivum springing (wildly out of scale) from the tiled roof of a house, a water lily backed by the blue ripples of a pool. But the early illustrations had been so formulaic, were so often misunderstood in copying, that this element – very close to our hearts in the twenty-first century – became of no practical use to herb-gatherers. Early manuscripts also often showed the insects, mad dogs or venomous snakes against which the herb supposedly offered protection. In added cartoons in earlier herbals[12] they showed herbs being gathered and prepared, patients being treated (see plate 42). Now, by separating the plant from its purpose in terms of the way it was presented on the page, the artists of this critical period in the first half of the fifteenth century prepared a way forward. Each plant became an object of interest in its own right, not just because it could be eaten, or turned into medicine or used in various rituals. Artists began to paint flowers because they were

Plate 43: A martagon lily (our Lilium martagon) *with accurate details of bulb and seed pod set alongside the flowering stem. From the Codex Bellunensis made in Belluno between* AD *1400 and 1425*

intriguing and beautiful, not just because some doctor or apothecary needed to be able to identify them. Wherever herbals had been produced, in Salerno, Padua or the Veneto, in Provence, Constantinople or Bury St Edmunds, they had shown only a tiny proportion of the plants that actually grew in each region. Model manuscripts were sometimes tailored for local consumption, but whether the illustrators were Italian, German or Anglo-Norman they had still shown only those plants which they considered useful in some respect.

The artist of the Codex Bellunensis, although not such a good draughtsman as Amadio or the artist of the Carrara Herbal, introduced another important innovation. He showed his plants in full flower, as was the convention, but he also included specific details, separately placed around them. The stem of his martagon lily (see plate 43) rears up straight out of the bottom of the page, the characteristic whorls of leaves clearly shown. Alongside, on the left, is the scaly bulb, with roots sprouting out of its flat base. On the right is the martagon in seed. It's a sketchy composition, but shows exactly how the flowers, which hang down on their stems, then turn into seed pods which stand upright, like the arms of a candelabrum. In presenting a Chinese lantern (*Physalis alkekengi*) the artist gives us a close-up of a papery orange calyx, broken open to show the cherry-like fruit inside. The herbal has begun a slow metamorphosis, to emerge triumphantly as a florilegium.

Pliny had been against illustrations in books about plants, on the grounds that repeated copying would gradually corrupt the images – he was right. What he could not have foreseen was the stylistic straitjacket that, in the years before the new way of looking, impelled medieval illustrators to turn plants into formal abstractions, patterns rather than living things. This took plants even further from the natural world than the bad copyists had done. Was it in the spirit of 'Look! We have come through!' that the artists of the late fourteenth and early fifteenth century turned their eyes, cleared of preconceptions, back to the beauties of the natural world? They had survived the Black Death. Was this a way of giving thanks, of celebrating the delightful manifestations of the here and now?

In their new freedom, plants escaped from herbals into tapestries.[13] They decorated prayer books and illuminated manuscripts. They invaded paintings. They bloomed on the great bronze doors that Lorenzo Ghiberti (1378–1455) made for the baptistry of Florence Cathedral. The primary work carried out by the illustrators of the magnificent herbals produced in northern Italy provided references for the painters that followed. The plants of the flowery mead behind the dancing girls at the Cappellone degli Spagnoli, Santa Maria Novella in Florence, painted in 1365 by Andrea di Bonaiuto, are stylised creations, varied in form, but unidentifiable. By *c*.1438–40, when Antonio Pisanello (*c*.1394–1455) painted his famous portrait of Margherita Gonzaga,[14] real

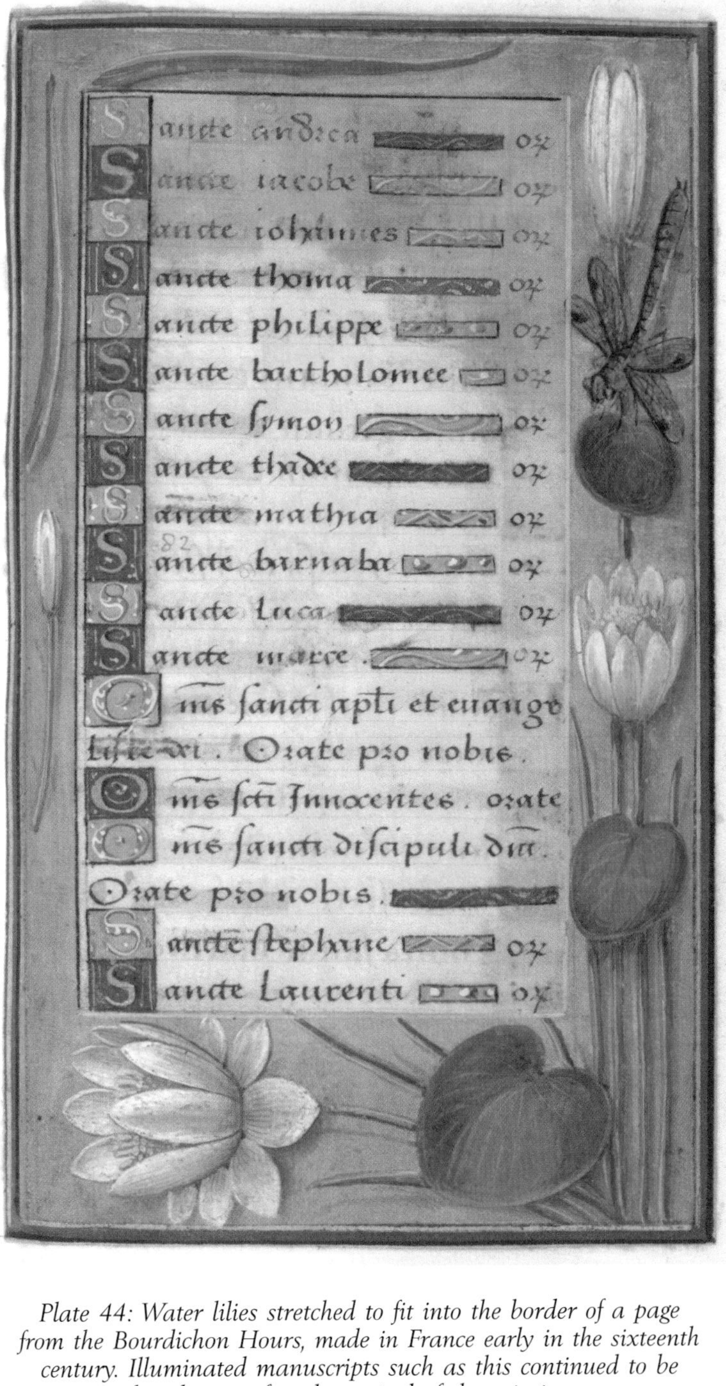

Plate 44: Water lilies stretched to fit into the border of a page from the Bourdichon Hours, made in France early in the sixteenth century. Illuminated manuscripts such as this continued to be produced even after the arrival of the printing press

columbines, real pinks with fringed petals and stamens as fine as the curled tongues of butterflies were scattered against the dark bosky background (see plate 45). Famous for his sketchbooks of animals, Pisanello produced plant studies too, observing, for instance, the different leaf forms of common plants such as violet, primrose, cinque-foil and dandelion.[15] The single blooms that Pisanello had scattered in the background of his Gonzaga portrait began to appear on the borders of the illuminated manuscripts produced in Bruges and Ghent, where Pisanello's columbines and pinks were joined by daisies, periwinkles and blue pimpernels.[16] In the Book of Hours (mid-1470s) made in Bruges for Charlotte of Bourbon-Montpensier by the Master of the Dresden Prayer Book, in The Vision made by Simon Marmion for Charles the Bold and Margaret of York (Valenciennes and Ghent 1475), a particular gallery of plants begins to emerge: cornflower, strawberry, harebell, vetch, thistle. Blue is a favourite colour, conspicuous consumption on the part of those who commissioned these costly works of art: an ounce of black pigment cost only two and a half *soldi*, an ounce of blue was ten. Only gold, at fifteen *soldi* an ounce, was more expensive. In the Book of Hours made c.1500–1508 for Anne of Brittany, the artist Jean Bourdichon even painted snowdrops and pinks in his favourite shade of blue. In the early manuscripts, painters such as Simon Marmion occasionally showed plants (such as the daisy on folios 7, 15v, 17, 27, 29 of The Vision) as though they were actually growing. The basal cluster of leaves, the stems are all there, as they are in his violet (folio 14v), as vivid as the violet in the Carrara Herbal – one of its most beautiful images. There are surprises in these illuminated borders too. Marmion includes a wild orchid (never to be seen again) in one of the borders of The Vision (folio 27).

By the mid-1480s most Flemish illuminated manuscripts featured the new kind of illusionistic border with flowers and insects[17] carefully placed on backgrounds of solid colour. These are not Simon Marmion's growing plants, but single flowers, often flat-faced ones such as viola, pink, daisy, forget-me-not, which suited this kind of treatment (see plate 44). A large collection of artist's models rapidly developed. Once again, nature was turned into patterns, *atelier* formulas. But this time, the artists had good patterns to work from. They also had better materials to work with. And their eyes had been opened to the natural world, even if the heavy-handed symbolism of the age meant that the same flowers tend to appear time after time in the illuminated manuscripts made between 1470 and 1560. The list of plants included in the early herbals was circumscribed by their usefulness. Religious conno-tations dictated the even smaller repertoire of the illuminators. Marmion's orchid was an aberration, with no symbolic part to play in this particular series of scripts.[18] But without the initial groundwork prepared by the flower painters, could the illuminators have produced such staggering (and lifelike) beauties as the tall iris in

*Plate 45: Pinks and columbines are scattered over the back-
ground of Antonio Pisanello's portrait of Margherita Gonzaga
painted between* AD *1438 and 1440*

a glass tumbler set on the ledge of an open window in the Hours of Mary of Burgundy (folio 14v) made by the Vienna Master of Mary of Burgundy *c.*1470–75? This was a far better way of using the flower than squashing it into a border of miniatures, as the same painter tried to do in his Hours of Engelbert of Nassau (folio 181v). The flower then becomes top heavy, too big for its space. To show itself off properly, it needs its long, strong stem and its sheaves of sword leaves, as Albrecht Dürer demonstrated in the painting he made of a similar bearded iris *c.*1503 (see plate 6).[19]

Petrarch was one of the first people to perceive a distinction between the beauty of nature and its utility. But in the 'startling marriage' of art and science that typified the Renaissance, the boundaries were blurred. It certainly wasn't a distinction recognised by Leonardo da Vinci (1452–1519) who, at thirty years old, was working as an engineer for the Duke of Milan. In his notebooks, he works out early prototypes for an aeroplane, a helicopter, a submarine, a parachute. He designs a dredging machine, analyses the flight of birds, sketches out a model city for another patron, François I, King of France.[20] He collects popular proverbs (and jots down an inventory of his household goods, including 'two large hatchets and eight brass spoons'). The structure of plants interests him just as much as the structure of buildings or machines. He makes leaf prints – physiotypes – by coating their undersurfaces with the slightly greasy soot produced by a candle flame and then pressing each leaf facedown on a sheet of paper. His painterly mind, though, is equally engaged in the way that plants actually look (see plate 46). Giving advice to other painters in his *Treatise*, he reminds them that, 'In autumn you will represent the object according as it is more or less advanced. At the beginning of it the leaves of the oldest branches only begin to fade – more or less, however, according as the plant is situated in a fertile or barren country. And do not imitate those who represent trees of every kind (though at equal distance) with the same quality of green. Endeavour to vary the colour of meadows, stones, trunks of trees, and all other objects, as much as possible, for Nature abounds in variety *ad infinitum*.'[21] In the Royal Collection at Windsor are wonderful studies of bramble, wood anemone, the drooping head of a columbine, a madonna lily (captured on paper in 1479).

Dürer (1471–1528), just twenty years younger than Leonardo da Vinci, knew exactly how to catch the habit of a plant – the way a flower is placed on a stem, the way a blade of grass emerges from its enclosing sheath – without overtly showing himself so interested in their structure. He does not share Leonardo's forensic interest in the insides of things. But he did share with the older man an absolute reliance on the evidence of his own eyes. 'Life in nature manifests the truth,' he wrote in his treatise on proportion.[22] 'Therefore observe it diligently, go by it and do not depart from nature arbitrarily, imagining to find the better by thyself, for thou wouldst be

Plate 46: Study of Flowers *(pen and ink over metalpoint) made*
by Leonardo da Vinci in about AD *1483*

misled. For verily, art is embedded in nature; he who can extract it has it.' Leonardo had proclaimed the same message in his *Treatise on Painting*: if a painter 'will apply himself to learn from the objects of nature he will produce good results . . . he who has access to the fountain does not go to the water-pot.' Truth to nature has become the yardstick by which a work of art is judged and the famous piece of turf that Dürer painted in 1503[23] came to be seen as the most extraordinary mirror of the natural world that any artist had ever produced (see plate 47). Dürer takes a worm's eye view, showing his plants almost life-size. It's a late spring scene, with smooth meadow grass, speedwell, dandelion, hound's tongue, cocksfoot, daisy, greater plantain, creeping bent, yarrow, springing fresh from the ground. The candour of this watercolour, its precision and its beauty became the gauge by which all other 'Dürer' paintings were measured. His paeony, his martagon lily, his anchusa (on paper at Bremen), his columbine, his violets (both at the Albertina, Vienna), his buttercup, his tuft of cowslips have all been demoted, the famous monogram analysed and found wanting – until the next generation of art historians comes along. But there they all are, these plant portraits, demonstrating that, even if they are not by the hand of the god himself, there existed a band of painters inspired by his genius. Together, they ensured that no one need ever again be at a loss for an image of a plant that showed it in its true form and exact colour.

Even in the fifteenth century, Nuremberg, Dürer's birthplace was famous for its gardens. 'About the windows of its houses, where reigns undying spring, innumerable flowers and foreign plants fill the air with their sweet scents, which the lightest breeze carries into the bedrooms and innermost chambers,' wrote one of its citizens in 1495. But why was it that artists could see those blooms, describe them on paper, while the writers remained dumb? It was almost as if Dürer and Leonardo were living in a different world from those who used words rather than paints for their pictures. Through all this long period, since the first pictures of plants were painted in Juliana's book, the images have been the only things that have moved on. The artists were the great naturalists of the period from the late fourteenth to the middle of the sixteenth century,[24] but they could be articulate only in one particular way. They could open eyes, but they could not, on their own, promote debate. For writers, there was a way out of the dark tunnel of the Middle Ages, but it depended on them creating new ways of describing things. The painters had been able to forge a new language of painting, but the lack of any agreed terminology for the parts of plants or the similarities and differences between them made informed exchanges between writers impossible. Theophrastus had been the first person to address these issues but even before the death of the Greek physician Galen in *c.* AD 200, Theophrastus had been forgotten in the West. It was time for his renaissance.

Plate 47: 'Das grosse Rasenstuck', the famous piece of turf painted with forensic accuracy by Albrecht Dürer in 1503

Plate 48: 'Hyppuris' (our common horsetail, Equisetum arvense) in a manuscript made in Lombardy c. AD 1440. The bulbous plant labelled 'Jacintus' is more likely to be the grape hyacinth (Muscari neglectum) found in France and Germany than the plant we call hyacinth (Hyacinthus orientalis) which had not yet come into Western Europe from Turkey

X

THEOPHRASTUS REBORN

1250–1500

WHEN THE OLD images became so corrupted as to be useless, a new generation of artists cast them aside and started again, with spectacular results. In the thirteenth century, one man had tried to do the same thing with the hideously corrupted classical texts with which he was familiar. It was a brave effort, but the times were against him. The man was Albertus Magnus (*c.*1200–1280) a monk from a wealthy Bavarian family who had studied at Padua University, then joined the Dominican order. During the 1230s he taught in Germany, then moved on to Paris and finally, in 1248, settled at Cologne. Some time before 1256 he produced his magnum opus *De vegetabilibus*, based, so he thought, on a treatise by Aristotle. Like Aristotle, Albertus was deeply concerned about the notion of a 'psyche' or soul in living things. He saw that plants fed, grew, reproduced and died, but could not conceive of them feeling, experiencing desire, or sleeping. But when ivy twined itself in a tree did the souls of the two plants unite in a similar way? He was clear that the root of a plant acted as the materfamilias, the vital source of supply to the family above. Like Theophrastus, he believed in the mutation of species. If a wood of oak or beech trees was razed to ground, he was perfectly prepared to suppose that poplars could rise up in their place. And he accepted the received wisdom that staffs made of medlar wood gave enchanters special powers. He did not question the fact that mugwort (*Artemisia vulgaris*) tied to a traveller's leg would relieve his weariness. His book was arranged in seven chapters, five of them theoretical. In the sixth was a list of plants useful in medicine; the seventh concerned itself with agriculture and horticulture. He divided his sixth book into two parts – the woody plants (about ninety) followed by herbaceous ones (about 180), both arranged in alphabetical order. Like some of the early Greek philosophers, he thought it slightly undignified, tasteless even, to come down from the philosophical heights of the first five chapters to the more literal level of the sixth.[1]

In his opinion, neither sexes nor sexual processes existed in the plant world; he thought all plants were of one sex, with male and female characters combined in the same plant. He used those words 'male' and 'female', but only in the sense of distinguishing between plants with particular characteristics. 'Male' plants had narrow leaves, were hard, dry and rough, and bore small fruits and seeds. His 'female' plants are relatively broad-leaved, soft, moist, smooth; they produce larger seeds and fruits than male plants. In his preoccupation with the soul of plants, his acceptance of some superstitious beliefs, Albertus reflected the spirit of the age. But he was unusual in the way that, like Theophrastus, he 'enquired' into plants, sought definitions. A tree (*arbor*), he classed as a woody plant with a single trunk rising from its root, which bore numerous branches (*rami*). A shrub (*arbustum*) on the other hand, had a number of stems rising from the root. He divides herbaceous plants into those with leafy stems of considerable size (*olus virens*) and the rest (*herba*), which are smaller. But immediately he sees a difficulty in his arrangement. Beet, for instance, is a *herba* in its first year but an *olus virens* thereafter. *Folium* (leaf) is used indiscriminately to describe a whole leaf, the leaflets of a compound leaf such as ash or walnut, but also a bract or a petal. The tendrils of plants such as vine or cucumber he calls *anchae*. He notes that bark is made up of two layers, the outer one hard and dry, the inner one softer and sappier. He sees clearly the difference between woody growth (*lignum*) and pith (*medulla*). He is particularly interested in the way that the trunk of the date palm developed, 'as if made up of stakes (*asseres*) rather than growing in circular layers'. He classifies flowers by their different shapes: bird-like, bell-shaped, star-shaped (the most common) or pyramidal. As far as he is concerned, the chief purpose of the flower is to signify the fruit to come (*indicia fructuum*). Along with classical authors, he classes fig and mulberry as oddities because they appeared to fruit without first producing flowers. Although he seems to be dismissive of flowers, he notes that, where they are made up of several whorls of petals, each petal on the outer whorl covered a gap between two petals of the inner whorl (if you look at a tulip, you see exactly what he means). He recognises stamens, and makes a distinction between their stalks (the filaments) and their tips (the anthers). These were remarkable observations and if anyone else in Albertus's circle had been remotely interested in the things which evidently fascinated him, perhaps texts which were already a thousand years out of date might have been

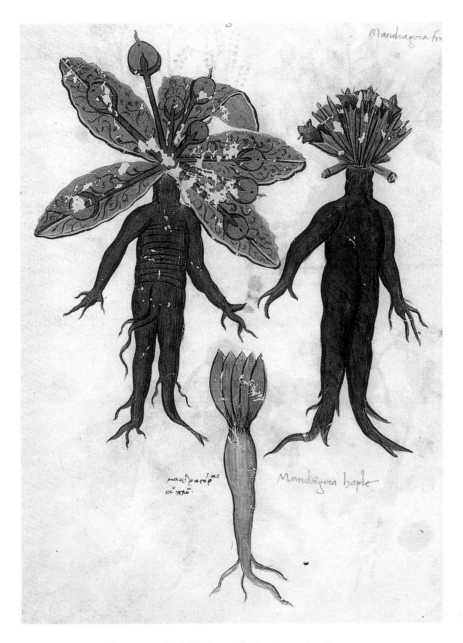

Plate 49: The fabled mandrake (our Mandragora
officinarum*), both male and female, in a manuscript made
in Constantinople between* AD *1406 and 1430. Though faithful
to the ancient device of showing the mandrake in human
form, the artist has shown clearly how the flowers grow on
separate stalks clustered in the centre of the plant and
the calyxes which clasp the orange berries*

jettisoned in favour of progress. Unfortunately, they weren't. But Theophrastus would have been proud of Albertus (who of course had never heard of him). Albertus's source was a text called *De plantis*, which he thought had been written by Aristotle. In fact, it is the work of Nicolaus Damascenus, a scholar working at the beginning of the Christian era. Like many other works of the classical period, Nicolaus's Greek text was translated into Syriac, then into Arabic, then into Latin which was the version on which Albertus based his own *De vegetabilibus*. But whose text had Nicolaus Damascenus used to create his own *De plantis*? Theophrastus's, as it turned out, though that serendipidity was revealed only in the second half of the fifteenth century when finally the *Enquiry into Plants*, the great work of the founding father, emerged again into the mainstream of the scholarly canon.

If Theophrastus's book had survived in Western Europe through the Dark Ages, might the medieval cast of mind have been different, more open to enquiry? Might Albertus have been the centre of a great web of scholars sharing botanical knowledge, as Luca Ghini was, later, in Renaissance Italy? Instead, the Middle Ages inherited works from the period of classical decline, such as Pliny's *Natural History*. Galen had been the last writer to quote Theophrastus at first hand.

A book needs an audience that is ready for it. It wasn't there during the Dark Ages or the Middle Ages, but in the revival of learning that characterised the fifteenth century, Pope Nicholas V introduced a scheme to translate a whole tranche of classical texts found stacked on the shelves of the Vatican Library. Among them was Theophrastus's *Enquiry into Plants*. Thirteen hundred years after Galen's death, Theophrastus was translated from Greek into Latin by Teodoro of Gaza (*c.*1398–*c.*1478), a native of Thessalonica who had fled to Italy *c.*1430 when Greece fell to the Turks (see plate 50). Teodoro of Gaza was a scholar typical of the early Renaissance. From his home in Thessalonica, he went to Constantinople *c.*1422 and opened a school there, just before Sultan Murad II laid siege to the city. When Teodoro was forced to flee, he came into Italy via Sicily. He studied Latin under Vittorino da Feltre at Mantua, taught Greek at Pavia, became a professor at the University of Ferrara where the Duke of Ferrara persuaded him to take over as rector. In 1451 he was called to Rome where the pontiff was putting into practice his plan of translating the best of the Greek authors into Latin. A chair of Greek had been established at the University of Florence in 1391, but right up until the end of the fifteenth century, knowledge of Ancient Greek was a rarity, even among the scholars of the early Renaissance. Teodoro was given two plums: Aristotle's animals and Theophrastus's plants. He completed his translations within five years, though it was not until 1483 that his Theophrastus found its way into print at Treviso. In his Preface to the *Enquiry into Plants*, Teodoro alludes to the difficulties

Plate 50: Teodoro of Gaza (c.1398–1478) who spent five years translating into Latin Aristotle's treatise on animals and Theophrastus's Enquiry into Plants

the work had presented to a translator. Latin had no words for the parts of plants that Theophrastus described, so he had had to invent them. Not being a plantsman himself, he could not always be sure that he had substituted the right Latin names for Theophrastus's Greek ones. Was his hemlock the same plant as the Athenian's hemlock? Did they both mean the same thing when they talked of laurel or lily? Inevitably, there were mistakes. But it was a triumphant new beginning for Theophrastus. At the time, nobody had built on his groundwork, but now, 1700 years later, with the help of Teodoro of Gaza, those same foundations are set out again, and this time they are not abandoned. Quietly, methodically, a building begins to grow. Later, it will acquire a name – botany. Teodoro became such a hero that the scholars of Ferrara took off their hats as they passed his house. Long after his death, they continued to salute him.

This rediscovery of Theophrastus typified the Renaissance scholars' enthusiasm for classical learning. At first this fervour was a reaction against the narrowness of the medieval mind. Then it turned into a critical evaluation of classical thought itself. And it was not long before Italian scholars began picking holes in the ubiquitous Pliny. For sixty years until his death, Nicolò Leoniceno (1428–1524) was professor of medicine at the University of Ferrara. For his students, the newly printed edition of Pliny was the most easily available source of information about plants. But when he and his scholars read Pliny in the original Greek, they realised how many mistakes had been introduced in translation. Teodoro of Gaza himself had confessed to problems. In 1492, Leoniceno published *Indications of Errors in Pliny and in Several Other Authors who Have Written on Medicinal Simples*, the first of a series of 'commentaries' on the ancient authors, which were made possible as further copies of Greek originals came to light. Even more damaging was the *Castigationes Plinianae*, published the same year by Ermolao Barbaro (1453/4–1493), who listed 2,500 mistakes he had found in the *Natural History*, (though he tactfully assumed that these were the fault of generations of amanuenses rather than the master himself). Having demolished Pliny, Barbaro moved on to Dioscorides. His *Corollarium Dioscorides*, published in 1516 after his death, is a kind of appendix to the works of the Greek army doctor, pulling together a ragbag of additional information about the plants that Dioscorides had written about in his *De materia medica* of c. AD 77. On iris, for instance, he adds a bit from Theophrastus, whom Dioscorides rarely mentioned, a bit from Pliny and then a bit (the most interesting) from his own experience. 'In his garden at Padua, Felix Sophia showed me an iris, the flowers of which smell like very ripe plums; on this account, they become very attractive to ants.' Is this the first mention in print of *Iris graminea*, a native of Southern and Central Europe and unmistakeable on account of its reddish-purple, plum-scented

*Plate 51: Madonna and Child set against a background of roses
by Domenico Veneziano, c.1445*

flowers? As Teodoro of Gaza had done, Barbaro too finds a problem with synonyms. '*Geranium* is one thing as described by the Greeks,' he says, 'and quite another thing as received by the Latins.'

Johannes Gutenberg had brought out the first book to be printed by moveable type between 1450 and 1455. The first edition of Pliny had appeared in 1469, an instant bestseller, quickly followed by multiple editions of Dioscorides and then a Latin translation of Theophrastus which appeared in 1483. There was evidently a market for herbals and by the time the printed book emerged as a commodity, superb plant portraits were being produced, particularly in northern Italy around the Veneto. Looking back into those years in the second half of the fifteenth century, it seems that here, at last, was an opportunity to create an entirely new body of work, marrying woodcuts made from the brilliantly true-to-life images of plants created by painters such as Andrea Amadio, with a fresh text that reflected the enquiring *zeitgeist* of the Renaissance. It didn't happen. The old classical texts were regurgitated and when the first printed illustration of a plant appeared, it was not an advance, but a retreat to the worst nonsense of the Middle Ages. The woodcut, (a landmark, though how I wish it had been a more worthy one) heads the fifth section of Conrad von Megenberg's *Buch der Natur*, printed by Hans Bamler of Augsburg in 1475 (see plate 52). In a frame roughly five inches by seven inches, it shows nine disparate, unrecognisable forms, even more useless to anyone interested in plants than the text, a rough jumble of extracts from the usual crowd: Avicenna, Galen, Dioscorides. Von Megenberg, who had studied at Erfurt and the University of Paris, wrote the book between 1349 and 1351, so it was already more than a hundred years out of date when it appeared. By 1475, the Vienna Master of Mary of Burgundy had painted his elegant blue iris standing, as though just cut, in a glass tumbler on a window sill. In the border of a Book of Hours made in Bruges and measuring scarcely three inches by two, Simon Bening had scattered pinks, double daisies, blue vetch, forget-me-not and blue pimpernel so real you want to scoop them off the page. By comparison, the illustration in the *Buch der Natur* is catastrophically awful. And it wasn't an aberration.

The next illustrated plant book sent out into the world as a printed text was a copy of one of the worst compilations of the Middle Ages, the *Herbarius* of Apuleius Platonicus.[2] The illustrations painted in the original manuscript had been worthless. Translated into a cruder medium, the woodcut, they became so spaced out as to be hallucinogenic. By 1481, anybody with the slightest interest in the natural world knew what a water lily looked like – the big rounded leaves spread horizontally on the surface of the water, the many-petalled cup-shaped blooms floating between them. And yet here is an illustration copied from a ninth-century original which

Plate 52: The first illustration of plants to appear in a book,
the Buch der Natur *by Conrad von Megenberg, published*
in Augsburg in 1478

turns the water lily into a trio of lollipops with vague pairs of feathery leaves marching up the stalks (see plate 53). It is a disaster. By 1481, Hugo van der Goes (*c.*1440–1482) had painted his famous Portinari altarpiece for the Medicis in Florence, setting in front of the Virgin and Child a vase and a tumbler, both filled with gorgeous, tangible, unfeigned flowers: an orange-red lily, blue and white irises, columbine, pinks, with violets strewn on the ground beneath them. The models were there, but the makers of plant books weren't using them (see plate 54).

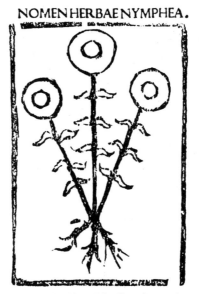

NOMEN HERBAE NYMPHEA.

A græcis diciſ Prothea. Alii Caccabus. Alii Lo tometra. Alii Androcanos. Alii Hidrogogos. Alii Heracleos. Alii Arneon. Itali Nvmpheā.

*Plate 53: An appallingly bad woodcut of a water lily (*Nymphaea*) in an Apuleius Platonicus herbal printed by Johannes Philippus de Lignamine in Rome c.1481*

There was certainly a hunger for knowledge about plants, and very quickly a system of distributing books emerged, as itinerant booksellers moved from town to town, advertising the titles they had in stock.[3] Already by about 1480, the Nuremberg printer Anton Koberer had produced a handbill advertising the twenty-two books he had for sale. In each new place they reached, the travelling booksellers displayed these advertisements, scrawling underneath the name of the inn where they and their wares could be found. There was, of course, a revolution in the number of copies available of any one work. Writing in 1475, a contemporary observer noted that three printers working for three months had produced 300 copies of a book,

Plate 54: *The central panel of the Portinari Altarpiece by*
Hugo van der Goes (c.1440–1482). Conspicuously set in
the foreground are vases with iris, columbines and a
bright red lily (probably Lilium bulbiferum)

each with 366 folios. In his estimation, three professional scribes working for the whole of their lives could scarcely have got through the same amount of work. And they would have introduced many mistakes along the way. That old problem of a text, insidiously corrupted by each amanensis who was set to copy it, could have faded away with the invention of printing. Here is the text, diligently set in lines of wood or metal characters. Here is Gutenberg's great machine, ready to disgorge as many copies of those locked-in characters as the printer might wish. Technically, it should be foolproof. But with copyright not yet established on the plant books that were being printed, pirated editions were commonplace. In the text, set and reset by competing printers even more times than it had been copied, mistakes actually got worse. By the time *Le grand Herbier* first published by Pierre Metlinger at Besançon *c*.1486–8 (but again based on an earlier manuscript) emerged in a new dress in England as *The grete herball*, forty years had passed and there had been many opportunities for error and distortion, most of which had been taken. And yet the process carried within it the seeds of its own redemption. In a printed text, the process of corruption was more visible to an ever-growing body of readers, some of whom had sufficient initiative to try to sort out the mess as Nicolò Leoniceno and Ermolao Barbaro did with Pliny.

The woodcut, as a medium for illustration, introduced fresh opportunities for error. The technique had been introduced into Europe *c*.1400, but compared with Amadeo's brush and Leonardo da Vinci's pen, the wood engraver's tools were blunt instruments (although no bar, one might have hoped, in getting at least the outline of common plants laid down in an appropriate form). Marie Boas argues that in the context of the time, the gulf that separates the crude, conventional woodcuts of the first printed books on plants from the work of the miniaturists and painters would not have been seen as remarkable. 'The woodcuts were copied from the illustrations of the manuscript whose text was also faithfully copied; the illustrations illustrated the text, not nature, a peculiar view, no doubt, but there was as yet no really independent botanical (or zoological) study. That was to be the contribution of the sixteenth century.'[4] In the earliest books, text and illustrations were all cut in the same wooden block but after moveable type had been invented, wood – tough, fine-grained stuff from apple, pear, medlar and quince – was used solely for illustrations. With text and illustration separated from each other, printers had the opportunity to introduce a new kind of muddle, by matching pictures with the wrong text. Woodblocks, a relatively expensive item for a printer to commission, had to work hard to earn their keep. They became worn and broken, but that didn't stop printers from using them again and again. The lacuna between a master drawing and the misshapen image derived from it was inherited from the age of scribes. Almost a hundred years passed by before a plant book was published that closed up that gap.

Like other Renaissance scholars wrestling with ancient classical texts, the first editors of the natural histories of Theophrastus, Dioscorides and Pliny had to work from worm-eaten manuscripts, which were themselves copies of copies of copies. Translation was a laborious process (it took Teodoro of Gaza five years to get through his quota of Aristotle and Theophrastus). But the plantsmen had a gift not available to those fighting their way through treatises on ethics or maths. They had the living plants themselves, flowering in their gardens, fruiting in their orchards, scattering the surrounding meadows in spring. They were not always the same plants as the ancient writers talked about (and it was some time before the plantsmen of the Renaissance understood that), but somewhere, these scholars were sure, they still existed in exactly the same form as Theophrastus had described in his seminal *Enquiry into Plants*.

In the 1480s, a wealthy German amateur set out to look for them. Nobody knows his name but on 28 March 1485, Peter Schoeffer at Mainz published the results of his labours in *Der Gart der Gesundheit* (The Garden of Good Health). It was a brave book because in it, several things were done that had never been done before. The text was written, not in Latin or Greek, but in an everyday language (a Bavarian dialect form of German). Of the 379 woodcuts, at least a sixth could be recognised as the plants they were supposed to be (see plate 55). That was a miracle, made possible perhaps because the blocks on which the illustrations had been cut measured five inches by seven inches, twice the normal size. The book also had a couple of decent indices, so that readers could find their way about it more easily. 'Since, then, man can have no greater nor nobler treasure on earth than bodily health,' wrote the author in his Preface,

> I came to the conclusion that I could not perform any more honourable, useful or holy work or labour than to compile a book in which should be contained the virtue and nature of many herbs and other created things, together with their true colours and form, for the help of all the world and the common good. Thereupon I caused this praiseworthy work to be begun by a Master learned in physic [this was Johann von Cube, the town physician of Frankfurt], who, at my request, gathered into a book the virtue and nature of many herbs out of the acknowledged masters of physic, Galen, Avicenna, Serapio, Dioscorides, Pandectarius, Platearius and others. But when, in the process of the work, I turned to the drawing and depicting of the herbs, I marked that there are many precious herbs which do not grow here in these German lands, so that I could not draw them with their true colours and form, except from hearsay. Therefore I left unfinished the work which I had begun, and laid aside my pen, until such time

Plate 55: 'Acorus' (our yellow flag, Iris pseudacorus)
from a German herbal Der Gart der Gesundheit,
published in Mainz in 1485

Plate 56: 'Canapus' (our hemp, Cannabis sativa)*, with the five-fingered leaves carefully delineated, in a German herbal* Der Gart der Gesundheit, *published in Mainz in 1485*

as I had received grace and dispensation to visit the Holy Sepulchre, and also Mount Sinai, where the body of the Blessed Virgin, Saint Catherine, rests in peace. Then, in order that the noble work I had begun and left incomplete should not come to nought, and also that my journey should benefit not my soul alone, but the whole world, I took with me a painter ready of wit, with a subtle and practised hand [his name was Erhard Reuwich]. And so we journeyed from Germany through Italy, Istria, and then by way of Slovenia or the Windisch land, Croatia, Albania, Dalmatia, Greece, Corfu, Morea, Candia [Crete], Rhodes and Cyprus to the Promised Land and the Holy City, Jerusalem, and thence through Arabia Minor to Mount Sinai, from Mount Sinai towards the Red Sea in the direction of Cairo, Babylonia and also Alexandria in Egypt, whence I returned to Candia. In wandering through these Kingdoms and lands, I diligently sought after the herbs there, and had them depicted and drawn, with their true colour and form. And after I had, by God's grace, returned to Germany and home, the great love which I bore this work impelled me to finish it, and now, with the help of God, it is accomplished. And this book is called in Latin, *Ortus sanitatis*, and in German *Der Gart der Gesundheit*. In this garden are to be found the power and virtues of 435 plants and other created things, which serve for the health of man, and are commonly used in apothecaries' shops for medicine. Of these, about 350 appear here as they are, with their true colours and form. And, so that it might be useful to all the world, learned and unlearned, I had it compiled in the German tongue . . .'[5]

So, in several ways, particularly the fact that it was the first plant book not written in Latin or Greek, *Der Gart der Gesundheit* broke into new territory. But it did nothing to further dispassionate appraisal of the plants themselves. They are still yoked to medicine, not studied for their own intrinsic interest. And the anonymous author disseminated a doctrine that thickened rather than dissipated the fug of superstition that had hung around healing since the Middle Ages. His work is based on the prevailing theory of the four elements and the four principles or natures deriving from them. The four elements are fire (hot and dry), air (hot and moist), water (cold and moist) and earth (dry and cold). The four different natures associated with each element are heat, cold, moistness and dryness. Physicians of the time believed that good health depended on a correct balance between all the elements and all the natures. Each herb acquired a set of characteristics, not about itself but about its effect. As the author of the Preface explained, 'One herb is heating, another is cooling, each after the degree of its nature and complexion.' Similarities and differences are being examined, but, for my purposes, they are not the right ones. Those laborious indices, though a breakthrough in one sense, do not group and list the plants in a way that takes forward the correct naming of names. I'm still waiting

Plate 57: A Lady in Yellow *by Alesso Baldovinetti*
(c.1426–1499) with a bold design possibly based on the
Chusan palm *(*Trachycarpus fortunei*) on the sleeve of her dress*

for the man who will start to understand and have the genius to re-create in words the vast, magnificent scheme of the natural world, set plants free from the pharmacy, strip them of the artificial order imposed on them on account of their usefulness. Meanwhile, fifteenth-century readers fell upon Schoeffer's book. Within five months, a pirated edition had been published by Johann Schoensperger at Mainz. Economising on the woodcuts, which subsequently appeared half-size, publishers in Strasbourg, Basel and Ulm brought out another seven plagiarised editions in the next four years.

But the world was opening up fast. On his travels between 1270 and 1295, Marco Polo had seen in their natural habitats plants such as rhubarb, cinnamon, turmeric, camphor, coconut and ginseng which previously had been known only as dry products, lined up on shelves of the apothecaries' shops. Although an account of that journey had been available in manuscript since 1298, its repercussions began to be felt only after his story was published in 1477. By 1487 explorers had reached the coasts of Africa and penetrated the interior of Abyssinia. By 1498, European ships reached India again, revisiting the Indus from where Alexander's generals had first sent back reports of the exotic banyan. By 1503, trade was opened up with the West Indies and the whole of the American continent. By 1511, Malacca and the East Indies were on the map. By 1516, seafarers had made their way to China and by 1542, they had reached Japan too. By the middle of the sixteenth century, European explorers and sailors had touched on most of the countries of the world, apart from Australia and New Zealand. The existence of plants totally unknown to the ancient authors had finally to be recognised. In less than a hundred years, twenty times as many plants were introduced into Europe as in the previous 2,000 years. Though the first exploratory voyages had been made by Portuguese mariners, funds to capitalise on the new discoveries were mostly provided by Italian merchants and bankers and it was in Italy that the first attempts were made to cultivate the onslaught of unfamiliar specimens. From the New World alone came such curiosities as maize, yams, potatoes, runner beans, French beans, the sunflower, the Jerusalem artichoke. In the gardens of the Medici in fifteenth-century Florence, there were already pineapples and mulberry trees among the olives and vines. By the time that Italian scholars of the sixteenth century began seriously to address the problem of sorting and organising the avalanche of plants coming into the country, they had three new tools to help them: the botanic garden, the *hortus siccus* or herbarium and, at last, some decent books on plants.

XI

BRUNFELS'S BOOK
1500–1550

FOR EARLY HUMANISTS, such as Teodoro of Gaza, the editing of classical texts by Pliny and Dioscorides was an end in itself. Repelled by the scholasticism of the Middle Ages and its obsession with logic and theology, the humanists saw the Middle Ages as an unfortunate hiccup between the great achievements of the classical past and the glorious promise of the secular present. They cared as much about man and his association with the living world as they did about his relationship to God. But the early scholars all agreed that if they were to understand classical authors correctly they had to produce accurate texts. Diligently comparing different versions of the classics, they restored lost passages, corrected wrong transcriptions, always attributing errors to the ravages of time, the copyists, never criticising the classical authors themselves. But when Constantinople fell to the Turks in 1453, this rich source of supply for Greek texts came to an abrupt end. 'The fount of the Muses is dried up for evermore,' proclaimed Cardinal Piccolomini to Pope Nicholas. Denied the distraction of fresh material, the next generation of scholars began to look more critically at the accumulated body of work newly translated into Latin. They dared question the fabled authorities. Nicolò Leoniceno published his *Indications of Errors in Pliny*; Ermolao Barbaro brought out his *Castigationes*. A thorough grounding in the classics was the standard apprenticeship for a humanist scholar but they soon began to find that the texts raised more questions than they answered. The Arab intermediaries, who had done so much to keep the old Greek texts alive, were now suspect. How much of their own thinking and writing had they interpolated into the hallowed texts of Dioscorides and Pliny?

Gradually, scholars began to untie the knots that bound them to the ancient texts. Looking back from our impatient age, full of arrogance, crammed with knowledge of things that had yet, then, to be discovered, we wonder why it took them so long. The humanists, after all, cultivated delight in nature, and insisted that it be understood and enjoyed for its own sake, not (as St Augustine had instructed) for its value in interpreting the Bible or as an allegory of the wonders of God. It was time for emancipation. It was time for original thinking.

It was time to look at the plants themselves, rather than what had been written about them 1,700 years previously. But the thinking could only happen after the looking. Fortunately, the opportunities to look at plants increased substantially in the sixteenth century as the first botanic gardens were established in Padua and Pisa, the first examples of the *hortus siccus* (collections of pressed, dried plants) were made and, above all, when the first quasi-serious books on plants were published. The first was Otto Brunfels's *Herbarum vivae eicones* (1530) and as the title (Living Portraits of Plants) suggests, the pictures in it are more important than the words.

In his Dedication, Brunfels (1488–1534) (see plate 58) wrote that he had no other end in view than bringing back to life 'a science almost extinct. And because this has seemed to me only possible by thrusting aside all the old herbals, and publishing new and really lifelike illustrations, and along with them accurate descriptions extracted from ancient and trustworthy authors, I have attempted both; using the greatest care and pains that both should be faithfully done.'[1]

Brunfels's illustrator was Hans Weiditz and with his 'new and really lifelike illustrations' Weiditz laid down a series of images of plants that meant that nobody need ever question again what a pasque flower looked like. Or a narcissus. Or an alchemilla. Or a water lily (see plate 62). Amadio had done that too (with a much more limited range of plants) but his paintings were one-offs. Here was a process that made it possible for scholars in Germany, France, Italy, Denmark, all to look at exactly the same image. The iconography of plants had begun. There was still a vast swamp to wade through before scholars agreed on the labels that should be attached to the icons, but Weiditz, who had been a pupil of Dürer's, provided 260 superbly lifelike plant portraits. He showed the broken stem of a teasel, the wilted leaves of a hellebore, the disease attacking the green leaves of his wild orchid. These were faithful images of individual specimens, not vague representations of types.

In his long Dedication, Brunfels does not mention Weiditz by name. He gets his credit, 'meyster Hans Weyditz von Strassburg', in the author's Introduction to the German language edition, the *Contrafayt Kreuterbuch* published two years later. Brunfels seems to resent rather than applaud the illustrator's extraordinary achieve-

Plate 58: Otto Brunfels (1488–1534), author of
Herbarum vivae eicones *(1530–36), illustrated by*
Dürer's brilliant pupil, Hans Weiditz

ment. He complains that on many occasions he has had to give way 'to the masters and journeymen-engravers' because they drew what they liked, when they liked. He explains that he hasn't been able to arrange the plants in any meaningful way because he only knew what was to be included when the block-cutters produced the images. The book was published in separate parts as sufficient material was gathered together; the first volume, which came out in 1530, was followed by a second in 1531–2 and a third, published posthumously, in 1536. From our perspective, we recognise Weiditz's pictures as being much more significant than Brunfels's text, but perhaps it was like this from the beginning. Perhaps the book was not Brunfels's idea at all but was instigated by his printer/publisher Johannes Schott of Strasbourg. Perhaps Schott saw an untapped market for a new, well-illustrated book on plants, commissioned Weiditz and throughout treated him as the most important contributor to the enterprise. Forty-seven of the plants that Weiditz chose to paint had never been illustrated before. They included common but beautiful native plants such as wood anemone, lady's smock, plantain, and the pasque flower, which inspires one of the most beautiful images in the entire book (see plate 59): the featheriness of the foliage, the soft hairiness of the stems, the flowers opening above a ruff of tendril-like growths, all caught to perfection by Weiditz. Brunfels was extremely grumpy about including the pasque flower, a 'herba nuda' with no proper Latin name, useless to apothecaries. The wood anemone was similarly dismissed as a wildwood herb, 'the name of which is unknown'. On the lily-of-the-valley, another wild flower that Weiditz painted, the authorities, said Brunfels, were 'as silent as fishes'. He didn't see the point of including plants that had no known use. No previous writers on plants had ever done so. He wasn't an innovator. But Weiditz, taught by the uncompromising Dürer, was evidently intrigued by the intrinsic diversity of plants, the various forms of leaves, the way a flower was positioned on its stem, the different receptacles that held seed. And because Weiditz produced these new images, which were then printed and distributed all over Europe, the plants he showed could no longer be ignored. Apothecaries may have had no use for them, but they existed, these 'herbae nudae', these no-name nonentities. In 1530, when the first part of *Herbarum vivae eicones* was published, there simply weren't enough plants in the pool to make sorting and categorising a viable exercise. Even so, Brunfels felt he ought to be imposing some order. He was irritated when he had to accept a plant name he didn't recognise simply because it was the name the artist had used ('Huic flori nomen inditum a grapheo accepimus cum pingeret').[2]

Brunfels's text was drawn together from all the usual sources. There were forty-seven of them and they included Theophrastus, Dioscorides, Pliny, Apuleius Platonicus and Arab physicians such as Serapion, Mesuë, Avicenna and Rhazes. The

A

B

Buchenschell.   Hackerkraut.

OTHO BRVNNFELSIVS.

CONSTITVERAMVS ab ipso statim operis nostri initio, quicquid esset huiuscemodi herbarum incognitarum, et de quarum nomenclaturis dubitaremus, ad libri calcem appendere, & eas tantum sumere describendas, quæ fuissent plane uulgatissimæ, adeoqȝ & officinis in usu: uerum longe secus accidit, & rei ipsius periculum nos edocuit, interdum seruiendum esse scenæ καὶ καιρῷ λατρύἱιν, quod dicitur. Nam cum formarum deliniatores & sculptores, uehementer nos remorarentur, ne interim ociose agerent & prȩla, cōacti sumus, quamlibet proxime obuiam arripere. Statuimus igitur nudas herbas, quarum tantum nomina germanica nobis cognita sunt, prȩterea nihil. Nam latina neqȝ ab medicis, neqȝ ab herbarijs rimari ualuimus (tantum abest, ut ex Dioscoride, uel aliquo ueterum hanc quiuerimus demonstrare) magis adeo ut locum supplerent, & occasionem prȩberent doctioribus de ijs deliberandi, qȝ

t 3

Plate 59: *The pasque flower* (Pulsatilla vulgaris), *one of the 'herbas nudas' that Otto Brunfels reluctantly included in his* Herbarum vivae eicones *(1530–36)*

elaborate frontispiece (see plate 60) is crammed with classical allusion: Dioscorides and Apollo (in a strange tasselled cloak) are set on plinths either side of the framed title, Venus relaxes in a sixteenth-century garden of raised beds, set round with boards, and the Hesperides frolic below in their orchard of golden apples. But Brunfels also gave credit to what he called the *vulgus*, as opposed to the *docti*. He has respect for their practical knowledge of plants, 'qui non ex libris sapiebant, sed experientia rerum edocti erant'.[3] It was the herb-women, the 'vetulas expertissimas' who told him about the spinach-like pot herb Good King Henry ('Praeterea et eam adpinximus quae vulgo Guot Heinrich vocatur, vel Schwerbel. Itsenim vetulae nos persuaserunt').[4] And he seems to take grim satisfaction in telling the story of a dinner given early in the sixteenth century by the physician-humanist Guillelmus Copus of Basel. Copus pulls a herb out of the freshly served salad and asks his guests, fellow physicians from the Paris faculty of medicine, if they know its name. None of them does and they suppose it to be a very rare exotic. Copus calls in the kitchen maid who tells them it is parsley.

Brunfels's own background perhaps gave him this natural empathy with the *vulgus*. He was born at Braunfels, near Wetzlar in Germany. His father, John, was a cooper, and strongly opposed his only son's desire to enter the Church. Around 1510 Brunfels took a Master of Arts degree at the University of Mainz, left home and became a noviciate in a Carthusian monastery at Königshofen near Strasbourg. He stayed there for about ten years but then, having converted to the Lutheran cause, escaped with a fellow priest, Father Michael Herr, and was taken in by the printer, Johannes Schott in Strasbourg. For the next couple of years, he travelled through south-western Germany, preaching as an evangelical Lutheran. When he returned to Strasbourg in 1524, he married and set up a school. For the next ten years everything he wrote and published was on theology, until in 1532, he took a degree as Doctor of Medicine at the University of Basel. He practised briefly in Strasbourg before becoming city physician in Bern. Only a year later, he died of consumption.

So he did most of the work on *Herbarum vivae eicones* when he was also running his own school and after a life dominated by theology. He gained his doctor's degree in 1532, the year in which the second volume of *Herbarum vivae eicones* was published. His course of study would have included lectures on *res herbaria*, the only way then available for a student to learn about plants. His teachers would have shown him how to navigate his way through the standard texts, gobbets of which he then regurgitated in the *Herbarum*. But this subject matter was almost as un-familiar to him as it was to his readers. And it was restricted. His teachers at Basel would have been lecturing only about plants of medicinal value. No wonder he was irritable when Weiditz presented him with pictures of plants on which the classical

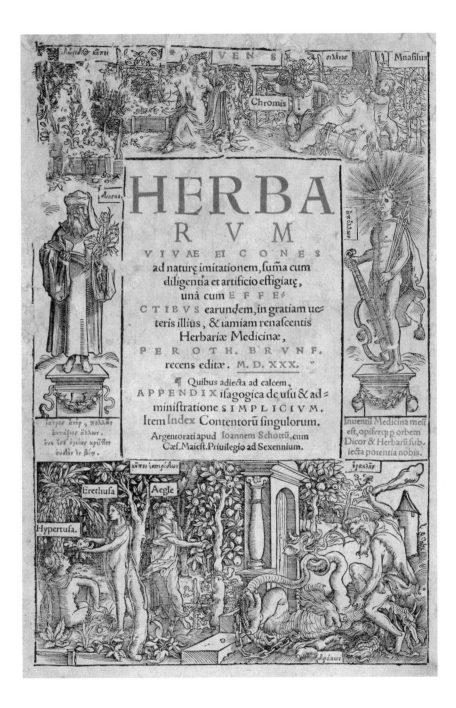

Plate 60: The title page of Herbarum vivae eicones *by Otto Brunfels, which included superb illustrations of plants by Hans Weiditz. It was published in Strasbourg in 1530*

authors had nothing to say. If they were 'silent as fishes' then he too was forced to be dumb, unless he could pick up information from local herb-gatherers or apothecaries. Uncritically, he accepts the 'doctrine of signatures', which laid down that the appearance of a plant was the best clue as to its use. Polygonum, for instance, was widely used to heal flesh wounds because of the blood-red blotch on each of its leaves. 'This herb,' wrote Brunfels, 'is also of two kinds, large and small, but both have a peach-like leaf which is blotched in the middle, just as if a drop of blood had dripped on to it, a mighty and marvellous sign which astonishes me more than any other miracle of the herbs.' Where a group of plants is in a muddle, with all kinds of disparate things lumped together as if they were different manifestations of the same flower, Brunfels replicates the mess, without adding any observations of his own. On narcissus he writes:

> There are, they say, two kinds of flower, namely, male and female, purple, yellow and white; also it flowers twice in the year, once in March and then in September; it sheds its seeds at Whitsuntide, and in the beginning of the year forsooth it springs up with white and yellow flowers, and in the winter with purple ones. They say that they have caught it in a miracle of nature; for if anyone tried to dig it up in March he could easily uproot it with a single finger, but from that time onwards it settles down daily deeper and deeper into the ground until September, when it can scarcely be dug up without a great deal of trouble. In the meantime, it lurks in the earth at the depth of one cubit, but in the winter it soon moves upwards again, so that it comes out even above the ground with its first bloom at the breath of spring. We also have found this, and have observed that the root is at first soft and bulbous and the leaves are like those of *Porrum* [leek] . . . , but soon the root hardens, and the leaves become more fleshy, coming from the root without a stalk. From September onwards it is quite hard and very deeply barked, but with a rather delicate and lily-like flower, opening about a hand's breadth above the ground, after the second mowing of the meadow.[5]

In fact there are three plants fighting to get out of this capacious hold-all: the yellow-flowered daffodil, the white-flowered spring snowflake and the purple-flowered colchicum or autumn crocus. Weiditz's illustrations of the daffodil and snowflake, set together on folio 129 of the first volume of the *Herbarum* (see plate 61), show that the flowers are entirely different. And in the list of names (Greek, Latin and German) that Brunfels gathers under his *Nomenclaturae*, he shows that in Germany, at least, the plants are known by two completely different common names. The March flower is called 'Hornungsblum', the September one 'Zeytloesslin'.

Though he uses the terms 'male' and 'female', it's not in our sense. There was

DeNARCISSO, & Hermodactylo,
Rhapfodia Vicefima.
NOMENCLATVRAE.
Graecae, νάρκισσος. ἀντογινίς. βόλβος ὁ ἱμεπινός. λείριον. ἄνυδρος.
Latinae, Narciffus, Hermodactylus.
Germanicç, in Marcio, Hornungs blům. In Septembri, Zeytlöflin.
PLACITA AVTORVM de Narciffo.
Hiftoria Narciffi, fecundum DIO=
SCORIDEM, lib.ρ.
NARCISSVS folia Porro fimillima habet, tenuia, multo mi=
nora, & anguftiora: caulis uacuus, & fine folijs, fupra dodrantem attolli=
tur: flos albus in medio, intus croceus, in quibufdam purpureus: radix in
tus alba, rotunda, bulbofa: femen uelut in tunica, nigrum, longum. Pro=
batiffimum nafcitur in montibus fuaui odore. Caetera Porrum imitatur,
atq haerbaceum uirus olet.

m

Plate 61: A wild daffodil or Lent lily (Narcissus
pseudonarcissus) and a spring snowflake (Leucojum vernum)
from Otto Brunfels's Herbarum vivae eicones (1530)

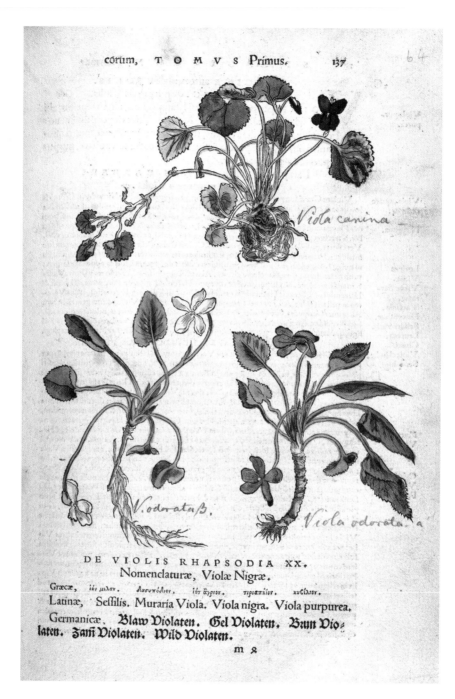

Viola canina

V. odorata β.

Viola odorata a.

DE VIOLIS RHAPSODIA XX.
Nomenclaturæ, Violæ Nigræ.

Græcæ, ἰὸν μέλαν. λευκόϊον. ἰὸν ἄγριον. πορφύριον. κυάνεον.

Latinæ, Sessilis. Muraria Viola. Viola nigra. Viola purpurea.

Germanicæ, Blaw Violaten. Gel Violaten. Brun Violaten. Zam Violaten. Wild Violaten.

m 2

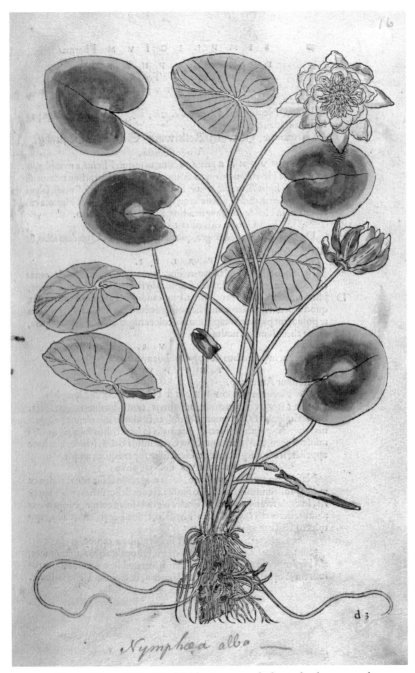

Nymphæa alba ——

Plates 62 and 63: *No lifelike images of plants had appeared
in a printed book until Hans Weiditz produced these illustrations
for* Herbarum vivae eicones *(1530). They included the white-
flowered water lily (*Nymphaea alba*) and various wild
violets (*Viola ssp.*)

still no understanding that plants had a sex life. These were just ways of distinguishing forms of plants which scholars such as Brunfels believed to be basically the same. The 'male' term was often used to separate dark flowers from pale 'female' ones. So Brunfels's male 'narcissus' would be the purple-flowered colchicum, his female, the white spring-flowering snowflake. He called the yellow water lily male, the white one female. Sometimes 'male' was used to represent what seemed to observers to be the standard, model form of a plant. 'Female' then became the way to describe an aberrant, though not necessarily lesser, form.

So in modern-day parlance, Brunfels did a competent 'scissors and paste' job, but contributed little that was new. Of the 258 species identified by Thomas Sprague in Brunfels's *Herbarum*, seventy-eight were known to Theophrastus, eighty-four to Dioscorides and other writers of the classical period, and forty-nine to medieval botanists.[6] The forty-seven 'new' plants, new only in the sense that they had not found themselves in a book before, seem to have been chosen by Weiditz for their looks, rather than by Brunfels for their scientific value. We can excuse him for not arranging the plants in any logical order as Schott, the publisher, who had spent a good deal of money in commissioning the engravings, evidently did not want to wait until the entire body of work was complete. As soon as he had a decent number of illustrations, he published them. Brunfels, though, could at least have devised some logical system for naming plants, but he didn't. He prefers a 'classical' name, if he can find one in his sources; if not, he chooses fairly indiscriminately from a variety of common names. That the ancient authors were mostly describing Mediterranean plants and knew very little about the native plants of transalpine Germany seems to him an impossible concept. If he has to deal with a German native plant that doesn't appear in the works of Theophrastus or Dioscorides, he dismisses it. Or he supposes that the plant must once have been known to the ancients, but that their descriptions of it have been misconstrued by *perfidissimi corruptores*. He doesn't bother with much description, but given such brilliant illustrations, the reader scarcely needs them. There was still no special vocabulary to describe the parts of plants. They were still characterised by comparison; the leaf of Brunfels's polygonum is 'peach-like', the foliage of his narcissus is 'like that of a leek'.

Why is the book important? Primarily because of Weiditz's illustrations. They provided a new base line which everyone with access to the book appreciated. All over Europe, scholars recognised that here was the start of a new journey towards a full knowledge of the plant world. Printing would eventually have a profound influence on the study of plants because it was the vehicle by which identical images of them could be spread. The existence, for the first time, of a body of lifelike pictures of plants provided a vital catalyst to study them and develop some way of classifying them into meaningful groups. So, if these naturalistic illustrations had such a galvanising effect (and they did), why were they so long in coming? Part of the problem lay with the reverence humanist scholars of the early Renaissance initially held for the classical texts they were recovering; ancient authors, such as Pliny, had maintained that a picture could only show a plant in one form, which could be misleading. But Weiditz got over that by including all kinds of minutiae alongside his main portrait: next to his picture of a daffodil plant in bud, for instance, is a drawing of an open flower. Slowly, though, the long-entrenched prejudice against illustrations faded away. The advantages of including them became too obvious. A second problem was technical rather than cultural. Artists had shown that they could portray plants, but it wasn't until Dürer's time that there were block-cutters (*sculptores*) sufficiently skilled to cut these images into the wooden blocks from which prints could be produced. Dürer's exacting demands ensured that a new tradition and craft of block-cutting was created in Germany. That is why the first decent herbals were produced by German printers and block-cutters, rather than Italian ones. Italy, seat of the Renaissance, quickly regained its pre-eminence, but in printing, Germany led the way.

Plate 64: Leonhart Fuchs (1501–1566) as he is shown
in his De historia stirpium (1542)

XII

THE IRASCIBLE FUCHS
1500–1570

ALTHOUGH THE ADVANTAGES of including images far outweighed the disadvantages, their presence introduced new possibilities for error. As Leonhart Fuchs (1501–1566) noted in 1542, when he brought out his own book on plants, *De historia stirpium*, the illustrations in Brunfels's book were not always matched up with the right block of text. But then Fuchs (see plate 64) never let slip an opportunity to be disobliging. Though there were some similarities between the two Germans – both were brought up as Catholics and converted to the Lutheran cause, both set themselves up as schoolmasters, both then took medical degrees, both depended overmuch on classical sources in compiling their books on plants, neither showed any inclination to travel, or to look at plants in any country other than their own – Fuchs had the advantage of perfect timing. He was, anyway, a better scholar and plantsman than Brunfels. But he was also born twelve years later, and benefitted by being part of a rapidly developing and brilliant network of scholars throughout Europe who all shared knowledge, swapped plants, engaged in endless debate about nomenclature. He had a secure position as professor of medicine at the newly established Protestant university at Tübingen. Brunfels died only a few years after he had taken his medical degree. And Fuchs was a fighter, opinionated, a driving force in any enterprise in which he involved himself. Brunfels had been rather at the mercy of his illustrator. Fuchs was entirely in charge of his *De historia stirpium*. Though he gave full and generous credit to Albrecht Meyer, who made the original drawings, to Heinrich Füllmaurer who copied the drawings on to woodblocks and to Veit Rudolf Speckle, who carved the blocks

Plate 65: The three craftsmen who prepared the illustrations for De historia stirpium *(1542). Albrecht Meyer made the original drawings, Heinrich Füllmaurer copied them on to woodblocks and Veit Rudolf Speckle (bottom) engraved them*

(he included pictures of all three of them at the end of his book [see plate 65]), it is evident from his Dedicatory Epistle that they are working to his instructions:

> As for the pictures themselves, every single one of them portrays the lines and appearance of the living plant [see plate 66]. We were especially careful that they should be absolutely correct, and we have devoted the greatest diligence that every plant should be depicted with its own roots, stalks, leaves, flowers, seeds and fruits. Over and over again, we have purposely and deliberately avoided the obliteration of the natural form of the plants lest they be obscured by shading and other artifices that painters sometimes employ to win artistic glory. And we have not allowed the craftsmen so to indulge their whims as to cause the drawing not to correspond accurately to the truth. Veit Rudolf Speckle, by far the best engraver in Strasbourg, has admirably copied the wonderful industry of the draughtsmen, and has with such excellent craft expressed in his engraving the features of each drawing, that he seems to have contended with the draughtsmen for glory and victory.[1]

The shaft was meant for Brunfels's illustrator Weiditz, driven by artistic vision rather than scientific expediency. Though Fuchs had criticisms to make of the *Herbarum vivae eicones* he credited Brunfels with rescuing herbal medicine 'from the thick darkness in which it was almost extinguished', and with trying to 'improve and illumine' the subject. There were 'many shortcomings in his writings', because he offered 'rather few and only common plants, and because he often did not give plants their true and accepted names. Nonetheless, he deserves praise for this reason alone, that he was the first of all to bring back the correct method of illustrating plants into our Germany, giving others something to imitate.'[2]

Fuchs's aim of course was not to imitate, but to surpass. And in terms of the number of plants he included, he did. His book contained nearly 500 full-page illustrations,[3] and though he leant heavily on Dioscorides for the content, he arranged information on the page in a more accessible way than Brunfels had done. The plants are grouped in 344 chapters in the order of the Greek alphabet. Though not ideal, this arrangement had historic precedents. In each case he arranges his subheadings in the same sequence: first *Nomina*, the various names by which the plant might be called, then *Forma*, a description of the plant's appearance, then *Locus*, an indication of where it may be found, followed by *Tempus*, its proper season, *Temperamentum*, its place in the moist/dry, hot/cold, strong/mild categories by which medical plants were rated in the system first proposed by Galen, and finally *Vires*, the properties of the herb as described by Dioscorides, Galen, Pliny or whichever other authorities Fuchs chose to include. Sometimes he follows these with an *Appendix* in which he notes his own observations about the plant in question. For

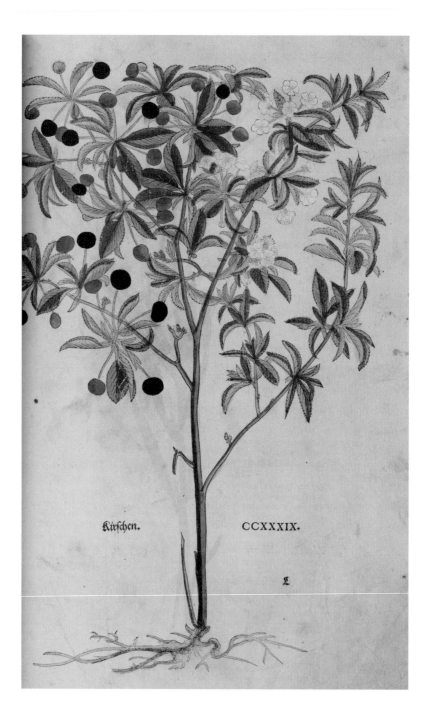

Plate 66: A cherry tree shown with its blossom and
three different kinds of fruit in Cap CCXXXIX of Leonhart
Fuchs's De historia stirpium (1542)

instance, after quoting what Pliny, Dioscorides and Galen have to say about *Cannabis sativa*, used since classical times for medicinal purposes, Fuchs adds 'Since it is clear . . . that *Cannabis* excites the mind and so injures it, those who unwisely, following a common error, administer potions made of this seed to those with mental ailments, especially the serious ones, do so with great risk to the patients.'[4]

He was less sympathetic to the practical experience and knowledge of the *vulgus* than Brunfels, noting in his Dedicatory Epistle that even among physicians,

> you will hardly find one among a hundred of them who has correct knowledge of [plants]. They appear to think that this kind of information does not belong to their profession, and to judge that it would be condescending from their proper dignity to entertain doubts about the accuracy and trustworthiness of those who buy and sell such things. And so it comes to pass that the druggists – God knows that they themselves are for the most part an illiterate set – leave all this to the foolish and superstitious old women who gather herbs and roots. Error is therefore heaped on error, and will be so long as the identification of vegetable medicines is left to rustic and vulgar ignorance.[5]

Fuchs was a precocious child and from this, perhaps, stems his later arrogance. He was the youngest of the three children of a prosperous burgomaster, who died when Fuchs was five. He was sent away to school in Heilbronn and was studying at the University of Erfurt by the time he was fifteen. Having emerged two years later with an arts degree, he opened a school in his home town, Wemding. Scarcely a year later he enrolled at the University of Ingolstadt to study medicine, took his degree on 28 June 1519, and was practising as a doctor in Munich before he was twenty-three. With his new wife, Anna Friedberger, 'a most virtuous maiden, of respectable station, well brought up', Fuchs returned to Ingolstadt to teach in the faculty of medicine. Two years later (18 May 1528), he was summoned to Ansbach by Prince Georg, the Margrave of Brandenburg (1484–1543), who shared Fuchs's Protestant sympathies. The Margrave hoped to establish a new Protestant university at Ansbach where Fuchs would teach. It never happened, but Fuchs continued in his post as the Margrave's personal physician for the next seven years. His reputation was greatly enhanced by his success in treating the sweating sickness that swept through Germany in 1529. 'As this plague spread, because a remedy was generally unknown, many thousands perished,' said Georg Hizler, a colleague of Fuchs's, in his obituary oration at Fuchs's funeral. 'At that time this doctor of ours, by the gracious favour of Almighty God, by his own skill saved many lives. For this he gained not only the favour and affection of the multitude, but also the praise and admiration of the most prominent men for his ability. That disease was commonly called English Sweat (*sudor Anglicus*), invading that island . . . in 1496.'[6]

A. Das Fürstliche Schloß.   B. S. Georgen Stifft.   C. Der Vniuersitel hauß.   D. Das Fürstliche Stipendium.   E. Das Rathauß.   F. Die Bürst.

*Plate 67: Tübingen, from a map made early in the sixteenth century.
In 1535, Fuchs accepted a position as professor of medicine at the town's
Protestant university and stayed there until his death in 1566*

Finally, Fuchs accepted an invitation to teach at Tübingen (see plate 67), then under the patronage of Duke Ulrich.[7] Having arrived on 14 August 1535, he stayed there for the rest of his life, making his home in a former nunnery of the fourteenth-century.[8] In the garden to the east of the house (now covered by an ugly block of flats) he grew sweet galingale, sowed seeds of tobacco, a newly introduced rarity, and grew many other plants that he later described in his *Historia*. It seems that he began work on the book shortly after he arrived at Tübingen, but he was also deeply involved in changing the way that medicine was taught at the university. Full of reforming zeal, like his patron, he banished all Arab texts from the curriculum: 'Since everyone knows that the Arabs copied almost all their material from the Greeks, henceforth they will be used very little in the teaching of this subject [medicine], which more advisably will be taught from the wellsprings of the art than by drinking from turbid waters.' That was no surprise. The first of Fuchs's writings had been an attack on Muslim physicians – the *Errata* published in 1530 while he was still at Ansbach. He was a Renaissance man; of course he backed the classical authors against their Muslim interpreters (though that didn't stop him, in the *Historia*, from quoting several times from the Arab scholar, Avicenna). There was a

ROSA Rosen.

*Plate 68: Roses, both single pink and double red in Cap CCLIIII
of Leonhart Fuchs's* De historia stirpium *(1542). 'The
domesticated variety occurs everywhere in gardens,' he wrote*

new requirement, instigated by Duke Ulrich, for teachers to lead field trips: 'in the summer season [the teacher] should often seek the countryside and the mountains with the students of medicine, and carefully observe the appearance of plants, and point out their living characteristics, and not, as many have been doing up to this time, to entrust the knowledge of medicinal herbs to those crude ointment peddlers and simple herb-women.'[9] This was a revolutionary idea, copied perhaps from Erfurt, where Euricius Cordus, one of Fuchs's teachers, had first introduced field trips as part of the curriculum for medical students, and it had profound consequences. Looking at live plants, being required to identify them, discussing their similarities and differences, as Theophrastus had done almost 2,000 years earlier, brought the whole subject of *res herbaria* into the limelight. As long as custom and snobbery dictated that a close, personal knowledge of plants be restricted to 'crude ointment peddlers and simple herb-women' the study of plants did not grow. Physicians had thought themselves too grand. Philosophers (at least, those since Theophrastus) had considered the minutiae of plant lore unworthy of their attention. Now it was required knowledge and for the rest of this glorious century an interest in plants became a defining characteristic of the age.

Fuchs was hired at Tübingen at a salary of 160 gulden a year, which in 1537 was increased to 200 gulden. That, added to a housing allowance of 15 gulden a year, made him one of the most highly paid professors at the university. After only two years at Tübingen, he was offered a post at Copenhagen, where King Christian III of Denmark was planning to open a university. But on 10 April 1538, Fuchs wrote turning down the offer. 'I have many small children,' he explained, 'and my wife is pregnant, so that I cannot make such a long trip at this time. I also have many books, which would be impossible to transport over such a long distance and that I could not leave behind, since I have to read medicine and give the public my services. Even if I accepted the condition proposed by Your Highness, I could not take a salary less than 700 or 800 gulden . . . Your Highness must be well aware that His Majesty will not spend that much money on me, and I ask that you will graciously accept my refusal.'[10]

Though the desire to increase his income was very real, the excuses he offered were weak. He did not want to move because he was already deeply preoccupied with his *Historia*. On 24 October 1538, the same year as he turned down the Copenhagen job, he wrote to Duke Albrecht that he had 'in preparation a Herbal, but it is not yet ready for the printer, containing pictures of over 350 plants (see plate 69). By the time the book came out, in 1542, the number of illustrations had passed the 500 mark. 'Notable commentaries on the history of plants', proclaimed the title page,

POLYGONATVM
LATIFOLIVM.

Weißwurtz.

585

*Plate 69: Solomon's seal (*Polygonatum x hybridum) *with its characteristically knobbly rootstock in Cap CCXXII of Leonhart Fuchs's* De historia stirpium *(1542). It is widespread in Europe, but Fuchs claimed it grew only on mountains*

prepared with great expense and diligence by Leonhart Fuchs, a physician by far the most distinguished in this our age, adorned with more than 500 lifelike pictures in imitation of nature, never hitherto drawn and printed with greater art.

Many others have visited foreign lands, some here, some there, at huge cost, with tireless effort, and sometimes not without peril to their lives, in order to acquire intimate knowledge of the substance of simples; all this substance you will be pleased to learn from this book, as in a living pleasure garden, at a great saving of money and time, far from any peril.

Added to this is an abbreviated explanation of the difficult and obscure words that occur here and there in this work; along with a four-fold index, containing the Greek names of the plants, the Latin names, those used in the shops of druggists and by herb-gatherers, and the German names.[11]

The portrait of the author included on the following page shows Fuchs, aged forty-one, in a flat black hat and a knee-length robe with an elegant reddish-brown fur collar (see plate 70). That was a practical accessory, but it may also have been a pun on his name (Fuchs means fox in German). He wears a ring with a red stone and holds not fuchsia, the plant that commemorates him, but germander speedwell (*Veronica chamaedrys*). The fuchsia had not yet arrived in Europe, and was named only in 1703, 137 years after Fuchs had died.

The book is dedicated to Joachim II (1505–1571), the current Margrave of Brandenburg, who had converted to the Protestant cause in 1539. With buttery self-interest, Fuchs writes that he 'can scarcely understand why almost none of our princes is eager to follow the example of the kings and heroes of old, and resolve at least to help those who are involved in investigating plants . . . It is within their power to make gardens planted with the very best plants, including those from faraway places, and to support at their own expense herbalists to look after the plants, increase and preserve them . . . There is no more likely way to acquire praise and fame . . . than by taking an interest in promoting the understanding of plants in this way.' Acquiring a powerful patron was the quickest path to success. The book was more likely to prosper if the Margrave took an interest in it. And since Tübingen lay within the borders of the Margrave's duchy, he also had the power to advance Fuchs's career at the university. With a letter to his friend and fellow plantsman, Joachim Camerarius (1500–1574), written a few months after the book had been published, Fuchs encloses a finely bound copy of his *Historia* and begs Camerarius to 'send a letter to Sabinus, or someone else, whose help can be an advantage . . . in getting easy access to the prince with the book . . . I have instructed the young

Plate 70: Leonhart Fuchs, wrapped in a sumptuous fox-fur collar for a portrait painted by Heinrich Füllmaurer in 1541

bearer to unwrap the book and show it to you.'[12] Camerarius, who taught at the university at Leipzig, was Fuchs's most stalwart correspondent, one of the few people he admired and trusted. Fuchs evidently consulted him about problems with nomenclature in the *Historia* and appreciated his advice: 'Far from being hurt by your differing strongly with me,' he writes,

> I am pleased by it. Would that such an adversary were my lot more often, one with whom I can argue about truth in a friendly and brotherly way. But even though I would have preferred to answer face to face the arguments presented to me by you, yet I do not know how I could manage to wait until I see you. For you know that it is implanted in my nature to accomplish immediately anything I have decided to do. But three times I have been called away by some country people, who today more than usual have overwhelmed me with their specimens of urine. But let me get to the subject . . .'

which was a discussion about anthemis and its proper identification.[13]

Like Brunfels, Fuchs expresses regret that he has not been able to group the plants of the *Historia* in any meaningful way, only 'tying related plants together here and there'. The need for a system, an order, a rationale, was now urgent. The more plants that were described and included in a book, the more compelling the need to classify them. Just occasionally, Fuchs shackles like with like: five kinds of buttercup, five kinds of mint, four kinds of cabbage. But it was not enough, and he knew it. He did, unlike Brunfels, accept that 'neither Dioscorides nor any other of the ancients' would know all the plants he included. After all, a hundred of them were exclusively German or middle European. A hundred were illustrated here for the first time, including imported exotics such as maize, pumpkin, and the African marigold. A desk man, parochial by nature, averse to travel, Fuchs had only the haziest notion of where they originally came from. He didn't know what grew in Greece, or Italy, home of the classical authors he relied on so heavily, let alone what was now coming in from the New World across the ocean. Unlike Brunfels, he feels no need to apologise for including pictures, used full-page in the *Historia*. 'We are all captivated by a painting', he writes, 'and those things that are set forth and pictured on canvas and paper are fixed even more deeply in our minds than those described in bare words.'

The book is another important landmark in the progress of *res herbaria*. Albrecht Meyer's pictures are nearly as good as Weiditz's, though less singular. There are almost twice as many of them and more have the details of flowers and seeds that had first begun to appear in Weiditz's illustrations. If you were wanting to identify the cuckoo pint (*Arum maculatum*), for instance, Meyer's portrait would tell you everything you needed to know (see plate 71). In the centre of the page, he shows the entire plant

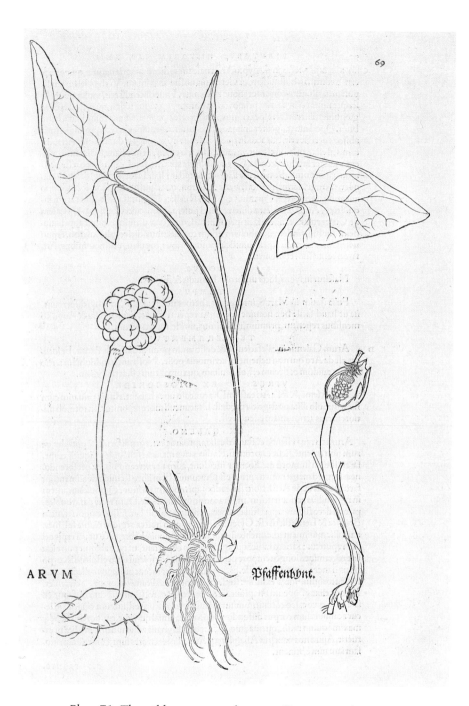

ARVM

Pfaffenbynt.

Plate 71: *The wild arum or cuckoo pint* (Arum maculatum) *in Cap XXII of Leonhart Fuchs's* De historia stirpium. *Its name was commonly 'misspelled, as usual, by the pharmacists' wrote Fuchs in typically cantankerous mode*

in full growth, from knobbly underground tuber to pointed arrow-shaped leaf and hooded spathe. The drawing on the left shows the plant at a later stage, when it is in fruit, the leaves and spathe now gone, the stem surmounted by a knob of bright berries. On the right is a cross-section (another innovation) of the bottom of the spathe, showing the complex arrangement of hairs and protuberances at the base of the spadix. Trees presented a greater problem than herbaceous plants. They couldn't be drawn in scale. But Meyer still includes an acorn alongside his oak, a wrinkled nut alongside his walnut. Fuchs's casual comments about plants – the walnut, 'widely planted every-where in Germany'; the hart's tongue fern, 'now prized in most gardens'; clove pink, 'widely grown in pots. You seldom find a house that does not have one displayed in front'; basil, which 'women everywhere raise in clay pots on the window sills of their homes'; chilli pepper, 'found almost everywhere in Germany now, planted in clay pots and earthen vessels. A few years ago it was unknown' – accumulate to provide a vivid picture of a mid sixteenth-century German garden. The picture was changing quite fast in terms of the plants that were being grown. And the uses Fuchs suggests for plants show a distinct change in emphasis from the herbals of the classical period and the Middle Ages. Poisons such as hemlock (and their antidotes) dominated the earliest texts; medieval herbals were peppered with pictures of mad dogs, poisonous snakes and venomous insects with instructions for treating their bites. Fuchs's herbal, compiled such a short time after the English sweating sickness had rampaged through Germany, provides copious recipes against the plague. Angelica 'wards off the contagion of devas-tating pestilence . . . drives out the poison in urine and sweat'. A conserve made of the flowers of clove pinks is equally effective. Gentian is 'of great use against the poison of pestilence'. Branches of rosemary must be burned inside to 'render a house safe during pestilence'. A powder made of the root of butterbur 'wonderfully bene-fits pestilential fevers' by stimulating the patient into a sweat. But there is also room now for cosmetic uses. Linen dipped in a potion of lady's mantle (*Alchemilla mollis*) makes sagging breasts hard and firm. Box, a common evergreen, can be used to dye hair red. Hair washed in flowers of the common marigold will become fairer. Cuckoo pint 'removes deformities of the face and skin'. Betony, which had been the cure-all for medieval herbalists, is replaced by juniper, widely distributed in Germany and long regarded there as a potent, sacred plant. Fuchs says it

> stops nosebleeds if applied to the temples and forehead crushed in egg white. The same suppresses vomiting, taken with a powder of frankincense and egg white. Likewise, rubbed on with the same, it settles diarrhoea. A powder of this in egg, taken by sipping, settles a stomach emitting bilious vomit, and stops bloody discharge of the belly. It digests phlegm that has collected in the stomach and intestines. Also it checks the

humour that gushes from the brain. It kills tapeworms and other animals in the belly. Applied, it dries up the wet crevices of fistulas. It staunches the menstrual flow. As a fumigant, it helps colds. Rubbed on, it benefits gaping cracks of the hands and feet. And, to sum up, it possesses the powers of *succinus* [amber, another cure-all], but a little more efficacious.

Pliny had recommended betony as a diuretic; modern research confirms that juniper does indeed cause an increase in the discharge of urine as its volatile oils influence the parenchyma of the kidneys.[14]

In defending the inclusion of pictures in his book, Fuchs pointed out that there were many plants that 'cannot be described in words'. The right words still aren't there. But he is the first writer on plants to include what we would call a glossary and what he calls a *Vocum difficilum explicatio*, an Explanation of Difficult Terms. This perhaps says as much about Fuchs's intended audience as his desire to forge a vocabulary that could be pressed into the service of a new science. He didn't invent these 'difficult terms' (there are 132 of them, arranged in alphabetical order). Many had first been used by Pliny – *bulbus* (bulb), *fructus* (fruit), *internodium* (internode). A few other words, most notably *stamen*, had been used before but not in the precise way that Fuchs employed them. He defines stamens as 'the *apices* that burst out in the middle of the cup'. But there was still no mention of 'petal', which was referred to as a kind of leaf, no word for 'pollen', the purpose of which was still not understood, and no glimmer of understanding that 'male' and 'female' had any real meaning in the world of plants. But occasionally a name crops up that is entirely familiar to us: *Angelica sylvestris, Aquilegia vulgaris, Digitalis purpurea*.[15] You see the same labels in garden centres; you find the same tags spelled out in gardening books. The surname/Christian name provides a neat shorthand to differentiate not only between kinds of plants, but between types within the same kind. Here was the germ of the system that finally prevailed, more than 200 years later. But Fuchs wasn't in a position to grasp its potential. Sometimes he used the two names, sometimes one, sometimes he used Greek names, sometimes Latin. But gradually there built up a vocabulary of simple, useful adjectives that we still use to describe plants today: *sylvestris* (of woods), *vulgaris* (common), *purpurea* (purple), *albus* (white), *germanicum* (German), *italicum* (Italian), *hortensis* (of gardens), *rotunda* (round), *angustifolia* (sharp-leaved), *odoratum* (sweet-smelling), *sativus* (cultivated). In a haphazard way, Brunfels had begun to use these two-name tags in his *Herbarum vivae eicones*. Fuchs continued the process, but there remained too much work to do for him to be able to mastermind a system. Each book that came out cleared a little more ground where plants could be seen more distinctly, but there were still thousands

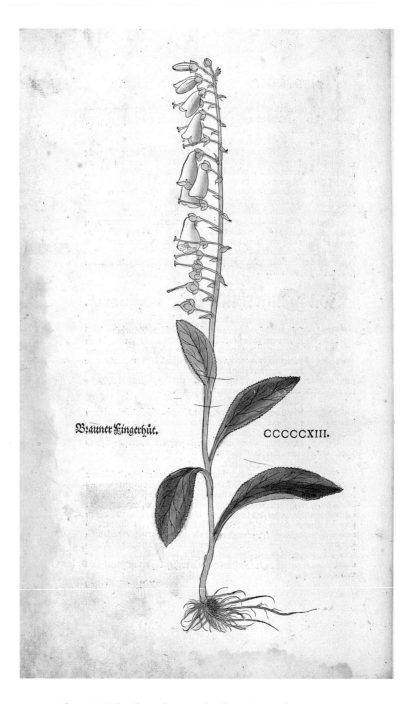

Blauner Fingerhut.

CCCCCXIII.

Plate 72: The 'fingerhut' or foxglove (Digitalis purpurea)
in the New Kreuterbuch (1543). It had previously appeared
as Cap CCCXLII in De historia stirpium, *the first
illustration of the plant ever made*

of plants that nobody had ever described at all. There were still too many wrong names attached to the wrong plants. Fuchs's account of the sweet-smelling shrub mezereon is typical of the prevailing mess:

At this point it should be noted that the apothecaries are greatly in error, because they use the leaves of *Daphnoides* instead of *Mezereon*, which, however, is the *Chamelea* of the Greeks, and differs entirely from *Daphnoides*. Its fruit is used instead of Cnidian berries, which are a fruit of *Thymelea*, too well known to need description. Thus the apothecaries are usually blind to the most obvious matters, while the physicians, every bit as ignorant of herbal matters as they, nicely back them up in their errors. That *Thymelea* is indeed not the plant today called *Laureola* can be ascertained from the fact that the latter itself, according to Dioscorides, was called *Linum* by some, for the sole reason that it bears a resemblance to cultivated flax, which everyone knows is quite different from *Laureola* . . .[16]

To use a favourite phrase of Fuchs's, 'Why say more?'

Fuchs was an organiser, rather than an innovator. His text is derivative (only twelve of the 344 chapters are his own work), and he mostly limits himself to plants of medicinal value. Thomas Sprague suggests that his main purpose was to 'reform the German pharmacopoeia' and characterises him as 'an industrious, methodical, and judicious compiler', rather than an investigator.[17] But Fuchs laid out his information clearly under an unchanging set of subheadings, the pictures were superb, and the book, prepared, as Fuchs wrote 'with great expense, and diligence', was a huge success.[18] The illustrations in the copy which Fuchs had sent to his patron, the Margrave of Brandenburg would have been hand-coloured. The original pages, of course, were printed in black and white; after the printing a coloured master copy was prepared under the author's supervision, with the flowers, foliage and fruit all painted in their proper shades. Mineral pigments such as verdigris produced an opaque green; cinnabar gave a rich red, lapis lazuli a deep ultramarine blue. Pigments derived from plants such as saffron provided more opaque colours. Coloured or plain, the book, in Fuchs's lifetime, went through thirty-nine imprints and was translated into German, French, Spanish and Dutch. In 1545, Fuchs's publisher Isingrin of Basel, brought out a pocket edition of the *De historia stirpium* with the same 'lifelike representations' of plants reduced in size, 'to the end that all those who cherish the desire to learn about plants thoroughly can carry them conveniently in their pockets when walking about or travelling, and can compare them with the growing plants'. Having introduced field trips into the curriculum at Tübingen, Fuchs had found a new market to exploit.

Vain, dogmatic, opinionated, strutting around his book like a turkeycock, Fuchs

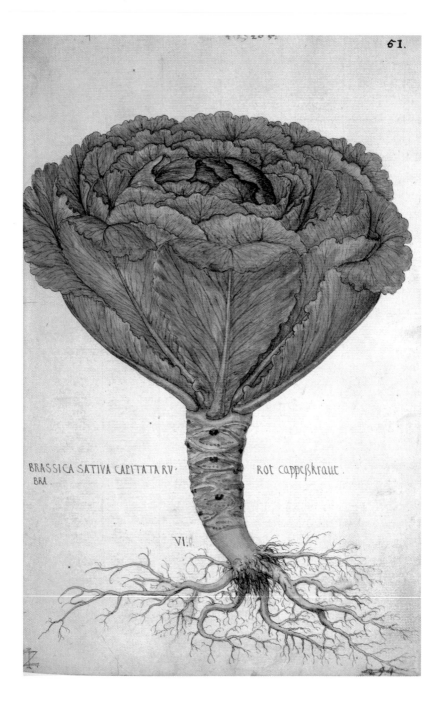

*Plate 73: 'Rot capperkraut', an early form of red cabbage
in an illustration prepared for Fuchs's unpublished
encyclopaedia of plants*

leaves no one in any doubt that he thinks his *Historia* a very good piece of work indeed. He has spared, he makes clear, 'neither expense nor labour' in preparing it. He has not begrudged frequent excursions through field and forest, 'clambering over the high ridges of mountains'. He has had to 'swallow down the numerous annoyances caused by the craftsmen, which the correction of their errors' gave him. Pointedly, he says that he is open to suggestion from other scholars 'provided only that they omit their insulting remarks, as becomes true seekers after truth, and refute and disprove our statements by reason instead'. Those who are quickest to disparage other people's labours, he points out,

> for the most part lurk in shadows, or hide themselves in corners and triumph marvellously among ignorant asses like themselves. But if these fault-finders should burst forth from the shadows and show themselves in the open, nobody would fail to recognise that they are puffed up with empty intellectual arrogance and are insolent humbugs. And we certainly would give these revilers such a reception that they would wish they had stayed in the dark, and never aspired to the light of day. For we would be sure not to lack either strength or skill to treat them as they deserve, and to dodge and return their spears and darts.[19]

The warning was well given; in subsequent years, the turkeycock charged out to peck furiously at any rivals who ventured on to his patch. The books produced by a rival printer, Christian Egenolff of Frankfurt were full of 'stupid errors'. Thaddeus Duno, who had criticised Fuchs for relying too much on Galen, was 'an ignorant young puppycock'. To Janus Cornarius, who had described the *Historia* as nothing more than a patchwork quilt, Fuchs replied, 'It's a dreadful thing when a madman masquerades as sane . . . Take yourself to the ravens until you get a sounder mind.'

The imprints rolled on, the book's fame spread and two years after its publication, the Italian Duke Cosimo de' Medici offered Fuchs 'a most generous and ample stipend' of 600 crowns a year to teach medicine at the University of Pisa. As Georg Hizler pointed out in his funeral oration for Fuchs, very few Germans had been offered the chance 'to go from Germany in the north down to Italy, which abounds in greatly learned men in every type of discipline and liberal studies'. The Medicis were used to getting their own way, but Fuchs turned down the offer. Still, the money was tempting, the idea more alluring than the prospect of moving to Copenhagen had been. In a letter dated 1 November 1544 to his friend Joachim Camerarius, he wrote of his dilemma: 'You can easily imagine in what conflict the appointment to Italy has placed me and how it has upset all my plans . . . Even though my thoughts are not turned toward Italy, this does not mean that on that account I am contemplating remaining here. Many things are urging me to consider

Plate 74: The hallucinogenic mandrake (Mandragora officinarum) in an illustration prepared for Fuchs's unpublished encyclopaedia of plants. 'Mountebanks and fakers hanging around the marketplace are peddling roots shaped in human form they claim are Mandragora,' wrote Fuchs, 'although it is quite evident that they are fashioned and made by hand from Canna roots carved in human likeness.'

thoughts of another position, especially my large flock of children, for whom I must definitely provide better.'[20] The 'flock' included four sons and six daughters, though two of them had died in infancy.

Was the 'flock' the real reason Fuchs turned down Duke Cosimo's generous offer? Was the thought of working in a predominantly Catholic country abhorrent to this staunch Lutheran? Or was it that, once again, he didn't want the upheaval of a move to spoil a work in progress? For as soon as his *Historia* came out, Fuchs started on a much more ambitious project: many more illustrations, many more plants, an encyclopaedic work that would embrace a far wider sector of the natural world than a manual on medicinal plants would allow. He spent the last twenty-four years of his life on this project and the first volume was ready for the press by 1550. Michael Isingrin, his original publisher, had died and, as Fuchs complained to his friend Camerarius, Isingrin's widow was unwilling to invest the necessary 3,000 florins in the new book. But this did not stop Fuchs from commissioning more illustrations and producing more text to go with them.[21] Heinrich Füllmaurer, who had copied on to woodblocks the original drawings for the *Historia*, had died in 1545; the engraver Veit Rudolf Speckle had died in 1550. For his new work, Fuchs used Jorg Ziegler, who left his mark on some of the original pearwood blocks still kept at the Botanical Institute in Tübingen. On the ends of some of the blocks, Fuchs has scribbled the names of the plants they show – a guide to the printer who now has no excuse to set the wrong text against the wrong illustration. The device of including magnified details of flowers, seed pods and seeds, begun in the *Historia*, was exploited much further in the new work (see plate 7). The manuscript is strewn with notes to Ziegler and the other unknown illustrators about details that need to be clarified. From his base at Tübingen, Fuchs built up a vast web of contacts, who fed him with news of discoveries and sent him seeds and specimens. Slowly he built up a body of work that covered more than 1,500 plants, laying out the information in just the same way that he had employed in the *Historia*.

The brilliant young Swiss scholar, Conrad Gesner (1516–1565) was engaged in a similar enterprise, but nevertheless wrote that he awaited the new work

with great eagerness. For although I disagree with it [the *Historia*] in some respects, pertaining to the imposition of plant names drawn from the ancients, nevertheless I do not doubt but that the author, when advised by me and others who have seen more regions abroad that are fertile in plants, will make certain changes for the better; and I praise vigorously the diligence of the man, his method of instruction, and finally the elegance and perfection of his figures, which even by themselves, if nothing else were added, would be of no small value.[22]

Gesner's point was well made. Although at this stage only twenty-nine years old, he himself had already travelled widely in Switzerland, as well as Germany, France and Italy. Fuchs knew only Bavaria and the part of south-western Germany around Würtemberg. When, in the *Historia*, he had mentioned localities for plants, they were always local ones: martagon lily on the Osterberg, yellow gentian and hart's tongue fern on the Farrenberg, spring snowflake in great profusion in the shady woods above the monastery of Bebenhausen, not far from Tübingen, radishes 'of stupendous size at Erfurt', anchusa at Nuremberg, bistort in the Black Forest.

In an attempt perhaps to deflect the publication of a rival work, Fuchs suggests that Gesner should send his research to be incorporated in his own forthcoming, expanded plant book. Coolly, but courteously, Gesner expresses his surprise that Fuchs should be 'frightening me away from the same field of investigation . . . There are infinite kinds of plants, a great part of which must be unknown to any one person on account of the differences between regions.' If everyone co-operated for the public benefit, it might indeed be possible to produce 'a single perfectly complete work'. He doubts, though, whether it is likely to happen in his lifetime. He hopes that many correspondents will indeed pass on their findings to Fuchs and that they will be helpful to his 'great and beautiful beginnings'. But he has things that he wants to say himself. Much of it is not yet written down or in an order that would be meaningful to anyone but himself. 'I beg of you,' he writes, 'to let me keep my freedom and my dearest delight.' In this field of investigation, he reminds Fuchs, 'there are many things left over for us to learn'. There's a veiled suggestion that Fuchs, unlike the French scholars Pierre Belon (1517–1564) and Guillaume Rondelet (1507–1566), is not always as generous in crediting his sources as he should be. That, as Gesner points out 'is the height of ingratitude or rather of ungracious self-seeking'.

Generously, Gesner outlines his own intention of publishing with Wendel Rihel, a Strasbourg printer. Even more generously, he writes that if his scheme 'is displeasing to you and Isingrin, I shall change my plan in your favour and wait until all your volumes have appeared.[23] But the handsome offer did nothing to mollify Fuchs. Years later, he had still not got over Gesner's desire to go his own way. 'I am greatly astonished', he writes in a letter to Camerarius,

> that Gesner's enormous work should be so extraordinarily anticipated by certain people, because he wrote to me almost a year ago that he had not yet prepared the bulk of it. Even if he does actually publish it before mine, I am not worried, since I under-stand that Gesner, a good friend who writes to me often, has a mind that flits around through almost every type of author and rejoices to weave together new wreaths fash-ioned from the unravelled garlands of others. Thus, recently, he repeated a whole book

Plate 75: The giant sunflower, believed to be from Peru.
This picture was based on a plant that Fuchs grew in his
Tübingen garden and was made c.1560 for his unpublished
encyclopaedia of plants

of Rondelet's in his own commentaries on fish. With the like intention, he has begged me, providing I let him use his own judgment about arranging the subject matter, to let him write a supplement to my Commentaries, once they are published. Let him arrange his own work as he wishes. I shall not permit him to arrange mine otherwise than I have done myself. Now he wants me to inform him about all my specimens. But I know what he is scheming, so henceforth I shall send him nothing.[24]

Fuchs's network, however, brought him into contact with others who were happy to share their findings. The young Augsburg scholar Leonhart Rauwolf (*c*.1535/40–1596), who had studied under the great Rondelet at Montpellier, lent Fuchs specimens from his *hortus siccus* of dried plants,[25] the first time that dried plants had ever been used to provide accurate descriptions. The technique had recently been refined in Italy and though Fuchs did not meet Rauwolf until 1563, when he had effectively finished work on his vast compendium, he nevertheless rearranged it to include forty-five of the plants Rauwolf had collected and pressed in the new manner on his long journey home from Montpellier, over the Alps at the St Gothard pass and so back, via Zurich and Tübingen to Augsburg. From Italy Francesco degli Alessandri (1529–1587) sent mandrake and the great teacher Luca Ghini (1490–1556) at Pisa sent a picture of the plum-scented *Iris graminea*. The English botanist, William Turner (*c*.1510–1568) contributed a starchy kind of pignut, *Bunium bulbocastanum*. From Antwerp, the 'zealous botanist' Samuel Quickelberg (1529–1572) sent comfrey. Within Germany, the web of contributors included the Margrave of Brandenburg, who sent young larch trees from his estate at Onoltzbach. Fuchs sent Guillaume Rondelet, professor of medicine at Montpellier, a list of sixty-two plants that he hoped Rondelet might be able to supply: black hellebore, smyrnium, solanum, epimedium, pignut (the *Bunium bulbocastanum* that he eventually got from William Turner) . . . 'Take care to have them come to me at the first opportunity,' he writes. 'You can send them to me either by way of Basel or by way of Strasbourg. In Basel, the printer Isingrin or Oporinus will forward them to me; in Strasbourg, the doctor of medicine, Sebald Havenreutter will do the same.' In a letter the previous August (it arrived with Fuchs four months later) Rondelet had evidently said that a promising young student, Carolus Clusius, was going to send him pictures and descriptions of some interesting plants. But Fuchs writes that he has

seen nothing of the medical students whom you recommended to me. Perhaps they went home by another route. Carolus Lucius [*sic*], the Fleming of whom you wrote, has not sent anything to me – neither pictures not descriptions. And I do not know whether he meant it seriously or not. If he does not undertake the work for my sake, my best hope is that he will keep his promise to you to do it. If I learn where he is, perhaps I will write to him myself. If he tells you where he is living, you would be doing me a great favour if you reminded him of this business.

Fuchs tells Rondelet he has now finished two volumes of his great commentary on plants and is about to start on a third. 'I so refute Mattiolus's nonsense,' he continues, '. . . that I shall not waste time on writing of that liar. If you cannot persuade him not to publish, or if he does, we will laugh at it.'[26] The Italian scholar Pier Andrea Mattioli (c.1501–1577) had bought out his own plant book, a commentary on Dioscorides written in Italian, just two years after Fuchs's *Historia* had been published. Fuchs evidently knew that Mattioli was preparing a handsome Latin version of this book with drawings by Giorgio Liberale and Wolfgang Meyerpeck and had asked Rondelet to do anything he could to suppress it. But Mattioli, almost exactly the same age as Fuchs, was not as compliant as the younger Gesner. He was the only one of Fuchs's contemporaries whose will, belief in himself, skill in trading insults, and unshakeable conviction that in any argument he was bound to be the victor, were a match for Fuchs's own formidable abilities.

'Why, as I recall, I refute him a hundred times in every volume,' exploded Fuchs in a letter to Camerarius. 'That pride-swollen Italian will understand without doubt that in Germany there are men who have noticed his nonsense and painted him in his true colours.'[27] Certainly, in his work-in-progress, Fuchs took every opportunity to lunge aggressively at his rival. Writing, for the first time, about tobacco, he considers the prevailing notion that it must be a kind of henbane. 'In his herbal book, Mattiolus also upholds this false opinion, just as, with no judgment, he always follows the mistaken guesses of others . . . It is clearer than the noonday sun that Matthiolus, Dodonaeus and certain others are wandering over the whole sky in suggesting this.'[28] Fuchs had commissioned his artists to prepare four pictures of tobacco, with their characteristic huge leaves, among the earliest pictures ever made of this New World oddity (see plate 76). He also coins, for the first time, the name *Nicotiana*, still in use today, perhaps in honour of Jean Nicot (1530–1600), the French ambassador to Portugal, who c.1559, sent seeds of tobacco to François II and other members of the French court. Famously, it had first been noted by sailors on Christopher Columbus's 1492 expedition, who watched the natives of Cuba and Haiti snuffing it up through a *tabaco*, shaped rather like a catapult. The handle or stem was held over the burning leaves, the smoke inhaled through the two arms of the Y, which fitted the nostrils. The Haitians themselves called the plant 'cohobba', the Aztecs 'quauhyetl', but local plant names such as these rarely made a successful transition into Europe. Language was too difficult a barrier; too often questions and answers were misunderstood,

199

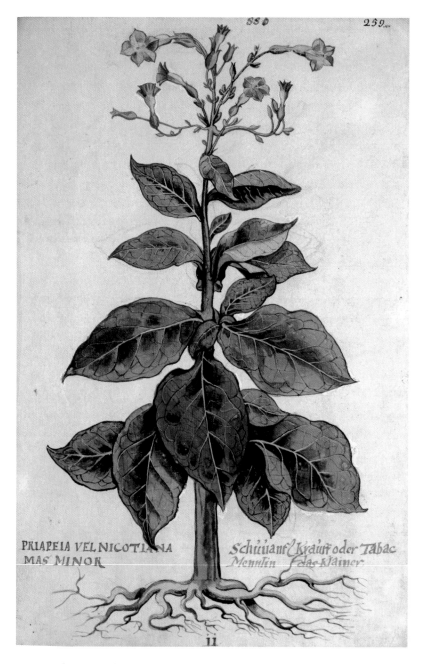

Plate 76: The unfamiliar tobacco plant (Nicotiana tabacum)
*gathering a portmanteau of different names in an illustration
prepared for Fuchs's unpublished encyclopaedia of plants. 'It has
recently been brought into Germany,' wrote Fuchs, 'having been
seen before by no one, as far as I know.'*

misinformation solidified into fact. Nicot, though, hadn't been the first to introduce the plant into Europe; it had already reached the Low Countries via Spanish merchants in the 1540s.

Fuchs's new work contained three times as many plants as the original *Historia*, and in it he finally makes the break from plants with a purpose and includes even more of the plants now flooding into Europe from the New World and the Near East. In the *Historia*, he had shown an aubergine for the first time. He christened it *mala insana*, since he could not match it with any plant described by the classical authorities. He described how 'they are eaten by some people, cooked in oil, salt and pepper, like mushrooms'. Pickle-makers preserved them in brine, but in Fuchs's opinion this was 'food for gourmets and those willing to taste anything'. In the new work, he introduced the tomato, one of the few plant names that has not strayed too far from its original roots – the Nahuatl '*tomatl*'. Mattioli had talked of its being in Italy in his *Annotationes* of 1544, but he hadn't included a picture and though Fuchs's illustration isn't very good, it is probably the first ever made of this Mexican rarity (see plate 77). He calls it *Malus aurea*, the golden apple, and shows the flowers and fruit springing singly from the junctions of leaf and stem, not hanging from the sprays that are so typical a feature of the plant. But Fuchs himself cannot have been satisfied with the drawing, for it is scratched all round with his comments. In the top left-hand corner of the manuscript, he draws the flower in more correct detail. At the bottom, next to a golden fruit, he makes a sketch, showing how it ought to include the characteristic green calyx on top. The plant, he writes is 'one of a number not mentioned by the ancient Greeks or Romans, or even the Moors'. Having fought hard to get the Arab scholars he despised struck off the curriculum at Tübingen, Fuchs now seems to readmit them, quoting in this new work from Mesuë, Avicenna and Serapion the Younger. He was dealing, of course, with many more plants than in the *Historia*, and a much higher proportion of them were, like the tomato, unknown in the classical literature; this, perhaps, forced him to cast his net wider.

Here, in Fuchs's massive compilation, is the earliest record of the African marigold (see plate 78), now the star of a million bedding schemes, but then a precious rarity. Introduced from Mexico by Hispanic exlorers following in Columbus's tracks, these annuals spread rapidly in Europe, as gardeners began to fill their gardens with decorative as well as useful plants. In his manuscript, Fuchs includes the earliest illustrations of the exotic day lily, introduced to Europe from China. He includes one of the first illustrations of the tulip, showing red, yellow and cream-coloured flowers. He doesn't call them tulips, simply *bulbus*, which suggests that the flower was still too new to have acquired a proper tag. The plants now streaming into

*Plate 77: Fuchs's annotations cover an illustration of the
tomato, a 'goldt apffelkraut'. It is possibly the first picture of
this fruit to appear in Europe and was made for his
unpublished encyclopaedia of plants*

*Plate 78: The African marigold (*Tagetes erecta*), which actually came from Mexico, in an illustration prepared for Fuchs's unpublished encyclopaedia of plants. The first published illustration of the flower appeared in 1565 in Pier Andrea Mattioli's* Commentarii

Europe, particularly from the Near East and America, produced a whole new series of problems and attributions for scholars to puzzle over.

Having amassed 1,529 illustrations and described about 1,540 plants, Fuchs finally addresses himself to the reader, who, he is sure, will benefit greatly from this expanded commentary on plants. Twenty years previously, he reminds his audience, 'at a time when the knowledge of plants was almost wholly extinguished and unknown, as if concealed in some prison,' he had published his *De historia stirpium*. 'The errors of the former', he points out, 'could scarcely be avoided by the author because of the incredible difficulty of the science of plants and its lack of organisation.' He doesn't doubt that 'as soon as some of the more long-nosed nit-pickers (of whom this age has too many) see that this work of mine on the subject of plants has come again into publication', they will have fresh opportunity for 'jeering and belittling'.

But the difficulties with his publisher Isingrin's widow continued. Already by 1557, Fuchs was writing to another publisher, Johannes Oporinus of Basel, talking of the new work in 'three volumes, each of which equals the first edition in size. I should rather give it to you than to anyone else, but I do not know what your resources may be.' Perhaps, he suggests, Oporinus could get the finished woodcuts from Isingrin's widow. 'If she should agree to this, it would not be too great an expense to prepare the rest.' But in 1563, Fuchs writes to his faithful correspondent, Camerarius: 'I am now taking the hot baths at Blasibad, which you enjoyed especially when you were with us. But now that I am a widower I cannot be away from home. As for my burning the midnight oil, I have long finished my Commentaries on the History of Plants, arranged in three massive volumes. Isingrin's widow and her son-in-law have broken faith with me, notwithstanding that she is bound in her own handwriting. So, my dear Joachim, no one anywhere can be trusted.'[29] Oporinus and other publishers had evidently considered the capital investment in type and paper too daunting a prospect. Paper was a big expense for publishers and the big, full-page illustrations of Fuchs's new work took up a lot of space.

Fuchs never got those firsts. Mattioli, the rival he loathed, got the first picture of an African marigold (and a hyacinth) into print in 1565, the year before Fuchs died. The Flemish scholar, Rembert Dodoens scored with the tomato and the day lily (1554) and later, the sunflower (1568). The Flemish scholar Lobelius (Matthias de l'Obel) had the honour of first showing the Western world what tobacco looked like (1570). Fuchs had already prepared pictures of all these exotics, but on 10 May 1566, he died. The massive, pioneering book, to which he had devoted the last twenty-four years of his life, remains unpublished.

XIII

IN ITALY
1500–1550

I T'S A SATURDAY morning, the 2nd of November, and I'm walking into Donnini from Santa Maddalena, where for the last six weeks, isolated in Italy, I've been trying hard to forget what I know. The two places are only a couple of miles apart and I can do the whole stretch on tracks through vineyards and olive groves, past crumbling barns and signpost cypresses without ever touching a road. The grapes have already been picked and all that's left are the dry leaves rustling on the vines. Now they are harvesting the olives. Some of the pickers use wooden tongs which they pull down over the branchlets, liberating the olives into the nets spread under the trees. Others just run their gloved hands down over the branches, making a noise like cows grazing in new, lush grass. Big, shallow, wicker baskets heaped with olives stand by the wooden ladders, alongside tidy piles of olive prunings, the low, young growth which they cut out from each tree as they harvest it.

Why am I here? Why am I trying to rid my mind of concepts such as evolution and all that it entails? Because in the sixteenth century, Italy was at the heart of the great quest to explore and understand the natural world. Germany, as represented by Brunfels and Fuchs, snatches the credit for publishing the first important books on plants. But almost all the other important discoveries and innovations happened here in Italy. The Renaissance in the study of plants had already begun to flower in the fifteenth century, in the painted pages of Benedetto Rinio's gorgeous herbal. The first edition of Pliny's *Natural History* had been published in Venice in 1469. Teodoro of Gaza's Latin version of Theophrastus came out in Treviso in 1483.

The earliest commentators on Pliny and Dioscorides were Italian scholars: Ermolao Barbaro, a member of the Venetian Senate, and Nicolò Leoniceno, professor of medicine at Ferrara University. Marcello Vergilio (1464–1521) had prepared a new translation of Dioscorides's *De materia medica* which appeared in 1518, when the paint on Michelangelo's frescoed ceiling in the Sistine Chapel was scarcely dry. And why am I trying to forget what I know? Because unless I can clear my mind of all that has happened since then – Linnaeus, Darwin, DNA – I won't be able to appreciate the scale of these achievements in Italy. The recovery of ancient learning had been the defining feature of the early Renaissance. The second half was more innovative: discovery rather than recovery. At Padua in 1533, Francesco Buonafede, the university's former professor of medicine, became the first ever professor of *simplicia medicamenta* – plants for medicine. We'd call it botany, but that word hadn't yet been invented. In the 1540s, the first botanic gardens were established at Pisa, Padua and Florence, where the Grand Duke Cosimo I of the Medici rented ground for a garden from 1 December 1545. At Pisa, the brilliant teacher, Luca Ghini (1490–1556) (see plate 79), found an entirely new way of studying plants when he made the earliest *hortus siccus*. By pressing plants and sticking the dry skeletons into a book, he invented the herbarium.

So I'm searching for the landscapes of their minds, walking slowly along this old cobbled track, lined with strong edging stones and made with an elegant camber that sheds rain- and flood-water into gulleys either side. Perhaps four hours' riding would bring a Florentine out into these forests, these paved tracks. Drifting in my direction is the comfortable smell of sheep. They are huddled under a small shelter, guarded by a dog tied to a tree; when he leaps out to bark at me, the tree (an elder) shakes and makes an old bell tied in its branches ring out a loud alarm. Set into a niche is a small glazed pottery plaque of the Madonna, painted blue, white and yellow. In a little pot underneath someone has put sky-blue flowers of chicory, white daisies and toadflax in acid-drop yellow. Behind me in the distance I can still see the very tall, very narrow tower of the church whose bell I can hear from my room at Santa Maddalena. Alongside the track are mounds of red rose hips, old man's beard, and occasional eruptions of spindle berries, the pink an extraordinary colour at this time of the year. Schiaparelli.

'Salve!' calls a man from the top of his ladder in an olive tree. 'Salve!' I reply, raising an arm to return his salute. I'm contemplating Luca Ghini and the sixteenth century, but here is a man addressing me in the language of Pliny. Ghini would have known all these things, I'm thinking, as I approach the elegant low curve of a single-span, stone bridge. Underneath, the river bed is paved with huge stone slabs, making a wide disgorge for the snow melt tipping down from the mountains. I sit on a

Plate 79: A portrait of Luca Ghini (1490–1556), the charismatic teacher at the University of Pisa who inspired an entire generation of plantsmen

grassy bank, eat prosciutto stuffed inside a fresh white ciabatta bought at the baker's in Donnini, pick wild apples and figs for pudding. Next to me, the pale celadon-green flower buds of the stinking hellebore are just beginning to show above the evergreen leaves. Behind, the early foliage of iris and narcissus pushes through the marbled leaves of wild arum – one of the plants that Hans Weiditz had illustrated in great detail in Brunfels's book of 1530. Everywhere around there's activity. But sporadic. The land here will be left alone for long periods, unlike England. There are few cows, few sheep, few arable crops. The landscape is mostly made up of vines (which have only to be pruned, and the grapes picked) and olives, which can be pruned and picked almost at the same time. Wonderfully suitable for wild flowers, I'm thinking, as I gaze out over the Valdarno. Our English arable creates too rest-less a system for many of them, though annuals such as cornflower and field poppy enjoy the yearly turning over of ground. Tufted tongues of wallflowers, pinks and marigolds lick out from the huge blocks of stone in the retaining wall along the track. It leads me past a farm with roosters scratching in the midden, turkeys, geese and hens in the yard and cobs of maize hanging upside down to dry in the barn. On the roof huge orange pumpkins cure in the sun. After a couple of hours, I turn back for Santa Maddalena, taking a different path through the woods. Though I can't see them, I can hear pigs grunting softly, snuffling up acorns. The bright red berries on the butcher's broom light up the undergrowth. Scuffling through beech leaves, I'm trying to sort out in my mind the endless feuds and vendettas between Italy's wildly competitive city states: Milan pitted against Venice, Rome set against Florence, Naples fighting Milan, Florence battling with Pisa, which controlled its access to the sea. But then I come into a clearing where colchicums are pushing out their last flowers, and two grazing deer look up, momentarily frozen as if in a fresco, before running off into the trees. Much later, as I'm approaching Santa Maddalena, I hear the hunters, shouting to each other, blowing their horns. 'Hi! Hi!' I shout, to make sure they know where I am. And in this way, our calls echoing each other across the valley, I make my way to the junction of the paths, where the hunters' rough-haired retriever bounds out, the bell round his neck ringing in a cracked, minor key.

These long, solitary walks in the strangely undisturbed country of the Valdarno are interspersed with train rides to Florence or Arezzo. From San Ellero, a two-euro ticket brings me into the heart of Florence, where, punch-drunk with painting, I ricochet from Giotto to Michelangelo, ending up often in the church of Santa Maria Novella, one of my favourite haunts. Though begun in 1485, the Ghirlandaio fres-coes in the Tornabuoni chapel (see plate 80) seem astonishingly contemporary: the easy, confident stance of the men leaning on the rampart overlooking the town,

Plate 80: A detail from The Visitation of the Blessed Virgin
Mary to Saint Elizabeth *by Domenico Ghirlandaio (1485) in
the Basilica Santa Maria Novella, Florence*

the quizzical way that people in the painted crowd look straight at you, like the old woman I met on the Donnini track, who was dragging three long sticks back to the village. The tall belltowers are entirely familiar, the hawk stooping on to a wild duck, the little hills erupting, sharp as molehills, from the landscape beyond the town. I could walk along that distant track and find similar trees, flowers, farms, pigs, hunters, vines (but not pumpkins – they were still a New World novelty when Fuchs wrote about them in the mid sixteenth century). At Santa Maria del Carmine, south of the Arno, I trawl dutifully through the art history lecture laid out in three languages on panels in front of the altar. The centrepiece is a wondrously grave thir-teenth-century Madonna by the Master of Sant'Agata, surrounded by fifteenth-century frescoes worked by Masolino, Masaccio and Fra Filippino Lippi. I'm looking through Lippi's painted door at a hill capped with tall thin cypresses, junipers, a poplar tree. From the train that brings me into Florence from San Ellero, I see just the same hills, just the same trees.

In the Medicis' palazzo in Via Cavour, I peer at the glowing fruit painted on Benozzo Gozzoli's tall, limbed-up trees. Pomegranates perhaps? Pier de' Crescenzi's *Liber cultus ruris*, first published in 1471, gives detailed directions for growing pome-granates, as well as almonds, filberts, chestnuts, cherries, quinces, figs, apples, mulber-ries, medlars, olives, pears, plums and peaches. The fresco Gozzoli painted here for the elder Cosimo de' Medici (1389–1464) covers three walls of the Medicis' private chapel and shows the three kings, Gaspar, Melchior and Balthasar making their way through a strange landscape, half dream, half real (see plate 81), with vast retinues of attendants and horses and hunting dogs, even a leopard. Cosimo, the banker and statesman who established the political power of the family in Florence, was also patron of the Confraternita dei Magi of San Marco; each year, on the day of the Epiphany, they organised a procession in costume along the city's Via Larga. The Medicis had banks in sixteen European cities and it was money, whether Roman, Venetian, Milanese or Florentine, that fuelled the Renaissance. The Medici money had come from wool and silk, for the company traded with Britain, Flanders and France, bringing in bolts of plain cloth to be reworked and dyed in the fabulous blues and crimsons I'd seen in Masaccio's paintings at the Casa Masaccio, San Giovanni Valdarno. Wool merchants, silk weavers, bankers, pharmacists were among the seven major guilds that controlled trade and the Medici metamorphosis was a classic one: from trade to money to *l'uomo universale*, endowed with wisdom, grace and all the other virtues that Florentines revered.

Italy's status as a country of largely autonomous city states produced a stream of rich patrons like the Medici, scholarly themselves and concerned with promoting scholarship, not only for its own sake, but as a way of gaining yet more power and

*Plate 81: A detail from the fresco (1460) by Benozzo di
Lese di Sandro Gozzoli (1420–1497) in the Palazzo
Medici-Riccardi, Florence*

prestige. By the sixteenth century, the university at Ferrara, founded originally in 1391 by Pope Boniface IX, was being extensively funded by Alphonsus and Hercules, Dukes of Ferrara. 'Ferrara is the city whither I would counsel any and everyone to repair who desires the most exact knowledge of plants,' wrote Joao Rodriguez de Castello Branco (1511–1568). 'For the Ferrarese, as if under some sort of Divine influence, are the most learned of all physicians, and most diligent in the investigations of nature.' It was the students at Padua University who had petitioned for the special chair in *simplicia medicamenta*, set up in 1533, but their appeal was enthusiastically endorsed by the Senate of the Republic of Venice. The city dominated an extremely profitable trade in spices; in terms of plant knowledge, there were commercial advantages in staying ahead of the competition. Dried roots, seeds, spices to make theriacs, treacles, poultices, and tisanes came in on the ships of the greatest navy in the Mediterranean (see plate 82). In the Venetian arsenal, a new galley was produced every hundred days. Ships moved along the quays as if on a watery conveyor belt, with masts, sails, oars, stores all loaded aboard as they passed the various warehouses. All the galleys belonged to the state; fixtures and fittings were standardised so that crews could easily move from one ship to another. The Venetian state had established trading communities in Acre, Alexandria, Constantinople, Sidon and Tyre and Venetian merchants were as familiar with the geography of the Black Sea as they were with that of the Adriatic. The Ferrarese physician Antonio Musa Brasavola (1500–1555) writes of a Venetian dealer he knows, trading under the sign of a bell, 'who never counted the cost of any enterprise', and who imported a kind of rhubarb, both dried roots and living plants, from the banks of the River Volga.[1] In the last years of the fifteenth century, Venice sent at least half a dozen galleys a year to Alexandria and Beirut and laid out more than half a million ducats in buying spices abroad.[2] There were Venetian ambassadors in cities as far apart as Cairo and Isfahan. Venetian travellers reached Sumatra and Ceylon before the Portuguese navigator Vasco da Gama (*c.*1469–1524) ever rounded the Cape of Good Hope. Venetians living in London, Paris and Bruges passed back intelligence to Venetian spymasters. But these travellers, ambassadors, ships' captains and merchants also brought in new and strange plants. In 1525, the Venetian ambassador Andrea Navagero, who had a villa in Selva and a garden of rare plants on the island of Murano, writes at length to Giovanni Battista Ramusio of the plants he has seen while travelling on horseback from Barcelona to Seville, noting the crops grown by Arab farmers. The Venetian patrician Pietro Antonio Michiel (b.1510), travels through the whole of Italy in search of rare plants. He makes a garden of exotics on the island of San Trovaso in Venice and keeps in regular touch with a whole web of Italian plantsmen, including Luca Ghini, Luigi Anguillara (*c.*1512–1570) and Ulysse Aldrovandi. Venetian ships

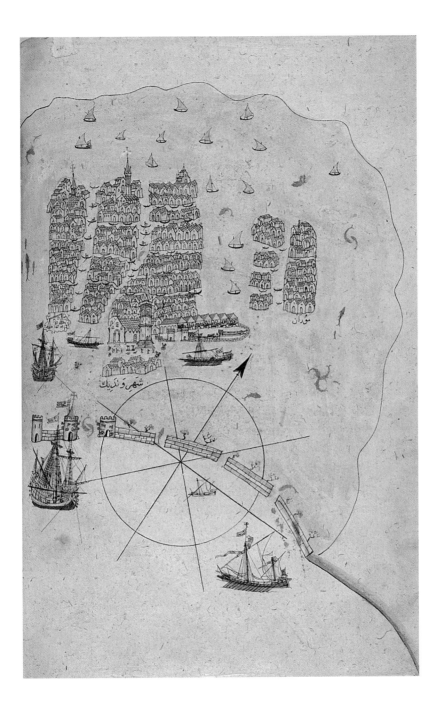

*Plate 82: Venice, as it appeared to navigators of the
sixteenth century*

bring him in specimens from Venetians serving in places as far flung as Constantinople and Alexandria. He gathers news, books, seeds from the French, German and Flemish travellers and merchants who pass through Venice. He has contacts in Crete, Dalmatia, the Levant. And he commissions a superb herbal with drawings by Domenico Dalle Greche.[3] Such productions seem to be a Venetian speciality: Benedetto Rinio, owner of the beautiful fifteenth-century herbal with paintings by Andrea Amadio, was also a Venetian. Great Venetian landowners such as Nicolò Contarini had for a long time taken a keen and intelligent interest in plants. And it had been a Venetian, Ermolao Barbaro (1454–1493), teacher of rhetoric and poetics at Padua and Venice, Venetian ambassador to the Holy See, who had produced the *Castigationes Plinianae* in 1492–3 and the *Corollarium Dioscorides* in 1516. The sack of Mainz in 1462 hastened the spread of printing through the rest of Europe and by 1480 there were presses in more than 110 towns, fifty of them in Italy. Most of those were in Venice, which quickly established a virtual monopoly of the printing business, cultivated and protected by the state. In Venice, Florence had a formidable rival, but the Medici were more than a match for the Contarini. Nicolò Leoniceno, in his Introduction to *Indications of Errors in Pliny*, pays a handsome tribute to 'the munificent Lorenzo di Medici', calling him 'the greatest patron of learning in this age, who, sparing no expense, has sent agents into every part of the world to collect manuscripts, so providing [himself] and other illustrious men with the most abundant means of study and the acquisition of knowledge.'[4] And the same dedication to learning had prompted Lorenzo's son, Cosimo the Great, the first Grand Duke of Tuscany, to invite Leonhart Fuchs to Pisa, which he was determined to establish as the greatest seat of learning in the land.

The universities – Ferrara, Bologna, Pisa, Padua, Florence – provided power bases for teachers such as Luca Ghini. But they also provided a structure within which the study of plants could grow. Not long after appointing Francesco Buonafede professor of *simplicia medicamenta* in 1533, the University of Padua took another pioneering step in appointing an *ostensor simplicium*, whose job was to lead students on guided tours round the university's new botanic garden. In the second half of the Renaissance there was a new emphasis on looking at plants; universities were the obvious places to establish living collections which students could study. It was a collecting age: minerals, strange shells, insects, corals, stuffed birds, dried snakes'skins, pickled fish. Plants fitted well in the prevailing mania to amass, assemble, convene; nature provided plenty of plants to accumulate and the numbers were increasing all the time with the exotics coming into the country from the Near East and the New World. By the early sixteenth century, there were already extraordinary collections of plants in Italy, but they belonged to rich patrons such as the Medici, who

*Plate 83: 'Oculis bovis', the carline thistle (Carlina acaulis)
a common plant in the alpine pastures of Southern and
Eastern Europe, in the Belluno herbal made in Italy early
in the fifteenth century*

grew pineapples from the tropics in their Florentine gardens. But the university gardens at Pisa and Padua, both established by the 1540s, were not private boasting booths. They were available to all and they included as many local plants as exotics, 'weeds' as well as the plants long used to supply pharmacists and apothecaries. There was a very real desire to understand the relationships between all these plants, to grasp the purpose of their myriad forms. 'The science of plants . . . owing to the continual and multifarious changes taking place in nature, was always difficult,' wrote the Florentine scholar Marcello Virgilio Adriani (1464–1521), 'and continues to be such, even to the present; because through lapse of time, diversities of location, the changes of the season, the influences of cultivation by man, and the perpetual mobility of all nature, plants seldom present the same appearance under these varying conditions. To these difficulties imposed by nature, there are added the differences of description used by writers of different nations. The perplexities embedded in these works are very great.'[5] There was a phenomenal amount of work ahead in unpicking the 'perplexities' but the availability, at last, of excellent pictures of plants (and, thanks to Ghini and others, of dried specimens which could be studied when the plants themselves had long disappeared underground) created a firm base for debate. It helped, too, that scholars in Germany, France, Flanders, Switzerland and Italy could communicate in a common language, Latin. Books were usually published in Latin before they were translated into vernacular languages.

But despite the pictures, despite the common language, muddles converged round even the most common of plants. In his *Examen omnium simplicium medicamentorum* (An examination of all plants), Brasavola of Ferrara writes, with pleasing parochial partiality, of a plant he calls *Primula veris*:

> The Florentines make use of this herb in salads and with us, at the very beginning of spring when all herbs are tender, it is edible. But then, the soil of Ferrara produces luxuriantly so many kinds of edible herbs that this one is there neglected. This is a small herb, with leaves spreading on the ground, and a flower resembling that of camomile, and white, except that the tips of the flowers are reddish. We of the Ferrara province, where the winters are mild, see it in flower all the year round. This is what your apothecaries take to be *Primula veris*, by our women called *petrella*, by some others St Peter's herb. Among recent names are *herba paralysis* and *margarita*, so much are people given to imposing names each according to his own fancy.[6]

For us, *Primula veris* is the official name of the spring-flowering primrose, but Brasavola's flower, white, tipped with red, doesn't sound in the least like a primrose. The clue lies in one of the common names he mentions – margarita. He's

Agave Americana

Plate 84: The American agave (Agave americana), *introduced in
1561 to the botanical garden in Padua. One of a series of
paintings of plants made between 1577 and 1587 by Jacopo
Ligozzi* (c.1547–1632) *for Francesco I de' Medici*

talking about a marguerite, a daisy, more specifically the common daisy *Bellis perennis*, weed of a million lawns. This plant had been growing in Europe for as long as people had inhabited it, yet still there was no consensus about its identity. The key lay in providing universally accepted tags to set alongside the common names of plants. The common names, of course, differed from country to country; even within one country, as Brasavola demonstrated, four or five different names might be attached to the same plant. They still are. *Galium aparine* is an irritating, widely spread weed with stems, leaves, and peppercorn-sized fruit all covered with tiny hooked hairs. As you brush by it, the plant sticks on to you, using you as a way to spread itself about. This clinging quality gives it its common name of cleavers, but it's also known as goosegrass, because it used to be chopped up and fed to newly hatched goslings. The common names are vivid, descriptive, and carry with them all kinds of baggage about their past. In a world that is increasingly homogenised, we see strengths in the local distinctiveness of such names. But they can't be exported and Renaissance scholars could already see that any system they devised had to be applicable everywhere. It had to have universal validity. They had a universal language at hand, and so the simplest thing was to use this language to forge a system that, eventually, could accommodate every thing that lived on earth. In their own way, artists such as Botticelli and Leonardo da Vinci had begun the process, by producing images of plants that all could recognise. The right words were more difficult to find. As Brasavola said, 'If it were possible to understand and comprehend matters without employing words, then there would be no need of names: but neither arts nor sciences can be understood or learned without using names. Therefore, it is preferable to use the words that the best authors choose, rather than barbarous ones, approved by no authority.'[7] In the Italian universities and their associated gardens, the great debate began, drawing in scholars from all over Europe. And, because the quest for order, for understanding, was a defining feature of the age, it engaged the attention of some magnificent minds.

'Look,' I want to say to the clusters of tourists in the Uffizi, being fed their gobbets of art history by German-speaking, Japanese-speaking, French-speaking, English-speaking guides. 'Look, it's not just about perspective or painterly techniques or the search for symbols. My men were riding through those landscapes, discussing those trees, their provenance, their cousinships with other plants. Students were petitioning, not for courses on art history, but for information about those plants you're looking at. By the time Botticelli died, Luca Ghini was already twenty years old. Those famous *Primavera* flowers aren't just ciphers. Scholars were growing them, writing to each other about them. They are central to this new beginning.'

Scholars such as Antonio Musa Brasavola had already realised that 'not a hundredth

Iris Susiana

Iris Xyphium

*Plate 85: Mourning iris (Iris susiana) from the Lebanon,
introduced to Europe in 1573 and Spanish iris (Iris xiphium)
from the Mediterranean. One of a series of paintings of
plants made between 1577 and 1587 by Jacopo Ligozzi
for Francesco I de' Medici*

part of the herbs existing in the whole world was described by Dioscorides, not a hundredth part by Theophrastus or Pliny, and we add more every day.'[8] By the middle of the sixteenth century, a map could be made of almost the whole world (with the important exception of Australia and New Zealand). It was now obvious that, as Sir Walter Raleigh put it, God had not 'shut up all light of learning within the lanthorn of Aristotle's braines'.[9] In Italy, with its long, hot summers, the first successful attempts were made to cultivate many unfamiliar plants: maize, sweet potatoes, potatoes, runner beans, French beans, pineapples, sunflowers, Jerusalem artichokes. By 1550, the first tomatoes were being enthusiastically grown, not for food but for their potential as aphrodisiacs. By 1585 peppers were fruiting abundantly all over Italy, as well as in Spanish Castile and Moravia (central Czechoslovakia). Just as the revival of anatomy in Italian universities had stimulated the renaissance of medicine, so the introduction of plant studies encouraged direct observation, rational criticism, intellectual scepticism and a long-overdue questioning of classical dogma.

XIV

THE FIRST
BOTANIC GARDEN

1540–1600

T HE BOTANIC GARDEN at Padua (see plate 86), proposed by Francesco Buonafede, was founded and funded by the Venetian Senate. The one at Pisa, developed by Luca Ghini shortly after he arrived in 1544, was funded by Cosimo de' Medici, the Grand Duke of Tuscany who, failing to get Fuchs, had lured Ghini away from the university at Bologna. Only two years after Padua had set up its special course on plants, Bologna had done the same thing and Ghini, who had been teaching in the medical faculty since 1527, got the job of *lector simplicium*, then *professor simplicium*. Dealing with the many questions raised by 'cognizione delle piante', he quickly became renowned as the best teacher in Europe. Born in Croara, Ghini himself had graduated at Bologna and when he started teaching the new course on plants had tried to persuade the authorities to set up a botanic garden there. Their delays and prevarications (it was not founded until 1567) provided him with a good excuse to move to Pisa, although he was already fifty-four years old.[1] The chosen site for the botanic garden in Pisa, the first in Europe, was on the right bank of the River Arno, close to the Arsenale, the naval shipyard of the Republic of Pisa. A map of the city (it's known as the 'Scorzi map' and was made some time between 1692 and 1737)[2] shows quite a large garden, extending on one side as far as the walls of the Guelfa Gate. In his capacity as professor at the university, Ghini was also *prefetto* or director of the botanic garden and held his demonstrations, his *ostensio simplicium*, here for the benefit of his students. Some of them – Luigi Anguillara of Latium (1512–1570), Andrea Cesalpino of Arezzo (1519–1603), Ulysse

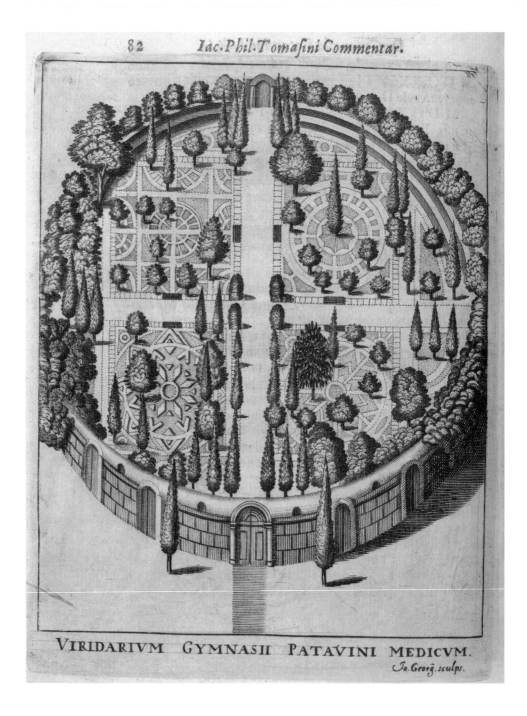

VIRIDARIVM GYMNASII PATAVINI MEDICVM.

Jo. Georg. sculps.

*Plate 86: The botanic garden at Padua, established in
1545 by Francesco Buonafede. From* Gymnasium patavinum *by
P. Tomasini (1654)*

Aldrovandi of Bologna (1522–1605), brilliant plantsmen themselves – had followed him to Pisa from Bologna. Twenty years before Galileo was born, Ghini established at Pisa a process of observation and experiment that made him a pioneer among his peers.

The first mention of the new garden (see plate 87) comes in a letter of 4 July 1545 written by Luca Ghini to Francesco Riccio, the Grand Duke's steward. In the course of a long journey from Pisa to Bologna, which took him over the Apennines near Pistoia, he says he has gathered 'molte piante da ponere nel giardino di Pisa' (many plants for the Pisa garden). He asks Riccio 'far acconzare il giardino pulita-mente' (to have the garden neatly arranged) so that it would please the Grand Duke, but also be 'utile alli scolari' (useful to the students). Ghini also mentions a trip he had made the previous June when he had gathered 'molte e bellissime piante, le quali ho fatto piantare con molta diligenza in un giardino di Pisa' (many beautiful plants which I planted very carefully in a Pisa garden).[3] A list from 1548 shows that there were already 620 different kinds of plant in the botanic garden.[4]

Ulysse Aldrovandi, one of Ghini's star pupils (and later the lucky owner of the superb Carrara Herbal) left a list of the lectures Ghini gave at Pisa. There are 103 of them and he evidently covered a wide range of topics and was as happy utilising the direct, practical knowledge of 'Greek soldiers in the service of our prince', or his Greek maidservant as he was quoting from Dioscorides. The problem with Dioscorides, says Ghini, is that he left 'so great a number of succinct, short, shabby and imperfect plant descriptions that, through such brief hints as he has given it may be impossible to identify the plants; we have such a variety of opinions, such seemingly opposite judgments about them, it must be doubtful whether they could ever be recognised, even if we could find them'.[5]

The plant Dioscorides calls 'crocodilium' presents a typical conundrum. Dioscorides had said that, 'It grows in wooded places, has a long, smooth, rather large root with a pungent smell. This root boiled and drunk causes copious bleeding at the nose. It is given to people who are splenetic and appears to help them. Its seed is round, double like a shield, and itself can be used as a diuretic.' Ghini writes to a friend that, for a long time, he has looked out for this plant, with the distinctive, shield-like seed that Dioscorides had described. Dioscorides had, at least, given a clue as to its habitat, so Ghini has been expecting to find it in some shady, woody place. But when he was down on the seashore, collecting plants and seed, he

came upon the blue-grey plant with spiny leaves which is commonly called *Eryngium marinum* and I saw that its seeds were double and rounded quite like shields. Then it came to my mind that Pliny describes 'crocodilium' as growing in gravelly (*sabulosis*)

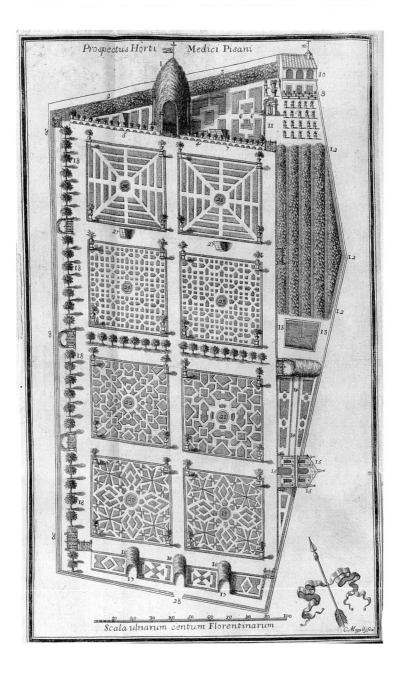

Plate 87: The botanic garden at Pisa, from Catalogus plantarum horti Pisani *by M. Tilli (1723)*

places. Although Dioscorides says wooded (*sylvosis*), I think he really meant to say *sabulosis*, but his text has been corrupted. I would not want you to take this as a decision, only an opinion, but all the same, I began to ask myself whether this might not be the very 'crocodilium' that I had been looking for. The dilemma is that the leaves of this plant, except for their spininess, are not very like the ones of the thistle that you consider to be *Chamaelon niger*, and which I have also until now taken for it. Still later, I recalled once having eaten the roots of that thistle in salads without any detriment to my health; this was in XXII [1522] on Monte Summano, when I was with the monks that live there. I never saw this plant down on the plains, much less along the seashore, but only in the mountains where the *Chamaelon niger* of Dioscorides was said to grow. And so I began to change my mind, and I now firmly believe that the thistle we speak of is not *Chamaelon niger* but something similar . . . I am sending you some seed of the plant which I now take to be the real 'crocodilium', but I would be more confident of being right, if I had tried drinking an infusion of its root and had found that it did indeed induce a nosebleed.[6]

The *hortus siccus*, the 'dried garden' that Ghini pioneered, made it very much easier for scholars in different countries to agree on the correct identification and naming of plants. Drawings and paintings were good, but the real plants, if carefully pressed to preserve their essential characteristics, were even better. Everyone interested in plants quickly saw the advantages of Ghini's herbarium. In 1551, Ghini sent a selection of dried plants to Pier Andrea Mattioli (*c.*1501–1577), who was then city physician of Gorizia. In a letter written 16 October 1553 to his former pupil, Ulysse Aldrovandi in Bologna, Ghini says he had once had a collection of more than 600 *erbe secche*, but more than half of them had been lost. The Flemish scholar, Matthias de l'Obel (generally known as Lobelius) and his friend Pierre Pena remembered also the wonderful paintings that Ghini had painted of Tuscan plants, recording the exact colours which, after a time, tended to be lost in the *hortus siccus*.

As well as providing a new means of documenting plants, the herbarium encouraged new ways of collating them. With his collection of Tuscan plants, Ghini was one of the first plantsmen to try to put together a local flora. He gathered plenty of material, but the book was never published. Instead, some of the illustrations he had commissioned of Tuscan plants – two kinds of bellflower, cistus, iris, ornithogalum, various wild orchids, were sent off to Fuchs in Tübingen.[7] While at Bologna, he had also planned to write a more comprehensive herbal, but in the year he came to Pisa, Mattioli's own massive *Commentarii* came out and was an immediate bestseller. As Mattioli explained in a letter written in 1558 to Ghini's former pupil, George Marius: '[Ghini] had intended to publish certain volumes which he had written about plants, together with the illustrations he had commissioned. But having read my commentaries, he wrote me a letter, congratulating me on anticipating him, and thus lightening his own labours. He also sent me a very great number of plants, and I felt duty bound to acknowledge this when I included pictures of them in my book.'[8]

And so Mattioli, the irritable bull elephant, gets a finite memorial. Ghini doesn't. Nor can Ghini claim credit for introducing any new plants, for he was not a great traveller, though he received plants from contacts in Calabria, Egypt, Sicily, Spain, Syria and also from his brother, Ottaviano, who was a lawyer in Crete. While his pupil, Anguillara, wandered through the wild regions between the Adriatic and the Black Sea, taking in Turkey, Syria, Greece, then moving on to Alexandria, Tripoli, Tunis on the northern shores of Africa, Ghini went no further than Elba. In his sixteenth-century book about the most beautiful houses and gardens in Italy, Bartolomeo Taegio of Milan had said that in the Pisa botanic garden 'verdeggiar si veggono infinite rare Piante, che altrove in Italia non sono vedute' (flourished an infinite variety of rare plants, not seen anywhere else in Italy).[9] But even that pioneering garden no longer stands as a monument to his brilliance. Seven years after Ghini's death, the botanic garden was requisitioned by the Knights of Santo Stefano so that the Arsenale could be expanded. A new garden, considerably smaller than the original, was laid out near the Calcesana Gate and the Convent of Santa Marta. But this was Andrea Cesalpino's garden, not Ghini's. Cesalpino, assisted by Luigi Leoni, oversaw its construction, but his academic responsibilities meant that he never had enough time to devote to the garden. It never flourished. The soil was poor. The site was largely overshadowed by the massive city wall.[10] Giovan Battista Fulcheri of Lucca writes to Aldrovandi in October 1571 that he is just on his way to Pisa to see the 'eccellente Cesalpino'. In a subsequent letter, he complains that, after making this special journey to Pisa, he had found neither Cesalpino nor his assistant Leoni and comments: 'Se tal horto per l'avenire non e atteso maggiormente, sene condurra a giardino di lattucha' (if this garden isn't more carefully looked after in future, it will be little better than a lettuce patch). Meanwhile Cesalpino, who like his master Luca Ghini had a great interest in crystals and ores, was wandering through Tuscany with one of his students, Michele Mercati, looking for minerals and fossils. Cesalpino's garden lasted scarcely more than thirty years (1563–1595). Added to its other problems was the fact that it was too far from the university to be useful to students, so Ferdinando I de' Medici ordered a third and final garden to be made, the one that exists today on land bordering the Via Santa Maria.

No book, no plants, no garden, no *hortus siccus* even (his original herbarium appears to have been lost), Ghini, who retired from the botanic garden in 1554 and died two years later, leaves instead a much more amorphous memorial: a reputation. His

Tab. 32

Jasminum Arabicum, Castanea folio, flore albo, odoratissimo, cuius fructus Caffe in Officinis dicuntur Boerh. Ind. Plant. 2. 217. N. 10

Plate 88: 'Jasminum Arabicum', the coffee bush, one of the exotic plants displayed in the botanic garden at Pisa and illustrated in the Catalogus plantarum horti Pisani *by M. Tilli (1723)*

altruism, his generosity, his unselfish desire to share with as many people as possible his devotion to his chosen subject, these are his gifts. He sent dried plants to Mattioli. He sent drawings and living plants to Fuchs. He was a giver, not a grabber. From a great distance, he drew people to him – the Englishmen John Falconer and William Turner were among his pupils. He enthused them, he sent them on their various ways with an understanding of and a regard for plants and their complexities that they would never lose. He was a catalyst. Without exception, his many pupils commend him as an exceptional, charismatic teacher. I look at his quizzical face with its strange little goatee beard, and wish that he had been my mentor too.

The herbarium made in 1563 by Ghini's pupil and successor Andrea Cesalpino (see plate 89) does still exist. Cesalpino actually made two examples of the *hortus siccus*, one (now lost) for his patron the Grand Duke, the other for Bishop Alfonso Tornabuoni, a powerful and important member of the Medici entourage. This is the one that's now kept in the Natural History Museum in Florence and it is the object of my first quest in the city. On an October day full of rain, I stand in front of two huge, locked panelled doors and ring the bell. There's a buzz, the catch is released and inside, seated behind a desk, is a uniformed custodian. Museo Botanico please, I say. No Museo Botanico, she replies. Just the Giardini dei Simplici, the botanic garden. Three euros. The Museo is shut. When will it be open, I enquire? She shrugs. But Cesalpino . . . I begin. She shrugs again. Could I perhaps speak to the museum's director? No, it isn't possible. So I buy a ticket for the garden and, nonplussed, walk slowly down one of the wide gravel walks to the circular pond in the centre. It's an enchanting garden, laid out in the classic way: a square, divided into four smaller squares by two main paths that cross in the centre. The pool at the intersection is surrounded by citrus in huge old terracotta pots. Vast azaleas, also in pots, line the walk from the pond to a handsome gate on the Via G. La Pira, the original entrance to the garden. Overhead are ancient chestnuts, acacias, limes. Tall buildings enclose the garden either side, the walls washed with ochre yellow. As sheets of rain drag the leaves off the lindens, I take refuge in the tall arcaded glasshouses shown in early maps of the botanic garden. Tender plants haven't yet been brought in for the winter and there are only a few permanent residents in the glasshouses: *Araucaria columnaris* from New Caledonia, *Araucaria cunninghamii* from Australia, both of them nearly touching the roof. Lumps of tufa are falling off the grotto. I watch a gardener sow seed in a line of clay pots, each about seven inches across. The seed has been gathered from the botanic garden, in white paper bags. He puts a handful of dried leaves at the bottom of each pot, fills it with compost from his

Plate 89: Andrea Cesalpino (1519–1603), the brilliant Italian plantsman who studied under Luca Ghini at Bologna and later succeeded him as curator of the botanic garden at Pisa

wheelbarrow, kneads it quickly and efficiently with his knuckles, carefully separates the seed from the stalks, chaff and seedcases, then sprinkles it on top of the compost. He writes names on labels – ribes, allium, chenopodium – then threads the ties through holes bored through the rims of the pots. He is absorbed, self-contained. That routine hasn't changed much since Cesalpino's day.

Also sheltering in the glasshouse is a tall, elegant man wearing a dark-blue collarless cardigan. He has a long, thin face and looks about seventy. He introduces himself: his name is Ivan Illich. I explain why I'm pacing the glasshouses, tell him about Cesalpino's herbarium, made in 1563 and now locked up, only seconds away, in a building I can't get into. The fault, he reveals courteously, is my own. The Museo Botanico is open only by request. I must make an appointment and if I contact him that evening, he will give me a name and a telephone number. Later, as instructed, I call him from a public phone booth near the Uffizi. Rain drums loudly on the perspex roof of the booth and the piazza is roaring with scooters. And two weeks later, I am on the second floor of the Museo Botanico, in a high-ceilinged room lined with cupboards piled with sheets of herbarium specimens. A faint smell of formaldehyde infuses the dense, ponderous silence. One glass-fronted cupboard is packed with shelves of handsome pots, late eighteenth century, early nineteenth century, glazed in a brilliant shiny green with a key pattern in black and white running round the top. Superimposed on each pot is the mask of a man holding a ribbon in his teeth from which is suspended a small oval frame. Written in black script in each frame is the name of the intricately modelled wax plant that each pot contains: *Passiflora quadrangularis, Pyrus japonica, Magnolia grandiflora, Hedychium gardnerianum*. The waxen colours have faded slightly to the buffs and olive greens of the funeral wreaths you see in Italian cemeteries. And there, laid out by the helpful curator, is the Cesalpino herbarium bound in three volumes of red morocco. For me, it has attained the status of an icon. I see it surrounded by an aura, a halo almost, glowing like the halos of the saints in Masaccio's frescoes.

Cesalpino's plants are stuck on sheets of thick handmade paper 29 cm x 43 cm. The handwritten dedication to Tornabuoni, Bishop of San Sepulchro, near Arezzo (Cesalpino's birthplace), covers two pages of small neat script. Tornabuoni was a keen amateur plantsman – already responsible for introducing tobacco into Italy – and would have understood Cesalpino's regret that so many scholars attempted to study plants 'without a grounding in philosophy, without which it is not possible to draw any profit from it'. After the dedication comes the index (see plate 90), the plant names set out in alphabetical order, first in Greek, then in Latin and Italian. He follows Luca Ghini's nomenclature and beside each name – 'digitalis', 'diosanthos', 'dipsacus' – is the folio number where each plant can be found. But

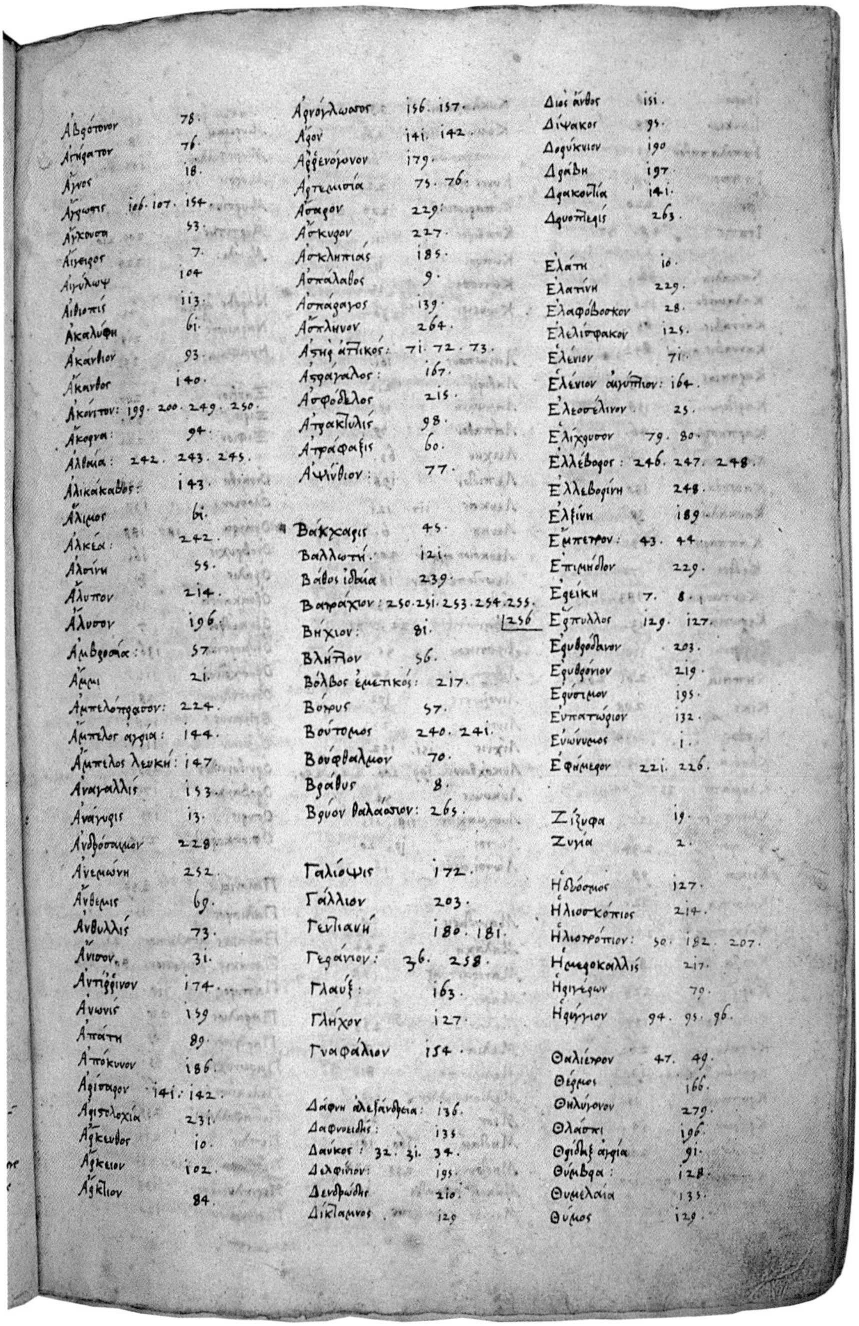

Ἀβρότονον	78.	Ἀγρώστωσος	156. 157.	Διὸς ἄνθος	151.
Ἀγήρατον	76.	Ἄρον	141. 142.	Δίψακος	93.
Ἄγνος	18.	Ἀρσένογονον	179.	Δορύκνιον	190.
Ἄγρωστις	106. 107. 154.	Ἀρτεμισία	75. 76.	Δράβη	197.
Ἄγχουσα	53.	Ἄσαρον	229.	Δρακοντία	141.
Ἄκειρος	7.	Ἄσκυρον	227.	Ἀριστέρις	263.
Αἰγίλωψ	104	Ἀσκληπιάς	185.		
Αἰθιοπίς	113.	Ἀσπάλαθος	9.	Ἐλάτη	10.
Ἀκαλήφη	61.	Ἀσπάραγος	139.	Ἐλατίνη	229.
Ἄκανθιον	93.	Ἄσπληνον	264.	Ἐλαφόβοσκον	28.
Ἄκανθος	140.	Ἀστὴρ ἀττικός	71. 72. 73.	Ἐλελίσφακον	125.
Ἀκόνιτον	199. 200. 249. 250.	Ἀστράγαλος	167.	Ἐλένιον	71.
Ἄκορνα	94.	Ἀσφόδελος	215.	Ἐλένιον αἰγύπτιον	164.
Ἀλθαία	242. 243. 245.	Ἀπαρκίνη	98.	Ἐλεοσέλινον	25.
Ἁλικάκαβος	143.	Ἀτράφαξις	60.	Ἐλίχρυσον	79. 80.
Ἄλιμον	61.	Ἀψίνθιον	77.	Ἐλλέβορος	246. 247. 248.
Ἀλκέα	242			Ἐλλεβορίνη	248.
Ἀλσίνη	55.	Βάκχαρις	45.	Ἐλξίνη	189.
Ἄλυπον	214.	Βαλλωτή	121.	Ἔμπετρον	43. 44.
Ἄλυσσον	196.	Βολβός ἰδαία	239.	Ἐπιμήδιον	229.
Ἀμβροσία	57.	Βατράχιον	250.251.253.254.255.	Ἐρείκη	7. 8.
Ἄμμι	21.	Βήχιον	81.	Ἕρπυλλος	126. 127.
Ἀμπελόπρασον	224.	Βλῆτον	56.	Ἐρύθρόδανον	203.
Ἄμπελος ἀγρία	144.	Βολβός ἐμετικός	217.	Ἐρύθρόνιον	219.
Ἄμπελος λευκή	147.	Βόρους	57.	Ἐρύσιμον	195.
Ἀναγαλλίς	153.	Βούτομος	240. 241.	Εὐπατώριον	132.
Ἀναγυρίς	13.	Βούφθαλμον	70.	Εὐώνυμος	1.
Ἀνθρόσαιμον	228.	Βράθυς	8.	Ἐφήμερον	221. 226.
Ἀνεμώνη	252.	Βρύον θαλάσσιον	265.		
Ἀνθεμίς	69.			Ζίζυφα	19.
Ἀνθυλλίς	73.	Γαλιόψις	172.	Ζυγία	2.
Ἄνισον	31.	Γάλλιον	203.		
Ἀντίρρινον	174.	Γεντιανή	180. 181.	Ἡδύοσμος	127.
Ἀνωνίς	139.	Γεράνιον	36. 258.	Ἡλιοσκόπιος	214.
Ἀπάτη	89.	Γλαύξ	163.	Ἡλιοτρόπιον	50. 182. 207.
Ἀπόκυνον	156.	Γλήχων	127.	Ἡμεροκαλλίς	217.
Ἀριστάριον	141. 142.	Γναφάλιον	154.	Ἡριγέρων	70.
Ἀριστολοχία	231.			Ἡρύγγιον	94. 95. 96.
Ἄρκευθος	10.	Δάφνη ἀλεξανδρεία	136.		
Ἄρκειον	102.	Δαφνοειδής	135.	Θηλίπτερον	47. 49.
Ἄρκτιον	84.	Δαῦκος	32. 33. 34.	Θέρμος	166.
		Δελφίνιον	195.	Θηλύγονον	279.
		Δενδρώδης	210.	Θλάσπι	196.
		Δίκταμνος	129.	Θρίδαξ ἀγρία	91.
				Θύμβρα	128.
				Θυμελαία	133.
				Θύμος	129.

Plate 90: The index of plants (here named in Greek) at the beginning of Andrea Cesalpino's herbarium, made in 1563. The plants are laid out according to similarities in fruit and seed

on the sheets of the herbarium itself, the plants are not set out in alphabetical order. They are arranged in groups, like with like, the first time anyone had attempted to do this. In his book, *De plantis*, published in Florence in 1583, Cesalpino explained what he was trying to do. In the main, his system depends on relationships – affinities – between different types of fruit and seed. He gathers together plants that seem to him to have similar fruits, distinguishing and separating them from those that are structured differently. 'All science consists in the gathering together of things that are alike', he wrote,

> and in the distinguishing and separating of the unlike, that is, distributing them into genera and species, as into companies, according to the difference that nature points out; and I now endeavour to introduce such system into the general history of plants, hoping thereby, though conscious of my limited ability, to offer something that may prove advantageous to the public. Among the ancients, Theophrastus first indicated the possibilities of such a method, though he did not follow it out. In our own time, Ruel has undertaken something similar, but never proceeded beyond Theophrastus, who had led the way. Dioscorides, being a physician, arranged things according to their medical qualities: juice, gum, root, seed.[11]

But Cesalpino also explains all this in the herbarium's dedicatory letter to Bishop Tornabuoni of San Sepulchro, dated 1563. This revolutionary way of looking at and arranging the plant world was fixed in his head twenty years before he ever published *De plantis*. Carefully I turn the pages of the herbarium, looking at Cesalpino's plants, now as crisp as well-grilled bacon. When Cesalpino was picking this agrimony, these verbascums and verbenas, Titian was painting his *Venus with a Mirror* and a new and terrible plague was breaking out in Europe. In London alone, it eventually killed more than 20,000 people.

On 260 sheets, Cesalpino has pasted down 768 plants, evergreen box, silvery artemisia, borage, broom, various ferns, elegant hellebores, spiky sea thistles, beech leaves, rush, water lily, viola, nettle (see plate 91). Like Theophrastus, he deals first with trees, moving on to shrubby plants and then flowers. On his first pages, he shows beech, hornbeam, ash and lime. The plants he planted in the botanic garden he created are looking back at me over a gulf of more than 400 years. He picked these things, pressed them and stuck them here, not randomly, but according to a carefully thought out method which was entirely his own. These sheets of plants are a living link back to my first hero, Theophrastus. Cesalpino, imbued with Aristotle's deductive method of reasoning, understood that Theophrastus was trying to do more than just list and describe; he was searching for essential similarities and differences between

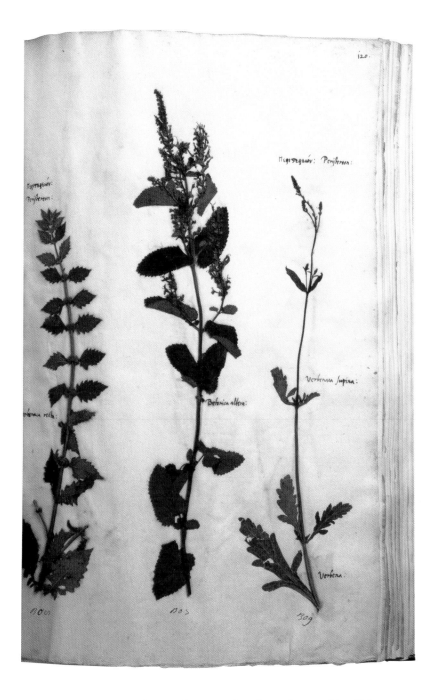

Plate 91: Betony and woundworts gathered together on folio 120 of Andrea Cesalpino's herbarium. It was made in 1563, twenty years before he published his book De plantis libri XVI, *setting out his revolutionary new theory of ordering plants in families*

plants. With Cesalpino, there emerged, finally, a scholar who understood the importance of the work that Theophrastus had started and who, 1,800 years later, picked up the dropped ideas and continued the debate. Curiously, that gap, between Theophrastus and Cesalpino, doesn't seem as enormous as the gap between Cesalpino and us. Cesalpino is perfectly at home in the classics. He sees nothing strange in the Aristotelian concept of *psyche* in plants. He agrees with Aristotle that this *psyche* or soul is most likely to be found at the point where the plant's underground root meets the shoot above ('qua scilicet radix germini coniunqitur, locus videatur cordi plantarum opportunissimus'). Cesalpino even thought that, at this critical juncture, he could distinguish soft tissue rather like an animal brain. He followed Theophrastus in believing that the ultimate goal of all plants was to produce seeds ('in ea propagatione, quae fit exsemine, plantarum finis consistat'). It followed therefore that the seeds themselves must be the key to grouping plants in a tenable, rational way. Plato had thought that male sperm must originate in the bone marrow. Following the same argument, Cesalpino supposed that seed must come from the inner pith of plants. He had noticed that seed tended to be produced from the thinner twigs on a tree, rather than from its thicker branches. This led him to suppose that it must be easier for the pithy stuff that made the seed to squeeze out from under the thin wrapping of a twig rather than through the dense woody bark that encased the bigger branches. The seed/pith notion may seem bizarre now, but it was accepted as an entirely valid concept for the next 200 years. In the context of what was known at the time, Cesalpino's argument was entirely reasonable.

Cesalpino argued for a system, an ordering that respected the true nature of plants and their characteristics. 'We look for those similarities and differences which make up the essential nature (*substantia*) of plants, not for those which are only accidental to them (*quae accidunt ipsis*); for things perceived by the senses become comprehended primarily from their essential nature and only secondarily from their accidents.'[12] The distinction between *substantia* and *accidentia* comes from Aristotle and persuaded Cesalpino that he was right in rejecting the artificial notions proposed by earlier writers. The doctor, Dioscorides, for instance, had grouped plants as though he were arranging a pharmacy, here the cough mixtures, there the feverfuges. Arranging plants by letters of the alphabet imposed a certain kind of order but precluded the possibility of establishing kinships, grouping plants in families which shared the same basic characteristics. Others had concentrated on plant roots, gathering together turnip, arum and cyclamen because each had a similarly rounded form. But the problem with roots, as Cesalpino pointed out, was that nature 'non posseva molto variare' (did not endow them with great variation). There were too few *differentiae* to be able to make meaningful distinctions. Believing, as he did, that the function of the leaf was merely to protect the fruit, Cesalpino ruled out forms of foliage as a possible way of classifying plants. No serious pattern could emerge by studying the size of plants, as that depended on soil, climate, the season of the year. Similarly, scent, taste and habitat were all dismissed as *accidentia*. Having so persuasively argued for fruits and seeds as the basis of his system, it was not surprising he should dismiss other characteristics as insignificant. He was looking for the most practical way to handle large groups of plants and believed his system provided it.

And so he groups together the trees that bear fruit similar to acorns – oaks, chestnuts, beech and hazel. He brings together hornbeam, birch, alder and ostrya, not because of their catkins (which would have brought hazel into their midst) but because of the fruit that develop from them. He gathers up the trees that produce one-seeded fruit with wings: elm, lime, plane, sycamore, ash. He distinguishes and assembles the trees that produce fleshy fruit with a stone in the middle – cherry, peach, plum. He noted the characteristic three-sided seed pod that develops on bulbous plants such as tulip and daffodil. He also noted that some plants, such as fungi and lichens, did not seem to set seed at all. 'These are the most imperfect, and spring from decaying substances; they have only therefore to feed themselves and grow, and are unable to produce their like; they are a sort of intermediate form between plants and inanimate nature (*media inter plantas & inanimata*).' As a system, it was better than anything that had gone before; it was supported by solid philosophical underpinning and, Cesalpino argued, by nature's own hand, 'for in no other parts has nature raised such a multitude of organs and distinguishing characteristics as are to be seen in the developing fruits'. Cesalpino searched for universals among the particulars of plants, tried to establish principles out of perceptions. His edifice, as it turned out, was built on the wrong foundations, but all the same, it was a powerfully persuasive piece of deduction, a landmark.

I'm struck, turning over the thick paper pages, by the familiarity of many of the plant names that Cesalpino uses. The language of plants is beginning to settle. Some consensus is being arrived at. Some names, of course, have come in a direct line, unchanged, from Theophrastus. He had been the first to use abrotonum, aconitum, adiantum, althaea, asparagus, asphodelus, balsamina, elleborum, silphium. At least forty of the names in Cesalpino's list can be tracked directly back to the *Enquiry into Plants*. But Cesalpino is also beginning to create the code that finally provided the answer to the correct naming of names. In the neat lists, handwritten at the beginning of his books of dried plants, he adds defining adjectives, to separate out one kind of plant from another which he believes to be closely related. So we have *Marrubium* (the white horehound, widely used to make cough mixtures) and *Marrubium nigrum*, the black horehound, which has purple flowers rather than white.

He distinguishes between *Edera spinosa*, a spiny ivy, and *Edera terrestris*, a ground-hugging one. He gives us both *Anagallis aquatica*, a pimpernel that favours damp, boggy ground, and *Anagallis sylvestris*, more likely to be found in woods. Though his method of classifying plants eventually turned out to be the wrong one, the two-name tags that he coined to link (and incidentally describe) similar kinds of plant provided a shorthand that all could understand and which could be used by scholars everywhere, Danish, German, French, English, as well as Italian.

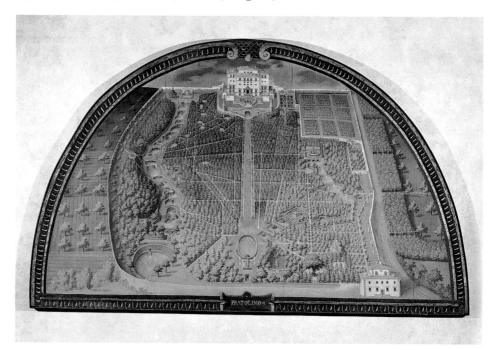

Plate 92: The ambitious garden and landscape at Pratolino as it appears in a lunette painted by Joost Utens between 1598 and 1601. The gardens, laid out for the Grand Duke Francesco I, had labyrinths of bay and meadows thick with flowers

Born in Arezzo, educated at the University of Pisa, Cesalpino took his MD in 1549. When Ghini died, his pupil succeeded him as director of the botanic garden in Pisa and taught botany, medicine and philosophy there for nearly forty years. Like Ghini, he gave regular *ostensione* in the gardens, even on public holidays. Cesalpino was in sole charge of the garden until 1558, when Cosimo appointed Luigi Leoni of Cividale (another of Ghini's students) as his assistant; Leoni was also made *prefetto* of the botanic garden in Florence, which had been set up in 1550. In 1555, the French nurseryman and traveller Pierre Belon visited the garden and was given several ever-green shrubs ('arbuscolis perpetuo virentibus'). The Flemish scholar Lobelius and his friend Pierre Pena came soon after and got some roots of papyrus 'expressly dug up for them', promising to send some on to Conrad Gesner in Zurich.[13] Papyrus was just one of the many exotic plants – tamarind, aloe, canna – that Cesalpino collected for the botanic garden from contacts in Constantinople, Egypt, Syria and other 'lontani paesi incert' (unknown distant countries). In 1592, Cesalpino left Pisa for Rome, peeved perhaps by the fact that the Grand Duke Francesco had invited Girolamo Mercuriale of Bologna to take over as *sovraordinario* of the Pisa botanic garden at a salary much higher than his own. In Rome Cesalpino took up the prestigious position of physician to Pope Clement VIII, taking care to point out in a letter to a colleague that his new job, combined with the post of lecturer on *medicina sopraordinaria*, would put him on an equal footing with his rival.[14]

Cesalpino had been forty-four years old when he made his *hortus siccus*, and another twenty years passed before he put his revolutionary theory into print. *De plantis libri XVI* was published in Florence in 1583 (see plate 93), just three years before the Arab physician Qasim ibn-Muhammad al-Wazir al-Ghassani published the first Arabic classification of plants.[15] Cesalpino's is an uncompromising book, written in Latin, of course, 621 pages of solid text, followed by an index and his corrections. He has refined his system of classifying plants since the *hortus siccus* and includes 1,500 plants divided into thirty-two different groups, including the *Umbelliferae* (plants such as hemlock and cow parsley that hold their flowers in umbrella-shaped heads) and the *Compositae*, many-petalled flowers that include the daisy and the dandelion. There are no pictures. In his Preface, Cesalpino tries to justify the lack of illustration: 'A picture', he writes, 'cannot provide more certain knowledge' than a good description because it cannot 'express all the *differentiae*' of the plant. He had often found that printed pictures to be incorrect; even illustrators as good as Hans Weiditz and Albrecht Meyer had different responses to plants and so produced disparate images. Woodblocks got cannibalised, could be (and were) used in the wrong place. But although Cesalpino in his Dedication talks of his work as 'most pure, unadulterated by any images', he also reminds his patron (the book is dedicated to the *Serenissimum* Francesco de' Medici, son of Cosimo the Great) that drawings have in fact been made 'thanks to your support, with such industriousness that they portray each one of the tiniest differences. They are almost alive and can offer very faithful evidence. If at some point, it should be decided to print these drawings, this should be considered an accomplishment which is not only distinguished, but also worthy of a great ruler.' In fact, Cesalpino had made desperate attempts to get these drawings included in his book. Writing in 1579 from Pisa to Belisario Vinta, secretary to his patron, Francesco I de' Medici, Cesalpino asks for information about a project that the previous Grand Duke, Cosimo, had promised to sponsor: the preparation of copperplate engravings from the drawings that Cesalpino had gathered

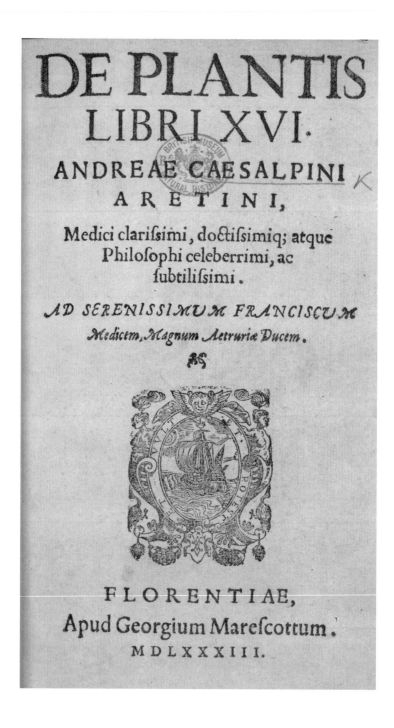

DE PLANTIS
LIBRI XVI.
ANDREAE CAESALPINI
ARETINI,

Medici clariſsimi, doctiſsimiq; atque
Philoſophi celeberrimi, ac
ſubtiliſsimi.

AD SERENISSIMUM FRANCISCUM
Medicem, Magnum Aetruriæ Ducem.

FLORENTIAE,
Apud Georgium Mareſcottum.
MDLXXXIII.

Plate 93: *The title page of Andrea Cesalpino's seminal book*
De plantis libri XVI *published in Florence in 1583*

together to illustrate his book. As he feared, Cosimo's successor abandoned the project and the illustrations have since been lost. *De plantis* was finally published, but the lack of any pictures made it a daunting prospect for a reader.

This long drawn out saga must be the chief reason that Cesalpino waited so long before publishing *De plantis* in 1583. He was sure of his system. The book, as he makes clear in his Dedication, had already been promised to Francesco's father, Cosimo. But he was also working in a time of massive flux. He has, he writes 'by no means been able to reach my goal, for, as the proverb goes, day after day Africa yields something new: not because nature produces new shapes, or forges new and beautiful kinds of things, but because new things are shown to us as the days proceed'. He mentions particularly the West Indies, whose plants had only recently been catalogued by 'that very learned doctor' the Spaniard Nicolas Monardes. The Portuguese scholar Garcia de Orta had already described China root in 1563 as 'a shrub of 5–6 ft high, root about 1ft, one thick root and one thin. The leaves are shaped like young orange leaves'. But it didn't find its way into Cesalpino's book. It was impossible to keep up with the torrent of new arrivals. Any attempt at an encyclopaedic account of plants was outstripped before the print was even set. In his *hortus siccus* Cesalpino had pasted 768 different plants. His book described and grouped 1,500. The ever-increasing number of plants made it all the more necessary to marshal them in a meaningful way. Cesalpino uses the analogy of an army. Unless plants are reduced to categories and 'just like the battle line of an army, are divided into their different groups, all these things are necessarily shaken by confusion and fluctuation'. In a time of such fluctuation and change, mistakes are bound to occur: 'some plant might by chance escape our notice and, in a way equivalent to those soldiers which at times move on to different groups, a plant can be placed in a category to which it does not belong. This might happen especially in the case of those curative plants which are foreign, and of which either only the root, or only the juice or only the wood or some other part is taken out for us, while we never get to see the whole plant.'[16] It was a valid point. Guaiacum was generally imported only in dried form, ready to use.

Drifting, intensely happy, out of the cool, still museum room, down the staircase with its curly handrail, past framed fossil plants, hung on the wall, trapped in slabs of rock, I'm once again thinking about the parameters of this sixteenth-century mind. This man thought seeds squeezed out into the open air from the inner pith of a plant. Imbued as he was with Aristotelian doctrines of form and matter, he believed that these principles provided all that was necessary to understand and organise the natural world. A plant could be described in the same terms as an animal: its *cor*

Plate 94: The cypress vine (Ipomoea quamoclit) *brought to Florence from the tropics of South America and included in the series of plant paintings made between 1577 and 1587 by Jacopo Ligozzi for Francesco I de' Medici*

was at the juncture of stem and root; the roots equated to the digestive system in an animal; intestines were represented by the pith; the stem provided a reproductive system, the fruit an embryo. Stepping into the sudden, brilliant light of the garden, it seemed perhaps not such an odd notion that the function of the leaves on these limes and citrus trees was to protect the fruit from the burning sun. Nobody knew yet about photosynthesis. Oxygen and carbon dioxide hadn't yet found names.

Outside, the gardeners are now buzzing about in forklift trucks, shifting the tender plants in their pots into the shelter of the glasshouse. That empty place where I sat looking at the rain is now crammed with exotic specimens that have come in for the winter: cycads from Africa, sweet-smelling datura from Mexico, bird of paradise plants from South Africa. Standing neatly in a square outside are the pots of seed that I had watched the gardener sow. The poppy (*Papaver rhoeas*) is already up, the seedlings brilliant green like duckweed on a pond. At the phone booth near the Uffizi, I call Ivan Illich to thank him for unlocking the door to Cesalpino and his herbarium. The number rings unobtainable. The operator denies such a number has ever existed. But there it lies, like Cinderella's shoe, written in his own hand in my notebook.

A few days after my tryst with Cesalpino's herbarium, I take the train to Arezzo, to look for his birthplace, unremarked in any guide I can find. It's a Sunday morning, and the stalls of the monthly antique market spill out into the streets surrounding the piazza at the top of the town – ancient gilded candlesticks, swatches of material, painted furniture, old books smelling of loneliness and damp. Beyond is the citadel, now an open grassy space, the Parco Il Prato, with big old holm oaks and a Mussolini-hideous statue of Petrarch – white marble – put up in 1928. Between the evergreen oaks are limes, pines and big puddings of clipped box. Wide stone steps lead down into Via Ricasoli, decorated with stone columns, topped with urns, the top limit of the antique market. My eyes flick up to a sign and quite by chance, I find I am at the corner of a street called the Via Cesalpino. A plaque marks the house where Petrarch lived, in exile from Florence. Close by is the Palazzo Chiaromanni with its sandy yellow-ochre front, scrolled windows, and bricked-in arches. I admire the church of San Pier Piccolo, the fifteenth-century stucco of the Madonna della Provvidenza, note the birthplace of the astronomer, Tommaso Ferrelli. But nothing (except the street name) commemorates my man, the great Cesalpino. The Commune di Arezzo Assessorato alla Cultura can shed no light on the matter. 'Cesalpino's book *De plantis* has been much in my mind,' wrote the fine scholar, Gaspard Bauhin later in the seventeenth century. 'I spent a long time reading it in order to use it for my classification. He is a learned man, but very obscure; I had great difficulty in understanding him, and doubt whether he would be intelligible to beginners and students.' Unfortunately he was right.

*Plate 95: A portrait of Pier Andrea Mattioli (1501–1577)
painted when he was sixty-seven*

XV

THE LONG-NOSED
NIT-PICKER

1540–1600

THE WRONG MAN won. Threading my way back to the station, through the antique market, it's not Cesalpino's book that I see displayed on a second-hand book stall, but a single folio (see plate 96) from the massive herbal *Commentarii in libros sex Pedacii Dioscoridis Anazarbei* first published in 1544 by Pier Andrea Mattioli (1501–1578) (see plate 95). The sheet offered for sale must be from a later edition, for most of it is taken up by a huge woodcut of a Chinese smilax, whirling with tendrils and small spherical fruit. These images were prepared from 1565 onwards, when the book had already established itself as a bestseller. In all, sixty-one different editions were produced: a French translation came out in 1561, a Czech one in 1562 (see plate 97), a German one in 1563 and the fancy Latin one in 1565, decorated with 932 handsome illustrations. In Mattioli's lifetime alone, the book in its various guises sold 32,000 copies, at a time when selling 500 was thought to be a prodigious achievement. It was disloyal, but I bought the folio anyway, for the sake of Giorgio Liberale's woodcut. His illustrations, heavily cross-hatched, don't have the immediacy of Hans Weiditz's, but they are bold and decorative. Weiditz drew exactly what he saw in front of him, mirroring nature. Liberale produced more stylised images, making patterns of his plants, stretching and spreading them all to fit into the same rectangular frame. Certainly, it wouldn't have been worth buying the fragment for the text, for Mattioli was a dinosaur compared with the brilliant, innovative Cesalpino. Mattioli hung on still to Dioscorides, making the work by the Greek doctor the basis of his own meandering commentary and

SMILACE ASPRA.

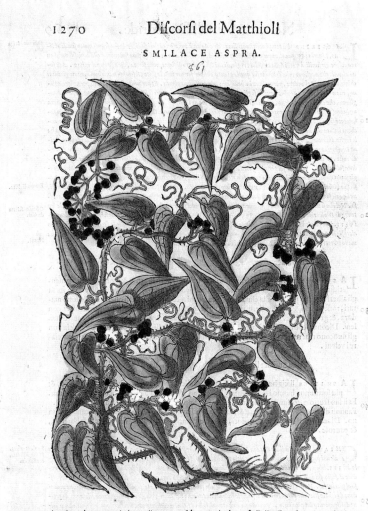

altra pianta che poco auanti mi uenne di Spagna; & se bene amendue hanno foglie di Smilace aspra, sono però minori,
ne sono spinose da rouescio, ne manco sono spinosi i suoi sarmenti. Onde posso ben hora assermare che sia qualch e diffe-
renza tra la Smilace aspra,& la zarza parilla, se bene io resto nella mia opinione che sieno piante congeneri, & d'vna
uirtù medesima. La Smilace liscia poi se non è quella, di cui è qui la figura, non so io altra pianta al presente che piu se
gli rassomigli di questa, in la quale si ueggono tutte le note dal seme in fuore, il quale non ha conformità veruna con i
lupini. Questa adunque nasce abondantissima in Toscana, & chiamasi Vilucchio maggiore. Questa produce le frondi
sue simili all'altra, & nascene similmente su per gli alberi; ma non sono i suoi sarmenti spinosi, ma lisci,& arrendenoli
I fiori son bianchi, simili à campanelle: & il seme nero, maggiore delle lenticchie. Chiamasi volgarmente nelle spetia-
rie Volubile, Di questa scriuono gli Arabici piu spetie, & tra ese connumerano anchora il LVPVLO. il quale quan
tunque sia à i tempi nostri per l'uso della medicina molto stimato, & necessario, nientedimeno non se ne ritruona men_ 10
tione alcuna appresso à Dioscoride, Galeno, & gli altri antichi Greci. Benche corsuamente chiamandolo Lupo sali-
ctario

Plate 96: *Giorgio Liberale's swirling woodcut of 'Smilace aspra',
our Chinese smilax (Smilax china) from an Italian edition of
Mattioli's* Commentarii in libros sex Padacii Dioscoridis
Anazarbei. *The full-page illustrations were first prepared
for the Latin edition of 1565*

completely overwhelming Dioscorides in the process. Dioscorides's own Preface to his work is contained in a single page. Mattioli's gloss, his interpretation of that Preface, runs on for fourteen, without a single paragraph break or pause for breath. The 600 plants that Dioscorides included in his original *De materia medica* are joined by several hundred new ones, and as each subsequent edition of Mattioli's book came out, the author included more and more of the novelties now pouring into Europe, particularly from Constantinople and the Near East. Cesalpino, well trained by his master, Luca Ghini, was a much better plantsman, but he didn't have Mattioli's aggressive determination to crush the opposition. Nor did he have his luck. Cesalpino had wanted to include illustrations in his own book, but the Medici patron who sanctioned them died before the book was produced; Mattioli, comfortably ensconced in Prague as private physician to Archduke Ferdinand, could call on unlimited grants to fund the always expensive process of producing images. Both had contacts all over Europe and overseas; both were well supplied with plants and information. Mattioli, though, was more ruthless in exploiting the contacts, putting his own stamp on work that had actually been done by others. While Cesalpino carefully built a framework for the plant kingdom, an entirely new method of appraising them, considering their similarities and differences, Mattioli contributed absolutely nothing to the great philisophical debate. And yet his book is the one that survives and flourishes. His book, out of all the work produced in this extraordinary century, is the one that is endlessly republished.

Shopping one day in Rignano, an ugly little town in the Valdarno rebuilt round a square with a pool and fountain, I pass the Farmacia Pratellesi owned by Dr Fiorella Galanti Massai. It's a shiny new shop with plate-glass windows, forming part of the ground floor of a block of flats. Dr Massai comes from a long line of pharmacists; her grandfather worked in the famous pharmacy at nearby Valombrosa. The windows of the shop are dressed with the ancient tools of a pharmacist's trade: a large marble mortar and pestle, pill moulds, palette knives, scales with tiny doll-size weights, forceps, distilling equipment, the decorated ceramic jars that once contained the apothecary's drugs, extracted from plants and minerals. A rubber plant with shiny oval leaves sprouts from a monstrous bronze mortar. On a stand centrally placed in one of the windows is a copy of Mattioli's book, bound in stained vellum, held together with Sellotape.

With great courtesy, Dr Massai invites me into her gleaming, brand-new office and fetches the book from the window. I sit at her curved desk in a futuristically elegant swivel chair, with perspex light and mobile phone to hand, reading the *Admonitio ad lectores* from a Latin edition of Mattioli, published in 1565. This edition has small illustrations, sometimes laid out four to a page. At the front is a list of

Plate 97: Yew (Taxus baccata) *illustrated in Pier Andrea Mattioli's* Commentarii in libros sex Pedacii Dioscoridis Anazarbei, *published in Venice in 1565*

plants – cyclamen, elleborus – followed by an alphabetical list of ailments – *Extremorum membrorum, Vulnerum, Venenorum* – with a concordance of the plants that Dioscorides and Mattioli recommend for their treatment. While, outside, the smartly white-coated assistants dispense laxatives, headache pills and cough medicine, I turn the pages on iris, tulips (still so new in Europe that Mattioli lists them as daffodils – *Narcissus Constantinopolitanus*), dracunculus and lilac. The first picture ever to be seen of lilac appeared in this edition of the *Commentarii*, produced in 1565. Though it's now one of the commonest of garden shrubs, it was then a rare novelty, having only recently arrived in Europe from the Near East. The French explorer and nurseryman Pierre Belon, one of the first Europeans to travel extensively in Turkey, had already described this 'petit arbrisseau qui porte les feuilles de Lierre, qui est vert en tout temps, et fait sa fleur presque d'une coudée de long, de couleur violette, entournant le rameau, gros comme une queue de Regnard'.[1] But Mattioli got the credit for picturing the plant and using its European name, lilac, for the first time. It was among a whole clutch of treasures introduced into Europe by Ogier Ghiselin de Busbecq when in 1562 he returned to Vienna from his embassy to the court of Sulaymān the Magnificent in Constantinople.

Dr Massai explains that her family have owned the volume as long as anyone can remember. Various users have scribbled their own annotations in the margins, updating the book as the author himself updated it in the thirty-three years that stretched from its first appearance in 1544 until his death in 1577. Why was it so successful? Lay readers were perhaps seduced by its encyclopaedic nature. The book gave the impression of delivering everything anyone needed to know on the subject of plants and their uses. The first edition of the book, though it was without illustrations, was published in Italian, which made it accessible to the widest possible local readership. Dioscorides's name was well known, and despite the careful criticisms published by Italian scholars such as Adriani, Manardo, Brasavola and Leoniceno, the name still carried weight. By hitching his own name to that of the man whom so many regarded as the ultimate authority on plants and their uses, Mattioli made sure that some of the old aura brushed off on himself.

And Mattioli lived a long time, longer than most of his contemporaries. Born at roughly the same time as Leonhart Fuchs, with whom he carried on a vicious battle in print, he outlived him by ten years. When Luca Ghini died in 1556, Mattioli still had another twenty years in front of him. He never quarrelled with Ghini, though. He needed him too much. In 1551, while working on an updated edition of his *Commentarii*, Mattioli sends Ghini a list of sixty-five plants in Dioscorides which he cannot name. One of them is *Medica* (our medick, or lucerne). Ghini, then still at Pisa, replies in a letter that he himself has not long known of its existence:

*Plate 98: Sea lavender (*Limonium latifolium*) carved into a block of pear wood, one of the illustrations prepared by Wolfgang Meyerpeck and Giorgio Liberale for Pier Andrea Mattioli's* Commentarii in libros sex Pedacii Anazarbei, *published in Venice in 1565*

'The Most Reverend Ludovico Beccadello, in our time sent as Legate of the Sovereign Pontiff to the Venetians, brought me seeds of *Medica*, which he had brought from Spain. I planted them and they grew . . . As cultivated in this garden, all the plants were at beautiful accord with Dioscorides's description of *Medica*. It puts forth flowers, what Dioscorides says nothing of, that are purple, seeds like lentils but smaller, in pods much incurved.'[2] Unlike Fuchs, who belligerently protected his own schemes, Ghini gives up the idea of publishing his book on plants and puts all his research at Mattioli's disposal. Cesalpino thought Mattioli owed more to Ghini than he ever admitted; though the debt was never publicly acknowledged, perhaps Mattioli knew that too. Writing in 1558 to George Marius, one of Ghini's many pupils, Mattioli acknowledges that 'Ghini's death was a heavy blow to me: his intellectual endowment was massive and brilliant: integrity, sincerity, loyalty to his friends were conspicuous. There was never a trace of jealousy.'[3] In a letter to the great scholar and plantsman Ulysse Aldrovandi (1522–1605), Mattioli said that Ghini's death has carried away half his heart.

In the same way that Camerarius had become Fuchs's most trusted correspondent, so Aldrovandi (who in 1550 founded in Bologna perhaps the first natural history museum in Europe), became Mattioli's. Their exchange of letters covers twenty-two years from 1550–1572. Luigi Anguillara (*c*.1512–1570), who, like Aldrovandi, had been a pupil of Ghini's, was not so lucky. Unlike Mattioli, Anguillara travelled, in the Levant, the Aegean and Crete, seeking out the plants that Dioscorides had described. In 1561, he published a small plant book, *Semplici* (see plate 159), in which he gently and courteously corrected some of Mattioli's nomenclature and suggested some different attributions for Dioscorides's plants. Enraged, Mattioli charged into print and was so vicious in his attacks on the scholarly Anguillara, so arrogant in his contemptuous dismissal of the other man's competence, that Anguillara, who was custodian of the Giardini dei Semplici in Padua, was forced to resign his post and retire, silenced, to Ferrara. But Anguillara was right to question the monopoly on plants that Mattioli was intent on establishing. Mattioli's arrogance bred a kind of carelessness. His picture of a banana palm (which he had never seen and included only on hearsay) was printed upside down. Other plants, sent to him pressed and dried, were soaked in water and 'revived' before being set before the illustrators, who then had to make considerable leaps of the imagination to interpret the soggy messes in front of them. The leap was not always in the right direction.

Though he spent much of his life travelling with Emperor Ferdinand's court between Prague, Vienna and Innsbruck, Mattioli remained fiercely Sienese, umbilically attached to 'Toscano mio nido'. His family had been established in Siena since the early fifteenth century and Mattioli was born there on 12 March 1501. He was

*Plate 99: The widow iris (*Hermodactylus tuberosus*) with velvety green and black flowers, painted by Jacopo Ligozzi between 1577 and 1587 for Francesco I de' Medici. What flower did he intend to include as its companion?*

ten when Botticelli died, nineteen when Leonardo da Vinci's febrile brain finally came to rest. Unlike most of the other great Italian scholars of this age, he never taught, but practised as a doctor in Rome. When, in 1527, the city was sacked by Charles V, King of Burgundy and the Netherlands, Mattioli established himself as city physician at Gorizia in north-east Italy. Then in 1555 he got called to Prague 'con salario honoratissimo'. After the death of Emperor Ferdinand I, who had lured him to the court, he was appointed personal physician to the Emperor's successor, Maximilian II. It was this court appointment that brought him into such close and useful contact with the Fleming, Ogier Ghiselin de Busbecq, Ferdinand I's ambassador in Constantinople. Writing from Constantinople in August 1557, Busbecq's private physician, Willem Quackelbeen says 'Whatever exact knowledge I have hitherto been able to arrive at concerning herbs and other simple medicaments, I owe entirely to your excellent commentaries on Dioscorides.'[4] This was exactly what Mattioli wanted to hear. Busbecq, based for seven critical years in the country from which so many brilliant new plants emerged, could give Mattioli first-hand accounts of the things he had seen. Writing just after his return to Europe in 1562, Busbecq says, 'I brought back from Turkey some drawings of plants and shrubs which I am keeping for Mattioli; but as to plants and shrubs themselves I have none, for I sent him many years ago the sweet flag and many other specimens.' Busbecq, who had arranged for the gorgeous Juliana Anicia codex to be brought out of Constantinople, also gave Mattioli two Dioscorides manuscripts which he had acquired in Turkey.

Mattioli jealously hoarded information, compiling, recording, but never stopping to see what deductions his great edifice of facts might lead to. He accumulated but did not infer. While Cesalpino worried away at his revolutionary theory of classification, Mattioli just continued to hoover up new plants for further, ever-expanding editions of his book. Cesalpino had thought hard about fungi, about their curious mode of life, their difference to most other kinds of plant. But writing of truffles, Mattioli blandly declares: 'Truffles are known to everyone. They occur abundantly in Tuscany everywhere – fine large ones of two sorts. In one of them the flesh under the skin is white; in the other it is dull. Nevertheless, both of them have rough, dark skin. In the diocese of Trent there is a smaller kind with a smooth, pale skin and an inferior taste.'[5] Yet in his will of 1637, the English diplomat Sir Henry Wotton left one of his most treasured possessions to Henrietta Maria, wife of Charles I – his sumptuously hand-coloured copy of the *Commentarii*: 'I leave to our most Gracious and Vertuous Queen Mary, *Dioscorides* with the Plants naturally colored, and the Text translated by Matthiolo, in the best Language of Tuscany, whence her said Majesty is lineally descended, for a poor token of my thankful devotion, for the honour she was once pleased to do my private study with her presence.'

XVI

WEAVING THE WEB
1500–1580

A T THIS WONDERFULLY fertile time, no one questioned the importance of the work at hand: the need to understand, describe, then sort and order the multifarious elements of the natural world. Like broadcasts beamed out from the first radio transmitters, the ideas debated in the Italian universities of the early sixteenth century gradually spread out over the rest of Europe. An extraordinary web of contacts was spun between scholars in Italy, France, Switzerland, Germany and the Netherlands, all of whom shared the same passion for *res herbaria*, things to do with plants. They had no clubs or other regular places to meet. There were no scientific journals where views could be exchanged and ideas disseminated, nor societies to which like-minded people could belong.[1] Nevertheless, the network spread ever wider, drawing in apothecaries, artists, clerics both Catholic and Protestant, physicians, humanist scholars and schoolmasters as well as wealthy men of leisure, their common interest in plants now stronger than the social prejudices that in previous ages might have kept them apart. Professional boundaries became blurred too. The Venetian Ermolao Barbaro had taught rhetoric and poetics at Padua and served in the Venetian Senate at the same time as producing new editions of Aristotle, Dioscorides and Pliny. Otto Brunfels had been a Carthusian monk, and a schoolmaster before he wrote his *Herbarum vivae eicones*. Ogier Ghiselin de Busbecq, responsible for introducing many superb Turkish plants into Europe, was in Turkey not as a plant collector but as Ferdinand of Austria's ambassador to the Ottoman Empire. These people could be poets as well as diplomats, politicians as well as clerics, doctors as well as historians. But they were bound together by these over-riding passions: the love of plants and the search for the most logical way of classi-fying them.

At the centre of the web were the universities, chiefly, at first, the Italian ones. The fame of the charismatic Luca Ghini spread far beyond his base at Pisa, and his successor at Bologna, Ulysse Aldrovandi, made sure that the study of plants remained at the heart of the university curriculum. Antonio Musa Brasavola (1500–1555) was equally successful in attracting students to the university at Ferrara. But soon, other inspirational teachers emerge in other universities, particularly at Montpellier, Zurich and Basel. Charles de l'Écluse (Clusius) and Matthias de l'Obel (Lobelius), pupils of Guillaume Rondelet (1507–1566) at Montpellier, both go on to be brilliant plantsmen. In Zurich, Conrad Gesner, who had so delicately crossed swords with both Fuchs and Mattioli, has friends at Montpellier and goes plant-hunting with Jean Bauhin, who had also studied under Rondelet. Jean's brother, Gaspard (1560–1624) is the first professor of anatomy and *res herbaria* at Basel University and visits scholars in Venice, Bologna, Rome, Verona and Florence. Very carefully he studies Cesalpino's *De plantis*, which one of his students brings him as a present from Padua, and in 1568, writes to a friend of the difficulties of fitting Cesalpino's plants into his own different system of classification. When, in the year before his death, he finally publishes his own book, *Pinax theatri botanici*, he lists sixty-three people – teachers, physicians, students, friends, correspondents – who have sent him seeds and plants.

But this web, which so intricately connected scholars across mainland Europe, did not at first include Britain. The universities at Oxford and Cambridge were slow to set up chairs for the study of *res herbaria*, or to establish botanic gardens to facili-tate the study of plants. The Oxford Botanic Garden, the first in Britain, was not established until 1621, nearly eighty years after those at Pisa and Padua. Nevertheless some Englishmen found their way to Italy and studied *res herbaria* at the great universities. Thomas Linacre was attached to Henry VII's embassy to the Vatican and had the opportunity to use the fine Vatican Library in Rome. He conferred with Ermolao Barbaro, at that time working on his new edition of Pliny's *Natural History*, then moved on to Padua, where he gained his MD in 1496. By 1499, he was back in Oxford, in time to meet the Dutch humanist Erasmus, who had come to the university to study Greek. Forty years later, John Falconer is learning from Luca Ghini how to press and dry plants and stick them in a book. When Falconer shows his new *hortus siccus* to the Portuguese explorer Amatus Lusitanus, it is reckoned to be a marvel. Lusitanus speaks of Falconer as 'a man fit to be compared with the most learned herbarists, a man who had travelled many lands for the study of plants and carried with him very many specimens ingeniously arranged and glued in a book'.[2]

Nobody in England, though, had written a decent book on plants. There was nothing that an English author could set against Fuchs's work in Germany, or even Mattioli's in Italy. *The grete herball* (see plate 100), which had been published in England in 1526, was a medieval throwback. It was no more than an English translation of a very bad French book, *Le grand Herbier*, dressed up with equally hopeless illustrations from a German herbal of the same period. Only in 1564, when the outspoken cleric William Turner (1508–1568) finally completed the last part of his book, *A new herball*, could Britain at last claim to have produced a good book on plants.

Born in Morpeth *c.*1508, Turner went up to Pembroke College, Cambridge, in 1526 and was awarded an MA in 1533. One contemporary describes him as 'very handsome in person and both witty and facetious, and withal a sound and elegant scholar', though another considered him 'very conceited of his own worth, hotheaded, a busy body, and much addicted to the opinions of Luther'. At Cambridge he fell in with a group of reformers who met regularly at the White Horse Inn to argue about religion with the passion of new crusaders. Among them were Nicholas Ridley (*c.*1500–1555), who taught Turner Greek, tennis and archery, and Hugh Latimer (*c.*1485–1555), whose brilliant sermons made Cambridge a pioneering centre of the Reformation in England. The inn soon acquired a local nickname – Little Germany – because of the staunchly pro-Lutheran views of the group that met there. Like Latimer, Turner believed passionately in justice, reason and the Church's duty to defend the oppressed. Like Latimer he argued furiously against the superstition and nepotism of the Catholic Church. Turner was scarcely ten years old when Martin Luther posted his famous *Ninety-five Theses* on the door of the Palace Church in Wittenburg. But Luther's disgust at the sale of indulgences later fuelled an equally strong loathing in Turner for the corruption that was endemic in the Church in England. Cardinal Wolsey managed to get his son four archdeaconries, a deanery, five prebends and two rectories, and was only brought to a halt when he tried to secure for him the bishopric in Durham.

Little is known about Turner's Northumbrian background, but his life's work, the *Herball* is stitched through with references to the plants that grew there and the local names by which they were known. 'I never saw any plaine tree in Englande saving one in Northumberlande besyde Morpeth,' he writes, 'and an other at Barnwel Abbey besyde Cambryge.' Speaking of wild hyacinth, 'called in Englishe crowtoes and in the North partes Crawtees', he remembers how 'the boyes in Northumberlande scrape the roote of the herbe and glew theyr arrowes and bokes

254

The grete herball

Ꮃhiche geueth parfyt knowlege and vnder
standyng of all maner of herbes & there gracyous vertues whiche god hath
ordeyned for our prosperous welfare and helth, for they hele & cure all maner
of dyseases and sekenesses that fall or mysfortune to all maner of creatoures
of god created/practysed by many expert and wyse maysters/as Auicenna &
other.&c. Also it geueth full parfyte vnderstandynge of the booke lately pryn
tyd by me (Peter treueris)named the noble experiens of the vertuous hand
warke of surgery.

Plate 100: The grete herball, *published in England in 1526, was not
an original work. It had been translated from a hopeless French herbal,*
Le grand Herbier, *and was decorated with unhelpful pictures taken
from a German herbal of the same period*

wyth that slyme that they scrape of'.[3] But by the time the first part of the *Herball* was published, Turner could draw on a much wider field of reference than Northumbria and Cambridgeshire, for in 1540, unable to preach the doctrines he so passionately believed in, he fled to Calais and did not return to England until the death of Henry VIII in 1547.

During that long exile, sustained by generous gifts from Ridley, he wanders through France into Italy, where he studies under Luca Ghini at Bologna. He goes to Cremona, Como, Milan, and Venice, where he later writes of seeing tamarisk 'in an yland betwene Francolino and Venish'. From Venice he proceeds to Ferrara, where he studies with Antonio Musa Brasavola 'som tyme my master in Ferraria'. Working his way back through Switzerland, Turner visits the young Conrad Gesner, whom he describes as 'a man most learned as most truthful'. In 1543, Turner is in Basel, a safe haven from which to launch religious tracts such as *The huntying & fynding out of the Romyshe fox* that he had been unable to publish in England. In the year that Mattioli brings out his *Commentarii*, Turner is in Cologne. There he practises medicine before moving on into Holland and East Friesland where he is appointed personal physician to 'the Erle of Emden'. He stays four years in East Friesland, where he 'bought two whole Porpesses and dissected them'. He dispenses bistort and feverfew to excellent effect but has a disastrous experience with opium: 'I wasshed an achying tooth with a little opio mixed with water, and a little of the same unawares went down, within an hour after my handes began to swell about the wrestes, and to itch, and my breth was so stopped, that if I had not taken in a pece of the roote of masterwurt . . . with wyne, I thynck that it wold have kylled me.' After the East Friesland adventure, he collects plants in Louvain and visits Pieter Coudenberg's famous apothecary shop at the sign of the Old Bell in the Burgerhout at Antwerp. Writing later to Gesner, Coudenberg says, 'I gave a sprig of Roman Wormwood formerly to William Turner who inserted its picture in his English Herbal: but then the plant died for me without seed, nor could I for all my care recover it.'[4] Moving on from Antwerp, where he first saw papyrus used as wrapping around loaves of sugar, Turner makes a diversion in order to see the pelican at Malines – a famous attraction of the age – and sends plants from Brabant to John Rich and Hugh Morgan, both apothecaries (and keen plantsmen) in the City of London. By the time he returned to England, by way of Dunkirk, he could boast (though he didn't) that no other Englishman had seen so many different plants growing in so many different places. His capacity to assimilate and remember the details of a plant's leaf, its stem or flower, his absorbed interest in the complex business of attaching the right names to the right species, his tireless ability to weave ever more complex links between scholars working in different languages, in different countries, but on

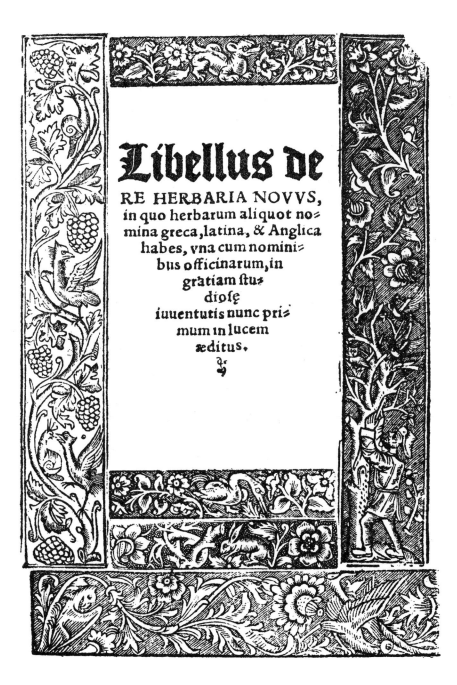

Libellus de

RE HERBARIA NOVVS,
in quo herbarum aliquot no=
mina greca, latina, & Anglica
habes, vna cum nomini=
bus officinarum, in
gratiam stu=
diosę
iuuentutis nunc pri=
mum in lucem
æditus.

Plate 101: The title page of William Turner's Libellus,
printed by John Bydell in 1538

similar casts of characters, made him a formidable confederate in an age that was full of extraordinary plantsmen. Ghini, Fuchs, Rondelet, Turner, Anguillara, Cordus, Gesner, Belon, Dodoens, Cesalpino, Aldrovandi, Clusius, Camerarius, Pena, Lobelius and Jean Bauhin were all born in the first forty years of the sixteenth century. Of course, their particular interest was not predestined. But the study of plants was the dominant preoccupation of the age. If you had a good mind, this is what you applied it to, in the same way that, in later ages, the best scientific minds turned to mathematics, nuclear physics and the search for DNA.

Turner complained that while he had been at Cambridge, he 'could learne never one Greke, nether Latin, nor English name, even amongest the Phisiciones of any herbe or tre, suche was the ignorance in simples at that tyme'.[5] The only English book available (*The grete herball* of 1526) was 'full of unlearned cacographees and falselye naminge of herbes'. Two years before his sudden departure from England, while he was still only thirty years old, he had published a little glossary of plant names, the *Libellus de re herbaria* (1538) which listed 144 plants with synonyms in Latin, Greek and English (see plate 101). 'You will wonder, perhaps to the verge of astonishment,' he wrote in his Preface, 'what has driven me, still a beardless youth, and but slightly infected with knowledge of medicine, to publish a book on herbary.' But, since nobody else in England seemed to want to take on the task, he thought it best to 'try something difficult of this sort rather than let young students who hardly know the names of three plants correctly to go on in their blindness'. It was the only book Turner wrote in Latin, a modest beginning, a first attempt to untangle the tangled skein of names by which the same plant was known in different languages: 'ATRIPLEX. Atriplex grece atraphaxis dicitur, anglice Areche aut red oreche. Atriplex hispaniensis quibusdam videtur nostra esse spinachia.' It was the trial run for *The names of herbes* (see plate 102), which came out very soon after his return to England. This book includes nearly three times as many plants as the *Libellus*, but its prime purpose is still to match the various names by which the same plant was known in different countries in Europe. This time, Turner is able to incorporate German and French names alongside the Latin and English ones: 'ATRIPLEX. Atriplex called in Greke atraphaxys, or Chrysolachano, in English Orech or Orege, in Duche [German] Milten, in Frenche arroches, is moyste in the seconde degree and colde in the fyrste, it groweth in gardines & in some Cornefieldes'. In *Names*, Turner also includes thirty-eight plants (among them alchemilla and foxglove) 'whereof is no mention in any olde auncient wryter'. Familiar flowers had always had common names, but these of course varied, not only from country to country, but also from county to county. Often the same common name was used for different plants that had no natural relationship.

Plate 102: The title page of William Turner's The names of herbes, *which gathered together plant names in Greek, Latin, English, German and French. It was published in 1548*

Turner had a natural aptitude for and interest in the identification of plants and their proper naming. If this was not instigated, it was at the very least massively encouraged by Ghini, who is constantly credited in Turner's final work, the *Herball*, as 'Lucas Gynus the reader [lecturer] of Dioscorides, in Bonony my maister'. There are references too to the trees and shrubs that Turner has seen on 'Mount Appenine besyde Bonony', including colutea, cyclamen and the *Rhus* which the Italians used to tan their leather. While he was in Italy he had been up the Po river as far as Milan where he saw 'Ryse growing in plenty.' On the road from Chertosa to Pavia he saw wonderful hops 'growyng wylde a litle from the wall that goeth . . . by a little rivers syde'. At Chiavenna he had found monkshood growing 'in great plentie upon the alpes'. From Chiavenna he had crossed into Switzerland and proceeded via Chur to Zurich and the company of Conrad Gesner. The two plantsmen remained faithful correspondents. Turner sent Gesner onions. Gesner sent Turner seed of rue. But there was still so much that was not known or understood. Turner lived in an age that believed in the existence of the phoenix, that considered a bat to be a bird. Even observers as careful as he was accepted that storks hibernated underwater on the beds of rivers. In that respect, little had changed since the thirteenth century. 'Cocks have a very liquid brain,' Alexander Neckham had written then in *De naturis rerum*. 'In their brain there are certain bones in the top of it, very insecurely joined together. A gross vapour rising from the liquor comes out through the cracks, and because it is gross it is enclosed in the upper part of the head and forms the comb.' In the sixteenth century it was commonly believed that gnats were generated from the dew on leaves, and that caterpillars simply appeared on cabbages. In an age that knew nothing of pollination, or metamorphosis, or migration, spontaneous generation seemed to be a reasonable explanation of nature's mysteries, the only one that their processes of deduction could lead to.

And yet this same man, who accepted that birds could hatch from barnacles and that rye could suddenly turn into cornflowers, also produced brilliantly pertinent reports of plants, some of which had never been described before. Writing of the strange, parasitic plant broomrape, he observes that it has 'a little stalke, somethynge red, aboute twoo spannes longe, sometyme more, rough, tendre, without leves: the floure is somewhat whyte, turnynge towarde yellow . . . I have marked my selfe, that thys herbe groweth muche aboute the rootes of broome, whyche it claspeth aboute wyth certayne lytle rootes on every syde, lyke a dogge holdying a bone in his mouth: notwythstandying I have not seen any broome choked wyth thys herbe: how be it I have seen the herbe called the thre leved grass or claver utterly strangled, al the naturall juice clene drawen oute by thys herbe.'[6] A twentieth-century field guide can scarcely do better: 'Common broomrape *Orobanche minor* neither seeds nor has any green colouring as it obtains its nourishment by parasitising the roots of other plants; it gets its name from a large but now uncommon species that thus "rapes" Broom. Common broomrape may be purplish, reddish or yellowish and parasitises pea flowers or composites; it flowers June–September in grassy places.[7]

Turner had hoped that his return to England would mark the beginning of a more settled life, with plenty of time to devote to his major work, the *Herball* (see plate 103). As the 1548 *Names* had built on the 1538 *Libellus*, so the *Herball* would build on the work that Turner had already gathered in *Names*. He accepted the position of physician in the household of Edward Seymour, Duke of Somerset, and took a house that belonged to the Duke at Kew. From here he made forays into the country, noting the camomile that grew 'viii myle above London in the wylde felde, in Rychmonde grene, in Brantfurde grene and in mooste plenty of al, in Hunsley [Hounslow] hethe'. But his new position kept him busier than he wished. 'For these thre yeares and a halfe,' he complains, 'I have had no more lyberty but bare iii wekes to bestow upon the sekyng of herbes, and markyng in what places they do grow.' Those three weeks were spent in the West Country, 'which I never sawe yet in al my lyfe, which countrey of al places of England, as I heare say, is moste richely replenished wyth al kindes of straunge and wonderfull workes & giftes of nature'. Many plants grew there that were not to be found anywhere else in Britain. On the Isle of Purbeck in Dorset, he mentions seeing the wild gladdon, 'a litle flour delice growing wylde'. The murky purple iris grows there still, in damp places along the hedges. He also noted a little periwinkle growing wild in the West Country and attempted the notoriously difficult task of distinguishing between the many kinds of fern that flourished there. Blechnum, the hard fern, he had seen 'oft both in Germany and in diverse places of Somerset shyre and Dorset shyre. It is muche longer than ceterach and the gappes that go between the teth, if a man may call them so, are much wyder then the cuttes that are in ceterach. And the teth are much longer and sharper'. He saw paeonies – 'the farest that ever I saw was in Newberri in a rych clothier's garden' – and talks too of 'Middow Saffron' round about Bath and, close to Chard, of finding the little orchid called autumn lady's tresses.

Anxiously, Turner tried to get the preferment in the Church of England that he felt he now deserved. In June 1549, he writes to Robert Cecil, thanking him 'for your paynes tayken about ye obteyning of my lycence'. His children, he says, 'have bene fed so long with hope that they ar very leane. I wold fayne have them fatter if it were possible.'[8] That begging letter produced the prebendary of Botevant, near York, but it was not enough and in November 1550, Turner was writing again to Cecil asking for permission to 'go into Germany & cary ij [iv] litle horsis wth me,

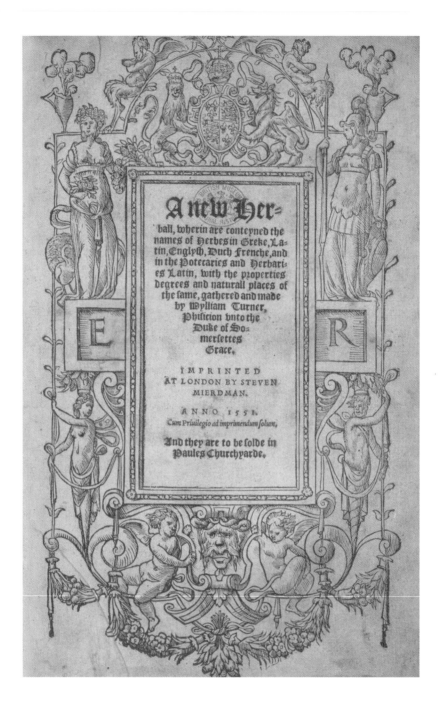

Plate 103: The title page of the first part of A new herball *by William Turner, printed by Steven Mierdman in London in 1551*

to dwell there for a tyme, whereas i may with small coste drynk only rhenishe wyne, & so thereby be delyvered of ye stone [his gallstones], as i was ye last tyme that i dwelt in germany if that i myght have my pore prebende cumyng to me yearly i will for it correct ye hold newe testament in englishe, and wryt a booke of ye causis of my correction & changing of the translation. I will also finishe my great herball & my bookes of fishes, stones & metalles, if god sende me lyfe and helthe.'[9]

Instead, Turner was awarded the deanery of Wells, though he had to go to court to get John Goodman, the previous incumbent, evicted. 'I am dene here in wellis,' he protested, 'but i can nether get house nor one foot of land . . . where i shuld have a dosen closes and medowes for my horses i can not get one.'[10] It's not the dispensation he cares about so much as a 'resting place for me and my pore chylder'; there were now three of these 'chylder': Peter, Winifred and Elizabeth. A year later, in May 1551, he was still 'pened up in a chamber of my lorde of bathes with all my hoholde servantes and children as shepe in a pyndfolde . . . i can not go to my booke for ye crying of childer & noyse that is made in my chamber.'[11]

Despite the noise, the children, the lack of anywhere to lay his books, Turner managed in 1551 to deliver the first part of his *Herball* (Absinthium–Faba) to his London printer, Steven Mierdman. Mierdman was a Fleming and, like Turner, a deeply committed Protestant; he had come to England from Antwerp to escape prosecution for printing heretical books. He must have had links with Fuchs's printer, for Turner's book was illustrated with 169 woodcuts, most of them lifted from Fuchs's *De historia stirpium*, which had come out five years previously. This time Turner wrote, not in Latin, as most of his contemporaries did, but in English. Some, he said in his Dedication 'will thinke it unwisely done, and agaynst the honor of my art that I professe, and agaynst the common profit, to set out so muche knowledge of Physick in Englyshe, for now (say they) every man . . . nay every old wyfe will presume not without the mordre of many, to practise Physick.' But, he asks in reply, how many physicians and apothecaries could read Pliny in the original? Dioscorides, after all, wrote in Greek for a Greek-speaking public. 'If they gave no occasion of murther, then gyve I none.' In *Names* he had arranged plants in alphabetical order, using the Latin name, *Arthemisia*, *Arum*, as the heading above each description. In the *Herball* the Latin headings are replaced by English names – mugwort, cuckoo pint (see plate 104) – and where Turner does not know an English common name, he provides one. These are often direct translations of the Latin names, so he gives us goat's beard from the Latin 'barba hirci', which 'groweth in the fieldes aboute London plentuously', and hawkweed from the Latin 'hieracium' which 'groweth in Germany about Colon'. Translation wasn't as easy an option as it might seem. The most commonly used dictionary of the period was Cooper's *Thesaurus Linguae Romanae & Britannicae*

Of cockoupynt.

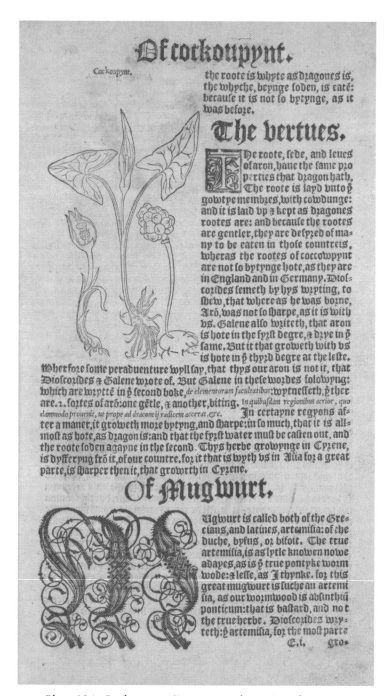

Cockoupynt.

the roote is whyte as dragones is,
the whyche, beynge soden, is eaté:
because it is not so bytynge, as it
was befoze.

The vertues.

The roote, sede, and leues
of aron, haue the same pro
perties that dragon hath.
The roote is layd vnto ꝑ
gowtye membzes, with cowdunge:
and it is laid vp & kept as dragones
rootes are: and because the rootes
are gentler, they are despzed of many to be eaten in those countreis,
wheras the rootes of coccowpynt
are not so bytynge hote, as they are
in England and in Germany. Dioscorides semeth by hys wzyting, to
shew, that where as he was boxne,
Arō, was not so sharpe, as it is with
vs. Galene also wzyteth, that aron
is hote in the fyzst degre, & dzye in ꝑ
same. But it that groweth with vs
is hote in ꝑ thyzd degre at the leste.
Wherfoze some peraduenture wyll say, that thys our aron is not it, that
Dioscozides & Galene wzote of. But Galene in these wozdes folowyng:
which are wzyttē in ꝑ second boke, *de elementorum facultatibus:* wytnesseth, ꝑ ther
are. 2. soztes of arō: one gētle, & another, biting. *In quibusdam regionibus acrior, quo-
dammodo prouenit, ut prope ad dracontij radicem accerat. &c.* In certayne regyons after a maner, it groweth moze bytyng, and sharpe: in so much, that it is all-
most as hote, as dzagon is: and that the fyzst water must be casten out, and
the roote soden agayne in the second. Thys herbe growynge in Cyzene,
is dyfferyng frō it, of our countre, for it that is wyth vs in Asia for a great
parte, is sharper then it, that growrth in Cyzene.

Of Mugwurt.

Mugwurt is called both of the Gre-
cians, and latines, artemisia: of the
duche, byfus, oz bisoit. The true
artemisia, is as lytle knowen nowe
adayes, as is ꝑ true pontyke wozm
wode: & lesse, as I thynke. foz this
great mugwurt is suche an artemi
sia, as our wozmwood is absinthiū
ponticum: that is bastard, and not
the true herbe. Dioscozides wzyteth: ꝑ artemisia, foz the most parte

C.i.   gro-

Plate 104: Cuckoo pint (Arum maculatum) *and mugwort*
(Artemisia vulgaris) *from* A new herball *by William Turner. The
illustration of the arum (reversed here and so most probably pirated)
had originally been prepared for Fuchs's* De historia stirpium

but it listed masses of English equivalents under each Latin term. Nuance was all. If you did not know the plant, it would be all too easy to reach for an entirely inappropriate English phrase. Where direct translation did not produce a sensible name, as with the Latin 'acanthium', Turner chose a tag that described the plant in some way: 'I have not hearde the name of it [acanthium] in englishe,' he writes in *Names*, 'but I thynke it maye be called in englishe otethistle, because the seeds are lyke unto rough otes, or gum thistle, or cotten thistle, because it is gummy and the leaves have in them a thynge lyke cotten, which appeareth when they are broken.' By writing in English, Turner hoped to spread his knowledge to the widest possible public. It was also another way of distancing himself from the Roman Church, with its Latin credos and canticles. As he said, a priest who did not preach in English was like a watchman on the walls of Berwick, the border town in the north of England: when a Scots raiding party surged down from the hills, there would be no point in him shouting 'Veniunt Scotii'; no one would take any notice. But Turner's aim, so in keeping with his fight for a fairer, more equitable society, did not have the effect that he had hoped. Of the three million people living in Britain at the time, perhaps half a million could read. But anyone who could read, read Latin as easily as they read English. And the fact that Turner's most important book was written in English meant that it never found an audience on the Continent, where he had gathered so much of his information on plants. Latin was the universal language.

He was also unlucky in his timing. Edward VI died before Turner had a chance to settle into his living at Wells and concentrate on part two of his great enterprise. In 1553, after only six years on the throne, Edward was succeeded by his Catholic half-sister Mary, so once again, Turner found himself on the wrong side of the religious divide and had to leave England in a hurry. He went back to Germany, a refuge for many English Protestants, and settled first in Weissenburg, where the local apothecary, Jacob Detter, became another vital contact. Mary's accession meant that, for a second time, all Turner's books were banned in England, which diminished still further his chances of finding a wide following. The first ban had been imposed on 8 July 1546 by Henry VIII, who had made it a crime to 'receive, have, take, or kepe . . . any maner of booke printed or written' by Turner and ten other contentious authors.[12] Mary reinforced and widened the scope of the ban with a similar proclamation, issued on 13 June 1555, the year in which Ridley and Latimer, Turner's compatriots at Cambridge, were both burned at the stake. The consequences of disobeying these draconian orders were all too evident, yet an inventory in 1556 of the 302 books belonging to Henry, first Baron of Stafford (1501–63) includes both the *Names* of 1548 and the *Herball* of 1551. From the Continent, Turner continued to publish his uncompromising tracts, denouncing the 'crowish stert uppes' of the new aristocracy, who enclosed commons and closed down hospitals. Still, he fought for a decent education for all, a decent standard of living for parsons and vicars, and an end to the entrenched practice of selling preferments to the highest bidder.

Turner's trenchant views kept him out of the country until Mary's death in 1558. The following year, on 10 September 1559, he preached to a vast and jubilant congregation in St Paul's, the old church, not yet consumed in London's great fire. After another protracted court case, he was at last able to evict the tenacious John Goodman and possess his deanery at Wells. Meanwhile, he settled in London and re-established contact with his apothecary friends, John Rich (*fl.* 1580s–1593) and Hugh Morgan (*fl.* 1540s–1613). Morgan's shop and garden were in Coleman Street, which runs north, parallel with Moorgate, from Lothbury up towards London Wall; he knew more about the plants then coming in from the West Indies than anybody else in London. He made a point of keeping in touch with the sea captains whose vessels came into the Port of London. He was also in regular contact with merchants in Venice, where so many novelties first appeared. Morgan's contacts included fellow apothecaries and pharmacists all over the Continent: Francesco Calzolari and Andrea Bellicocco in Verona; Alberto Martinello and his brother the Syrian doctor Cechino Martinello in Venice; Jacques Raynaudet in Marseilles; Jacques Farges in Montpellier; Valerand Dourez the Fleming in Lille; Wilhelm Driesch and Turner's friend, Pieter Coudenberg in Antwerp. They exchanged letters, often carried by itinerant booksellers, with news of new discoveries, new names, new treatments, but also sent each other seeds and roots of the plants themselves, the raw material of their trade. It was in Hugh Morgan's shop that Turner first saw 'plentye of righte oke miscel [mistletoe]', which had been 'sent to hyme oute of Essex'. Spinach was another novelty, 'an herbe lately found and not long in use'. Turner felt it was a useful addition, though likely to cause stomach ache and wind.

In 1562, the second part of the *Herball* came out, dedicated to the second Baron Wentworth, 'whose father with his yearly exhibition did help me, being student in Cambridge of physic and philosophy'. By this time, Turner had already been back in England for four years, but his work was published not in London but in Cologne. His publisher Mierdman, had, like Turner, been forced to leave England when Mary came to the throne but he had not returned. Here was another piece of bad luck. For reasons completely beyond his control, the printer of the first part of the *Herball* was not able to continue with the rest of it and Turner had no way of knowing when (or even whether) he would be able to come back to England. After being in Weissenburg, Turner had spent the latter part of his second exile based in Cologne, and this is presumably where he had become acquainted with Arnold Birckman who finally published the second part. Birckman, like Mierdman, had access to the illustrations from Fuchs's book, so Turner could continue to use them (see plate 105). But publishing in Germany a book written in English severely compromised its chances of success: few on the Continent could read it; few in England could get hold of it. Undaunted, Turner pressed on with the great work, conscious, as all who tried to produce these encyclopaedic works were, that he could scarcely keep up with the vast amounts of new plants arriving in Europe.

Outspoken as always, defiant of ecclesiastical control, Turner also continued to preach in his old uncompromising way. Bishop Berkely complained in a letter (1563) to William Cecil and Archbishop Parker at Canterbury that he was 'much encombred with Mr Doctor Turner, Deane of Welles, for his indiscrete behaviour in the pulpitt: where he medleth with all matters and unsemelie speaketh of all estates, more than is standinge with discressyon. He contendeth utterly all Bishops and calleth them White Coats, tippet gentlemen, with other words of reproach much more unsemelie and asketh, who gave them authority, more over me than I over them.'[13] The Marprelate Tracts, published in the 1580s by the Puritan underground press, tell how, when the Bishop came to dinner, Turner called up his well trained dog: 'the dog flies at the Bishop and takes off his corner cap – he thought belike it had been cheesecake – and so away goes the dog with it to his master.'[14] Despite efforts to get rid of him, Turner hung on to his deanery, and the third and final part of his *Herball* is dated from Wells, 24 June 1564, four years before his death in London. It was printed, like the previous instalment, by Birckman in Cologne and included many novelties such as nutmeg, 'from an Ilande of Inde called Badon', and cassia, which came from 'the Weste newe found Ilandes, out of Hispaniola'. Hugh Morgan would have kept him informed of the new and unfamiliar things arriving by ship in the Port of London: caraway, cucumber, fenugreek and hemp were among the strange seeds unloaded from the *Cock* which arrived in London via Bruges on 29 April 1568; the cargoes of the time also included exotic goods such as oranges, lemons, almonds, nutmeg and aniseed.[15] Plants that had been dealt with very briefly in the earlier *Names* received longer (though not necessarily kinder) treatment in the *Herball*. Speaking, for instance, of the poisonous oleander, Turner had written in *Names* that 'I never sawe it but in Italy.' In the *Herball* he is more elaborate: 'I have sene thys tre in diverse places of Italy but I care not if it never com into England, seying it in all poyntes is lyke a Pharesey, that is beuteus without, and within, a ravenus wolf and murderer.' On dead nettle, he had been brief in *Names*, giving synonyms, habitat and little else. In the *Herball* he provides a vivid description: 'Lamium hath leaves like unto a Nettel, but lesse indented about, and whyter. The downy thynges that are in it like pryckes, byte not, ye stalk is four-square, the floures are whyte, and have a stronge savor, and are very like unto litle

267

Of Anagyris.

Nagyris groweth not in Englande that I wote of/but I haue sene it in Italye. It may be called in English Beane trifolye/because the leaues growe thre together/and the sede is muche lyke a Beane. Anagyris is a bushe lyke vnto a tree with leues and twigges/like vnto Agnus castus of Italy. But the leaues are greater and shorter/and growe but thre together/where as Agnus hath euer fyue together/and excedinge stinkinge/wherevpon riseth the Prouerb/Præstat hanc Anagyrim nō atrigisse. It hath the floures lyke vnto kole. It hath a fruyt in longe horned coddes/of the lykenes of a kidney/of diuerse coloures/firme and stronge/whiche when the grape is ripe wexeth harde.

The properties of Anagyris.

Plate 105: Anagyris (Anagyris foetida) 'groweth not in Englande that I wote of / but I have sene it in Italye' wrote William Turner in the final edition of A new herball, printed by Arnold Birckman in Cologne (1568)

coules, or hoodes that stand over bare heades. The sede is blak and groweth about the stalk, certayn places goyng betwene, as we se in horehound.' Though he still describes them in terms of the four 'humours' – choleric (hot and dry), melancholic (cold and dry), phlegmatic (cold and moist), sanguine (hot and moist), he includes more uses for the plants he mentions, even if he disapproves of them: some women 'springkle the floures of Cowislip in whyte wine, and after still it and washe their faces with that water to drive wrinkles away, and to make them fayre in the eyes of the worlde rather than in the eyes of God, whom they are not afrayd to offende with the scluttishnes, filthines and foulnes of the soule.'[16] Honeysuckle would cure hiccups, but had to be used sparingly for it could induce impotence. Nutmeg was a useful aphrodisiac 'for cold husbands that would fain have children'. Water lily was the suitable corrective to prescribe for 'wiveles gentlemen or husbandles gentleweomen agaynst the unclene dremyng of venery and filthy polutiones that they have on the nyght. For if it be dronken continually for a certayn tyme it weykeneth much the sede.'[17]

The *Herball* also provided, for the first time, recognisable descriptions of 238 British native plants.[18] Both Turner's religion and his science depended on interpreting words with forensic accuracy. Like Dioscorides, he was extremely good at linking plants with their natural habitats: he noticed, for instance, how water lilies favoured 'standyng waters', that wood sorrel was most often to be found 'in woddes aboute tree rootes and amonge busshes', that absinthium or wormwood 'groweth commonly in diches whereinto the salte water useth at certeyne tymes to come' and that the yellow-horned poppy was most likely to be seen in 'places by the sea syde'. By writing in English Turner had hoped to make his work more easily accessible to an English audience. Mattioli, too, had written in his native tongue, but his book was quickly translated into several other languages and a Latin edition was produced within twenty-one years of the book's publication. Perhaps, though, Turner felt a kind of patriotic pride in abandoning Latin for the vernacular. Certainly, in the Preface to *Names*, he had written that he wished to 'declare to the great honoure of our countre what numbre of sovereine & strang herbes were in Englande that were not in other nations'. Perhaps he was articulating a desire to make the English language a medium fit for scientific discourse. Perhaps he felt that if enough important books were published in English, scholars in other countries would have no option but to learn the language. It happened in the end. But, like the brilliant Cesalpino, though for different reasons, Turner was ahead of his time. Cesalpino was unread because he was so far ahead of his contemporaries in the thinking that underpinned the divisions of his *De plantis*. Turner was unread because he was unlucky in his timing. Produced in a foreign country in a foreign tongue, his books were never translated.

The title *Herball* became associated not with him but with a man of much less intellect, probity or vision, the slippery John Gerard. Throughout his life he worked in difficult circumstances. Even in the Preface to the final part of his *Herball* he complains that 'beyng so much vexed in the sickness and occupied with preaching and the study of Divinity and exercise of discipline, I have had but small leasure to write Herballes'.

No portrait of Turner exists, no plant was named after him, as they were for both Fuchs and Mattioli. But after his death in July 1568, his widow, Jane, the daughter of a Cambridge alderman, put up a memorial to him in his parish church, St Olave's, Hart Street, in the City of London. On a hot summer's day, 436 years later, I make my way through the crowds of commuters spilling out of Fenchurch Street station, with a small bunch of West Country flowers for Turner. Sadly it does not include the thorow-wax he had admired in fields between Somerton and Martock in Somerset; once widespread in the arable land of the West Country, it is now extinct in the wild. Turner's church, just along the street from his house at Crutched Friars, was founded in the eleventh century. The present building, which dates from 1450, is the third one on the site and was badly damaged in the Blitz of April 1941. Miraculously, the memorials inside survived and a board by the church entrance notes the most significant of them: Sir James Deane (1608) merchant adventurer, Samuel Pepys (1669) diarist, Sir Andrew Riccard (1672) chairman of the East India Company . . . There is no mention of William Turner. Inside, Pepys and Riccard face each other across the chancel of the superb small church, both extravagantly commemorated in stone. On the south wall is the brightly painted bust of Peter Capponi, an exiled Florentine 'of ancient lineage', who died of the plague in 1582. Unexpectedly, someone is playing a Schubert sonata. Tiptoeing round the grand piano set in front of the altar, I finally find Turner, completely overshadowed by Deane, the merchant adventurer, who has a huge showy memorial. As befits a man who railed against the extravagant vestments of sixteenth-century clerics and taught his dog to snatch the caps from the heads of visiting bishops, Turner's memorial is a very plain, small rectangle of creamy marble, bordered in black, like a Victorian mourning card. In densely lettered Latin, the inscription stresses Turner's piety, and marks how he 'fought against the enemies of the Church and the Commonwealth, chiefly the Roman Antichrist'. There is no mention of his *Names* or his *Herball*, the first original works on plants ever written by an Englishman.

Unlucky Turner. Too soon after he finally found himself in the right place at the right time, he died. And, like so many pioneers, he died before the worth of what he was doing was recognised. His patient synthesising of plant names – Greek, Latin, English, French, German, Italian – banished much of the confusion that was bound to exist when common names were the only common currency. By way of his extensive travels, he set England on the intellectual map of Europe. The intellectual isolation that had marked the few English plantsmen of the first half of the sixteenth century had completely vanished by the second half. After Turner's death, England became a magnet for anyone interested in the study of plants. In 1540, Turner had fled to the Continent to escape Catholic persecution. Thirty years later, and for the same reason, the Flemish scholar, Matthias de l'Obel (Lobelius) came in the opposite direction and, in terms of plantsmanship, found a country very different from the one Turner had been forced to leave. Turner laid the foundation for the pre-eminence of this later generation of English plantsmen: John Goodyer, John Parkinson, John Ray. He was the vital link between the early scholar-botanists and the later generation of more practical, experimental gardeners, many of whom were based in London. But as is the way with foundations, Turner's were, all too soon, buried and forgotten. His name ought to be on that board at St Olave's.

XVII

PROTESTANTS PREVAIL

1530–1580

TURNER'S EXILE IN Europe at various times in the sixteenth century was typical of the disruption and turmoil inevitable then in the lives of those with strong views on religion. In the first half of the century, Turner, an English Protestant, had fled to the relative safety of Germany and the Netherlands. Later, Flemish Huguenots, harried by Philip II of Spain and his Catholic armies, came the other way, escaping across the Channel to an England that once again had a Protestant on the throne. Only in comfortable retrospect can we see gain as well as adversity in this ebb and flow of populations, forced for the sake of their beliefs to abandon known lands and landscapes and face the unknown. But new ideas travelled with these exiles; that was the benefit. New contacts were established between scholars in new cities. At Basel, the intellectual life of the university was hugely enriched by an influx of scholarly Protestant refugees, driven out of Italy and France. Massacres and martyrdoms strengthened bonds between Protestants. Though indirect, the Reformation had a palpable impact on the study of *res herbaria* because it forced scholars to live different lives in different landscapes, surrounded by different plants. Until the Reformation, universities had paid little attention to the natural world; it was acknowledged that peasants probably knew more about plants than professors. But Luther himself urged his followers to consider the beauty, the intricacy, the evidence of God's concern, in even such minute confections as a peach stone. Gradually, reforms were initiated that introduced a close study of plants into faculties of medicine. It happened at the new Protestant university of Tübingen under

Leonhart Fuchs, who fought hard to change the antiquated syllabus. At the equally new Lutheran university at Marburg, Fuchs's near contemporary, Euricius Cordus (1486–1535) published a reforming *Botanologicon* (1534), prompted by his concern that the ingredients stored away in the jars and packets of the apothecaries' shops were often wrongly labelled. The sick and injured could be given useless (or worse, dangerous) medicines made up from the wrong ingredients. Cordus attempted to show (as others had tried to do) that the plants described by the Greek army doctor, Dioscorides, were not necessarily the same plants as grew in the cooler climates of Germany, France and the Netherlands. Dioscorides, armoured in infallibility, proved difficult to dislodge from his pedestal. But during the late fifteenth and early sixteenth century, the shift slowly came about; Cordus's reforming zeal was just one of the landmarks in that gradual journey towards seeing the natural world clear and plain and ordering it in a rational way.

Protestant reformers insisted on the equality of all men in the eyes of God. All, however humble, were potentially worthy of salvation. Similarly, the new wave of Reformed scholars – Carolus Clusius in France, Euricius Cordus and his son Valerius in Germany, Conrad Gesner and the Bauhin brothers, Jean and Gaspard, in Switzerland, William Turner in England – thought all plants equally worthy of attention. So-called 'weeds' were now described with as much care as the plants known to be useful in medicine. Fortunately, differences in faith did not stop scholars in Northern Europe corresponding with those in Italy. But scholars studying the natural world tended to become reformers in spirit, even if they could not publicly acknowledge the shift. Andrea Cesalpino at Pisa and Ulysse Aldrovandi, who founded the botanic garden at Padua, were both suspected of heresy by the Catholic Church. In the sixteenth century, the University of Padua was teeming with Averroists, followers of the Arab philosopher and physician, Averroes (1126–88), who had attempted to reconcile Arisotelian philosophy with Islam. The doctrine was particularly attractive to those who studied medicine.

In France, the divide between Catholic and Protestant institutions was more overtly laid down. Refused entry to the university in Paris, Protestants, particularly Huguenots, made their way south and enrolled instead at Montpellier in the Languedoc (see plate 106). Whereas in Paris students learned medicine almost entirely from books, the courses at Montpellier had a more practical basis. The medical school there had first received a charter and the right to confer degrees in 1220, though its origins were even earlier.[1] By the middle of the fourteenth century, a syllabus was laid down with twenty set texts, including Avicenna, Galen and Hippocrates. Later, a new statute at Montpellier decreed that half the money collected from student fees was to be spent on books for the library. And any student who would not give the customary

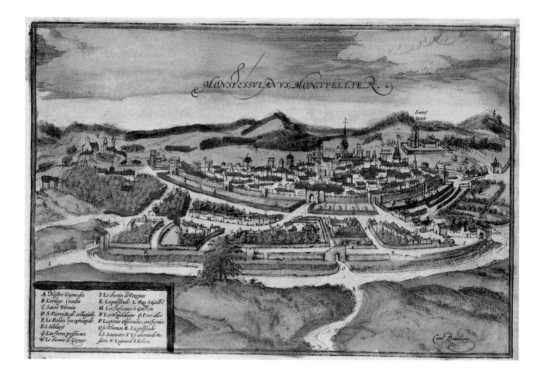

feast to celebrate the start of his course had to give a handsome donation to the library instead.[2]

In 1530, the student proctor there was Guillaume Rondelet (1507–1566) (see plate 107), the son of a local spice merchant or *aromatarius*.[3] Rondelet had spent four years studying the liberal arts in Paris before enrolling in Montpellier's medical school. He practised as a doctor first in the Auvergne, then back in his home town. Like Euricius Cordus, Rondelet was disturbed by the hazards his patients faced when the medicines he prescribed were made up by pharmacists with the wrong ingredients. Even such a popular remedy as syrup of chicory invited disaster. The syrup was prescribed for obstructions or chills of the liver and a typical recipe would include ingredients such as *taraxicon*, *cicerbita*, *endivia* and *scariola*, all of them derived from the plants that pharmacists knew by those names. But the names being in such a muddle, *endivia* itself was sometimes called *scariola*, or *intybus domesticus*. So if they meant the same thing, why did the recipe call for both *endivia* and *scariola*? And if they didn't, what should the pharmacist use instead? And was *cicerbita* perhaps a misprint for *cucurbita*, a kind of cucumber? Or was it really *cicerbita*, called *sonchus* by the ancient Greek authors, pig-snout by the peasants. Unfortunately, though, there were two kinds of *sonchus*, hard and soft . . . It was hardly surprising that French pharmacists killed several of Rondelet's patients by substituting, not always knowingly, the wrong ingredients in his prescriptions: *cucurbita* for *cicerbita* (the handwriting not being plain), *polypodium* for *dryopteris* (they were, after all, both ferns).

Rondelet did not make a success of his medical practice in Montpellier. He was hopeless with money, and caused an uproar in the town when he dissected the body of his baby son to try to find out why he had died. The scandal, however, did not prevent him joining the medical faculty in Montpellier as a teacher in 1539, just a few years before plague broke out in the town. By 1543, only three students were left in the university's medical faculty and the law faculty had moved out entirely. Rondelet also decided to leave Montpellier and took up a post as private physician in the entourage of a powerful cardinal, François de Tournon. While travelling with the Cardinal, Rondelet visited the Italian universities, exchanging information with Luca Ghini, then newly installed at Pisa, with Antonio Musa Brasavola at Ferrara, Ulysse Aldrovandi at Padua and with Cesare Odo, who had taken over from Ghini as lecturer on 'simples' at Bologna.

When he resumed his duties at Montpellier, it was as holder of one of the four lucrative and influential regencies first established at the university by Louis XII. Well travelled, well read, well connected, he attracted some of the most talented students of the time, all devoted, as he was, to the proper study of plants. It was as

Plate 107: Guillaume Rondelet (1507–1566) who gathered around him a clutch of brilliant students in the medical faculty at the university of Montpellier. This portrait appeared as a miniature in his Livre des Poissons *(1554)*

glittering a bunch as Ghini gathered about him at Pisa. The young Swiss scholar Conrad Gesner stayed briefly in 1540, but, unable to find suitable lodgings, moved on to Basel. In the early 1550s Rondelet taught Carolus Clusius (Charles de l'Écluse), who went on to become the first director of the new botanic garden at Leiden. Jean, the elder of the two Bauhin brothers, came to Montpellier in 1561, after studying at Tübingen under the splenetic Fuchs.

In 1552, the eminent scientist Felix Platter, then just fifteen years old, rode his pony all the way from Basel to Montpellier to begin a six-year course of study under Rondelet's guidance. In his letters to his father, which he later published as a journal, Felix Platter (see plate 108) leaves a vivid picture of day to day life at the university under Guillaume Rondelet's regency.[4] Like Rondelet, Platter was a Protestant, but unlike him, he took care to keep his religious principles to himself. Already by 1528, a Montpellier student, Stephanus de Templo, had been prosecuted by the Inquisitor of the Faith in Toulouse 'for the crime of the Lutheran heresy'. Elections to the regencies, overseen by Guillaume Pellicier, Bishop of Montpellier, became a focal point for religious divisions in the university. Fortunately Pellicier and Rondelet shared a passion for plants that overrode their ostensible differences of religion. In his *Life* (1599), Rondelet's student, Joubert, reinforced the generally held opinion that Rondelet hated violence. 'Even when he travelled, he never carried so much as a dagger.'[5] When his friend Pellicier was imprisoned, Rondelet burned all his theology books in a despairing protest. But as the reformers gained ground in the university, statutes were brought in that improved the way the faculties operated. Students had complained that their professors kept leaving town to attend to their rich private patients. Now lectures had to start promptly at the feast of St Luke (late September or early October) and continue uninterrupted until Easter. Lecturers were forbidden to charge for lectures given privately in their homes, nor could they make students pay for accompanying them on visits to patients or apothecaries' shops. The new statutes emphasised the practical side of the students' studies in medicine. During the summer months, one of the lecturers had to search for 'simples' in the city of Montpellier and its surroundings, and then 'demonstrate' them to the students.

As a newcomer in 1552, Felix Platter benefitted immediately from these rules and innovations. His father, a schoolmaster and printer in Basel, had borrowed the money to send his son to Montpellier and to buy the pony that carried him there. Felix leaves home on 10 October, his father having 'wrapped up two shirts and some handkerchiefs in a waxed cloth for me'. At Fribourg, Platter writes, 'we began to eat and to sleep in the French fashion', and by the twentieth of the month, he and his travelling companion are close to Lyons where he sees 'several men hanging from gibbets and others exposed on wheels . . . As we entered the town we met a Christian

Plate 108: Felix Platter (1536–1614) in a portrait painted by Hans Bock the Elder in 1584. In a series of letters to his father Platter left a vivid account of his years as a medical student at the university of Montpellier

who was being led out to be burnt outside the gate; he was in his shirt with a truss of straw fastened on his back'. After fording the Rhone in flood, Platter comes to Pierrelatte, where he tastes his first olives, finding them 'nasty and sour'. By the time he reaches Orange, he is 'miserable and dejected . . . I felt such a desire to return home that I went to the stable to my little horse and threw my arms round its neck and burst into tears.' The whole journey from Basel to Montpellier, he reckoned to be ninety-five German miles (roughly four times as long as an English mile). It took Platter twenty days and, what with stabling and fodder for his pony, tips, lodgings and tolls across the rivers, cost him more than ten livres.

At Montpellier, he lodges in a house on the Place des Cévenols belonging to Laurent Catalan, the town pharmacist.[6] Platter writes to tell his father of his safe arrival, adding that 'large numbers of Bibles and other religious books that our people had had printed and which had been found at a bookseller's, had been burned publicly in the street'. He enrols at the medical faculty and makes 'arrangements for a course of serious study' in the building which is still a school of pharmacy today.[7] On 6 November he goes with some German companions to Villeneuve where he is 'very surprised to see rosemary growing in the fields as freely as juniper does with us. There were marjoram and thyme as well, filling the fields, and so common that no one pays any attention to them. Rosemary is used for heating, there is so much of it. It is carried into the town on the backs of donkeys, and burned in the hearths.'

His favourite place to read and study in M. Catalan's house, he recalled later, was 'a fine terrace, or platform, reached by a stone stair. It commanded the whole town, and one could see as far as the sea, the sound of which could be heard when the wind was in the right quarter. I grew an Indian fig-tree there in a vase.' At Lent he discovers that 'meat and eggs are forbidden under pain of death', but tells his father 'we Germans did not stop eating them. I learned how to cook eggs in butter on a piece of paper held over live charcoal. I did not dare use any utensil for this purpose.' Throughout Lent Platter hides the eggshells in his study, but as the heap gets bigger, they are discovered by a servant who reports the matter to Madame Catalan. She is 'very annoyed' but fortunately does not take the matter any further. The Catalans were Marans, Christian Jews. Platter celebrates Pentecost with a new pair of breeches, 'red in colour. They were tight, slashed and lined with taffeta, and pleated so low that I almost sat on the gathers. They were so tight that I could scarcely bend'. On 23 May he gathers pomegranate blossom outside the walls of the town, and without a change in pace or style, tells his father about five martyrs burned at the stake, 'who had studied at Lausanne, and who on their return had been arrested, thrown into prison, and condemned to the fire'.

On 25 July, Platter and some friends go to Grammont to collect plants. There is a little monastery there, in the middle of a copse of evergreen oaks, and it is one of the best places he knows to find wild flowers. His father is delighted to hear that his son is spending so much time assiduously seeking out plants and herbs ('in scrutandis simplicibus et stirpium inquisitione'), but warns him, in such dangerous times, to choose his companions carefully. On St Bartholomew's day, 24 August, a huge onion market is held in Montpellier. 'The onions are bound into strings with straw', Platter explains to his father, 'stacked up like so many faggots, in piles two feet high. The whole square is covered with them, and only narrow passages are left for people to walk about. The onions are of all kinds, some very large and others white and sweet, but none of them are as strong as ours are.'

The university term started again on St Luke's day, 18 October. The professors had given up teaching during the summer, except, said Platter, 'for a few who had conducted private courses for extra fees'. On 6 November 1553, he sends a quantity of fruit and seeds to his father in Basel, together with the news that the Turkish fleet has arrived off Aigues Mortes. 'We perceived it plainly at sea.' In the New Year, there are more grim executions: Guillaume Dalençon, an unfrocked priest, and a local cloth-shearer who refused to recant. Like Dalençon, the cloth-shearer was to be burned at the stake, but as Platter writes to his father, 'It had rained on that day, and the fire would not burn. The victim, who was not completely strangled, endured great suffering. At last the monks of the neighbouring monastery brought some straw, and the executioner took it and sent for oil of terebinth from my master's pharmacy to ignite the fire. Afterwards, I reproached the assistants who had given it to him, but they advised me to hold my tongue, for the same fate could befall me also, as a heretic.'

For six years the Platter letters make their laborious way backwards and forwards from Basel to Montpellier, sometimes taking as much as three months in passage. The father's are anxious, exhortatory, urging his son to yet more study, pointing out repeatedly that there are already seventeen doctors in Basel and reminding him of the difficulty of his ever finding a niche among them. The son's letters are full of serenades, drinking, dancing. He asks for more lute strings to be sent (he is teaching the lute to Rondelet's daughter, Catherine). He encloses for his father Dr Saporta's prescription for strengthening the memory. These quotidian events are set against a continuing backdrop of terror and religious persecution: on 23 March 1554, 'a commissioner came from Toulouse, and in company with the bailly searched the town for Lutherans. At that time all reformed Christians were called by this name, and the names of Calvinist and Huguenot were unknown. It was cried throughout the town, to the sound of a trumpet, that all who knew of any must denounce them, or be themselves severely punished.'

Towards Christmas Platter sends a box of curiosities to his father:

> two langoustes without claws, and an enormous crab, as big as a plate, and quite dried up. There was also a leaf of the Indian fig, for my father to plant; it came from the one that I grew in a vase on the roof, and which had flourished and put out several leaves. One of these plants in my master's garden had become a real tree, with several branches, and produced fruit; nevertheless it had grown from a single leaf from Italy. Further, I included a quantity of shells, as well as ninety-five large pomegranates, some sweet and some acid, which I had bought in the market . . . also sixty-three beautiful oranges, a basket of dried grapes, and some figs . . . Finally there was a large pot of compounded mithridate and a small skeleton and a letter.

Platter collects plants, and arranges them 'properly on paper', amassing what his father called a vast 'domestic thesaurus'. Perhaps Rondelet had learned the technique from Luca Ghini at Pisa and now, in turn, passed it on to his own students. Platter has a suit made from two skins, tinted green, sent by his father, recalling later how he 'paraded in it at the ball, and aroused the admiration of every man, for leather breeches were then quite unknown in that country. The tailor had made them a little tight, claiming that he had not had enough leather, but I found afterwards that he had robbed me of a good-sized piece and had made a bag out of it for his wife.' In November 1556, Platter and his fellow students complain that the professors are not giving them the statutory number of lectures. 'We went to the parliament house. We elected a spokesman and he made a complaint in our name against the negligence shown by the professors, and demanded our ancient right to have two proctors authorised to withhold the salaries of professors who did not fulfil their duties as they should.' Their claims are admitted and peace returns to the medical faculty.

On 27 February 1557, Felix Platter leaves Montpellier for ever and returns home by way of Narbonne, Poitiers, Orléans and Paris, where he stays for more than a month. From Paris, he goes on to Dijon and Montbeliard before sighting at last the two familiar towers of the cathedral at Basel (see page 109). The whole street celebrates his safe return. Despite his father's anxieties, Platter establishes himself as an extremely successful physician in his home town and is appointed professor of practical medicine at the university. He builds a big house 'most painted and ornate, with arabesques in the French style'. In the garden are many rare plants, including the Indian fig which he had first cultivated as a cutting on the roof of his master's

BASILEA Basell.

M. D. I.

*Plate 109: Basel, Felix Platter's home town, in a map that
appeared in Bauer and Hogenbergius's sixteenth century
compendium 'All Cities of the World', printed in Cologne c.1550*

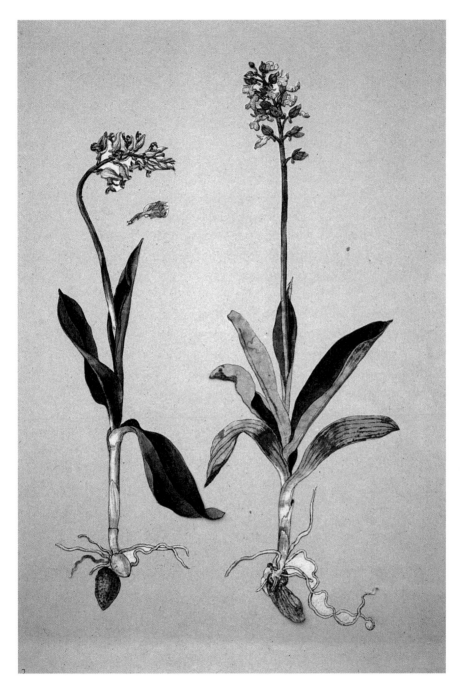

Plate 110: Purple and military orchids from Felix Platter's herbarium in which, alongside pressed and dried specimens of plants, he stuck images cut out from the drawings that Hans Weiditz had prepared for Brunfels's Herbarum vivae eicones

house in Montpellier. A collection of exotic animals, including a wild ass and a marmot, are housed in the stables and in the house Platter amasses a famous collection of curiosities. The French essayist, Michel Montaigne (1533–1592) was one of the many travellers who made their way to Platter's private museum, and in 1580 noted that 'Amongst his other work he was preparing a book of simples . . . and it was his practice, instead of painting like other botanists the plants according to their natural colours, to glue the same upon paper with so great care and dexterity that the smallest leaves and fibres should be visible, exactly as in nature . . . he showed us certain simples which had been fastened therein more than twenty years ago.'[8]

By a curious trick of fate, Platter's treasures included the exquisite illustrations of plants that Hans Weiditz had originally made for Brunfels's *Herbarum vivae eicones*. Nearly 500 years on, we value these not only for their beauty, but also for their iconic significance as the first body of work in Western Europe that showed plants in their true guise. Platter was more pragmatic. In the *hortus siccus* that Montaigne describes, he arranged Weiditz's drawings opposite the pressed and dried flowers that they represented. But Weiditz's original drawings had been done on both sides of his sheets of paper. In order to use as many images as possible, Platter cut out each drawing (see plate 110), pasted it in his book and then retouched the bits that were missing. Looking at the cannibalised results, now in the Felix Platter Herbarium at the University of Bern, I can't help wishing he hadn't.

XVIII

GESNER'S MASTERPIECE
1530–1580

THE WEIDITZ ILLUSTRATIONS had been the first important set of plant portraits to be published in Europe. They were followed twelve years later by the drawings that Albrecht Meyer made for Leonhart Fuchs's *De historia stirpium*. A third important body of illustrations emerged in Italy with Giorgio Liberale's bold, decorative images, commissioned by Pier Andrea Mattioli for his *Commentarii*. Now a fourth collection of plant pictures was amassed by Conrad Gesner (see plate 111), the young Swiss scholar. There were nearly 1,500 of these images, some painted by Gesner himself, some by an artist he employed, all surrounded with scratchy annotations, constantly updated, with information about the plant's source, its colour and natural habitat. He intended the pictures for a massive *Historia plantarum*, to follow on from the equally monumental *Historia animalium* which he had published with 1,200 woodcuts in four folio volumes between 1551 and 1558.[1] The plant book was never published and Gesner's drawings passed from hand to hand, until in the eighteenth century, they were acquired by Dr Trew, the city physician of Nuremberg, who in turn gave them to Casimir Schmiedel, the professor of botany at Erlangen, Bavaria. There, at the university founded in 1743, they were quietly forgotten until by chance they emerged from the attic of the university's library. More than 400 years after Gesner's death, the drawings, acutely observed, finely executed, were finally published in their entirety.[2]

Gesner's non-book is the greatest might-have-been in the whole of this story, its non-appearance even more to be regretted than Luca Ghini's silence (or indeed

285

D. CONRADUS GESNERUS.

ARCHIATRUS TIGURINUS. PROFESSOR PHYSICUS,

Obijt Aº 1565.   Æt. 49.   13. xbr.

Plinius alter eram: per me vis iam liquet omnis
Naturæ, ingenij vi superata mei.

Conrad Meyer fecit.
Aº 1662.

*Plate 111: Conrad Gesner (1516–1565) who died before he
could publish the monumental* Historia plantarum *that
occupied the last ten years of his life. Shown here in an
engraving made in 1662 by Conrad Meyer*

Guillaume Rondelet's; he produced a fine book on fish, but never published anything about plants). Precociously, when he was only twenty-six, Gesner produced a brief *Catalogus plantarum* with plant names in four languages which he hoped might be a useful tool for students on the plant-hunting expeditions recently introduced into the curricula of universities such as Bologna, Pisa, Fuchs's Tübingen and Rondelet's Montpellier. The *Catalogus* did a little more than William Turner's *Libellus* of 1538 and a little less than Turner's *The names of herbes* published ten years later. But though this was Gesner's first publication, his Preface already shows the measure of his soaring mind, his inexhaustible enthusiasm for research, his innate gift for collating and commenting, guided always by the evidence of his own eyes. In the Preface, he seeks to define 'the essence of the infinitely questing spirit', in effect, his own spirit. Gesner had trained as a doctor but he could equally well be called a zoologist, a plantsman, a philologist, a bibliographer, an encyclopaedist or a linguist (he read Latin, Greek and Hebrew, spoke French and German as well as his own Swiss dialect). He was a one-man search engine, a sixteenth-century Google with the added bonus of critical evaluation. He did not just collect facts; he weighed them, came to a view about them and set them on the page with the kind of reasoned judgment that made those who read him, trust him. From the beginning he was a man in love with systems, arrangements, categories, classifications, order, method, patterns, pigeonholes. He loved to sort and file and organise. And though a Protestant himself, he took care not to antagonise those of a different persuasion. When he asked for help, or wanted plants to be sent, his correspondents were happy to help him. He was charitable, compared with Fuchs and Mattioli, both of whom recognised a serious rival in the young Gesner. Both tried to silence him by suggesting they incorporate his work in their own. 'I agree with him and forgive his faults,' Gesner had said of Mattioli. 'He accepts my friendship so long as I don't criticise.'

Three years after the *Catalogus*, Gesner produced a remarkable pandect, a *Bibliotheca universalis*, an alphabetical index of all known authors who had written in Greek, Latin or Hebrew. He dug out obscure works buried in the library of Diego Hurtado de Mendoza in Venice and in the Marciana where Cardinal Besarion (1403–72) had deposited a priceless collection of Greek manuscripts. He checked the Laurenziana catalogues in Florence, the catalogues of the Vatican Library and the church library of San Salvatore in Bologna. He sent for catalogues from printers and booksellers in Germany, Italy and France: Aldus Manutius of Venice, Cratander of Basel, Wechel in Paris. 'Where are the 700,000 books from Ptolemy's library?' he asks rhetorically in his Dedication to the *Bibliotheca*. 'Destroyed by the soldiers at Alexandria.' Another 120,000 had been lost as Byzantium burned, but, crammed into 1,264 folios, Gesner still amassed a list of about 10,000 titles produced by nearly

3,000 authors.[3] His lists were not just simple inventories of content; he commented too on the form and style of the books he was cataloguing. Then, he systematically ordered the titles he had collected into different categories: arithmetic, astrology, astronomy, dialectics, divination, geography, geometry, grammar and philology, history, music, natural philosophy, poetry, rhetoric. Yawn, yawn, you might think. How tedious. Tedious in the extreme. But it wasn't. Systems were desperately needed. Knowledge was increasing at a dizzying rate in this questioning, exploratory age: just two years before Gesner brought out his *Bibliotheca*, the Polish astronomer Copernicus had published his revolutionary thoughts about the solar system; in the same year the Flemish doctor Andreas Vesalius produced his seminal research on human anatomy; news was flooding in about Columbus's New World. This torrent of new information had to be codified in some way before it could be assimilated and slotted into its most useful place. Only when systems had been built could scholars analyse and compare the information they contained.

If Gesner had only put plants before animals, his method would have immeasurably enriched the process of understanding and ordering the great pantheon of European plants. But perhaps he wanted to follow the example of Aristotle, the only other person who had ever attempted such an encyclopaedic work. Eighteen hundred years previously, Aristotle had addressed the animal kingdom first, leaving the world of plants to his pupil, Theophrastus. Gesner started serious work on his plant book only in the last ten years of his life. But reports of new plants poured in at a rate that threatened to overwhelm a man such as himself, pursuing single-handed the goals of universal knowledge, encyclopaedic understanding of the natural world. On 13 December 1565, aged only forty-nine, Gesner died in the plague that swept through Zurich in the 1560s. 'Toward the middle of the night of the fifth day of the progress of the disease, he asked to be helped from his sleeping apartment to his work room and study. That same day he had caused a couch to be placed there, and, conducted to it, within a few moments, Gesner expired.'[4] His great work on plants was unfinished. No gravestone marks his burial place in the cloister of the Zurich Grossmünster; no plaque records his name.

What drove this extraordinary man? The Protestant ethic? Poverty? Perhaps a little of these, but most of all it was that 'infinitely questing spirit' he had written of in the Preface to his first book. His father, a furrier, had been a poor man who died fighting for the Protestants in the civil war that broke out in the early sixteenth century between the Protestant and Catholic cantons of Switzerland. The young Gesner was educated by his uncle, Johannes Frich, a canon who had a small garden of interesting plants. Later, the city fathers of Zurich sent Gesner to Paris to broaden his mind. There, in the Bibliothèque du Roi, as he wrote in his *Bibliotheca universalis*,

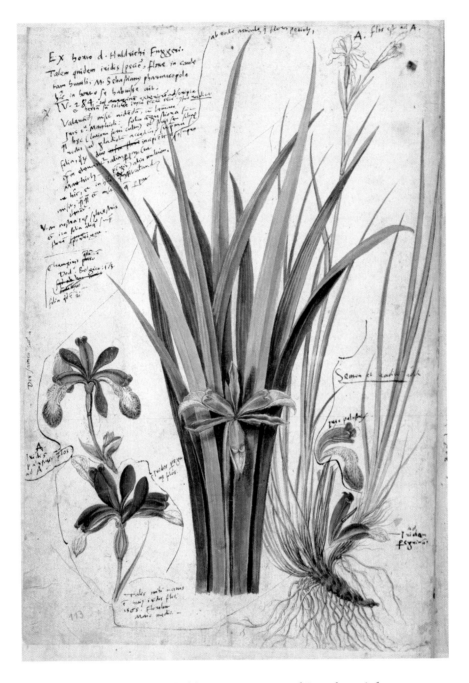

Plate 112: Iris (probably Iris graminea *and* Iris sibirica) *from the garden of Huldrich Fugger who employed Conrad Gesner as tutor to his sons. One of the many drawings that Conrad Gesner collected and annotated for his never-to-be-published encyclopaedia of plants*

he 'devoured' books, particularly the classics: Aristotle, Dioscorides, Galen, Plato, Hippocrates, Sophocles, Theophrastus. Fleeing Paris on 9 December 1534, when Protestant students were being seriously persecuted by Catholics, he returned to Zurich, opened a school, and, still scarcely nineteen years old, married a girl from a family as poor as his own. By this act, he forfeited the patronage of the city fathers, but his marriage did not prevent his being appointed, two years later, as professor of Greek at the University of Lausanne. It was the first and last properly paid job he ever had and he stayed there three years before setting off for Montpellier, then Basel to continue his medical studies. When he graduated in March 1541, he returned to his native city, Zurich, and rarely left it again, building around himself instead a world constructed and construed from letters, visits from his correspondents, parcels of skeletons, fossils and dried plants sent to him by fellow enthusiasts in Italy, France, England, Germany and the Netherlands. 'If you have any rare plants to be named,' he wrote to Dr Kentmann in Dresden, 'it is sufficient to send me the dried flower and leaf.' Information poured in to Gesner in Zurich, but he also poured it out again. He passed on to Jean Bauhin news of what Mattioli was doing in Italy; he discussed with Thomas Penny in England the new plants that he had heard about in Germany.

He produced a guide to the most important plant collections in Switzerland, Germany and northern Italy (*De hortis Germaniae*, 1561), aimed, as he explains, at the 'natural philosopher'. It would not suit those 'in quest of the utilities of things or their pecuniary values; nor ought recognition of any, even the most minute natural objects to be regarded as mere idle curiosity. I include collections of a particular kind, such as you might find in the garden of a liberal-minded and comprehensively scientific man, not that of a greengrocer, or a florist, or an epicure, or a physician, or a vendor of drugs.'[5] Although university botanic gardens had by now been established at Pisa, Padua, Florence and Ferrara, most of the plant collections that Gesner included belonged to private enthusiasts, men such as Matthias Curtius, a merchant in Libau, and Caspare de Gabrieli, a nobleman of Padua. He noted, too, how particular garden flowers were now being collected in a great number of varieties. Italian gardeners were especially keen on anemones: 'All are much admired for the form and colour of their flowers, not for any scent, and they have no use in medicine.' It added a new complication to the naming of names. What were all these things to be called? Had each tiny variation to be honoured by a separate tag? As enthusiasts collected and sowed seed of their favourite varieties, the scenario became ever more complicated. The varieties produced a whole chorus of slightly different plants, some showing characteristics of one parent, some the other. But nobody yet knew how seed was produced or what the difference was between a species and the varieties that can emerge from it.

Gesner did not know the answers, but he was aware of the issues. 'I think that there are practically no plants which do not form some group that is divisible into two or more kinds,' he wrote in a letter to Jean Bauhin.[6] 'The ancients described a single *Gentiana* but I have observed ten or more different sorts.' Gesner also thought it worth sowing seed of different plants to test which characteristics were true and fixed and which were 'accidental' variations. He had noticed that double flowers never bore seed, but supposed (a reasonable supposition given the mind-set of the time) that this must be because the food available to the plant to set its seed had been used up in producing extra petals. He had an intuitive understanding of what we now call ecology, recognising that 'plants differ as to their birthplace'. Some favour the tops of mountains, others their sides. Some grow in meadows, others near walls and hedges. Some like stony ground, others prefer shady woods. Some will grow only in fallow ground, others prefer cultivated. The water lily grows entirely in water, while the maidenhair fern likes a home that is damp but not drowned. He was also a pioneer of what is now called phenology – the study of recurring phenomena. Carefully he noted when leaves unfurled, flowers came out and seed was set on more than a thousand different plants. Busily gathering information on the plants now arriving in Western Europe from the Indies and Central Asia, he was the first to name the canna, the fritillary, and, famously, the tulip.

The careful illustrations of 1,500 plants he prepared over the last ten years of his life (see plate 113) make it clear that, both in identifying and in sorting plants into groups, he considered the flowers, fruits and seeds much more useful than the foliage. The Italian scholar, Andrea Cesalpino, just three years younger than Gesner, was following the same line in Pisa, arranging the plants in his herbarium of 1563 according to similarities in fruit and seed. Gesner's pictures include separate, detailed images of petals, pollen sacs, seed pods, which must have been made with the help of a magnifying glass. These minutiae, technical as well as beautiful, represented a completely new approach. Gesner had moved on from thinking of the image purely as a way of identifying a plant. He was now using it to understand more clearly the physical structure, particularly the way flowers and seed pods were arranged. Dürer's iris had been a mirror image of what he saw in front of him. Gesner's watercolour fractures a Siberian iris into half a dozen parts (see plate 112), a sheaf of the sword-shaped leaves, three flowers shown at different angles and at different stages in their development, the fleshy rhizome with roots hanging below.[7] He shows the anthers of the flower, the pollen sacs carefully positioned to brush pollen on the backs of visiting insects. They are working drawings, with spidery lines separating one detail from the next, or marking off rough boxes of scratchy writing, recording, for instance, in the case of the iris, that it came from the garden of Ulrich Fuggers of Augsburg,

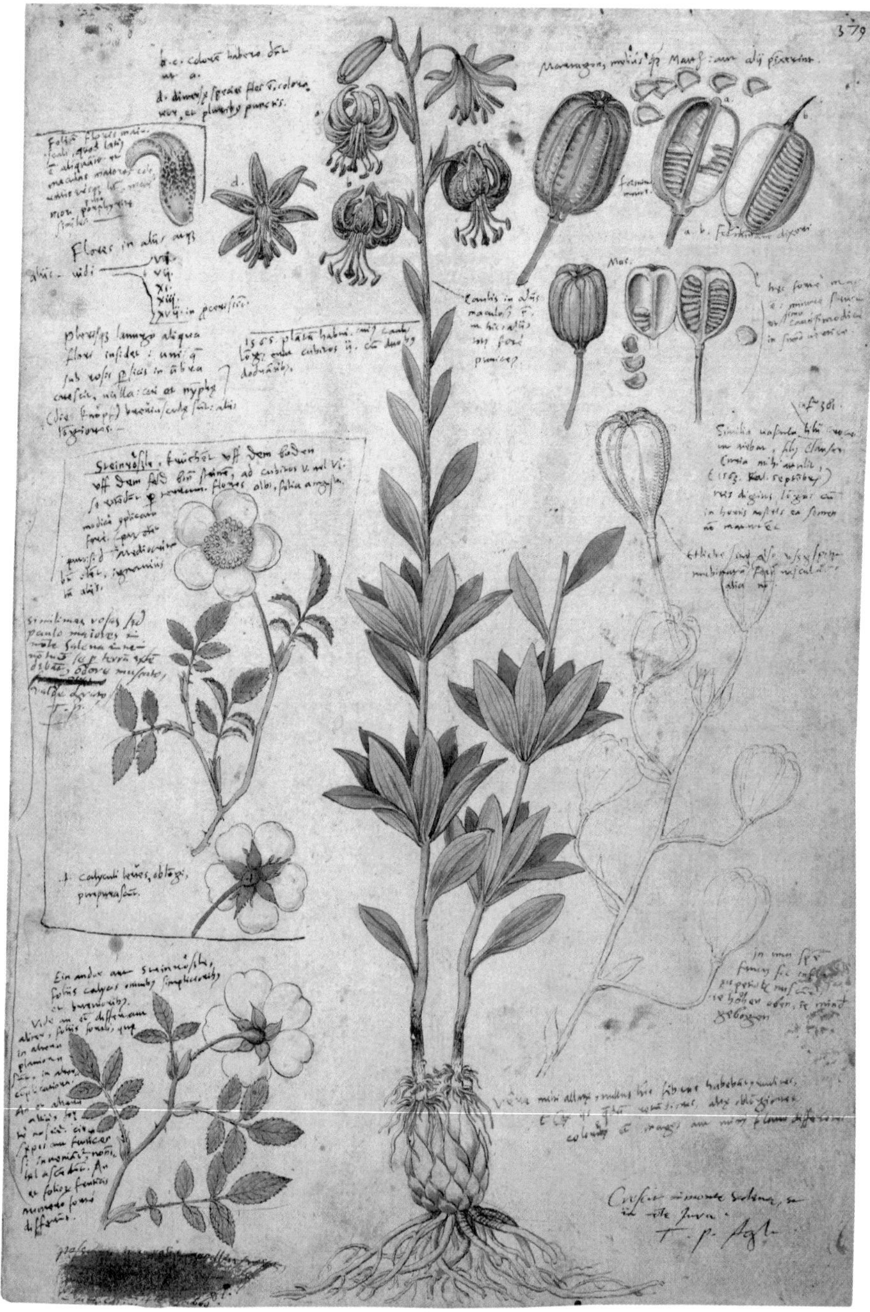

Plate 113: The drawings of plants that Gesner amassed were
endlessly reworked and annotated not only by him, but also by
his English friend Thomas Penny, whose signed notes can be
seen on this drawing of a lily and a white-flowered rose

who in 1545 had hoped to engage the young Gesner as tutor to his family. The elegant martagon lily, which he shows with its characteristic whorls of leaves and seed pods like upturned candelabra, came originally from Mattioli. On this folio (and others) additional, initialled notes have been written by Gesner's English friend, Thomas Penny, who had also studied at Montpellier.

Gesner evidently hoped, through his close study of the structure of flowers and seeds, to find a way of sorting and classifying plants that would make their dazzling diversity easier to understand and appreciate. Too poor to travel far, he became more and more dependent on his correspondents for specimens. In the last few months of his life, Gesner worked tirelessly, as he recounted, to get 'the innumerable dried specimens received from Jean Bauhin painted as quickly as possible so as to return them to their owner'. Dried, pressed plants also came from Felix Platter, whom Gesner had also known at Montpellier. When Gesner needed a branch of white poplar to draw, he asked Theodore Zwinger, rector of Basel University and one of his most faithful correspondents, to send one of his students to pick some from the garden of Felix Platter's father, where he had remembered seeing it years before. Only a month before his death he writes to Zwinger: 'If you have any rare or foreign plants, or any parts of such laid away, I should be glad if you would send me at least the names of them at your earliest leisure; also that in the case of each you inform me whether, over and above the stem with its leaves, any flower, or fruit, or root, either one or two of these or all are represented; for these three parts I almost always insist on having when figuring from a live plant; for by these rather than by the foliage do the natural affinities of plants become apparent.'[8]

After his death, Gesner's friends and colleagues did their best to commemorate his achievements. His drawings were acquired by Joachim Camerarius the Younger (1534–1598), who published about forty of them in his own *Hortus medicus* (1588). Jean Bauhin published Gesner's extensive correspondence with him. But when, for three years in a row, Jacob Zwinger searched at the Frankfurt book fair for Gesner's *De hortis Germaniae*, he learned that the booksellers had long ago returned their unsold copies to the printer in Strasbourg, who had used them to make blotting paper.[9]

XIX

NEW PASTURES
1550–1580

G ESNER'S DEATH IN 1565, followed the next year by those of Rondelet and Fuchs, brought to an end a particular phase of research into *res herbaria*. In the first half of the sixteenth century, four great sets of plant illustrations had been accumulated, circulated, annotated, compared. Four important botanic gardens had been established in Italy, providing a model for those that followed later in the rest of Europe: Leipzig had one by 1580, Leiden in 1587, Basel by 1588, Heidelberg by 1593, Montpellier in 1597. Thomas Platter, Felix's younger brother, who studied medicine at Montpellier between 1595 and 1599, described how the new garden (see plate 114) had been created there by Rondelet's successor, Pierre Richer de Belleval,

> between the gates of the Peyrou and Saint-Gely, a gunshot away from the walls of the town. He has had a large well or cistern dug there, beside which have been built several grottoes that are deliciously cool in summer; here aquatic plants are cultivated in humid and mossy earths brought here by his order. Everything is perfectly managed for other species too; he has even built a mound for them, with several high terraces one above the other. Each part of the garden has its own entrance . . . If the King does not reimburse him for all his expenditure, he must be a ruined man.[1]

In the summer of 1596, Thomas Platter and his friends went hunting for plants on

*Plate 114: The botanic garden at the University of Montpellier
as it looked in 1596. From Charles Martin's*
Jardin des Plantes *(1854)*

the shoreline at Montpellier, as his brother had done forty years before, but the monastery in the woods at Grammont was now in ruins, and the little church had become a farmhouse. As a young student in the 1550s, Felix Platter had witnessed at first hand the massacres that followed the persecution of French Protestants; the religious wars in the Languedoc persisted almost to the end of the century. By the time of Gesner's death, the first religious refugees from Flanders had already settled in England; by 1562, a Huguenot colony was trying to establish itself in Florida. The Montpellier garden, so carefully planned and planted by Richer de Belleval lasted scarcely thirty years, for Louis XIII did not share Henri IV's tolerance towards the Montpellier Protestants. In the winter of 1621–2 his army laid siege to the town. The soldiers made their camp in the botanic garden and left it 'entierement desmoly et mis en ruyne'. The irony was that Rondelet had been a Protestant who never lost his Catholic friends; Richer de Belleval was a Catholic who saw his life's work destroyed by a Catholic army.

In an intellectual sense, the Counter-Reformation had closed Italy in on itself. Gradually France, Germany and the Low Countries took the lead in producing scholars with the ability to take forward the pioneering work that, from the early Renaissance onwards, had been focused in Italy. The Reformation encouraged Protestants to rediscover a delight in 'the works of the Lord', to reaffirm a symbiosis with the natural world. By the middle of the sixteenth century the shift was almost complete. Italy still produced great plantsmen but the names that dominate the field in the latter part of the sixteenth century are all from the Low Countries: Rembert Dodoens (1517–1585) born in Mechlin, Belgium, Charles de l'Écluse (1526–1609) born at Arras, and Matthias de l'Obel (1538–1616) born at Lille, both then in Flanders. Together they produced an avalanche of plant books, most of them published in Antwerp by the Flemish printer Christophe Plantin (*c*.1520–1589) who commissioned another important set of illustrations, the fifth to be produced between 1530 and 1590. No woodblocks have ever worked harder than Plantin's, recycled in a whole series of volumes which culminated in the compendium of 2,173 illustrations that appeared in the *Icones stirpium seu plantarum tam exoticarum* of 1591.

The new botanic gardens helped create a taste for the rare and the strange; rich men now laid out gardens which were intended purely for pleasure and filled them with the exotic fritillaries, tulips, narcissi and lilies that had begun to appear in Europe from Constantinople. The catalyst in this instance was the Fleming, Ogier Ghiselin de Busbecq (1522–1592), the traveller, linguist, scholar and antiquarian who from 1554 to 1562 was Emperor Ferdinand's ambassador at Constantinople, the centre of the Ottoman Empire. In a series of letters addressed to his friend

Nicholas Michault,[2] Busbecq, a keen plantsman, describes the country he and his entourage passed through on their way to the Ottoman court:

> We stayed one day in Adrianople and then set out on the last stage of our journey to Constantinople, which was now close at hand. As we passed through the district we everywhere came across quantities of flowers – narcissi, hyacinths and *tulipans* as the Turks call them. We were surprised to find them flowering in mid-winter, scarcely a favourable season. There is an abundance of narcissi and hyacinths in Greece, and they possess so wonderful a scent that a large quantity of them causes a headache in those who are unaccustomed to such an odour.[3]

The Anglo-French jeweller Sir John Chardin, who travelled in the Near East in the 1660s, left a similar account of the rich flowers he saw, so desirable to Western eyes:

> By the vivacity of their colours [these flowers] are generally handsomer than those in Europe, and those of India . . . Along the Caspian coast there are whole forests of orange trees, single and double jasmine, all European flowers, and other species besides. Towards Media and the southern parts of Arabia, the fields produce of themselves tulips, anemones, single ranunculus, of the finest red, and imperial crowns. In other places, as round about Isfahan, the jonquils grow of themselves . . . they have in the proper season seven or eight sorts of daffodils, and there are flowers blooming all winter long . . . white and blue hyacinths . . . dainty tulips and myrrh . . . in spring, yellow and red stock and amber seed of all colours and a most unusual flower called the clove pink, each plant bearing some thirty blooms.

Chardin also noted

> the lily of the valley, the lily and violets of all colours, pinks and Spanish jasmine of a beauty and perfume surpassing anything found in Europe . . . There are beautiful marsh-mallows and, at Isfahan, charming short-stemmed tulips . . . The rose which is so common among them is of five sorts of colours besides its natural one, white, yellow, red and others of two colours viz red on one side and white or yellow on the other . . . I have seen a rose tree which bore upon one and the same branch roses of three colours, some yellow, some yellow and white, and others yellow and red.[4]

Merchants soon discovered that the plants that grew from bulbs and corms – crocus, cyclamen, fritillaries, hyacinths (see plate 115), lilies, tulips – were not difficult to transport from East to West because they died down soon after they had flowered

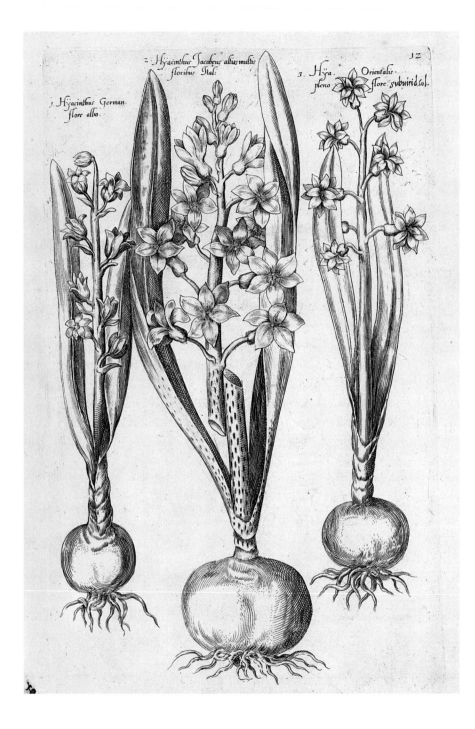

Plate 115: Hyacinths, both single and double from
Emmanuel Sweert's Florilegium *(1612)*

and remained dormant until the following growing season. And avid collectors in the West also discovered that these treasures were not too difficult to grow, if you kept mice away from the bulbs and dried them off in summer. The rarity value of novelties such as the crown imperial and the prices paid for them obliged gardeners to watch their new acquisitions closely and try, instinctively, to guess what they most needed to survive in a climate that was damper, cooler, less extreme in its heats and chills than their natural habitats.

The arrivals, these infidel flowers, the first great wave of foreign plants to arrive in Western Europe, were shocking in their glamour, their outrageous colours, their charisma and allure. Until the 1560s, most flowers grown in European gardens had been natives of Europe and the Mediterranean: calendulas, different coloured columbines, violas, odd kinds of primrose. But in April 1559, under grey Bavarian skies, a tulip from the East suddenly erupted in brilliant scarlet in the garden of a rich Augsburg silversmith. With equal drama, in the 1570s the first crown imperial (see plate 116) pushed its thick fleshy stem through the bare earth of spring to produce a flower that was disgracefully, flagrantly set to seduce. From the top of its thick stem, it produced orange bells, symmetrically arranged in a perfect circle, thick and fleshy, the central pistil hanging like a clapper inside. 'In the bottom of each of these bels,' wrote the English plantsman John Gerard, 'there is placed six drops of most cleare shining sweet water, in taste like sugar, resembling in shew faire orient pearles; the which drops if you take away, there do immediately appeare the like, notwithstanding if they may be suffered to stand still in the floure according to his owne nature, they will never fall away, no not if you strike the plant until it be broken.'[5] On top of the bells small green leaves arranged themselves in a topknot, an arrangement quite unlike any other flower that had ever been seen in Europe. The crown imperial was a self-made centrepiece and demanded attention. The soft, fleeting scents of the European spring – primroses, violets – were now overlaid by the heavier, insistent, rocking smell of the hyacinth: musky, almost overpowering in its intensity.

Busbecq, though, was only part of a flourishing export trade which, during the reigns of Sultan Selim I and Sultan Murad I, fostered strong links between Turkey, Austria and the Netherlands. Most new plants coming from that quarter quite quickly found their way to Charles de l'Écluse (known to his contemporaries as Carolus Clusius), who had a particular interest in bulbs. Clusius (see plate 117) had studied under Rondelet at Montpellier; then, in the same way that Cosimo I de' Medici had persuaded Luca Ghini to come to Pisa, Maximilian II of the Holy Roman Empire induced Clusius to look after the Imperial Botanic Garden in Vienna. Clusius's contemporary, Rembert Dodoens, was also summoned, as the emperor's personal

*Plate 116: The showy crown imperial (*Fritillaria imperialis*)
introduced into Europe from Constantinople in the second
half of the sixteenth century. This illustration was made
in the 1630s by Pieter van Kouwenhoorn*

physician. Ferdinand, Maximilian and his successor Rudolf collected rare plants and other oddities with the furious zeal so typical of the age. Coins, medals, manuscripts, fossils, gemstones, skulls, shells, the *gran libro della natura*, animal, vegetable, mineral, were crammed into cabinets of curiosities, the *wunderkammern* that became such a feature of the late sixteenth and early seventeenth centuries. Philip II of Spain, Archduke Ferdinand II of Tyrol, Duke William V and Duke Maximilian I of Bavaria were all equally infected with this *cultura della curiosita*. The collections were microcosms of the natural world, its curiosities and treasures, and all over Europe tremendous hoards were built up by private collectors such as Ferrante Imperato in Naples, Ulysse Aldrovandi in Bologna, Canon Manfredo Settala in Milan, Olao Worms in Copenhagen, and the Tradescants in London.

At the heart of one of the richest and most powerful courts of the age, Clusius had to ensure that the Imperial Botanic Garden held at least as many rare plants as any other in Europe. The emperor's ambassadors were primed to send back novelties from the various countries in which they served. In 1576 Clusius received a huge consignment of rare trees and shrubs from David von Ugnad, who had succeeded Busbecq in Constantinople. Unfortunately, most were dead; only a horse chestnut and something that von Ugnad called a Trabison curmasi, the date or plum of Trebizond, had survived the long journey. Travelling was naturally more stressful to large plants than it was to bulbs, perfectly packaged and, in their dormant season, eminently portable. But the surviving horse chestnut and the Trebizond plum both settled like natives in Europe and were quickly spread between enthusiastic gardeners. Those who grew the foreign plants did not always understand that they were used to tougher conditions than they found in their new homes. In 1629, the English plantsman John Parkinson described a Trebizond plum (or cherry laurel as it became known in England) flowering in the Highgate garden of James Cole 'which hee defended from the bitternesse of the weather in winter by casting a blanket over the toppe thereof every yeare, thereby the better to preserve it'.[6]

Clusius also travelled widely himself, introducing at least 200 new plants from expeditions in Spain and Portugal. All these were described in his first original work, *Rariorum aliquot stirpium per Hispanias observatorum historia*, which was published by Christophe Plantin in 1576. The book contained an important Appendix which had nothing to do with Spain, but gave a detailed list of the plants that Clusius had up to that time received 'ex Thracia', that is, from the east Balkan peninsula. Plantin had woodblock illustrations cut especially for the book, but in the end they were used in a work of Dodoens's before Clusius ever got hold of them. Fuchs would have burst several blood vessels over the matter; Clusius merely commented that he and Dodoens were 'united by friendship of old', and that 'whatever friends possess

Plate 117: A portrait of Carolus Clusius (Charles de l'Écluse
1526–1609), a key figure in the web that connected plantsmen
of the sixteenth century. The portrait is by Filippo Paladini

ought to be freely shared'. In 1571, on his first trip to England, Clusius went plant-hunting around Bristol with Lobelius (Matthias de l'Obel). William Turner had posited the West Country as a kind of Mecca for plant-lovers and Clusius tracked down West Country specialities such as colchicum, scurvy grass, tutsan, yellow wort, a rare pimpernel, lady's mantle and a special kind of pignut. In London, where Lobelius was at that time based, Clusius met the poet Sir Philip Sidney and listened to Francis Drake's account of his adventures in the New World.

It was in London, too, that Clusius came across a work that had recently been published in Seville by a Spanish physician, Nicolas Monardes (1493–1588), the first book ever to describe the strange and unknown plants of the Americas. Called *Dos Libros* . . . (see plate 118), it described the extraordinary things coming into Spain from what were then known as the Occidental Indies, the brave new world that lay west over the *Oceano Occidentale*. One of Monardes's sons had settled in Peru and the various forays made by Spanish conquistadores in South America brought dispatches from these previously unchartered territories directly into Cadiz and the cities of southern Spain. 'And as there is discovered newe regions, newe kyngdomes, and newe Provinces by our Spanyardes,' wrote Monardes, 'thei have brought unto us newe Medicines and newe Remedies.' The plants that came into Western Europe from Constantinople and the Near East had been rated by plantsmen for their beauty and rarity, but the plants that, shortly after, began to flood into Europe from the New World were valued chiefly for their medicinal qualities. The pox had arrived in the Old World with Christopher Columbus and swept through Europe faster than the plague. The drugs extracted from the new South American plants were far stronger and more effective against syphilis than any cure distilled from European ingredients. Intrigued by *Dos Libros* . . . and Monardes's descriptions of plants that few Europeans had ever seen, Clusius translated it into Latin and Plantin published the new edition in 1574. Three years later it was available in English, published under the winning title *Joyfull newes out of the newe founde worlde* by John Frampton, a merchant who had spent much of his working life in Spain. In Monardes's book, he promised, readers would find 'declared the rare and singuler vertues of diverse and sundrie Hearbes, Trees, Oyles, Plants, and Stones, with their applications, as well for Phisicke as Chirugerie, the saied being well applied bryngeth such present remedie for all deseases, as maie seme altogether incredible . . .' The book, in its various editions, was an immediate success, entrancing European readers with its descriptions of

that countrie, whiche thei cal the newe Spaine, as in that whiche is called the Peru, where there are many Provinces, many Kingdomes, and many Cities, that hath contrary

❧ DOS LIBROS, EL V-

NO QVE TRATA DE TODAS LAS COSAS
que traen de nueſtras Indias Occidentales, que ſiruen
al vſo de la Medicina, y el otro que trata de la
Piedra Bezaar, y de la Yerua Eſcuerçonera.
Cõpueſtos por el doctor Nicoloſo de Monardes Medico de Seuilla.

IMPRESSOS EN SEVILLA EN CASA DE
Hernando Diaz, en la calle de la Sierpe.
Con Licencia y Priuilegio de ſu Mageſtad.
Año de 1 5 6 9.

*Plate 118: The title page of Dos Libros in which the Spanish
doctor Nicolas Monardes gave some of the first accounts of the
plants of the New World. It was printed in Seville in 1569*

and divers customes in them, whiche there hath been founde out, thynges that never in these partes, nor in any other partes of the worlde hath been seen, nor unto this daie knowen: and other thynges, which now are brougt unto us in greate aboundance, that is to saie, Golde, Silver, Pearles, Emeraldes, Turkeses, and other fine stones of great value . . . And besides these greate riches, our Occidentall Indias doeth sende unto us many Trees, Plantes, Herbes, Rootes, Juices, Gummes, Fruites, Licours, Stones that are of greate medicinall vertues . . . And this is not to bee merveiled at, that it is so, for the philosopher doeth saie that all Contries doeth not give Plantes and Fruites alike: for one Region yeldeth suche Fruites, Trees and Plantes, as another doeth not.[7]

The close trade links between Spain and England meant that the goods brought out of the New World by Spanish merchants quickly found their way 'hether into Englande, by suche as dooeth daiely trafficke thether'.

Monardes talked of 'the Islande of Cuba', where 'certine Fountaines at the Seaside . . . cast from them a kinde of blacke Pitch' which, mixed with tallow, the Spanish sailors used to tar their ships. He described the resin that the native Indians gathered 'by waie of Incision, by giving cuttes in the Trees of whiche forthewith the licour doth droppe out'. The resin, 'called in the Indians' language, Caranna', came into Spain by way of Cartagena and Nombre de Dios, and the Spaniards continued to call it by its South American name. The Americas also provided a source of balsam, the aspirin of the Renaissance pharmacy. The drug had previously been imported from Egypt, but as Monardes explained, 'it is many yeres that it failed, because the Vine from whence it came, dried up'. When balsam initially came into Spain from the Americas it cost a small fortune, 'one ounce was worthe tenne Duccates and upwardes'. Later, merchants 'brought so muche and suche great quantity, that it is nowe of small valewe'. But of all the plants that the New World produced the three most important were guaiacum, the bark of a tree that grew round Sancto Domingo; China, a root rather like ginger; and sarsaparilla, 'a thyng come to our partes after the China. It may be twenty yeres that the use thereof came to this City.' All were considered extremely effective against syphilis[8] 'except the sicke man doe returne to tumble in the same bosome, where he tooke the firste'.

Famously, the Americas also produced the tobacco plant, a picture of which decorates the title page of the second part of Monardes's book. Though he fills sixteen pages with the 'greate vertues' of tobacco, it was a while before the smoking habit caught on in Europe; at first tobacco was used 'to adornate Gardeines with the fairenes thereof, and to geve a pleasaunt sight'. Monardes explains that among the American Indians the plant is known as 'peciels' ('tobacco' came from the Spanish, after the island of the same name) and that they for their pastyme, doe take the smoke of the Tabaco, for to make theimselves drunke withall, and to see the visions and thinges that doe represent to them, wherein thei dooe delight . . .

The blacke people that hath gone from these partes to the Indias, hath taken the same maner and use of the Tabaco that the Indians hath, for when thei see theimselves wearie, thei take it at the nose, and mouthe, and it dooeth happen unto theim, as unto our Indians, liying as though thei were dedde three or fower howers: and after thei doe remaine lightened, without any wearinesse, for to laboure againe: and thei dooe this with so greate pleasure, that although thei bee not wearie, yet thei are very desirous for to dooe it: and the thyng is come to so muche efecte, that their maisters doeth chasten theim for it, and doe burne the Tabaco, because thei should not use it, where-upon thei goe to the desartes, and secrete places to dooe it, because thei maie not bee permitted, to drinke themselves drunke with Wine . . .

When thei use to travaile by waies, where thei finde no water nor meate: Thei take a little baule of these, and thei put it between the lower lippe and the teethe, and thei goe chewyng it all the tyme that thei do travell, and that whiche thei doe chewe, thei doe swallowe it doune, and in this sorte thei dooe journey three or fower daies, without havyng neede of meate, or drinke.[9]

Frampton, in his translation of Monardes's work, added that the herb was known among the French as 'nicotiane' and explained how 'Maister Jhon Nicot, Counseller to the Kyng, beeyng Embassadour for the Kyng in Portugall, in the yere of our Lorde 1559, went one daie to see the Prysons of the kyng of Portugall and a gentleman beeyng the Keeper of the saied Prions presented hym this hearbe, as a strange Plant brought from Florida. The same Maister Nicot caused the saide hearbe to be set in his Garden . . .' Already by 1570, Lobelius was writing about tobacco in his *Stirpium adversaria nova*, undecided whether to call it by its French name (*Nicotiana gallorum*) or its Spanish one ('Sana sancta Indorum'). He shows a picture of the plant (see plate 119) very similar to the one that Monardes had used, but sets alongside it a bizarre vignette of a vast horn-like cornucopia issuing from the mouth of an American Indian, with an alarming amount of smoke and flames coming out of the top of it. It was scarcely surprising then, that smoking, as a 'pastyme', was not an immediate attraction in Europe.

Monardes also writes of coca, 'that hearbe so celebrated of the Indians', which was used as a kind of currency to buy 'Mantelles, and Cattell, and Salte, and other thinges whiche doe runne like to money amongest us'. The coca seed was sown, he explained 'as we doe put here a Garden of Beanes, or of Peason' in carefully tilled

Nicotiana inserta infundibulo ex quo hauriunt fumũ Indi & nauteri.

Plate 119: The tobacco plant (Nicotiana tabacum) *as it appeared in Lobelius's* Stirpium adversaria nova *(1570). The illustrator has taken a fanciful view of the way that tobacco was smoked by the 'Indians' of South America*

earth. The use of coca among the Indians was 'a thing generall', and Monardes describes the Indians' method of preparing the drug:

> Thei take Cokles in the shelles, and they doe burne them and grinde them, and after they are burned they remaine like Lyme, verie small grounde, and they take of the Leves of the Coca, and they chawe them in their Mouthes, and as they goe chawing, they goe mingling with it of that powder made of the shelles in suche sorte, that they make it like to a Paste, taking lesse of the Powder than of the Hearbe, and of this Paste they make certane small Bawles rounde, and they put them to drie, and when they will use of them, they take a little Ball in their mouthe, and they chawe hym . . . and so they goe, using of it al the tyme what they have neede, whiche is when they travaill by the waie, and especially if it be by waies where there is no meate or lacke of water. For the use of their little Bawles dooe take the hunger and thurste from them, and they say that they dooe receive substaunce, as though that they did eate. When thei will make themselves dronke and bee out of judgemente, thei mingle with the Coca the leaves of the Tabaco, and thei doe chewe them all together, and thei go as thei were out of their wittes, like as if thei were dronke whiche is a thyng that dooeth geve them great contentment to bee in that sorte.[10]

Unlike tobacco, coca didn't find its way into Lobelius's book, nor in any other of the wordy torrents published in the second half of the sixteenth century. The coca leaves came from a semi-tropical South American shrub, *Erythroxylon coca* that could never grow in the European climate. Like cinnamon and cloves, it remained fixed in the European mind as an ingredient rather than a living plant.

But European gardeners very quickly took to the 'Hearbe of the Sunne' that Monardes described (see plate 120) and which he said had been grown in Spanish gardens for some years past. 'It casteth out the greatest flowers, and the moste perticulars that ever hath been seen,' he wrote. 'It is greater then a greate Platter or Dishe, the whiche hath divers couleurs. It is needfull that it leane to some thyng, where it groweth, or ellese it will bee alwaies falling: the seede of it is like to the seedes of a Melon, sumwhat greater, his flower doth tourne itselfse continously towardes the Sunne, and for this they call it of his name, the whiche many other flowers and hearbes do the like, it showeth marveilous faire in Gardines.'[11] Gerard was equally enthusiastic, especially about the centre of the sunflower, 'made as it were of unshorn velvet, or some curious cloath wrought with the needle'. When the plant was mature, the seed appeared 'set as though a cunning workman had of purpose placed them in very good order, much like the honycombs of Bees'. The seeds, though, were so numerous (sometimes more than 2,000 in a single head) and the plant itself so

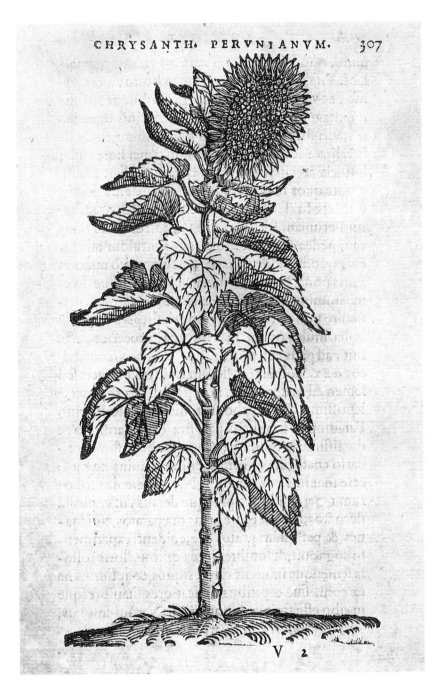

Plate 120: *The sunflower* (Helianthus annuus) *which created a sensation when it was first brought into Europe from South America. The illustration comes from Rembert Dodoens's* Florum et coronarium, *printed in Antwerp in 1568*

easy-going in its habits, that later in the seventeenth century the sunflower became a common flower and so fell out of favour in smart gardens. 'Not at all respected' said John Rea, dismissively in 1665. But in 1606, Johann Conrad von Gemmingen, the Prince-Bishop of Eichstatt, had been proud to include it in the fabulous collection of flowers he grew in his garden at Eichstatt, south of Nuremberg. Under the name of 'Flos solis major' it blazes on the page of the *Hortus Eystettensis*, an illustrated record of the Prince-Bishop's garden with 367 plates illustrating more than a thousand of the plants in his collection.

The sunflower, sacred to the Aztecs, carved as an emblem on Inca temples, had its own long-established indigenous name, as did tobacco. Those names may have travelled back with the plants when they were first brought to Europe. But they were not adopted, or even adapted for European use, though the tags hung on them sometimes acknowledged their origin. The sunflower, which Frampton in 1577 had translated from Monardes as 'the herbe of the sunne', had already appeared in the second edition of Rembert Dodoens's book *Florum et coronarium* (1569) under the label 'Chrysanthemum Peruvianum'. Dodoens writes that the plant, still then rare, had already flowered in the gardens of the Royal Palace in Madrid and also in the botanical garden at Padua. Philip Brancion, an avid amateur grower, had not been so successful in the cooler climate of Malines. His plant had been cut down by frost before it ever reached flowering size. But in an amazingly short time after its introduction, the sunflower had already collected a whole bagful of epithets. Lobelius uses three different names in his *Plantarum* of 1576: 'Solis flos Peruvianus', 'Sol Indianus' as well as Dodoens's 'Chrysanthemum Peruvianum'. All these alternative names were gradually sorted and sifted, abandoned and taken up again until it was finally settled that the sunflower should be christened *Helianthus*, because it followed the sun.

In Europe, only the Spaniards sometimes continued to use the original names for the plants they brought in from the New World. Though brutal colonisers, they had unusual respect for the plant knowledge of the indigenous people of Mexico. The vast manuscript, *Rerum medicarum Novae Hispaniae thesaurus*, presented to Philip II of Spain by the king's physician, Francisco Hernandez (*c.*1514–1587), adopts many of the authentic Mexican names for the plants described in the text (they included the first description of the 'cocoxochitl' or dahlia). The original names are preserved too in a manuscript (see plate 121) made in 1552 at the Roman Catholic College of Santa Cruz by two Aztec authors: Martin de la Cruz, an 'Indian physician . . . who is not theoretically learned, but is taught only by experience', and Juannes Badianus, who translated the work into Latin. It includes a picture of the showy marvel of Peru which quickly became a favourite in European gardens. Usefully, it also recommends plant extracts guaranteed to cure 'the fatigue of men working in government departments'.[12]

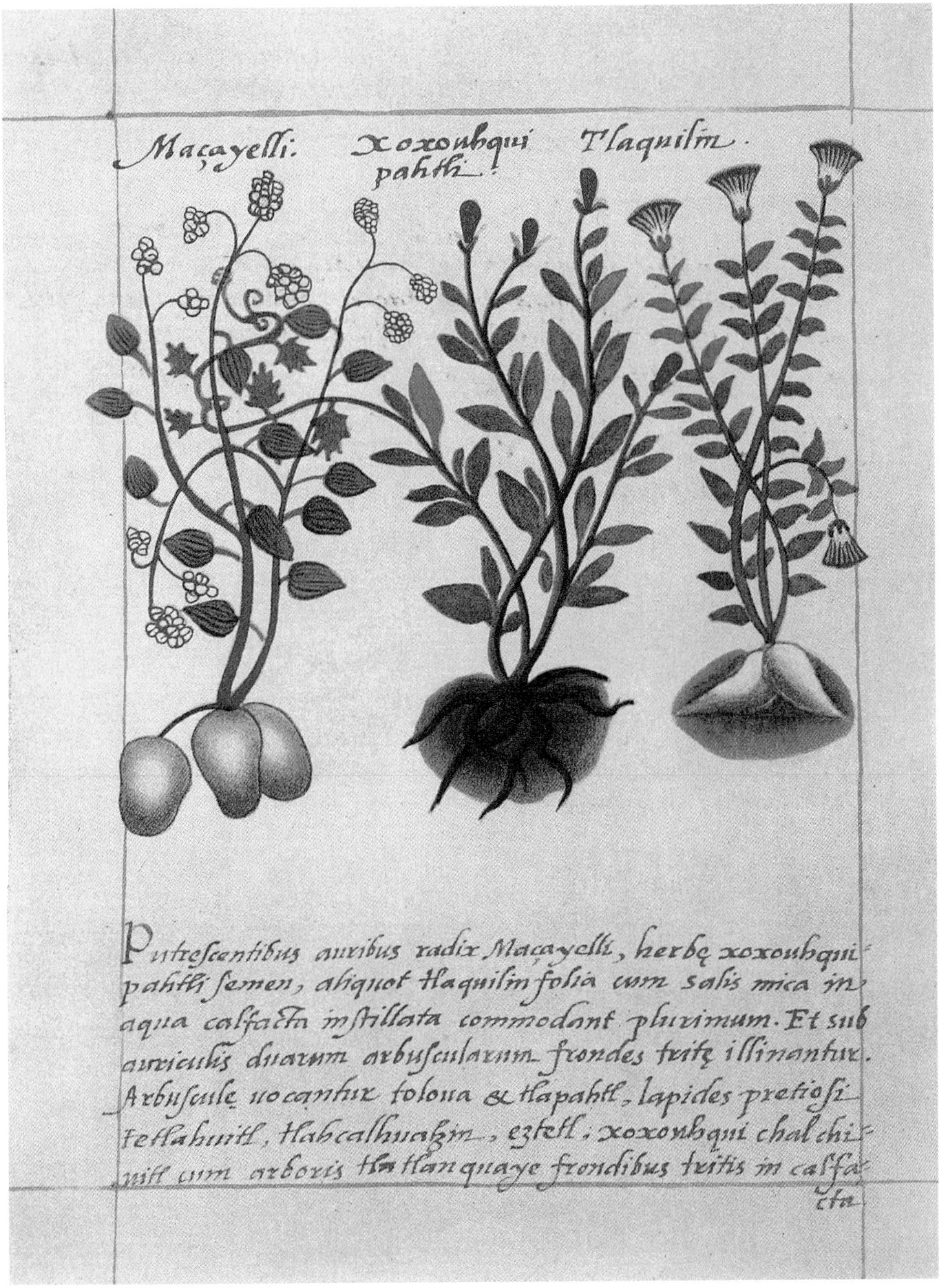

Macayelli.   *xoxouhqui pahth.*   *Tlaquilm.*

Putrescentibus auribus radix Maçayelli, herbę xoxouhqui
pahtli semen, aliquot tlaquilin folia cum salis mica in
aqua calfacta instillata commodant plurimum. Et sub
auriculis duarum arbuscularum frondes trite illinantur.
Arbusculę uocantur tolona et tlapahtl, lapides pretiosi
tettahuitl, tlahcalhuatzin, eztetl. xoxouhqui chalchi-
uitl cum arboris tla tlanquaye frondibus tritis in calfacta

Plate 121: Marvel of Peru (Mirabilis jalapa) *and other plants
from an Aztec manuscript, the Badianus Herbal, made in 1552*

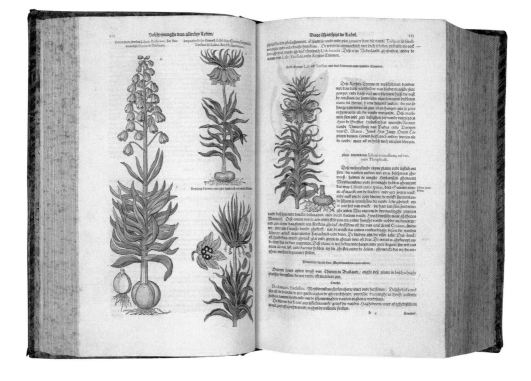

*Plate 122: Fritillaries (*Fritillaria persica *and* Fritillaria imperialis*) from Lobelius's* Kruydtboeck *of 1581, printed by Christophe Plantin in Antwerp and hand-coloured in his workshop*

XX

PLANTIN'S TEAM
1560—1620

F ROM THE 1570s onwards, Christophe Plantin's virtual monopoly on the printing of plant books in the Low Countries fudges the distinctions between the charismatic Clusius and his near contemporaries, Dodoens and Lobelius. Plantin, a native of Tours, had learned printing and bookbinding at Caen. Later he moved to Antwerp to escape Henri II's energetic persecution of French Noncomformists. While Bruges as a financial centre was slowly dying as its lifeline, the River Zwyn, silted up, Antwerp was booming, partly as a result of the amount of trade now flowing in from the New World. The annual movement of capital in the city was reckoned to be worth around 40 million ducats. 'In Antwerp one lives sumptuously, and possibly rather more so than the dictates of reason warrant' wrote the Florentine merchant Ludovico Guicciardini in the 1560s.[1] By the time Plantin arrived, there were already forty printing houses in the city, responsible for more than half of the 4,000 books printed in the Low Countries in the first forty years of the sixteenth century.

Initially, Plantin worked as a bookbinder, but on his way to deliver a leather case for a jewel intended for the Queen of Spain, he was attacked by a drunken gang. One of them ran him through with his sword, injuring Plantin so severely that he could not return to his former trade. By 1555 he had set himself up as a printer, issuing, as his first book, a bilingual edition (Italian and French) of a treatise dealing with the education of young girls of good family, written by the Italian humanist, Giovanni Bruto. By 1557, he had adopted his famous logo: a pair of compasses (he's

313

holding them in the portrait that now hangs in the Museum Plantin-Moretus in Antwerp; see plate 123), the symbol of the firm's motto 'Labore et Constantia'. One arm of the compass stands still (constancy), the other does the work.

French was Plantin's mother tongue, Flemish the language of his adopted country, but at his printing house, Plantin brought out books written in Latin and Greek, Italian and Spanish, German and English, all of which demanded a prodigious number of typefaces. Already by 1567 there were forty-two different sorts of type at the works. By 1585 there were ninety. At his height, Plantin employed 150 men, including thirty-two printers and twenty typesetters, who were paid about 165 florins a year. His many daughters were expected to be competent proofreaders in several languages by the age of five. Sixteen monumental hand presses were installed at his head-quarters near the Marché du Vendredi in Antwerp.[2] The presses cost him about sixty florins each, which compared with the price of one of his splendid polyglot bibles (seventy florins) was not expensive. So, at the sign of the golden compasses, Plantin's business flourished. Letters, he said, came into the business headquarters as thick as flocks of sparrows. In a career spanning thirty-four years, he printed an average of seventy-two books a year, usually about a thousand copies of each. He was a capitalist pioneer of the Renaissance, turning what had been a laborious handcraft into something more like a production line. Twice a year, he went to the important book fair at Frankfurt, sending barrels packed with books to the fair by way of the barges that plied up and down the Rhine. It was a cut-throat business. Printers would regularly pay bribes to the censor to delay the publication of rival books so that their own editions could come out first. 'Went to Brussels on business connected with my printing house,' notes Plantin in a paper dated 1 March 1565, 'and to secure the interest of the Chancellor and others who might be useful to us.' The Chancellor's pay-off included four Auvergne cheeses which cost the printer three florins, as well as eight baskets of plums and pears which cost him half as much again. Cheeses and fruit also went to the local priest as well others who could cause difficulties, if they chose.

The problem, as always, was religion. Plantin had left Paris to escape religious persecution, but found censorship almost as rigorous in Antwerp. Almost 300 titles appeared in the catalogue of condemned books drawn up by the University of Louvain in 1546. Another sixty-nine works were added in 1551 and by 1559 the papal index listed 650 banned books. In 1545 an Antwerp printer, Jacob van Liesvelt was beheaded for printing Lutheran bibles. When Philip II of Spain's representative, the Duke of Alva arrived in Flanders, four Antwerp printers were banished, one sentenced to the galleys, and one hanged. Plantin had to be careful. More than a third of his business depended on printing breviaries, missals, prayer books and bibles

Plate 123: A portrait by an anonymous artist of the printer
Christophe Plantin (c.1520–1589). He is holding the compasses
that became the famous logo of the printing house that he
established in Antwerp in the middle of the sixteenth century

for the Catholic Church, but his own sympathies lay secretly with an Anabaptist sect, The Family of Love (very Sixties).

On 1 March 1562, the Margrave of Antwerp received a difficult letter from Philip II's half-sister, Margaret, Duchess of Parma: 'There has been delivered to us here,' she wrote,

> the little book I am sending with this letter, and which, it is maintained, has been printed in the house of Christopher Plantin, printer in the town of Antwerp, although he has put neither his name nor his address. On comparison with other books printed by the said Plantin, the type is found to be similar. And inasmuch as in this he has contravened the enactments and public edicts of our sovereign lord the King, and whereas he who sent us this book has also warned us that the said Plantin and those about him are tainted with the heresies of the new religion, with the exception of a corrector and a servant, it has seemed proper that we should send you the said book in order that you may proceed to the house of the said Plantin to confront him with this type and to see whether you can find in his house any further copies similar to the one we are sending you, and which, we are assured, were still there on the 23rd of this month. And according to what you may there discover, you shall proceed towards him as the law and the enactments of His Majesty require, advising us as to what you find there and what steps you are taking.[3]

Plantin slipped away to Paris, and waited there for a year until the unpleasant enquiries had run their course. Two of his workers were found guilty, but the business survived. Perhaps an extra cheese was added to the Chancellor's gift list.

Less controversial were books about plants, which became a speciality of Plantin's press. With the help of the artist, Pieter van der Borcht (c.1540–1608) and the engraver Arnaud Nicolai (c.1525–c.1590), Plantin gradually built up a huge hoard of woodblock illustrations. After the death of the printer Jan van der Loe, his chief rival in Antwerp, Plantin acquired from his widow the 715 blocks that van der Loe had commissioned to illustrate Rembert Dodoens's Flemish *Cruydeboeck* of 1554, published before Plantin himself had arrived in Antwerp. The illustrations were of course printed in black and white but Plantin kept three women – Myncken Liefrinck, Lyncken Verhoeven and Lisken Zeghers – fully employed at his press, hand-colouring the images in the deluxe editions of his books. Plantin treated his collection of botanical woodblocks like a vast bran tub to be dipped into for whatever book was in hand at the time. The same blocks were repeatedly used to illustrate books by different writers. It was an expensive business, commissioning illustrations, and Plantin, recognising that his readers now expected pictures, was keen to realise the

Plate 124: The title page of the Flemish Cruydeboeck *(1554) by Rembert Dodoens. Heracles attacks the dragon, Ladon, who guards the garden of the Hesperides and its golden apples*

Plate 125: Black pepper, in an illustration originally made for Christoval Acosta's Tractado de las drogas y medicinas de las Indias Orientales *(1578). This version is the copy that appeared nine years later in the second volume of Jacques d'Aléchamps's* Historia generalis plantarum *(1587)*

maximum return on his investment. Muddles, however, arose when Plantin used the same image to portray a whole range of completely different plants in a succession of different publications. Visually, it became difficult to distinguish one author's book from the next, since all were issued in similar typefaces and with the same pictures.

There was a sameness about Plantin's output, too, because Dodoens, Clusius and Lobelius were constantly engaged in revisions of their own works in an effort to keep up with the continuous flow of plants coming into Western Europe. More than forty new bulbous plants – narcissi, crocus, alliums, lilies, colchicums, erythroniums – appeared in Lobelius's *Plantarum seu stirpium historia* of 1576, a revised edition of the book he had published six years earlier. Nevertheless, there were important differences between the three men. Rembert Dodoens was particularly knowledge-able about the plants of the Low Countries, while Clusius's strong suit was Spain, Austria and Hungary. Lobelius, who like Clusius had studied at Montpellier, plant-hunted in the Languedoc for several years after he graduated and had an intimate knowledge of the plants of southern France. He and Pierre Pena were the last of the glittering group of students who had studied under Rondelet.[4] When Lobelius later settled in London, he added to his knowledge of French plants an equally formid-able grasp of English native plants. Dodoens, nine years older than Clusius and, like him, employed at the Imperial Court in Vienna, retained always the mindset of a physician. His books were still cast as herbals. Insofar as he classified at all, he did so by pharmacology and function, though in his last great production *Stirpium historiae pemptades sex* (1583), a few plants – lilies, iris, orchids, daisies, umbellifers – were treated together in family groups.

Clusius, handsome, elegant, quizzical as the portrait painted in 1606 by Filippo Paladini shows (see plate 117), was in many ways the most gifted of the three men. He, though, was so busy staying ahead of the pack, making sure he knew more, had seen more and possessed more than any other scholar in Europe, that he scarcely had time (or indeed the inclination) to make philosophic sense of all that he knew. He liked to be closely involved in the production of his books. He wrote to Plantin about a carpenter he'd found in Frankfurt 'qui scache faire bonnes planches de poirier bien assaisonné et net, a dix pfennings pour planche'. He fussed about the accuracy of the illustrations, standing beside the artist van der Borcht as he drew the portraits of the plants to be included in each new compendium.

Plantin printed three of Clusius's original works and eight of his translations. Clusius, who could read Flemish, French, German, Greek, Italian, Latin and Spanish, taught himself Portuguese so that he could translate into Latin the Portuguese trav-eller, Garcia de Orta's account of his journey to Goa.[5] De Orta (*c*.1490–1570), a physician born in the Portuguese frontier town of Elvas, near Badajos, had made his journey in 1534, taking six months to sail from the Tagus to India. In Goa, now the capital of Portuguese India, he took up a position as personal physician to Alfonso de Sousa, a Portuguese naval officer. He stayed for more than thirty years and in 1563 wrote an account of the plants and medicines he had become familiar with there. His *Coloquios dos simples, e drogas he cousas medicinais da India*, published in Goa by Joannes de Endem, was one of the first European books ever printed in India and the first to describe the plants of the subcontinent to a European audience. The book is cast in the form of a dialogue between de Orta and a fictitious Dr Ruano and includes accounts of the betel nut, clove, mace, nutmeg, ginger, camphor and cinnamon that formed such an important part of the trade between East and West. He also wrote about bhang (*Cannabis sativa*), which he said was used by women who wanted 'to dally and flirt with men', and by anyone seeking rest, sleep and escape from the cares of the world. The Sultan Bahadur took it 'when he wished to journey about the world at night'. It's a hotchpotch of a book, with instructions for taming elephants as well as preparing drugs. Only occasionally does it deal with plants in terms of their own intrinsic interest, but it was the first book to make clear the original source of the drugs that reached the West through Alexandria, Constantinople and the bazaars of Syria. Goa had made Garcia de Orta fabulously wealthy, but it had also given him intellectual freedom. 'Even I, when in Spain, did not dare to say anything against Galen or against the Greeks,' he wrote. De Orta gathered plant names in various Eastern languages – Persian, Hindu, Malay – and wrote about their sources, techniques for preparing them, the customs of his adopted country. Clusius's Latin edition was published in 1582, with yet more illustrations, hastily supplied by Plantin.

After fourteen years with the Imperial Court, Clusius accepted an invitation to go to Leiden as *horti praefectus*, director of the botanic garden. He was already sixty-seven years old, but with extraordinary energy he began to lay out the new garden, and from a fresh hub spun a web of contacts to supply him with plants, or at the very least reports and pictures of them. The Florentine collector, Matteo Caccini, sent him day lilies, ranunculus, the curious marvel of Peru from the New World and from Constantinople the elegant pink and white tulip that was later given Clusius's name, *T. clusiana*. Clusius sent Caccini hyacinths, lilies and colchicums. From the botanic garden at Pisa, where a fellow Fleming Joseph Godenhuize (known in Italy as Giuseppe Casabona) was now in charge, he received Cretan seeds, bulbs and plants: berberis, broom, the beautiful white-flowered paeony endemic on the island, thyme, sage, various narcissi. Casabona had recently made an expedition to Crete where he had been delighted at last to meet 'the fig tree of Mount Ida and the aconite of Theophrastus'. He had dragged an unwilling German soldier round the

Plate 126: An early drawing of the potato, newly brought in from South America and sent to Clusius in Vienna in 1589 by Philippe de Sivry, governor of Mons. Clusius described the plant in his Rariorum plantarum historia *(1601)*

island to paint the plants they saw and some of these paintings too found their way to Leiden.[6]

Clusius is indefatigable. He gets hold of some of the sketches made by the Flemish painter, Jacques le Moyne de Morgues (c.1533-1588), who in 1564, had set sail from Le Havre as cartographer and artist/recorder on Lieutenant René Goulaine de Laudonnière's exploratory expedition to Florida.[7] By September 1565, the Huguenot colony in Florida had been overrun by Spaniards, but de Morgues escaped and returned to France with some of his paintings. After he settles in London, Clusius keeps in touch with him there and with other plantsman-emigrés such as the Huguenot apothecary James Garrett whom he describes as 'my dear friend, a man of honour, greatly delighting in the study of herbarism'. From Garrett in October 1599, Clusius gets a dried specimen of a kind of acacia brought back from San Juan de Puerto Rico by the Earl of Cumberland. In London he inspects the herbarium made by Thomas Penny, whose annotations appear on so many of the drawings made by Conrad Gesner for his never-to-be-published encyclopaedia of plants. The 'learned and kindly' Richard Garth, Chief Secretary of the Chancery in London, brings him some plants of a floury-leaved primula he has never seen before, said to grow wild near Halifax. He packs them up and sends them to friends in Antwerp. He corresponds with the two Royal Druggists, Hugh Morgan and John Rich. He translates into Latin the French nurseryman and traveller Pierre Belon's account of his journey through the Levant in 1546. The book, *Les Observations de plusieurs singularités*, first published in Paris, had been an immediate success. Clusius's version of 1589 was a typically opportunistic venture by Plantin.

But Clusius, though a scholar (and the first plantsman to describe and illustrate a wide selection of fungi), is not much interested in the search for order. By nature he is a describer, a disseminator, a collector. By the time of his death in 1609 he has added more than 600 plants to the known canon, but he has not contributed to the debate, more urgent now with the influx of so many previously unknown plants into Europe, about the right way to group and categorise them. Lobelius, twelve years younger than Clusius, was different. Throughout his life, he was searching for a method of grouping plants that seemed rational and could be tested by a series of empirical observations. In his first book, *Stirpium adversaria nova* (A New Notebook of Plants), written with his friend Pierre Pena in 1570, Lobelius chooses the form of the leaf as his preferred method of pigeonholing plants. Was he aware of the different method that Cesalpino in Italy had chosen? Cesalpino's herbarium, ordering plants by way of their fruits and seeds, was made by 1563.

Plate 127: The title page of Stirpium adversaria nova by
Pierre Pena and Matthias de l'Obel (Lobelius) which
was published in London in 1570

Lobelius and Pena had themselves visited the botanic garden at Pisa. Surely they would have been shown the great *hortus siccus* and discussed a matter of such interest and concern to them both? Though Cesalpino turned out to be closer to finding the key than Lobelius, Lobelius, taking the differences between leaves as his guiding principle, made in his *Stirpium* a fundamental and historic observation. He noted that some plants such as grasses, rushes and bulbous plants like iris had leaves with long straight veins running from top to bottom of the leaf. Others (the majority) had leaves netted all over with veins that connected the central midrib with the edge of the leaf. Lobelius had homed in on the difference that in our own age has made profits of billions for the manufacturers of weedkillers. The herbicides sprayed annually on to the lawns of the temperate world depend entirely on active ingredients that can distinguish between grass-like plants with long straight parallel veins and the broad-leaved plants – plantain, dandelion, daisy – netted all over with veins, that grow among them. The distinction between the two now rests not on the trait that Lobelius had seized upon, the way that they are veined, but on the way these two different kinds of plants germinate. While scientists of the twenty-first century describe the two in concepts and words (monocotyledon and dicotyledon) that hadn't been framed when Lobelius wrote out his painstaking observations, our monocots are Lobelius's grass-like plants, so-called because just one leaf emerges from the seed when the plant first germinates. Our dicots are the broad-leaved plants, which on germinating produce their first leaves as a pair.

Lobelius starts his *Plantarum* of 1576 with grasses; the title page, featuring a splendid architectural portico dreamed up by Plantin, wild countryside beyond, promises 'Nominum & opinionum Consensus & Harmonia' in the pages to come, but full consensus and harmony in the matter of names and opinions about them were still a long way off. Even the simplest plant, such as the charming purplish corncockle, then still widespread in arable land, was weighed down with a dictionary's worth of alternative names. Lobelius decides to call it 'Pseudomelanthium' but includes the quite different attributions of other plantsmen before him. Dodoens has called it 'Nigellastrum'; Fuchs has preferred 'Lolium perperam'; Moroni chooses 'Lichnioides segetum'; the German scholar Tragus tries 'Gitago'; to the Spanish it's known as 'Neguillia' or 'Allipiure'. Yet though the use of pictures has made it easier for Lobelius to match his corncockle to the plants that other authors are also thinking of as corncockle, and though they are mostly using the same language, Latin, wheat, perhaps one of the most essential of European plants, still has no commonly agreed name. Lobelius calls it 'Siligo spica mutica'[8] and follows that with names in German (Weyssen), English (weet), Belgian (Terwe), French (Froument, Bled), Italian ('Fourmento', Grano and Solina) and Spanish (Trigo).

324

After grasses, Lobelius moves on to iris, inventing over-complicated Latin names such as 'Iris perpusilla saxatilis ferme acaulis' (small, nearly stemless iris that grows on rocks) in his attempt to pin down accurately the differences between one species and another. Over the previous hundred years, a two-name routine had evolved more or less naturally. Tags such as *Iris latifolia*, where *Iris* denotes one group of plants and *latifolia* (broad-leaved) the particular type within the group, provided a useful and commonly understood shorthand. Now that process was in danger of being swamped by labels that were not so much names as descriptions. The pernicious procedure continued in Plantin's picture book, the *Icones* of 1581, where a small hoop petticoat daffodil staggers under its newly given name 'Narcissus montanus iuncifolius minimus alter flore luteo' (a small, rush-leaved daffodil with a yellow flower that grows in the mountains).

The *Icones*, a compendium of all the pictures that Plantin had used in the books written by Dodoens, Clusius and Lobelius, published just five years after *Plantarum*, shows how quickly a taste for bulbs had grown among European collectors. The number of iris portrayed has almost doubled from eight to fifteen. Twenty narcissi are shown, compared with eight in *Plantarum*. Tulips, then still called 'Lilionarcissus', have exploded from six to twenty-six. There are twice the number of lilies in the *Icones* as appeared in the *Plantarum*. Plantin includes iconic flowers such as the crown imperial and the fabulous black-flowered fritillary recently imported from Persia.[9] The illustrations that Pieter van der Borcht made for Plantin are accurate but they don't have the immediacy of Weiditz's work for Brunfels or the elegant beauty of Liberale's illustrations for Mattioli. The pictures Plantin commissioned are workmanlike; there is none of the sympathetic identification with habit and form shown by the artist of the Carrara Herbal. But Plantin's illustrator adopts Gesner's useful innovation, setting against the image of the thing in its entirety, details of the plant he is drawing – the construction of a flower, the particular aspect of a bulb, seeds massively magnified. The compound microscope, invented by Zacharias Jansen in 1590, would make accurate realisation of these details even more important in the plant books of the early seventeenth century, once Galileo had refined Jansen's first proposals. By 1665, when the English scholar Robert Hooke published his *Micrographia*, the invention had changed for ever the way that man viewed the previously hidden secrets of the natural world.

There are plenty of names in Lobelius's *Plantarum* that we still use today: leucojum, campanula, aster, *Papaver corniculatum* for the horned poppy, *Papaver rhoeas* for the Shirley poppy, *Pulsatilla vulgaris* for the pasque flower, cyclamen, which has been constant in its name ever since it was painted in Juliana's book in the sixth century AD. Plantin packed in plenty of pictures (sometimes four to a page), which should have

Martagon hoc floruit aftate Annj 1613
Francofurti ad Moenum in horto D. Iacobi
de Fay, civis & mercatoris ibid.

84

*Plate 128: A martagon lily (*Lilium martagon*) which flowered in
1613 in the Frankfurt garden of Jacob de Fay, illustrated in
Johann Theodor de Bry's* Florilegium novum. *The book was first
published in 1612, but went through several editions*

been a help with identification. But, because of the carelessness with which he married up image and text, adjustments sometimes needed to be made after the books were printed. In the copy I'm reading in the rare books room of the University Library, Cambridge, alternative images have been pasted over some of the ones originally printed. Finally the right image is matched with its description on the printed page. 'Another job for the five-year-old daughters' I think, as I turn over the flimsy pages of the battered, leather-bound book.

There were many different incentives to study plants in the sixteenth century: some people were motivated by piety; some enjoyed the opportunities it offered to explore foreign lands; some hoped to arm themselves against the prevailing ignorance of pharmacists; some were driven by a kind of lust, a collector's greed, a compulsion to possess; some hoped that plants would further their quest for occult knowledge; some regarded plants as just one aspect of a wider delight in the beauty and fascination of the natural world; some admired above all the artistry of the painters who portrayed flowers. National pride was perhaps one of the driving forces behind Lobelius's preoccupation with plants. Born at Lille in Flanders, he makes a special case for Flemish supremacy in terms of plant knowledge. He points out that the Flemish were the first to introduce plants from Constantinople and the Near East, and that in Flemish gardens there grew more rare plants than could be found in the whole of the rest of Western Europe. Some of these gardens had been destroyed in the civil wars of the sixteenth century, but the *Plantarum* is full of flowery tributes to dedicated Flemish collectors: Carolus de Croy, Prince of Chymay, the *generosi* Joannes de Brancion, Dr Joannis of Limoges, the *clarissimae matronae* Maria de Brimeu, the wife of Conrardi Scetz, the illustrious doctor, Joannes van der Dilf. The drawback of all this collecting was its effect on plants growing in the wild. Already in 1570, Lobelius and Pena noted that the plant they called *Panax Heraclium Herculea* used to 'grow naturally on that stony hill on the left as you go from Montpellier to Frontignan, close behind the ruins of Saccellum, as we were shown by Doctor Assatius, professor at Montpellier, who labours greatly and untiringly at this. But, thanks to the traffic of the students, who avidly preserve this plant on pieces of paper, this plant has been almost completely destroyed.'[10]

Though intensely proud of his homeland, Lobelius found that Flanders was no longer a place he could live. It was impossible, he observed, to make a home on a sea tossed by incessant tempests, or indulge his peaceful love of gardens and flowers on lands watered with human blood. From 1569 onwards, he had travelled throughout in Britain with his friend Pierre Pena. Later, he settled more or less permanently in

London. As superintendent of Edward Zouche's garden at Hackney, he became an important link between the scholar-botanists of the Continent and the new generation of more practical, experimental gardeners emerging in England, particularly in the capital. Until the Oxford Botanic Garden was set up in 1621, Britain had no equivalent to the great European centres of learning at Padua, Vienna or Leiden. Plant collections were amassed by rich aristocrats and, among these, Lord Zouche was paramount. His Hackney garden was a gathering point for all the best botanists, including fellow Flemings who had 'come for religion' as contemporary records put it, and who, like Lobelius, had settled in London. By 1607, through Zouche's influence, Lobelius is established in the post of *botanicus regius* to James I. He sends plants, including seaweeds, to Jean, the elder of the two Bauhin brothers, and in turn, receives seeds from the younger brother Gaspard, which he grows in Lord Zouche's garden. He stays in close contact with Jean Robin, botanist to the French king, who in 1602 had sent him a cyclamen from the Pyrenees. He writes to Clusius about a limonium he has found at Colchester. He has a particularly good trip to Wales, enjoying the yellow and orange Welsh poppies spread widely in the countryside. He collects Welsh names ('Cambro-British' he calls them) to add to the indices of his plant books. At Drayton, near Portsmouth in Hampshire, he visits Jane, the widow of Richard Garth, who had given Clusius the floury primulas. She plies him with metheglin, a wildly alcoholic kind of spiced mead. From Sir John de Franqueville, whose father had fled from Cambrai to England after the Edict of Nantes, he gets his first sight of the roots of sugar cane. He receives regular parcels from Wilhelm Boel, a Frieslander who supplies him with seeds and plants acquired on trading trips to North Africa, Spain, Portugal and the south of France. Hieronymus Winghe, the canon of Tournay in Flanders, sends him melon seeds. And, after a lifetime's study, he makes a profound distinction between the leaves of different plants. But his method of arranging plants, using foliage as his criterion, leads him up some blind alleys, and persuades him to make some reckless decisions. He submerges all pears into the apple family, for instance, on the basis that it is 'useless to try and name any character by which pear trees are distinguishable from apples'. Any greengrocer could give him a lesson on that. But with the 'nieuwe ordeninghe', the fifty tables gathered in his *Kruydtboeck* of 1581, he has at least tried to classify the unwieldy mass of plants with which scholars now had to deal. He had shown up some of the problems inherent in his method and perhaps dissuaded others from following the same way. After his death in 1616, he was well placed from the comfortable eminence of his grave in the churchyard of St Denis, in the heights of Highgate, to oversee the progress of his protégés in the opening years of the seventeenth century.

Plate 129: Different varieties of anemone were much collected in the late sixteenth century. Francesco Caetani, the Duke of Sermoneta, was said to have 29,000 in his garden at Cisterna. This illustration comes from Crispin de Passe's Hortus Floridus *(1614)*

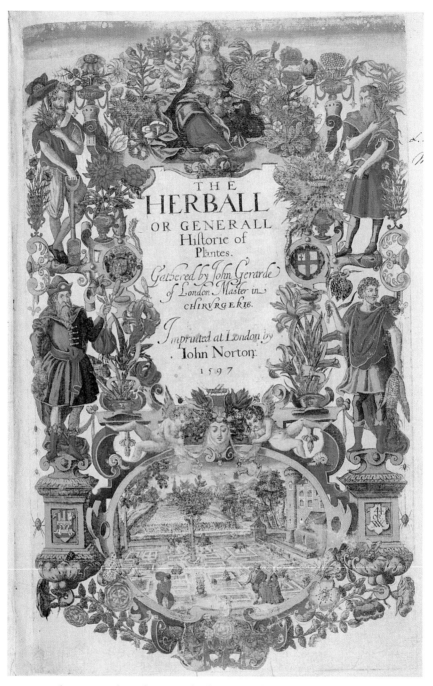

THE
HERBALL
OR GENERALL
Historie of
Plantes.

Gathered by John Gerarde
of London Master in
CHIRVRGERIE.

Imprinted at London by
John Norton.
1597

*Plate 130: The title page of John Gerard's Herball, printed in 1597
by John Norton in London. The surrounding garland shows
exotic plants such as the crown imperial from Constantinople
and maize, recently introduced from the New World*

XXI

THE LAST OF THE HERBALS
1560—1640

THE ACADEMIC CARAPACE that fostered the study of plants on the Continent – botanic gardens attached to universities, newly established faculties of *res herbaria*, scholarly books issued by well-established printers, inspirational teachers – did not exist in Britain, even towards the end of the sixteenth century. When Lobelius came as an exile to London, no English university had a faculty devoted to the study of plants and the only botanic gardens to be found were the private collections built up by interested amateurs such as his employer, Lord Zouche. Lord Burghley had equally fine gardens in the Strand, London, and at Theobalds in Hertfordshire, looked after by John Gerard (1545–1612). The professional power base for plantsmen in England, in so far as there was one, rested with bodies such as the Society of Apothecaries of which Thomas Johnson and his *socii itinerantes* were members, the College of Physicians and the powerful Barber-Surgeons' Company. All had an interest in acquiring knowledge about plants, though of a very specific kind. Rich amateurs such as Lord Zouche and Lord Burghley could afford a more disinterested view, collecting plants for their rarity value, rather than their medicinal qualities. John Gerard (see plate 131), apprenticed in 1562 to barber-surgeon Alexander Mason, had a foot in both camps. He rose rapidly in the hierarchy of the barber-surgeons, becoming a freeman by 1569, but he was also well known as a collector. In 1596 he published a list of all the plants (1,039 different kinds) in his Holborn garden, where he grew 'all manner of strange trees, herbes, rootes, plants, floures and other such rare things, that it would make a man wonder, how one of his degree, not having the purse of a number, could ever accomplish the same'.[1] It was the first such catalogue ever produced. He had a wide circle of influential friends, including Lancelot Browne, physician to Queen Elizabeth, and George Baker, Master of the Barber-Surgeons' Company. He knew and exchanged plants with the apothecaries James Garrett, Hugh Morgan and Richard Garth, all of whom had fine gardens in the City. Garth, described by Gerard as a 'worshipful gentleman and one that greatly delighteth in strange plants', had useful connections with South America and imported strange rarities from Brazil. Garth was also friendly with Clusius and in exchange for South American plants, Clusius gave him a root of Solomon's seal, which Garth in turn passed on to Gerard. Gerard cultivated other useful contacts, such as 'Captain Nicholas Leet of the Turky Company', a leading merchant who imported plants from Syria and Turkey, which Gerard was among the first to grow. He went out to Twickenham to see Richard Pointer whose garden and nurseries were noted for their trees. Pointer kept conies in his orchard, not for food but 'onely to keepe downe the grasse low'.[2] Gerard knew Master Fowle, keeper of the Queen's house at St James's, and champion melon-grower. He kept in regular touch with Master Huggens, keeper of the garden at Hampton Court. He sent his servant, William Marshall, on an expedition to the Mediterranean sea, where he saw plane trees and the Indian fig (*Opuntia ficus-indica*) 'in an island called Zante, about a day and nights sailing with a meane winde from Petrasse'. Jean Robin, botanist to the King of France, sends him nasturtium seeds from his garden in Paris 'at the signe of the blacke head in the street called Du Bout du Monde'.

So it was not surprising, perhaps, that when the English publisher John Norton had it in mind to bring out an English translation of one of Dodoens's seminal works, the *Pemptades* of 1583, he should turn to John Gerard. Henry Lyte (1529–1607) had already made a great success of his translation of Dodoens's *Cruydeboeck*, which had appeared in England in 1578 as *A Niewe Herball*. Norton evidently felt the market could take more of the same. (By the middle of the sixteenth century, the population in Britain totalled about three million, rising to five million by 1651. At least half a million of that three million could read and increasingly books became the way by which ideas spread. Though it was slow to get established in England, printing gradually forced the pace of change.) Lyte, though, was an honest amateur, who in his final printed work carefully distinguished between his translation of Dodoens and his own added amendments. Gerard, whose *Herball* was published in London by John Norton in 1597 (see plate 130), was a plagiarist and a crook. He had not been Norton's first choice as translator. The work had been started by a Dr Priest of the College of Physicians, who had died before completing his task. Among his other posts, Gerard was curator of the physic garden that belonged to the College,

Plate 131: *John Gerard (1545–1612) in his fifty-third year, the portrait that appeared in his* Herball *of 1597*

so would surely have known Dr Priest, and the nature of the work he was engaged in. Yet in his preliminary address to the reader, Gerard writes 'Doctor Priest, one of our London Colledge, hath (as I heard) translated the last edition of Dodonaeus, and meant to publish the same; but being prevented by death, his translation like-wise perished.' In fact, Gerard pirated the translation, reordered the material to fit more closely the arrangement pioneered by Lobelius, and then brought out the book under his own name, 'the first fruits of these mine own labours'.

Gerard conceded that 'faults . . . have escaped, some by the printer's oversight, some through defects in my selfe to perform so great a worke, and some by means of the greatnesse of the labour'. He ended his address with the pious hope that his 'good meaning will be well taken, considering I do my best, not doubting but some of greater learning will perfect that which I have begun according to my small skill, especially the ice being broken unto him, and the woode rough hewed to his handes'.

Very rough-hewed, thought some of his contemporaries, including James Garrett, the clever Huguenot apothecary in whose garden at London Wall Gerard had seen the first tulips to bloom in England. While Gerard was still at work on the *Herball*, Garrett quietly warned Norton that it was full of mistakes.[3] Gerard was an avid collector, an assiduous cultivator of people as well as plants, but he was not a scholar. In an attempt to repair the damage, Norton brought in Lobelius to edit the first version of the text. The two men were good friends and had often been 'simpling' together – Lobelius had been with Gerard when they discovered the red-flowered prickly poppy at Southfleet in Kent. He had written a generous introduction to the 1596 *Catalogue* of plants in Gerard's Holborn garden.[4] Lobelius found more than a thousand mistakes in the manuscript of the *Herball* before Gerard, in a huff, whisked it away from him. Lobelius, he said, being a Fleming, did not understand the English idiom. The truth was that Gerard could not match Lobelius's erudition and had no ready defence when Lobelius accused him, rightly, of plundering material from his own *Stirpium adversaria nova*, which Plantin had published in 1570. But, faults and all, Norton decided to print the book that had already suffered so many setbacks. A further problem arose over the question of illustrations. No body of plant pictures had been built up in England to match the five great sets of illustrations amassed in Europe between 1530 and 1590. Norton could have raided the Fuchs images that William Turner had used in his own books, written more than thirty years earlier, but there were not enough of them to fill Gerard's work. Many of the plants Gerard was writing about hadn't even been introduced when Turner was at work. The obvious thing would have been to use the illustrations that Plantin commis-sioned for Dodoens's original work, the *Pemptades*. That, however, would have high-lighted Dodoens's claim as author, rather than Gerard's. Instead, Norton rented a

Battata Virginiana siue Virginianorum, & Pappus.
Potatoes of Virginia.

Plate 132: Potatoes, not from Virginia, but probably from Cartagena in Colombia, brought back to England by Francis Drake in 1586. Best 'boiled and eaten with oile, vinegar and pepper, or dressed some other way by the hand of a skilfull Cooke,' wrote John Gerard in his Herball *(1597)*

hoard of woodblocks belonging to a Frankfurt publisher, Nicolaus Bassaeus. There were more than 2,000 of these and about 1,800 were used for the new *Herball*. They provided the opportunity for another grand muddle, as Gerard, unable to identify the plants carved on the blocks, matched them with the wrong decriptions.

Only about sixteen of the illustrations were original, including one of the earliest pictures of the potato (see plate 132), which, Gerard wrote, 'groweth naturally in America, where it was first discovered . . . I have received roots hereof from Virginia, otherwise called Norembega, which grow & prosper in my garden as in their owne native country'. Less wisely, he finished his book with a new illustration and description of the barnacle tree (see plate 133), a miraculous thing that bore geese rather than leaves. The tree, he writes, is 'one of the marvels of this land (we may say of the World)'. In northern Scotland and islands such as the Orkneys, there are 'trees whereon do grow certaine shells of a white colour tending to russet, wherein are contained little living creatures: which shells in time of maturitie doe open, and out of them grow those little living things, which falling into the water do become foules, which we call Barnacles; in the North of England, brant Geese; and in Lancashire tree Geese: but the other that do fall upon the land perish and come to nothing'.

All this is hearsay, as Gerard concedes, but he can describe a similar phenomenon, which his own 'eies have seene, and hands have touched'. On an island called the Pile of Foulders in Lancashire, the timbers of wrecked ships breed a kind of spume or froth, which in time turns into shells,

> in shape like those of the Muskle, but sharper pointed, and of a whitish colour; wherein is contained a thing in forme like a lace of silke, finely woven as it were together, of a whitish colour, one ende whereof is fastned unto the inside of the shell, even as the fish of Oisters and Muskles are; the other ende is made fast unto the belly of a rude masse or lumpe, which in time commeth to the shape and forme of a Bird: when it is perfectly formed, the shell gapeth open, and the first thing that appeareth is the foresaid lace or string; next comes the legs of the Birde hanging out and, as it groweth greater, it openeth the shell by degrees, til at length it is all come foorth, and hangeth onely by the bill; in short space after it commeth to full maturitie, and falleth into the sea, where it gathereth feathers, and groweth to a fowle, bigger than a Mallard and lesser than a Goose, having blacke legs and bill or beake.[5]

Back in the thirteenth century, Albertus Magnus had already written firmly that barnacle geese hatched from eggs like all other birds. Gerard was less rational, more credulous. But, like other observers at this time, he was trying to explain natural phenomena that were not yet understood. Nobody knew that birds migrated each year. Where then did these flocks of geese suddenly come from? In the context of the time, the barnacle tree seemed to provide as good an explanation as any other.

Plate 133: The barnacle tree, endowed with a spuriously important tag 'Britannica concha anatifera' in John Gerard's Herball *(1597)*

Gerard was a practical man, a populist. The speed with which he rose through the hierarchy of the barber-surgeons (in August 1608 he was elected Master) suggests a clubbable type of fellow, but compared with Lobelius and Turner, he had seen very little outside London. In his early years, he made his one and only trip abroad, travelling, possibly as ship's surgeon, on a merchant vessel that traded between Russia, Denmark, Sweden and Poland. But he had none of Turner's close experience of European countries and their plants, none of Lobelius's easy mastery of foreign languages and scholarship. Turner had studied at Cambridge, Lobelius at Montpellier; Gerard did not have that early academic discipline. His formal education ended with his schooling in Nantwich, where he was born in 1545; he was just seventeen when his apprenticeship as a barber-surgeon began. He was a doer, not a thinker. The *Herball* is dedicated to Lord Burghley, his patron, and in the fulsome Dedicatory Letter, Gerard sets out what he sees as his own particular achievements:

> To the large and singular furniture of this noble iland I have added from forren places all the varietie of herbes and floures that I might any way obtaine, I have laboured with the soile to make it fit for the plants, and with the plants to make them to delight in the soile, that so they might live and prosper under our clymat, as in their native and proper countrey: what my successe hath beene, and what my furniture is, I leave to the report of them that have seene your Lordship's gardens, and the little plot of my speciall care and husbandrie.[6]

It is the testament of a gardener, not a scholar. Gerard's *Herball* is a celebration of plants, their variety and beauty, with scarcely a nod at the theory underlying their study. In the first part of his book, he roughly reorders his material to take account of Lobelius's shift towards foliage as a means of classifying and ordering plants. But as for himself, he says that it would be tedious to introduce 'any curious discourse upon the generall division of plants' or 'to speak of the differing names of their severall parts, more in Latine than our vulgar tongue can well expresse'. He was not, by nature, interested in the search for order or the characteristics that most clearly defined the differences between plants. The *Herball* is divided into three parts, starting with 'Grasses, Rushes, Reeds, Corne, Flags', and the 'Bulbous or Onion-rooted Plants . . . such as with their brave and gallant floures deck and beautifie gardens, and feed rather the eies than the belly'. In the second book, Gerard puts 'most sorts of Herbs used for meat, medicine, or sweet smell'. The third is a ragbag: trees, shrubs, bushes, fruit, 'Rosins, Gummes, Roses, Heaths, Mosses, Mushrooms, Corall, and their severall kindes'.

No great breakthroughs there. So why is Gerard important? A significant part of his appeal at the time was his accessibility. He used words vividly, describing white hellebore (our veratrum) with leaves 'folded into pleits like a garment plaited to be laid up in a chest', or the seed pods of honesty with the innermost skin 'thinne and cleere shining, like a shred of white Sattin newly cut from the piece'. He favoured showy florists' flowers such as anemones and pinks, which were beginning to be collected with tremendous enthusiasm by gardeners of the late sixteenth century. He had good contacts which meant that he could include details of the intriguing new plants coming in from the Americas, all of great interest to plantsmen in England: the potato, marvel of Peru, maize (see plate 134), tobacco, sunflower and tomato, still then thought of as an aphrodisiac, The Apple of Love. The tomato 'bringeth

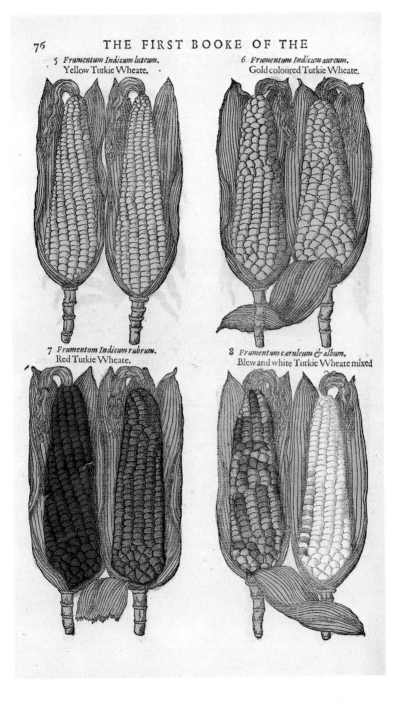

5 *Frumentum Indicum luteum.*
Yellow Turkie Wheate.

6 *Frumentum Indicum aureum.*
Gold coloured Turkie Wheate.

7 *Frumentum Indicum rubrum.*
Red Turkie Wheate.

8 *Frumentum cæruleum & album.*
Blew and white Turkie Wheate mixed

Plate 134: *Turkie Wheate, which is not wheat from Turkey but maize* (Zea mays) *from South America in John Gerard's* Herball *(1597)*

forth very long round stalkes or branches, fat and full of juice, trailing upon the ground', wrote Gerard.

> The leaves are great, and deeply cut or jagged about the edges . . . amongst which come forth yellow floures growing upon short stems or footstalkes, clustering together in bunches: which being fallen there doe come in place faire and goodly apples, chamfered, uneven, and bunched out in many places; of a bright shining red colour, and the bignesse of a goose egge or a large pippin. The pulpe or meat is very full of moisture, soft, reddish, and of the substance of a wheat plumme.[7]

By including very specific localities for his plants, Gerard (though it was not his purpose) contributed to the gradual building up of a map of the British flora and an understanding of its distribution. Most of the locations he mentions are in London, or close to it: Margate, Rye, Harwich. The kidney vetch for instance, he found on Hampstead Heath, 'right against the Beacon, upon the right hand as you goe from London, neere unto a gravelle pit. They grow also upon black Heath, in the high way leading from Greenwich to Charleton, within half a mile of the towne.' Sea lavender grew 'in great plenty upon the walls of the fort against Gravesend', by the king's storehouse at Chatham and 'fast by the King's ferrey going into the Isle of Sheppey'. He mentions a saxifrage growing 'upon the bricke wall in Chauncerie lane, belonging to the Earle of Southampton', and a fine plane tree 'in my Lord Treasurer's garden at the Strand'. He found brilliant yellow loosestrife 'along the Medowes as you goe from Lambeth to Battersey neere London' and the pink-flowered skullcap 'upon the bog or marrish ground at Hampsteed heath neere unto the head of the springs that were digged for water to be conveied to London 1590 attempted by that carefull citizen Sir John Hart, Knight, Lord Mayor of the Citie of London, at which time my selfe was in his Lordship's company and viewing for my pleasure the same goodly springs I found the said plant not heretofore remembred'. In the east he does not seem to have got farther than Cambridge, where he talks of the beautiful purple pasque flower, which grew 'very plentifully in the pasture or close belonging to the parsonage house of a small village six miles from Cambridge, called Hildersham'.[8] Cheshire, Gerard's birthplace, was the most northerly county he knew and he mentions the pennywort he found there, growing on the walls of Bieston Castle.

The book succeeded, too, because it was printed in English, in a fine, light type, less daunting on the page than the heavy, Germanic black letter type that had been the norm in Turner's day. It was widely distributed, thanks in part to Gerard's own wide circle of contacts, but also because of the growing number of booksellers in

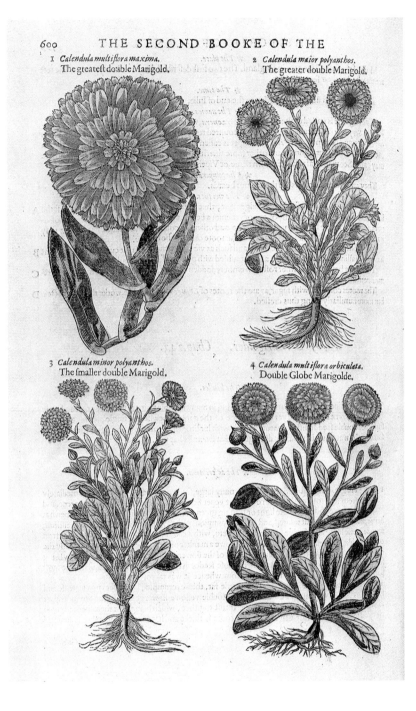

1 *Calendula multiflora maxima.*
The greatest double Marigold.

2 *Calendula maior polyanthos.*
The greater double Marigold.

3 *Calendula minor polyanthos.*
The smaller double Marigold.

4 *Calendula multiflora orbiculata.*
Double Globe Marigolde.

Plate 135: English marigolds (Calendula officinalis) *of various forms in John Gerard's* Herball *(1597)*

the country. Those who owned the *Herball*, men such as Sir John Salusbury (1567–1612) of Lleweni in Denbighshire, annotated their copies with details of local plants, adding new localities and differing flowering seasons. Beside Gerard's picture of the sunflower, Salusbury noted with satisfaction that 'This galant greate sunflower grewe in Sir John Salusbury's Garden at Llewenye & cam to the full perfection of this portraiture the year 1607.' All this swapping of knowledge, the annotating, the commentaries, contributed to the laborious but necessary process of identifying plants and coming to a consensus about their correct names. Gerard's book, flawed though it was, was part of that.

Gerard died without ever seeing a flower on his yucca, one of the earliest plants to be introduced from the New World into Europe. He was immensely proud of possessing this rarity but the honour of its first flowering in Britain went to William Coys of North Ockendon in Essex. Gerard's yucca had been brought to him in 1593 'by a servant of a learned and skilfull Apothecarie of Excester, named Master Thomas Edwards'. He had wrongly called the plant yucca because he believed it to be the manihot or yucca that the Amerindians of South America used to make cassava. In the *Herball*, he described its leaf which 'with advised eie viewed, is like a little Wherrie or such like bote', evergreen 'notwithstanding the injurie of our colde climate, without any coverture at all'. Gerard's yucca perished with him, but during his lifetime he had passed on a little piece of it to Jean Robin in Paris. Robin's son, Vespasien, in turn passed a 'pup' from that plant to another of Gerard's former correspondents, Sir John de Franqueville (Lobelius knew him too). Franqueville, in whose London garden were many rarities such as sugar cane and the Jerusalem artichoke, then gave a piece of Gerard's yucca to John Parkinson (1567–1650), a fine gardener and apothecary to James I. Parkinson tried to set right the wrong name, but by then it was too late, and yucca it has been ever since.

Parkinson's own book, the *Paradisi in sole paradisus terrestris* published in 1629 (see plate 136), was the first plant book to be produced since Gerard's *Herball* and in the Introduction he says that, if the present book was well received, he intended to follow on with another, *A Garden of Simples*, more clearly designed to supercede Gerard's work. Alerted to Parkinson's intention, Adam Islip, Joice Norton and Richard Whitaker, the printers who had taken over Norton's firm, decided that they could not leave the field to Parkinson and must bring out a revised edition of Gerard to fill the gap that Parkinson had identified. Urgently, they began the search for an editor who would agree to their condition that the work be produced within a year. It was a demanding stipulation, but it was fulfilled and in 1633 the new edition was published, at 42s 6d unbound, 48s bound. The book was half as long again as Gerard's original, with 2,765 woodcuts almost all now borrowed from Plantin's bran tub. It

Plate 136: Spring- and autumn-flowering cyclamen
(probably Cyclamen coum and Cyclamen hederifolium)
in an illustration from John Parkinson's Paradisi in
sole paradisus terrestris (1629)

is the biggest collection of illustrations yet printed in any herbal. The editor is Thomas Johnson, the same Thomas Johnson who in 1629 had arranged a plant-hunting trip to Kent with companions from the Society of Apothecaries.

At the time he made his record-breaking journey, Johnson, aged about twenty-eight, had only just finished an eight-year-long apprenticeship to the apothecary William Bell. On 28 November 1628, he had been 'examined and found sufficient, was made free, paid his fees and gave a spoone'. He was friendly with John Parkinson, to whose *Paradisi* he contributed a laudatory address, but his chief interest was not in the garden flowers that so delighted Parkinson and Gerard. With the help of correspondents throughout the land, Johnson's long-term aim was to produce a complete list of all the plants known to grow in Britain. The Kentish trip alone produced about 150 accounts of plants not previously recorded in the country. His role model was the young Italian plantsman, Ulysse Aldrovandi, whose 1557 plant-hunting expedition into the Sibylline mountains of Italy had been the first of its kind ever made. In his short life Johnson published four accounts of his various journeys into Kent, the West Country, Wales and the Isle of Wight. The *Iter* (1629) covered his first expedition in Kent and a subsequent exploration of Hampstead Heath. The *Descriptio itineris plantarum* (1632) dealt with later travels in Kent. The *Mercurius botanicus*, published in two parts in 1634 and 1641, recorded Johnson's journey to the West Country, Wales and the Isle of Wight. The ambitious expedition to the West Country and Wales was undertaken after his work on the *Herball*, the others before, the earliest accounts of plant-hunting expeditions ever to be published in England.

Much progress had been made in the matter of correctly identifying plants in the thirty-six years since Gerard's *Herball* had first been published and Johnson carefully distances himself from the original work: 'For the author Mr John Gerard I can say little,' he writes. 'His chief commendation is that he out of a propense good-will to the publique advancement endeavoured to perform therein more than he could well accomplish; which was partly through want of sufficient learning.'[9] The title page of Gerard's edition shows four vaguely classical figures, clutching anemones, a crown imperial and some anachronistic maize. Flanking the title of the 1633 edition, 'Very much Enlarged and Amended by Thomas Johnson Citizen and Apothecarye', are Theophrastus, soulful in sandals, and Dioscorides in a suitably warlike outfit. Johnson's enlarging and amending provided about 2,850 descriptions of plants, at least 800 of them new additions. He also used 700 new illustrations, including one (drawn by himself) of a bunch of bananas (see plate 137), the first ever published. It had come to him on 10 April 1633, a present from Dr John Argent, President of the College of Physicians, who had received it from a contact in Bermuda.

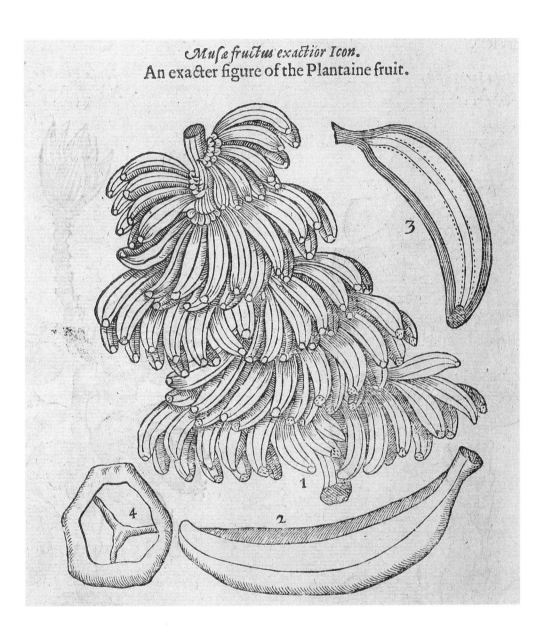

Muſæ fruitus exactior Icon.
An exacter figure of the Plantaine fruit.

Plate 137: The 'Plantaine fruit', as Thomas Johnson called the bananas that he hung outside his apothecary's shop – the first bananas that had ever been seen in London. He prepared this picture of them for his 1633 edition of Gerard's Herball

Johnson hung the bananas outside his London shop where they caused a sensation. Nobody had seen anything like them before and Johnson's drawing shows exactly the structure of the fruit, the seeds laid lengthways along the midrib, and the strange three-cornered marking underneath the stalk. The famous bananas were also included in the title page of Johnson's edition of the *Herball*, making a triumphant centre-piece in the vase of flowers set to the left of Gerard's portrait. The bananas, wrote Johnson, 'became ripe about the beginning of May and lasted until June: the pulp or meat was very soft and tender and it did eate somewhat like a Muske Melon'.[10]

XXII

ENGLISH ACHIEVEMENTS
1629—1664

WILLIAM TURNER, who had written the first plant book ever published in English, had been unlucky in his timing. Throughout his life, he found himself in the wrong place at the wrong time; his books had scarcely a chance of finding an audience. Thomas Johnson, on the other hand, was brilliantly placed to exploit the spirit of the age. The old beliefs were not sufficient for this new generation of plantsmen, who questioned fables, unmasked superstition, gradually threw nonsense aside. The barnacle tree found no place in Johnson's edition of the *Herball*. Increasingly knowledge was based not on tradition but on observation; a study of plants became a necessary part of a gentleman's education. Edward, Lord Herbert of Cherbury was typical of this new breed of amateur connoisseurs:

I conceive it is a fine study and worthy a gentleman to be a good botanic, that so he may know the nature of all herbs and plants, being our fellow-creatures and made for the use of man; for which purpose it will be fit for him to cull out of some good herbal all the icones together, with the descriptions of them and to lay by themselves all such as grow in England, and afterwards to select again such as usually grow by the highway-side, in meadows, by rivers, or in marshes, or in cornfields, or in dry and mountainous places, or on rocks, walls, or in shady places, such as grow by the seaside; for this being done, and the said icones being ordinarily carried by themselves or by their servants, one may presently find out every herb he meets

Plate 138: Various forms of daisy (Bellis perennis) *from Theodor de Bry's* Florilegium renovatum et auctum *of 1641*

withal, especially if the said flowers be truly coloured. Afterwards it will not be amiss to distinguish by themselves such herbs as are in gardens, and are exotics, and are transplanted hither.[1]

The newly enlarged *Herball* found a ready market among men such as Sir Henry Wotton, Provost of Eton. On 2 July 1637, he writes to Johnson, addressing 'this my servant unto you at the present with two or three requests. First, that you would direct him where he may buy one of your Gerrards, well and strongly bound; next, where I may have for my money all kinds of colored pinks to set in a quarter of my garden, or any such flowers as perfume the air.'[2]

The same spirit of rational enquiry prompted the summer 'simpling' expeditions that Johnson instigated and undertook with fellow members of the Society of Apothecaries. This Pickwickian crew includes William Broad, who had contributed laudatory verses to John Parkinson's *Paradisi*, and John Buggs, later thrown into prison for practising medicine without a licence (Buggs then abandoned medicine for the stage and joined the Queen of Bohemia's players instead). The first journey into Kent (13 July 1629) produces records of about 270 plants. Johnson does not include trees or shrubs, but concentrates on the smaller plants of the pasture, arable and shoreline typical of the landscape around Rochester and Gravesend (see pages 5–10). His account of the expedition (the *Iter* of 1629) is written in Latin, rather than English. Perhaps he felt it added *gravitas*. Perhaps he felt it was what would be expected of him by his fellow apothecaries, for whom the account was chiefly made. Perhaps there was a general consensus that Latin was somehow more 'scientific' than English and a more appropriate language to use in a work that was intended as a serious contribution to scientific research. There was, as yet, no Royal Society to promote such enquiry and it was the Warden of the Society of Apothecaries, Thomas Hicks, 'knowing that we had for several years past been in the habit of undertaking a journey of three or four days for the sake of traversing the natural habitats of the plants', who in 1632 'not only encouraged us as usual to spend some days on it, but promised himself to take his fair share of the work and more than his share of the expenses'. Johnson and his companions 'agreed forthwith, and thanked him for thinking us worthy of such an honour'. So, on the first of August that year, the *socii itinerantes* – Johnson and his friends William Broad, Leonard Buckner, Robert Larking and James Clarke – gather at Hicks's house where they have a celebratory breakfast. They then

went to the barge, boarded it, spread our sails to the wind, and left London. In the course of ten hours we covered sixty English miles, so that at the first approach of night we put to shore by the chalk cliffs of the isle of Thanet and the bay of Margate, where piles have been driven in and tied together and rocks thrown into the water so as to make a mole or pier for the more convenient berthing of ships. Here we left our own ship and went to our inn, where we found everything fit and ready, including our most attentive host, whose name is Richard Pollard. While we were in the island, he never left us, nor did he, like most others, plunder us when we departed.[3]

This, Johnson's second plant-hunting expedition into Kent, takes him and his crew into a more easterly part of the county than before, moving on from Margate to Sandwich by way of Quex Park, whose garden Gerard had known well. Johnson goes off to look at Sandown Castle, which Henry VIII had built in 1539. Guided by a local schoolmaster, the others explore the walls and bastions 'now partly ruinous with age'. They visit Caspar Niren, a Fleming settled in the town, in whose garden they admire sweet cicely, liquorice, bistort and a pink-flowered guelder rose. They pay their respects to the local apothecary, Charles Duck, who shows them 'a thing worth remembering':

the 'spoils' (if I may so call them) of a serpent fifteen feet long and thicker than an arm. As far as I can hazard a guess, it was a sea serpent; for it was caught by two men among the sandhills near the seashore, after its head had been shattered by small shot discharged from a fowling piece. It was hunting the rabbits, of which there is a vast abundance there, for food; for one or two were extracted from its stomach. These men, as I have said, brought the dead beast to our good friend Charles Duck, were duly rewarded and handed it over; its skin stripped from the flesh and stuffed with hay he still keeps with him as a memento of the event.

From Sandwich, the party moves on to Canterbury, and explores the cathedral, 'once world-famous for the shrine of Thomas Becket, of which the least costly part was of gold.'[4] Turning back homewards, they make their way on more familiar territory to Faversham where they pay their respects to the local apothecary, Nicholas Swayton. Swayton's garden is planted for pleasure as well as profit: Michaelmas daisies from America, Brompton stocks, columbines, cotton lavender, opium poppies, cyclamen, feverfew and tall melilot, much in demand for plasters and poultices. After 'waiting for an opportune moment at Gravesend, at the first of the tide on the river we entered a splendid boat driven by eight oars that happened to be left there and so returned to London, giving heartfelt thanks to God for His many benefits conferred on us: and we pray that on the works undertaken by us and all men for the public good He will bestow the desired fulfilment. Amen.'

The public good – that was what motivated this energetic and ambitious young apothecary. He was proud of his profession, but conscious that, while they knew so little about the plants they used to prepare their medicines, they could easily be duped by unscrupulous suppliers. The immediate point of the journeys 'undertaken for the discovery of plants' was to understand what these things really looked like, since native plants still made up the greatest part of an apothecary's pharmacopoeia. But it is evident from the Introduction to his published account of this second Kentish journey (the *Descriptio itineris plantarum* of 1632), that not everyone in the Society agreed with him. Perhaps it was the older generation, more moulded by custom and practice, whom he had in mind when he complained that 'some folk not only ridiculed our labour as vain and superfluous but derided all more precise knowledge of plants as useless, supposing that it is enough to know them merely by name and from reading. It is very certain', he continued, 'that the men of old who founded medicine were not so indolent and ignorant.' Johnson never loses an opportunity, either in the four accounts of his journeys, or in the amended *Herball*, to point out how easily apothecaries can be held to ransom by their own lack of knowledge. Speaking in the *Herball* of the hemlock water dropwort, he notes that it 'groweth amongst oysiers against Yorke House a little above the Horse ferrey against Lambeth . . . Pernitious and not excusable is the ignorance of some of our time that have bought and (as one may probably conjecture) used the roots of this plant instead of those of Peionie; and I know they are dayly by the ignorant women in Cheape-side sold to people more ignorant than themselves by the name of Water Lovage'. The water dropwort, widespread in ditches and damp places in the south and west of the country, was much easier for the herb-women to find than the lovage or the paeony. But all parts of it – roots, stem, flower – are highly poisonous. There was, as Johnson recognised, a pressing reason for apothecaries to be better informed.

Johnson's references show him to be a well read man: he refers to classical authors such as Dioscorides, Italian sources such as Giovanni Pona's catalogue of plants on Monte Baldo and Prospero Alpino's 1592 book on Egyptian plants, the works of the French nurseryman and explorer, Pierre Belon, and Jean Robin's *Catalogus stirpium lutetiae* of 1597, English authors such as William Turner and John Parkinson as well as the great trio of Clusius, Dodoens and Lobelius. But the consensus that plantsmen in England were slowly achieving in the first half of the seventeenth century depended as much on extensive networks of sympathetic friends as it did on book learning. Johnson's new edition of the *Herball*, which he began to work on immediately after his second journey into Kent, pays tribute to a mass of these contacts. The Gentleman Usher, Sir John Tunstall, drew his attention to a strange colchicum growing in his

Within the illustration:

DELICIÆ·DOMIN
NEC·QVID·SPERABE
HABEBAT.

Plate 139: A seventeenth-century garden scene from Daniel Rabel's Theatrum florae *(1633)*

garden 'at Edgcome by Croydon'. Thomas Glynn of Glynllifon sent a red-flowered mountain avens from his garden in Caernarvonshire. William Coote, chaplain to Lord Herbert, reported a hawkweed growing 'in the Lady Briget Kingsmill's ground at Sidmonton not far from Newberry in an old Roman camp close by the Decuman port'. Leonard Buckner, who had been with Johnson on both the journeys into Kent, supplied details of a marestail which he had found 'three miles beyond Oxford, a little on this side Euensham ferry, in a bog upon a common by the Beacon hill neere Cumner wood in the end of August 1632'. Without maps to reference, establishing the exact locations of plants was a cumbersome business. In Essex with Nathaniel Wright, Johnson found a new kind of pimpernel, 'among the corne at Wrightsbridge being the seat of Mr John Wright his brother'.

Johnson was more of a plantsman than his calling as an apothecary strictly required. Adding the ambitious Welsh journey to his travels, he had visited twenty-five English and Welsh counties by 1641, when he described that last epic journey (it included an assault on Snowdon, where the party picnicked among thymes and sedums, saxifrages and violets) in his *Mercurii botanici pars altera*.[5] Collecting and cataloguing was Johnson's forte and it was work that had to be done if the study of plants was to go forward – a study that had been later starting in Britain than on mainland Europe. But the constraints imposed by editing an existing work did not give him the opportunity to impose a major rearrangement. Perhaps at the time he was working on Gerard's *Herball* he was not anyway sufficiently interested to push on the great Lobelius's work in sorting and arranging plants in particular groups and families. He must, though, have appreciated and admired the work that Lobelius had done, for he quoted him more often than any other author, both in the *Herball* and in his own accounts of the apothecaries' journeys. And yet, in his chapter 'Of Rushes', he is able to write briskly: 'I do not here intend to trouble you with an accurate distinction and enumeration of Rushes; for if I should, it would be tedious to you, laborious to me, and beneficial to neither.'

Johnson's edition of the *Herball* was reprinted in 1636 but Johnson himself felt obliged to place an advertisement on the last page, apologising for the fact that so little new work appeared in it. This, he said, was because of his plan 'to travell over the most parts of this Kingdome . . . for I judge it requisite that we should labour to know those plants which are and are ever like to be inhabitants of this isle; for I verily believe that the divine Providence had a care in bestowing plants in each part of the earth fitting and convenient to the foreknowne necessities of the future inhabitants; and if we thoroughly knew the vertues of these we needed no Indian nor American drugges'. Helped by his friends he now had it in mind to produce a complete flora of Britain. The lists of plants published in the accounts of his various journeys broadcast a kind of *status quo*. Correspondents could then add new information about areas of the country Johnson had not yet visited himself. Unfortunately, in 1642, the Civil War brought his travels abruptly to an end. Johnson left his apothecary's shop on Snow Hill and entered the company of London Royalists at Oxford. From there, he joined Colonel Rawdon at Basing House, the seat of the Marquis of Winchester, where, as the fellow Royalist Thomas Fuller relates in his *Worthies* (1662), he was 'no lesse eminent in the Garrison for his valour and conduct as a Souldier, than famous through the Kingdom for his excellency as a Herbarist, and Physician'. In a sortie during September 1644, he was wounded in the shoulder, 'whereby contracting a Feaver he dyed a fortnight after'.

There was one man in England who could have carried on the great work that Johnson had in mind, the publication of a complete flora of Britain, and that was John Goodyer. Goodyer, eight years older than Johnson, had already collaborated with him, sending much of the information used in the revised edition of Gerard's *Herball*. In the Preface Johnson freely acknowledged the great contribution made by Goodyer 'the onely Assistant I had in this Worke' and arranged for each of Goodyer's paragraphs to be signed with his own name (there were more than a hundred of them). But Goodyer was an amateur, a country gent, who never lived more than a few miles from his Hampshire birthplace. He was thorough, methodical, an obsessive taker of notes, a demon indexer, a maker of concordances, an autodidact, observant, interested, steady, pedantic even, but he lacked Johnson's drive. Together, he and the more extrovert, energetic Johnson would have made a perfect editorial pair. Alone, wrapped in the calm of his Hampshire study, he collected, corresponded, listed, kept meticulous accounts (thirteen shillings and eightpence for lodgings in Guildford on his way to London in 1631, together with outlay on oats and hay for the horses, grease for the coach – sixpence, a shilling tip for the ostler, and ferry charges at Lambeth) but, on his own account, published nothing.[6]

Like Johnson, he makes regular summer journeys in search of new plants (horse hire, one shilling; expenses at Weymouth, three shillings). While Johnson's expeditions were sponsored by his fellow apothecaries, Goodyer's are less focused. But he does realise how unsatisfactory it is to try to cram British plants into a straitjacket cut for a different time and a different place. William Turner, the pioneer, had been chiefly concerned with matching English names to the plants that Dioscorides and other classical authors had already described. His book, though an important landmark, did little to increase knowledge about British plants that the ancients did not know of. Gerard's *Herball* grew out of a Continental book, Dodoens's *Pemptades* of 1583, and had been illustrated with pictures that also originated on the Continent. Johnson's edition of 1633 added British locations and more British plants, but was

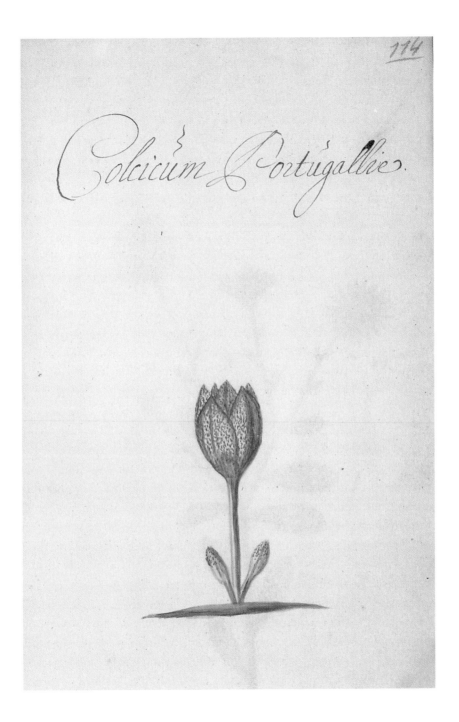

Colcicum Portugallie.

Plate 140: A single chequered colchicum (possibly Colchicum agrippinum) *in a painted florilegium produced by a Dutch artist in the first half of the seventeenth century*

still constrained by its source. In his early twenties, Goodyer seems to want to do something about this lacuna and for five years produces a storm of notes, diligently collecting information about British plants: herb Paris at Chawton, sea holly at Tichfield, white and purple colchicums at Warminster, a narrow-leaved lungwort in the New Forest, sea heath on Hayling Island. He records information about oak, walnut and chestnut trees that Johnson later uses in his edition of the *Herball*. After this flurry, he retreats to his study and in 1622 begins his laborious interlinear translation (Greek into English, for no English edition yet existed) of Theophrastus's *Enquiry into Plants*. One of the first books he had ever bought had been Theophrastus in the Aldine folio edition of 1497.[7]

In 1631 he goes to London ('wyne wth. Johnson 6d'), possibly to discuss the new edition of the *Herball*. He stays at the Angel, near Denmark Street off the Strand and visits his bookseller, Dr Dale in Long Acre. He drafts letters to various foreign plantsmen with a view to exchanging seed of English plants for foreign ones he has never grown: 'Sir, I have made a short Catalogue of some plants which growe for the most p[ar]te wild in Fraunce; you may acquaint anie herborists there that you please yf they will helpe me to seeds of them, or any other.' The plants are cross-referenced with the page numbers of the plants as shown in Lobelius's *Stirpium adversaria nova* of 1570 'that there may be no mistakinge'. Aged forty, Goodyer marries Miss Patience Crumpe, spinster of St Giles in the Fields, Middlesex, and buys a present of edging lace for his new wife (tenpence). A Royalist, of course, he does not fight in the Civil War but defends himself as best he can with a Protection Order granted on 9 December 1643 by Lord Hopton of the King's garrison at Petersfield. His Majesty's soldiers are to 'defend and protect John Goodyer of Petersfield in the County of Southton Gent: his house horses servants family goods chattels and estates of all sortes from all damages, disturbances & oppressions whatsoevere'. When the war is over he settles to an interlinear translation of Dioscorides's *Materia medica* which fills 4,540 pages; later he arranges for it to be bound in six quarto volumes (three shillings). On 26 September 1661, he sends to the binders the Theophrastus translation he had made nearly forty years earlier ('The bindinge – the cleane paper – the claspes, four shillings'). At his death in 1664, twenty years after Johnson's, he leaves 'all my books de plantis which I do give and bequeath to Magdalen College in Oxon to be kept entirely in the library of the said College'. Those books, carefully inscribed by Goodyer with the date he bought them and the price he paid, encapsulate the entire history of the study of plants from Theophrastus to John Ray. Gathered on the shelves of that quiet Hampshire study are Aristotle and Dioscorides (bought on 10 November 1631 for 1s 6d), Brunfels, Fuchs, six different editions of Mattioli's *Commentarii*, Lancelot Browne's copy of Cesalpino's

De plantis (bought on 17 November 1627 for four shillings), Turner, Gesner's *Historia plantarum*, Bauhin's *Phytopinax* of 1596, six books by Clusius, seven by Dodoens, six by Lobelius, copies of all Johnson's accounts of his plant-hunting expeditions. There's a ten-year moratorium on book buying around the period of the Civil War, but then he begins again: '22 March 1651 £3 2s 6d sent Dr Dale for Bauhin 3 vols, one shilling for the portage to & from Dr Dales, a shilling to John Symonds to carry up the money, one shilling and fourpence to William Mychell for bringing the bookes down.[8] Almost as soon as it is printed, he buys Hernandez's account of Mexican plants and John Ray's iconic catalogue of the plants of Cambridgeshire, published in 1657. John Goodyer's library contains everything of importance that has ever been written about plants. But like a logjam that has built up in a river, the time has come for that great, congested accumulation of facts to sweep on and be reassembled in a more coherent way.

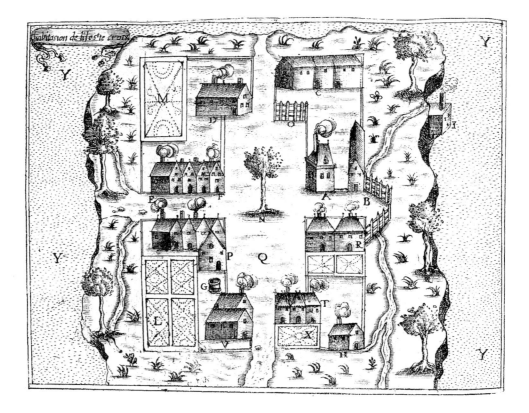

*Plate 141: Samuel de Champlain's sketch of the settlement at
La Croix, Maine, as it appeared in the first edition of
his* Voyages *(1619)*

XXIII

THE AMERICAN
CONNECTION

1620–1675

BY THE TIME of Goodyer's death, some progress had been made in answering the first question that Theophrastus had posed in the Athens Lyceum almost 2,000 years previously. 'What have we got?' he asked, noting and describing the plants then known to the classical world and setting them out in his seminal work, the *Enquiry into Plants*. In that book he includes about 500 plants; Gaspard Bauhin's *Pinax theatri botanici*, published in 1623, describes 6,000. Theophrastus's second question, 'How can we most usefully differentiate between these things?' proved more tricky to resolve. Theophrastus never doubted that harmony, method, a grand plan must exist in the natural world. The difficulty lay in finding the correct key, the cipher that would transform chaos into order, reveal a system, a pattern in the turmoil. Theophrastus suggested some possible ways of arranging the 500 plants he describes. They could be divided into trees, shrubs and herbs; they could be classed as cultivated or wild; they could be sorted into flowering or flowerless plants; they could be deciduous or evergreen. He also considered the habitats of particular groups of plants: some plants seemed to favour high places, others rocks, others ditches or streams. But he saw that each of the divisions and categories he proposed threw up problems. He defined a tree as having a single trunk, not easily uprooted, while a shrub had multiple stems. But the pomegranate was often trained to grow with several trunks rather than one. Did this then make it a shrub rather than tree? And though, on the face of it, it seemed easy to distinguish between plants that dropped their leaves in autumn and those that didn't, he had heard that in some places figs and vines, deciduous in Athens, actually kept their leaves right through winter.

Theophrastus put trees at the head of the plant kingdom because he felt that they most truly expressed the essential nature of plants. Pliny starts with trees because of their great value and importance to man. That shift in attitude had a profound effect on the search for order begun by Theophrastus. Utility became the driving force in man's relationship with the plants around him; the consequence was a flood of herbals whose chief concern was to list the various medicinal uses to which plants could be put. That over-riding concern obscured Theophrastus's grander purpose and dominated man's interest in plants for the next 1,500 years. The detailed, reliable and beautiful images that began to appear in sixteenth-century books such as Leonhart Fuchs's *De historia stirpium* (1542) provided an invaluable tool in recognising and distinguishing between one plant and another. At the same time, plantsmen in Europe began the long slow process of matching synonyms, eliminating wrong attributions, agreeing identities. Starting in Italy, that work involved a vast network of scholars based in Germany, Flanders, France, the Netherlands, Switzerland and finally England.

To some there seemed a logic in listing plants in alphabetical order as Galen had first done in the second century AD, but by the middle of the sixteenth century, the German plantsman Hieronymus Bock (1498–1554) had reverted to the classical divisions of trees, shrubs and herbs: 'I have placed together, yet kept distinct, all plants which are related and connected, or otherwise resemble one another and are compared, and have given up the former old rule or arrangement according to the ABC which is seen in the old herbals. For the arrangement of plants by the alphabet occasions much disparity and error.'[1] Indeed it did, but the lack of any better and universally accepted arrangement meant that Gerard's *Herball*, published at the end of the sixteenth century, was still arranged with plants set out in alphabetical order. Even Theophrastus had understood that plants such as oaks or willows could be treated together in a group. They had certain characteristics in common, but at the same time, there were enough differences between types to distinguish one oak from another, one willow from a neighbour with distinctly different qualities. Early on, scholars such as Conrad Gesner were using the Latin terms, *genus* and *specie* to denote first the larger groupings and then the various members of each particular group. 'I think that there are practically no plants which do not form some group that is divisible into two or more kinds,' Gesner had written in a letter to Jean Bauhin.[2] There was also a vague appreciation of the fact that the various *genera* could be gathered together into even larger groups, to form families such as the Umbellifers, plants such as hemlock and Queen Anne's lace all of which had big, flat, umbrella-shaped heads of flower. Plant form dictated that particular grouping,

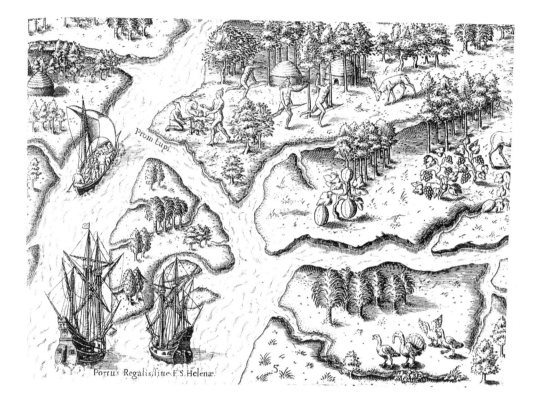

*Plate 142: Theodor de Bry's engraving of the coast of Florida,
showing the unfamiliar plants and animals of the New World in*
Brevis narratio eorum quae in Florida *(1591)*

but early scholars found it extremely difficult to establish these important overarching categories. The brilliant Andrea Cesalpino came closest in 1563, with his perception that an enduring system had to depend on *substantia*, characteristics that were part of a plant's essential nature, not *accidentia* such as scent, taste or usefulness. Cesalpino arranged plants into fifteen different classes, starting with trees bearing fruit with solitary seeds, such as oak, beech or laurel, and moving briskly on to a second class of trees that bore fruit with several seeds, such as fig, mulberry and vine. Herbaceous plants were not so easy to categorise and of them he made thirteen different groupings, some no more than ragbags. That was the problem. There was always some bit of the puzzle that didn't fit.

While physicians and apothecaries were content with books that arranged plants according to their use in magic or medicine, scholars had always seen that, although it had a certain logic, any classification that depended on utility was anthropocentric, inherently unsatisfactory. Clusius understood this, but his gifts were for describing, not classifying. Lobelius, in *Stirpium adversaria nova* (1570) wrote of 'an order, than which nothing more beautiful exists in the heavens, or in the mind of a wise man'. He worked out an ingenious system of grouping plants according to the structure of their leaves. There was a clear guiding principle here, but Lobelius struggled to make it fit all the plants he knew. Most writers put forward schemes that were a mixture of sometimes conflicting precepts. In his *Historia plantarum Lugdunensis* of 1586 for instance, the French plantsman d'Aléchamps uses three different axioms – habitat, utility and structure – to order the plant world into eighteen separate groups. Habitat dictates nine of those classes: trees which grow wild in woods, plants that grow in marshes, plants that grow by the sea, or in the sea itself. Three of his groups (including the cathartic plants in Group XVI and the poisonous plants in Group XVII) are circumscribed by their medical virtues. Morphology dictates the rest: plants with beautiful flowers, plants that are fragrant, plants that climb or that have spines and prickles. His ragbag, a big one, contained 'Foreign Plants'. In his *Theatrum botanicum* of 1640, John Parkinson groups plants into seventeen classes, but they are as meaningless as d'Aléchamps's: 'Venemous, Sleepy and Hurtfull Plants' (Class III), 'Strange and Outlandish Plants' (Class XVII).

As new areas of the world opened up to trade, strange and outlandish plants poured into Europe in ever-increasing numbers. It was too unwieldy simply to describe separately all these acquisitions. They needed to be grouped, filed under headings that could be generally agreed upon by the scholars now intent on this task. The first significant influx of plants into Western Europe had been from the Turkish Empire and included the savage, vivid bulbous plants – crocus, cyclamen, erythronium, fritillary, hyacinth, lily, ranunculus, tulip – that dominated European flower gardens from the middle of the sixteenth century onwards. Some New World curiosities such as the sunflower and the yucca had arrived in Europe before 1600, but in the 1620s the trickle of American plants became a flood, which flowed unabated for the next hundred years. From America came the Michaelmas daisies that in 1632 Thomas Johnson had admired in the apothecary Nicholas Swayton's Faversham garden as well as the Virginia creeper and persimmon cherry that William Coys cultivated in Essex. John Goodyer had visited him there and was pleased to get seeds and cuttings of Coys's American rarities to grow in his own Hampshire garden. Goodyer already grew two kinds of tobacco, noting that 'The whole plant perisheth at the first approach of winter, if it be not planted in an earthen pott or other fitt vessell, and putt into a close place to defend it from the injurie of the cold.' From Coys too came the ivy-leaved toadflax, a common weed now, but a New World rarity then. 'I never saw this growinge but in the garden of my faithfull good frend Mr William Coys in Northokington in Essex,' wrote Goodyer, adding that it grew in his own garden at Droxford from seed that Coys had sent him in 1618. Coys already had an impressive list of plants from Virginia – sumach, golden rod, solanum – that had settled at Stubbers, his Essex home. A little later, John Parkinson carefully lists the 'Virginia seeds recd from Mr Morrice 18 March 1636', twenty-four different items including:

> A scarlet flower requiring a moist ground . . . A poisonous berrye black rugged round berry with blackish seede straked like a tick . . . A black round rugged berry like large peper cornes with 3 square black shining seeds sent for a running vine yt bears no flowers . . . A kind of Hawes much eaten by the Indians . . . Virginia silke growing in a long white thick cod . . . A kind of Persicaria but higher by much then ours . . . The berrye of a plante whose juice is good red incke . . . Seede of the herbe Carales, so called from a Captain that said it was much eaten in East India & in a tyme of scarsitye there also: a small black shining seade like Amaranths purpureus, not Milium nigrum . . . Water melons flat darck graye seede like Citrulls . . . Red water melons flat darck graye seade like unto the other but a little longer pointed.[3]

Here Parkinson seems to be copying out the notes that perhaps arrived with his seeds – two dozen strangers with no names, no descriptions, no pictures showing what they were likely to turn into. The American Indians certainly had names for all these things, and knew more about their virtues and vices than anyone else alive. But this valuable information too rarely found its way back into England, though by 1643 Roger Williams had produced a *Key into the Language of . . . natives in that part of America called New England*, a sketchy compendium that

Flos Solis maior.

Plate 143: The sunflower (Helianthus annuus) *as it appeared in*
the Hortus Eystettensis *(1613), a record of the superb collection
of plants in the garden of the Prince-Bishop of Eichstatt*

gave English gardeners an occasional glimpse of the way that American plants were used by indigenous Americans. Indian corn, or maize, which had saved the early pilgrims from starvation in their first winter in the Promised Land, was properly called 'ewachimneash'. The Indians planted four seeds to a hillock and manured the plants with dead fish. 'If the use of it were known and received in England,' wrote Williams, 'it might save many lives in England, occasioned by the binding nature of English wheat, the Indian corne keeping the body in a constant moderate looseness.' He was equally enthusiastic about the Virginian strawberry: 'the wonder of all the fruits growing naturally in these parts. It is of itself excellent, so that one of the chiefest doctors of England was wont to say that God could have made, but God never did make, a better berry. In some parts where the natives have planted, I have many times seen as many as would fill a good ship within a few miles compass. The Indians bruise them in a mortar and mix them with meal and make a strawberry bread.'[4]

Parkinson's list provides only the briefest of clues about the newcomers and their characteristics: 'found on small trees in the woods . . . flower is an excellent sallat . . . milke more bitter than aloes . . . found on small lowe imbracing vines'. It was not much to go on, but yet these things had to be tagged, differentiated, assimilated. And sometimes treated warily. Parkinson had poison ivy from the New World in his garden by 1640 but nearly thirty years later Richard Stafford still thought it worth reminding English gardeners of its dangers. Writing from Bermuda in 1668, he warned: 'You shall receive of Captain Thomas Morly, the Commander of our Magazeen-ship, such things as I could at present procure. Among which you shall find of the Leaves and Berries of that Weed you enquire after, which we call Poyson-weed, growing like Ivy. I have seen a Man, who was so poyson'd with it, that the skin peel'd off his Face, and yet the Man never touch'd it, onely look'd on it as he pass'd by.'[5] Francis Higginson, who arrived in Salem in 1629 as 'reader' to the Reverend Skelton, immediately seizes in the New World on what is familiar to him from the Old: strawberries, sorrel, brooklime, watercress. Higginson was employed by the Company of New England, whose stated objectives were 'the propagation of the Gospell of Christ, the conversion of the Indians, and the enlargement of the King's . . . dominions in America'. But merchants' pockets had also to be enlarged, if the new colonies were to succeed, and from the beginning ships' captains and settlers were encouraged to send back plants that might possibly be exploited commercially. Higginson's report, sent the following year to England, describes the 'sweet Herbes delightful to the smell, whose names we know not', and the 'Plentie of single Damask Roses verie sweete', but he also takes care to note the 'two kinds of Herbes that bear two kinds of Flowers very sweet, which

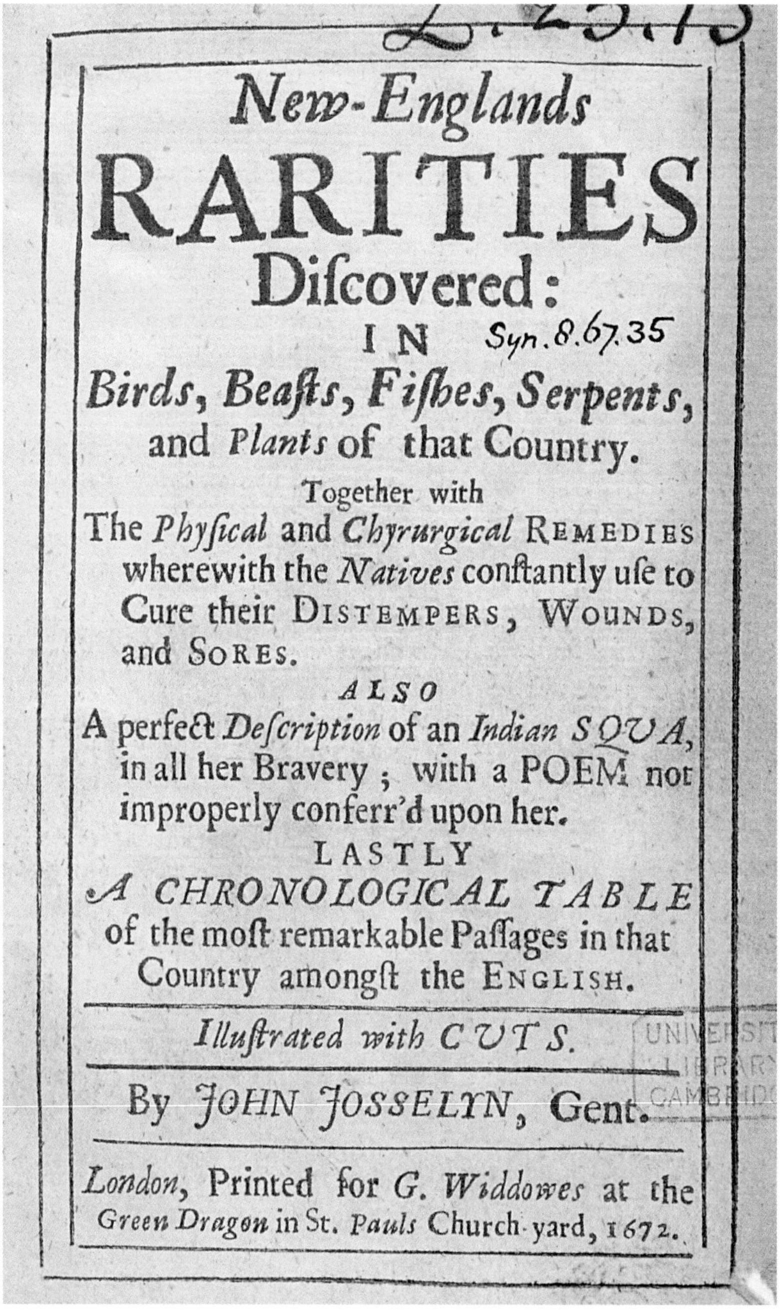

New-Englands
RARITIES
Difcovered:
IN
Birds, Beafts, Fifhes, Serpents,
and *Plants* of that Country.

Together with

The *Phyfical* and *Chyrurgical* REMEDIES
wherewith the *Natives* conftantly ufe to
Cure their DISTEMPERS, WOUNDS,
and SORES.

ALSO

A perfect *Defcription* of an *Indian* SQUA,
in all her Bravery ; with a POEM not
improperly conferr'd upon her.

LASTLY
A CHRONOLOGICAL TABLE
of the moft remarkable Paffages in that
Country amongft the ENGLISH.

Illuftrated with *CUTS*.

By *JOHN JOSSELYN*, Gent.

London, Printed for *G. Widdowes* at the
Green Dragon in St. *Pauls* Church-yard, 1672.

Plate 144: The title page of New England's Rarities Discovered
*by John Josselyn, printed in London in 1672. It contained a
'perfect Description of an Indian squa' with 'a POEM not
improperly conferr'd upon her'*

they say, are as good to make Cordage or Cloath as any Hemp or Flax we have'.[6]

Thomas Johnson had added 300 plants from New England to his edition of Gerard's *Herball*. 'Had they been in New England,' wrote John Josselyn, one of the 'spare kindred' that Captain John Smith had urged the gentry of the Old World to send over to the New, 'they might have found 1000 at least never heard of nor seen by any Englishman before. Tis true, the Countrie hath no Bonerets, or Tartar-lambs, no glittering coloured Tuleps; but here you have the American Mary-Gold, the Earth-nut bearing a princely flower [he is speaking of the ground nut, *Apios americana*], the beautiful leaved Pirola, the honied Colibry. They are generally of course of (somewhat) a more masculine vertue than any of the same species in England, but not in so terrible degree as to be mischievous or ineffectual to our English bodies.'[7] The pilgrims had hoped to earn money by sending back wild herbs from America to England, but found that French settlers in Canada had already scooped the market. Many plants native to New England grew also in Canada and had quickly found their way into the royal botanic garden in Paris. In his book *New England's Rarities Discovered* (1672) (see plate 144), Josselyn tries to impose a kind of order on the plants he finds by sorting them into five different categories. First he groups together plants such as stitchwort, wild sorrel and herb Robert, that though native to New England, seem familar to the settlers from England. Then he deals with 'Such plants as are proper to the country': Indian wheat, maidenhair fern (see plate 145) (which, as Josselyn noted, grew so abundantly in America the apothecaries had no need to adulterate it with wall rue, as they did in England), treacle berries, bilberries ('very good to allay the burning heat of Feavers and hot Agues, either in Syrup or Conserves'), the ague tree or sassafras and cranberries. These are mostly plants used for food or medicine. But that left him with a mass of wild plants that, because they had no English tag, he considered anonymous and so categorised simply as 'Such Plants as are proper to the Country and have no Name known to us'. Few of the Indian names were used. Sarsaparilla and sassafras were both derived from Spanish words. Much larger was Josselyn's section on 'Such plants as have sprung up since the English planted and kept cattle there'. With the settlers came weeds such as couch grass, groundsel, dandelion, stinging nettle and plantain, which the Indians with their gift for vivid imagery called English-Man's Foot, as though, wrote Josselyn, it was 'produced by their treading'. He also produced a long list of 'Such Garden Herbs (amongst us) as do thrive there and of such as do not': cabbage, lettuce, sorrel, parsley, marigold, chervil, thyme, sage, radish, turnip. Rue, he says 'will hardly grow' though parsnips grew to 'a prodigious size', as did peas 'of all sorts, and the best in the World; I never heard of, nor did see in eight years time, one Worm eaten Pea'. Pests had not yet caught up with the newly imported plants. Southernwood, rosemary,

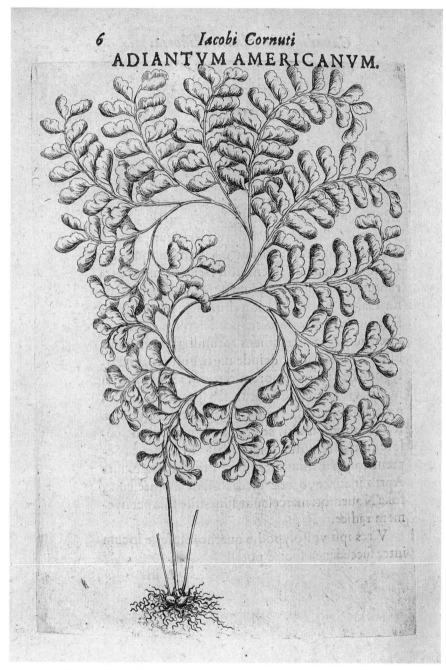

ADIANTVM AMERICANVM.

*Plate 145: 'Adiantum americanum' the American maidenhair
fern as shown in Jacques Cornut's* Canadensium plantarum
. . . historia *(1635). It grew so abundantly in
the New World that apothecaries had no need to
adulterate it, as they did in England*

bay, lavender all struggled to survive. Clary only lasted one summer as 'the Roots rot with the frost'.[8]

Writing from the New World in March 1631, John Winthrop, who had arrived at Salem on the *Arabella* in the summer of 1630, advises his son, who is planning to join him in America, to bring 'meale and pease, and some otemeale and Sugar, fruit, figges and pepper, and good store of saltpeeter'.[9] Winthrop's son sailed that summer on the *Lyon*, captained by Mr Pierce, bringing hogsheads of oil and vinegar, books and cloth, gunpowder and butter, leather, rope, alchemical equipment and garden seeds purchased from Robert Hill on 26 July 1631 – angelica, cabbage, fennel, hollyhock, leeks, wallflowers, sweet marjoram, poppy, rocket, 'spynadg' at twopence an ounce, and violets.[10]

It was, as the English scholar and plantsman John Ray writes in the Preface to his *Synopsis methodica stirpium Britannicarum* (1690),

> an age of noble discovery, the weight and elasticity of air, the telescope and microscope, the ceaseless circulation of the blood through veins and arteries, the lacteal glands and the bile duct, the structure of the organs of generation, and of many others – too many to mention: the secrets of Nature have been unsealed and explored; a new Physiology has been introduced. It is an age of daily progress in all the sciences, especially in the history of plants: to this end have been devoted the energies not only of private individuals but of princes and magnates, eager to find new flowers for their gardens and pleasances and to send plant-hunters to the furthest Indies: they have travelled over mountains and valley, forest and plains, exploring every corner of the earth, and bringing to light and to our view all that is hidden.[11]

The English physician William Harvey had announced his discovery of the circulation of the blood in 1619; the Oxford Botanic Garden had been established in 1621 and the Jardin des Plantes in Paris in 1626; Galileo had published his *Dialogo sopra i due massimi sistemi del mondo* in 1632; the Academie Française had been set up in Paris in 1635, the Royal Society in London granted a Royal Charter in 1662; on the orders of Van Diemen, governor of the Dutch East India Company, Tasman had left Batavia in 1642 on a voyage which led to the discovery of Tasmania and New Zealand; Robert Hooke had described his experiments with a microscope in his *Micrographia*, published in 1665; Isaac Newton had constructed the first reflecting telescope in 1668, and in 1687 published his *Principia mathematica* establishing the laws of motion and gravitation; the Greenwich Observatory had been set up in 1675; Nehemiah Grew had described the function of the stamens and pistil in a plant in 1676 (though his work was not published until 1682); Dampier had begun his voyage

Plate 146: Albert Eckhout's Mameluka with
Basket of Flowers, 1641. *She is surrounded by the strange
products of the New World*

round the world in 1683. Reviewing these astonishing achievements in his *History of England*, Macaulay suggests that the civil troubles of the age 'had stimulated the faculties of the educated classes and had called forth a restless activity and an insatiable curiosity . . . the torrent which had been dammed up in one channel rushed violently into another.'

XXIV

THE BEGINNING
OF THE END

1650–1705

RAY, THE SON of a village blacksmith, is the final protagonist in this story. He was just five years old when Thomas Johnson brought out his edition of Gerard's *Herball*, twelve when John Parkinson published his *Theatrum botanicum*, seventeen when Johnson died in the Siege of Basing House. After a lifetime of study and observation, John Ray (see plate 147), solitary, modest, principled, persistent, was the man who, two years before his death in 1705, provided the means to answer Theophrastus's second question.[1] His Six Rules for Classification finally showed how future scholars must proceed in this ever more complex investigation.[2] In a series of propositions, carefully revised over more than twenty years, he set out his principles for a method of classification that could embrace not only the known plants of Europe but also the vast numbers of plants from the tropics and the New World that were now finding their way to England. In an age badly infected with astrological absurdities, he understood that the study of plants should not be tied to magic, but could in itself be a profound and philosophical discipline. Once 'one of the handmaids of physick' as William Coles described it in 1656, the study of plants had now outgrown this constraint. Like Theophrastus, Ray understood that a method (and method had to come before system) was only likely to be valid if it was suggested by the plants themselves, not imposed upon them. Like Theophrastus, he looked for innate similarities, distinct differences, the most important characteristics of the plants he surveyed. Though fully acknowledging the achievements of both Cesalpino and Lobelius, he saw that their systems had foundered because both had relied on a single characteristic to delineate their various groups of plants. They had forced the plant to fit one over-riding idea, rather than allowing the idea to arise naturally from the plant. Lobelius had tried leaf form, Cesalpino was closer to a valid scheme in fixing on seed and fruit as the defining features. In his *Pinax theatri botanici* of 1623, Gaspard Bauhin, professor of medicine at Basel, had already set out the different synonyms attached to plants, made a choice between them, introduced more compact descriptions, and tried to stem the prevailing tendency to long plant names – *Lilium montanum rubrum praecox* (an early red lily generally found in mountains), *Jasminum indicum flore rubro et variegato* (a jasmine from the Indies with flowers that can be either red or striped) – names that described rather than denoted. Bauhin used the binary system of nomenclature with a great degree of consistency: a generic name (a kind of surname), followed by a specific epithet which becomes the distinguishing mark, as our own Christian names are. That was a great advance, a preliminary clearing of the jungle for subsequent explorers such as John Ray. But like all those who had gone before him, Ray was hampered by the lack of a specific vocabulary to describe and evaluate plants. There was still no word, for instance, to describe such a simple concept as 'petal'. It was John Ray who, from Fabio Colonna's notes on Hernandez's *Rerum medicarum Novae Hispanicae thesaurus* (1649), took the suggestion that 'flower leaves' as they were called, could be distinguished from true leaves by a new term taken from the Greek *petalon*. Then, in 1682, the year that Ray published his first thoughts on the correct classification of plants,[3] his contemporary Nehemiah Grew made a huge leap forward with the startling suggestion that the stamens of a flower were in fact male sexual organs. Cesalpino had called them *flocci* and thought they must be the means by which plants breathed. Subsequent writers had frequently described stamens and stigma – Gerard, for instance, had noted the centre of the potato flower and its 'pointell, yellow as golde, with a small sharpe greene pricke or point in the middest thereof' – but nobody had given them names before and nobody before Grew had worked out their significance. But where Grew exploded like a rocket, scattering unconnected bright stars of insight randomly over the universe, Ray's intellect burned more discreetly, more methodically, less showily perhaps but in the end to greater purpose.

John Ray was unusual in that he became a plantsman not because he had trained as a physician or an apothecary or pharmacologist, but because of a deep, quietly passionate response to the beauties of the natural world. At Cambridge, where he arrived with a scholarship in 1644, he studied theology and made himself a master of Hebrew and Latin composition. Like William Turner before him, he searched in vain for a mentor who might teach him something about plants. And like Turner,

Plate 147: The English plantsman John Ray (1627–1705),
whose Synopsis methodica *of 1690 laid down the rules for a*
modern system of nomenclature

he was largely self-taught. 'I had been ill, physically and mentally,' he writes in the Preface to his first book, the *Catalogus plantarum circa Cantabrigiam nascentium* of 1660, 'and was forced to rest from more serious studies, and to spend my time in riding or walking. I had leisure in the course of my journeys to contemplate the varied beauty of plants and the cunning craftsmanship of Nature that was constantly before my eyes, and had so often been thoughtlessly trodden underfoot. First I was fascinated and absorbed by the rich spectacle of the meadows in spring-time; then I was filled with wonder and delight by the marvellous shape, colour and structure of particular plants. While my eyes feasted on these sights, my mind too was stimulated. I became inspired with a passion for plants.'[4]

With his Cambridge *Catalogus*, Ray finally achieved what Thomas Johnson had set out to do twenty years previously. Johnson's purpose had been to publish a series of books listing and describing the plants that grew in the different areas of England. His expedition to Kent in 1629 was the first English journey ever undertaken with the specific purpose of recording plants. His death in the Civil War left a gap that took a long time to fill. Johnson, though, could not have wished for a better successor than Ray, who, before publishing his list, spent six years plant-hunting in the fields and fens around Cambridge; another three years passed as he put the resulting material in order. He had hopes that his 'little book' would encourage others to make similar surveys of their own localities. United, these would then give a complete picture of all the plants in Britain. 'I should like to enter a plea', he wrote, 'that men of University standing to whom God has given leisure and a suitable education and intelligence, should spare a brief interval from other pursuits, and, without in any way neglecting their other studies, that they should develop the habit of examining Nature, and compile a comprehensive account of its creatures so that they can begin to gain wisdom by their own experience rather than from somebody else's brain, and learn to read the leaves of plants and interpret the characters impressed on flowers and seeds.'[5]

Ray's purpose in his Cambridge *Catalogus* was to identify and describe plants, rather than to arrange or order them. In this first book, he set out his plants in alphabetical order, not because he thought that was the best way to organise them, but because he had not yet worked out any better method. At the end of his list (it finished with the plant he called *Xyris* and which we call *Iris foetidissima*, the gladdon or stinking iris) he included an Outline Classification, almost identical to the one that Jean Bauhin, elder brother of Gaspard, had laid out in his *Historia plantarum universalis* published posthumously in 1650. Jean Bauhin had trained at Tübingen under Leonhart Fuchs and later at Montpellier under Rondelet; though his scheme presented difficulties, Ray was not alone in considering him 'the Prince of Herbarists'.

Plate 148: Compact grape hyacinth (Muscari botryoides)*,
love-in-a-mist* (Nigella damascena)*, geranium* (Geranium
phaeum) *and knapweed* (Centaurea montana) *enclosed in a
border of gooseberries in a French florilegium of 1608*

Following Bauhin, in a fundamental division that had remained unchanged since Theophrastus, Ray splits the plant world into trees, shrubs, sub-shrubs and herbs. He points out that trees could be evergreen or deciduous and then, taking their fruit as the defining characteristic (as Cesalpino had done) divides them into eight groups: *Pomiferae*, which bore fruit without stones (apple, lemon, fig, pomegranate etc.); *Pruniferae*, which bore fruit with a stone (plum, peach, date, olive etc.); *Nuciferae*, which bore nuts (walnut, chestnut, hazel, nutmeg, pistachio etc.); *Bacciferae*, which bore berries (laurel, mulberry, juniper, box, myrtle, elder etc.); *Glandiferae*, which bore acorns (oak, ilex, beech); *Coniferae*, which bore cones (pine, fir, larch, cypress, cedar etc.); *Siliquosae*, which bore their fruit in pods (laburnum, Judas tree, cassia etc.); and then, at the end, the difficult ragbag containing trees such as birch, willow, ash, elm and lime that did not fit neatly into any of the other categories. Shrubs he disposes of very quickly, dividing them merely into those with thorns (berberis, buckthorn, gooseberry etc.) and those without (broom, jasmine, privet etc.). He understands how unsatisfactory this is and hints at other possible divisions: shrubs that flower, shrubs that bear fruit, shrubs that climb. Nowhere does he admit groups based on *accidentia* such as scent or taste. The sub-shrubs can be lumped together into one group, as they are mostly aromatic garden plants such as lavender, wormwood, hyssop, savory and sage. Herbaceous plants, being so numerous, are the most difficult to sort. It was, as he acknowledged, difficult if not impossible to arrange them 'so that no plant belongs to more than one class, or is classified ambiguously'. The pack could be dealt in many different ways, but for the moment, Ray follows Bauhin in proposing twenty-two groups, some defined by their roots, some by the form of their leaves, some by flower, some by usage, others by habitat.

By the time the *Catalogus* was published, Ray was well established in his Cambridge life. He had been appointed as a tutor at Trinity in 1653, where he lectured on Greek, mathematics and humanities. He had begun the series of long summer journeys in search of plants which he undertook in the company of similarly minded friends such as his young patron, Sir Francis Willughby (1635–1672), the heir to extensive estates in the Midlands. On 23 December 1660, Ray was ordained. A comfortable life stretched ahead of him: paid employment, secure lodgings, good libraries, social status, the company of men with whom he could discuss the pioneering work in which he was engaged. But on 24 August 1662, he forfeited his Fellowship and all the comforts it promised. Proud, independent, moral, principled in a way that is scarcely understood in our less honourable age, he found himself unable to take the oath required by the Act of Uniformity that Charles II had brought in at the Restoration. Both in a spiritual and an intellectual sense, he was a man of the Commonwealth and, rather than giving lip service to an Act of which he disapproved, he resigned from Trinity and left Cambridge, his home for the past eighteen years. For the next seventeen years, he was effectively without a base, relying on the kindness of friends such as Willughby who, at his Middleton estate, provided as much of a home as Ray could call on. Only in 1679, after the death of his mother, did he move to the house that he had built for her at Black Notley, the Essex village in which he himself had been born. Called Dewlands, it is commemorated now only in the name of a close of modern brick houses leading off the main street through the village. Close by the village hall, a Millennium Green has been dedicated to Ray's memory. Though his picture is already fading from the information board, oak and hornbeam, poplar and ash, white campion, creeping buttercup, tufted vetch and cranesbill flourish in the grass. The forge and adjoining cottage, Ray's birthplace, stand on the northern edge of this scattered village, a couple of fields away from the small flint church with its shingled spire.

Free of Cambridge, Ray intended, he wrote, to cast himself 'upon Providence and good friends'.[6] Providence, aided by his good friend Willughby, almost immediately afforded him the opportunity of a Continental tour through the Low Countries, Germany, Italy and France, which occupied the next three years. Leaving Dover on 18 April 1663, Willughby and Ray went by way of Calais and Dunkirk to Ostend. From there they moved on to Rotterdam, Delft, Haarlem and Amsterdam. In Germany they 'first began to have feather-beds laid upon us instead of blankets' and travelled up the Rhine 'in a boat drawn by men'. They went to Heidelberg, Strasbourg, Basel, Zurich, Munich and Augsburg, by boat to Vienna, then by coach to Venice, the coachman hiring 'ten oxen to draw his coach to the top of the hills'. From Venice they went to Padua, where Ray attended anatomy lectures at the university. Then they moved on to Ferrara and Bologna, where they visited Aldrovandi's famous museum. They missed the great Marcello Malpighi, lecturer at the university, whose illustrations of plants (see plates 149 and 157), showing their anatomy in unprecedented detail, were published just five years after Ray returned to England. Via Parma, they went to Milan, Turin and Genoa, then on to Lucca and Pisa. They sailed to Naples, and climbed Vesuvius, where Pliny had lost his life in AD 79. From Naples, Willughby returned to England, where on 4 January 1665, he gave a report of the journey to the Royal Society. Ray went on to Sicily, Malta, and then to Salerno, site of the famous medical school. In Florence, an English doctor, John Kirton, treated him with cucumber pulp for a fever. On 1 September he started for Rome, where he stayed until the following January. Then, crossing the Apennines, he went by way of Bologna, back to Venice and from there on to Trent, Lucerne, Berne, Lausanne, and Geneva where he arrived on 20 April 1665. By late July he was in France, visiting Lyons, Avignon and Montpellier, still a centre of intellectual life, still a magnet

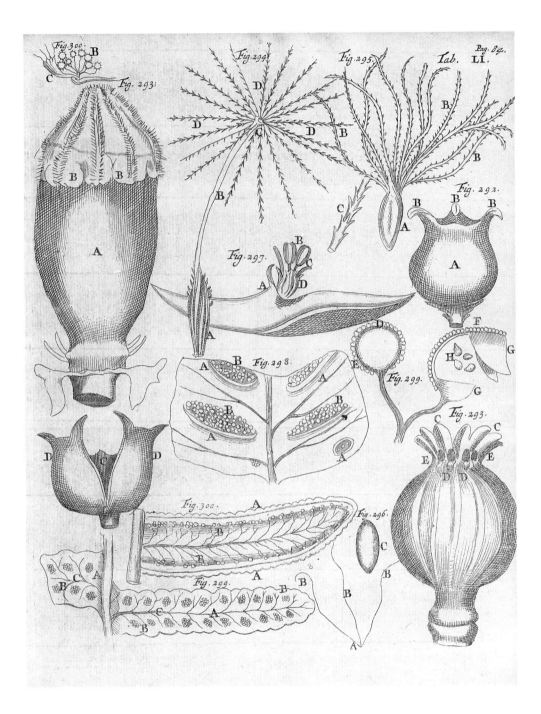

Plate 149: Various forms of fern spores and seed vessels in the Italian plantsman Marcello Malpighi's Anatome plantarum *of 1675*

for English scholars. Pierre Magnol, successor to the great Rondelet at Montpellier, impressed Ray greatly and he might have stayed longer at the university had not Louis XIV ordered all Englishmen to leave France within three months. On 26 February 1666, Ray left Montpellier for Paris and got finally to the ferry at Calais, travelling from the capital in a fish cart.

The Royal Society, founded to promote research in the sciences, provided to some extent a new fulcrum for Ray's intellectual life. Formally set up in 1660, it had its origins in the Oxford Philosophical Society and a nucleus of men with enquiring minds who had met regularly in London since 1645. The Society offered its members a meeting place, the opportunity for regular discussion and debate, a vehicle for the publication of research (its magazine *Philosophical Transactions* appeared on the first Monday of each month). John Evelyn and Ray's friend Sir Francis Willughby were founder members, Samuel Pepys its president. The Society encouraged a direct approach to the natural sciences, insisted on studies in the field. It embraced astronomy, chemistry, engineering, mathematics, physics, physiology, as well as the study of plants and animals. The 200 members were mostly gentlemen rather than players, too few of them capable of initiating work of real worth; they needed John Ray, who was elected to the Society on 7 November 1667. In accordance with the rule that required members 'to entertain the Society once a year with a discourse grounded upon experiment', Ray sent his 'Discourse on the Seeds of Plants' and 'The Specific Differences of Plants' to the Society on 30 November 1674. He apologised for his first paper being 'inchoate and imperfect', explaining that he hoped in the following year 'to prosecute and perfect' his plan 'of distinguishing plants by the content of the seed'.[7] Nehemiah Grew (see plate 150), who had been working on the structure of plants since 1664, had already in May 1671 submitted a paper on 'The Anatomy of Vegetables Begun' to the Society.

The first draft of Ray's thoughts on plant species and the differences between them had appeared in the Preface to his *Observations and Catalogus Stirpium in Exteris Regionibus* (1673), an account of the plants he had seen on his European travels ten years previously. 'Whether my readers will enjoy these bare lists of names, I do not know,' he wrote. 'To me to gaze at the plants themselves freely growing on the lavish bosom of mother earth was an unbelievable delight; I can say with Clusius that I was as pleased to find for the first time a new plant as if I had received a fortune; to discover very many daily that were unknown to me and strangers to our Britain was an ample reward for travel.'[8] The Alps had been particularly satisfying. But the paper presented a year later to the Society crystallised even more cogently his argument for fixing different species. 'Having observed', he writes in his paper, 'that most herbarists, mistaking many accidents for notes of specific

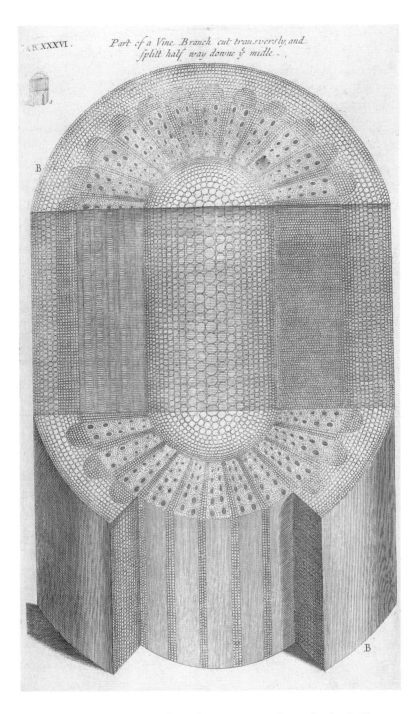

TAB. XXXVI.

Part of a Vine Branch cut transversly, and splitt half way downe ye midle.

Plate 150: 'Part of a vine branch cut transversely, and splitt half way downe ye midle', one of the illustrations in The Anatomy of Plants (1682) by Nehemiah Grew

381

distinction, which indeed they are not, have unnecessarily multiplied beings, contrary to that well known philosophic precept; I think it may not be unuseful, in order to the determining of the number of species more certainly and agreeably to nature, to enumerate such accidents and then give my reasons why I judge them not sufficient to infer a specific difference.' We are back with the all important difference between *substantia* and *accidentia* debated at length by Andrea Cesalpino. The vast numbers of new flowers – anemones, ranunculus, auriculas – now being raised by enthusiastic gardeners, were in danger of swamping such systems as presently existed. Some scholars made a species out of each new arrival, a tulip flamed more outrageously than another, a ranunculus of a different colour from its predecessors. A good proportion of the 6,000 plants listed by Gaspard Bauhin in his *Pinax theatri botanici* (1623) were no more than varieties of existing species, though the concept of a variety was only slowly beginning to be understood. Ray saw that the rush by some plantsmen to ascribe new species names to each slightly modified flower had to be stopped. Differences in size, scent, taste, colour, the doubling of a flower, the variegation of a leaf, were not in themselves characteristics of sufficient importance to determine a separate species. 'God having finished his work of creation', he believed (and it was then a staple of Christian belief) that the number of species is 'in nature fixed and determinate'. Though it was possible that a species might have been lost, it was, he argued in that optimistic age, 'highly improbable'. They could be found, of course – no age had found more – but they could not be made.

During his long journey through Europe, Ray had seen and noted more wild plants growing in their native habitats than any other man in England. The dried plants he collected at that time and sewed on sheets of paper fill twenty large books.[9] No one perhaps was better equipped to find a method of organising them into a system. Method was the key and Ray was in no hurry to rush into print. Writing earlier to his friend Martin Lister, whom he had first met at Montpellier, he had resolved 'never to put out anything which is not as perfect as possible for me to make it'.[10] Nine years after his preliminary notes in the Preface to his *Observations*, and now with a settled, permanent home in Black Notley, Ray brought out his *Methodus plantarum nova*. 'Nothing is more helpful to clear understanding, prompt recognition and sound memory than a well ordered arrangement into classes, primary and subordinate,' he wrote in the Preface.

> But I would not have my readers expect something perfect or complete; something which would divide all plants so exactly as to include every species without leaving any in positions anomalous or peculiar; something which would so define each genus by its own characteristics that no species be left, so to speak, homeless or be found

*Plate 151: The exotic produce – bananas, pineapples, coconuts –
of a market stall in the East Indies, painted in the mid-
seventeenth century by Albert Eckhout*

common to many genera. Nature does not permit anything of the sort. Nature, as the saying goes, makes no jumps and passes from extreme to extreme only through a mean. She always produces species intermediate between higher and lower types, species of doubtful classification linking one type with another and having something in common with both . . . In any case I dare not promise even so perfect a Method as Nature permits – that is not the task of one man or of one age – but only such as I can accomplish in my present circumstances; and these are not too favourable.[11]

As well as showing, way ahead of Darwin, that he grasped the concept of the evolution of species, Ray reviews the three possible ways in which plants might be grouped and sorted: by habitat, by use or 'from the likeness and agreement of the principal parts'. Our concerns in the twenty-first century make sorting by habitat an attractive option. But, in the very different parameters of the late seventeenth century, Ray rejects the first two options because they separated plants that were obviously alike and united those which had equally obvious differences. He pays a generous tribute to Andrea Cesalpino 'the first so far as I know to classify plants by the number of seeds and seed-vessels developed from each flower', but gives cogent reasons why he cannot agree wholeheartedly with his method: the form of the flower, the corolla and calyx must also be taken into account. He is too modest to suppose that his own new Method can be comprehensive, for he understands that thousands of plants are not yet known or described. The third of Ray's introductory essays deals with the structure of the seed and its embryo. He makes a seminal distinction between plants such as the lily, whose seeds produce seedlings with one leaf, and those such as mustard or cress, which sprout with two. The two different groups acquired names – monocotyledon and dicotyledon – still in use today. Lobelius had arrived at a similar distinction when he differentiated beteen plants whose leaves had long thin parallel veins, like those of the grasses, and those whose leaves were netted all over with veins leading to a central, strong midrib. But Ray knew that the outward appearance of a plant's leaves did not provide a strong enough foundation for the method he was seeking. The distinction between the two types of embryo he described put the difference on a more profound footing. It is as valid today as it was in 1682. He sees that the traditional divisions of trees, shrubs, sub-shrubs and herbs, are 'popular and accidental rather than accurate and philosophical' but accepts the customary usage, though he abandons sub-shrubs as a separate section. He divides trees into eight classes, shrubs into six (an improvement on the previous cursory separation into spiny and non-spiny). Herbs, always a problem, have expanded from the twenty-two classes listed in the Cambridge *Catalogus* to an unwieldy forty-seven. Only Nehemiah Grew, Secretary of the Royal Society by

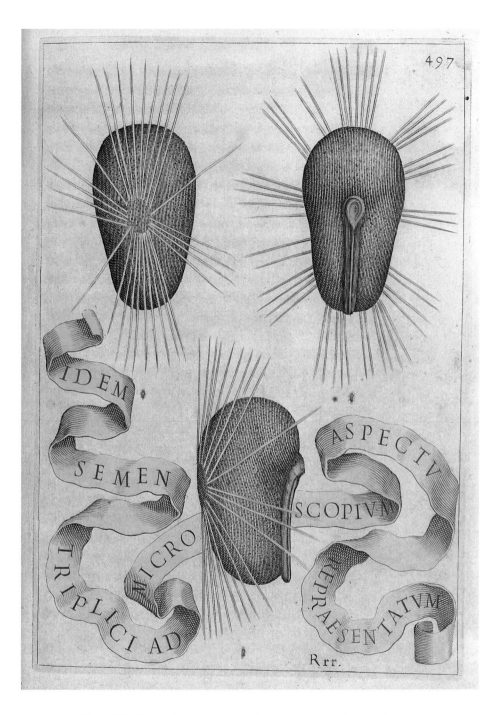

Plate 152: *Three different views of an hibiscus seed, seen through
the magnifying lens of a microscope. From Giovanni Battista
Ferrari's* Flora, *published in Rome in 1638*

1677, came anywhere near Ray in effecting a sound method of sorting plants into coherent groups. Grew, though, was still using the colour of a flower or the number of its petals as a basis for classification, characteristics which Ray had expressly dismissed as *accidentia*. Unlike Grew, Ray was working alone, unsupported by the facilities of a university or botanic garden, under conditions which, as he himself acknowledged, were 'not too favourable'. He was always overworked, frequently ill, and the cures recommended by Benjamin Allen, the young Braintree doctor who treated him (crushed woodlice for colic, a decoction of peacock's dung for epilepsy) exacerbated rather than relieved his complaints. The Braintree carrier made weekly trips to London, but travel was still uncomfortable and slow.[12] The immediate neighbourhood was, he wrote to John Aubrey, 'barren of wits, here being few of the gentry or clergy who mind anything that is ingenious'.[13]

Ray, though, maintained a massive correspondence and in these last twenty-five years at Black Notley patrons and supporters such as Sir Hans Sloane, who in 1693 became the new Secretary of the Royal Society, and Tancred Robinson, the *amicorum alpha* who had studied under Tournefort in Paris and with Magnol at Montpellier, became increasingly important to him.[14] Both Sloane and Robinson were important in providing Ray with the motivation and incentive now, in his fifties, to begin the monumental *Historia plantarum*, which eventually filled three volumes of close-set print and ran to more than 2,000 pages. 'Yours and some other friends' opinions and expectations from me do inspire me with such force and courage as not to despair of my abilities,' Ray wrote to Tancred Robinson, 'but to contemn all difficulties and contend even to excel and outdo myself.' Other nations were busy and active in the field, he noted, and he wished to show that 'the English are not altogether idle or asleep but do at least endeavour to contribute something'.[15] Ray intended his work to be an encyclopaedic overview of all the plants known to man. His list of sources includes Willem Piso's *De Indiae utriusque re naturali* published in Amsterdam in 1658, as well as the six volumes of the *Historia naturalis Indiae* written by Jakob de Bondt, who in the 1620s had spent six years working as a doctor in Batavia. He consulted the eight volumes of the *Historia naturalis Brasiliae*, written by Georg Marcgraf, physician to Prince Moritz of Nassau, and published in Amsterdam in 1648.[16] He worked his way through an even earlier work, Francisco Hernandez's *Plantas y Animales de la Nueva Espana* published in Mexico in 1615. He read the Italian author, Paolo Boccone's *Icones et descriptiones rariorum plantarum* (1674) as well as the *Catalogus Monspeliensis* prepared in 1676 by Pierre Magnol, the young lecturer whom he had so admired at the University of Montpellier.

Until this time Ray (and indeed everyone else with an interest in the field) had hoped that the task of compiling a complete encyclopaedia of plants would be accomplished by Robert Morison (1620–1683), who since 1670 had been Professor of *res herbaria* at Oxford. Morison seemed ideally equipped for the task. After fighting with the Royalists against Cromwell, he left England for Paris, where he studied under Jean Robin, director of the royal gardens. He returned to England as physician to Charles II; the *Plantarum umbelliferarum distributio nova* he published in Oxford in 1672 was to be the first of a series of ambitious monographs, each dealing with one particular family of plants. Eventually, they would cover the entire plant kingdom. The *Plantarum umbelliferarum* (see plate 153) is a large handsome folio with superb copperplate engravings of various umbelifers, which included careful representations of the separate parts of the flower and seed.[17] Tipped into the front of the volume is Morison's PROPOSAL, addressed to the 'Noblemen, Gentlemen and others' who may be willing to subscribe towards his 'New Universal Herbal, ordering Plants, according to a new and true Method never mentioned heretofore'. Morison explained that he was now 'desirous, for the advancing and facilitating that part of Natural History, which hath hitherto been so tedious and discouraging to Students of that Science', to publish his encyclopaedia with all possible speed. Unfortunately the 'Excessive Charge of Designing, Graving, and Printing' means that he cannot proceed 'without the assistance of such Noblemen and Gentlemen as are desirous to further and encourage this Great Work. He therefore doth Engage hereby to every Nobleman and Gentleman, or other, who will be pleased to favour him with one Plate of Five Pounds, that an Honourable Memorial shall be made of him, by Engraving his Coat of arms on their respective Plates.' Morison had in mind a work that would eventually cover 2,450 plants with fine plates cut in Taille Douce. When they had laid down their five pounds, Morison contracted to supply his sponsors with a complete set of the 'Great Work'. But following the Proposal is a slightly desperate Addendum. Morison explains that it has taken nearly three years to complete the first section of 108 plates. For the first two years, work was extremely slow, 'partly for want of good or excellent, yea, and the more diligent Gravers; and now this last Year, finding some Strangers both diligent and able, who join'd with some of our own, we want now onely Encouragement of Subscribers, for the paying of the Painters and Gravers, to finish the whole Work, in as short time as can be possibly allowed'. Despite the delicate appeal to the aspirations and snobbery of those who might back his project, Morison's great enterprise collapsed. In the year following the publication of Ray's *Methodus*, he died.

Ray, too, had hoped that his own massive *Historia plantarum* would be illustrated. He understood how helpful pictures could be, how much easier they made an understanding of the various parts of plants. A history of plants without illustrations was, he felt, as opaque as a book of geography without maps. But Morison had bankrupted

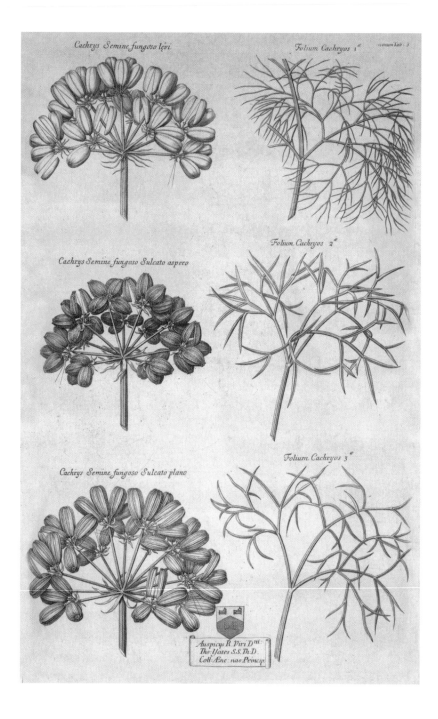

Plate 153: Various umbellifers, beautifully engraved in Robert Morison's doomed Plantarum umbelliferarum distributio nova, *published in Oxford in 1672*

himself in producing the fine copperplate engravings for his book on umbellifers. The Royal Society was too stretched to be able to help. 'I am so teased about cuts for my History of Plants,' Ray wrote to Tancred Robinson on 12 May 1685, 'all my friends condemning wooden and telling me I had better print it without any.'[18] So Ray was persuaded to do without illustrations, but he never ceased to hope that they might be included in future editions. On 15 September 1685, Samuel Pepys, President of the Royal Society, issued an instruction to Henry Fairthorne, the Society's printer, to put the *Historia plantarum* in hand. Every week for next six months, bundles of copy were taken by the Braintree carrier up to the London printer, and bundles of proofs returned to Ray in the country. The first volume was published in June 1686; at the end of the book was an appeal for subscriptions to fund the engraving of plates family by family, as Morison had hoped to do. It never happened.

'I know that there are other species, new and undescribed, in the gardens of Universities and of the great,' Ray wrote in his Preface. 'These must some day be published: I have dealt chiefly with those already recorded: even here I am conscious of omissions through lack of enquiry, negligence, forgetfulness or haste: my readers will perhaps notice more such: what else can be expected from one mere man who had not even a secretary but must needs plough the whole field with his own hand.'[19] He had not seen the tropical plants now being grown by Jacob Bobart, curator of the Oxford Botanic Garden.[20] He had, however, grown persicaria and sneezewort from Virginia,[21] as well as the now ubiquitous golden rod.[22] In the matter of plant descriptions, he acknowledges a major debt to the books of the Bauhin brothers, the Italian plantsman, Fabio Colonna, and the industrious Carolus Clusius. He recapitulates the reasons for sticking to the method of classifying plants that he had already proposed and published four years earlier. His first volume covers four classes of what he calls the 'imperfect plants' (corals, seaweeds, fungi and mosses) and follows on with a treatment of ferns. Then he turns to the vast tribe of flowers, finishing this first volume with the pea family, the *Leguminosae*. In his second volume, published in 1688, he considers trees, first the monocots such as palms and then the dicots. He goes right back to Theophrastus for an account of the way in which female palm trees can be fertilised by the male, finishing with his own opinion 'that the apices supported by the stamens take the place of male seed in plants and serve for fertilising the females'. It was one of the boldest statements about the sex life of plants that anyone had yet made in print.[23] Although products such as quinine, sago, chocolate, coffee and tea were now familiar in England, (Samuel Pepys wrote of his first taste of tea, taken on 25 September 1660; Ray describes how its leaves can be prepared as an infusion, but evidently does not regard it as a safe drink), the trees from which they came were not. Often there were no reports or accurate descriptions on which he could rely. Though he does not know them at first hand, he is, nevertheless, filled with a general sense of wonder at the strange exotics of the tropics, so different from the plants of the temperate world. 'If a man were carried there in his sleep he would not believe his eyes when he woke up,' he wrote and I remember how it was on the trail to the Orinduik waterfall, how unreal, how disorientating, how mesmerisingly strange. 'If any European travelling through woods saw the bark of trees shining by night so brightly as to light up the path and enable him to read letters, would he not be astounded?' he asks.[24] But once again he states his conviction that the number of plant species in the world must be fixed and limited, 'constant and unchangeable from the first creation to the present day'.

When, in September 1687, Ray had finished work on the second volume of his mammoth encyclopaedia, he went up to London to look at the collection of foreign seeds and nuts that William Courten had amassed at his private museum in the Middle Temple.[25] He also admired the exotic trees and shrubs newly planted in Bishop Compton's garden at Fulham Palace, then the finest arboretum in England. Tancred Robinson writes to Sir Hans Sloane, now in Jamaica, promising to send him a copy of Ray's book on the next available ship. But the vast enterprise (a third volume was finally printed in 1704, a year before Ray's death) did not have the popular success that Ray, in those long years of lonely labour, must have hoped for. Like his other books, it was written in Latin, now not so exclusively the language of scholarly discourse. William Turner, writing more than a hundred years earlier in the middle of the sixteenth century, had the opposite problem: he published a book written in English that was all but inaccessible to the Continental scholars among whom he spent so much time.[26] But at this end of the seventeenth century, Ray complained that there was scarcely a printer left in London who could be trusted to set up accurate text in Latin. Ray's book was dauntingly enormous and it was set in very small type, unrelieved by any pictures. And, like others before him, he was perhaps unlucky in his timing. Many of the Englishmen to whom Ray's great work might have appealed were preoccupied with politics. (The first volume of the *Historia plantarum* came out the year after the Duke of Monmouth's rebellion; the second volume was published in the year that the Whig Lords invited William of Orange to take over the English crown.) And, after its promising start, the Royal Society had got into difficulties. Ray's friend Tancred Robinson resigned as Secretary, and shortly after signing the order to print Ray's *Historia plantarum* Samuel Pepys had resigned as President, to be succeeded by the third Earl of Carbery, whom Pepys called 'one of the lewdest fellows of the age'. There was no money to commission research and no new papers were published in the *Philosophical Transactions*. The Society only recovered when, after his return from Jamaica, Sir Hans Sloane took

Plate 154: 'Flos Africanus' the African marigold from De Koninglycke Hovenier, *a Dutch treatise on gardening published in 1676*

on the job of Secretary. 'As for cuts for my *History of Plants* there are none to be expected,' wrote Ray to his friend Edward Lhwyd on 2 August 1689. 'The book sells not so well as to encourage the undertakers to be at any further charge about it. The times indeed of late have not been very propitious to the booksellers' trade.'[27] Ray got twenty free copies of the *Historia* and was paid £30 for each of the first two volumes.

Ray's final, seminal word on order (the *Methodus plantarum emendata* published in Amsterdam in 1703) was honed by a sharp exchange of views with the French plantsman, Joseph Pitton de Tournefort (see plate 155). He'd read Tournefort's new book, the *Élémens de botanique* during the summer of 1695, though in the French language, Ray was, he said, 'but a smatterer'. Tournefort was an important adversary – professor at the university in Paris, curator of the Royal Garden – and Ray was dismayed that Tournefort, who had read his *Historia* closely, dismissed his method and was proposing a system he could not agree with.[28] The whole cause for which he'd fought so long could be set back if it was adopted. He had to reply. Tournefort's chief criticism was that Ray used too many characteristics to define his various groups of plants. Tournefort was proposing one single defining feature: the number and relative symmetry of the petals of a flower. It wouldn't do, argued Ray. It forced too many unnatural groupings: the narcissus with the reed, the rose with the poppy. Tournefort could not ignore the wider structure of plants, or disregard their natural relationships. And so, his legs now covered in running sores which he bathed in a mixture of dock root and chalk, and with gangrene spreading on the undersides of his feet, Ray, isolated in his Essex cottage, set down his last words on the subject that had intrigued and sustained him for more than thirty years. In the *Methodus plantarum emendata*, he lists his rules for grouping plants according to their natural affinities. Plant names must be changed as little as possible to avoid confusion and mistakes; the characteristics of a group must be clearly defined and not rely on comparison (this had been a marked feature of early descriptions when there were no agreed standards – leaves were 'bigger than box' or 'not so indented as ivy'); characteristics must be obvious and easy to grasp; groups approved by most plantsmen should be preserved; related plants should not be separated; the characteristics used to define should not be unnecessarily increased. The six Rules Ray proposed provided the vital underpinning of a new discipline which would later acquire a new name – taxonomy.

And is that it, you may ask? Yes, that is indeed it. No fireworks, no claps of thunder, no swelling symphonic themes mark Ray's achievement. It is a quiet, lonely, dogged consummation, and, in its insistence on the importance of method before system, critical in shaping future thinking on the subject to which he had devoted

Joseph Pitton de Tournefort
Con.er du Roy, pensionnaire de l'Académie Royale
des Sciences, Docteur en médecine de la faculté
de Paris, Professeur en Botanique au Jardin du
Roy, &c. né à Aix en   Prov.ce   en 1656. mort
à Paris   en 1708.

A. Paris chez

E. Desrochers.

Louis 14. le fit Chevalier de S.t Louis en consideration de ses grands voyages; il revint dans cet habillement

Consommé dans la Botanique
Nous verrions encor Tournefort,
Vivre et nous enseigner leur vertu spécifique
Si les simples pouvoient garantir de la mort.

*Plate 155: Joseph Pitton de Tournefort (1656–1708), John Ray's
rival, whose* Élémens de botanique *set out a new system of classifying
plants according to the form of the flower*

the whole of his adult life. After his death, Tournefort's system flourished for a while. So did that proposed by the Swedish taxonomist, Carl Linnaeus. But thinking men came inexorably back to Ray. We are so far now from where he was then that it is difficult to fit our minds to his seventeenth-century accomplishments. But he foresaw that too. I have to go, of course, to Black Notley, now almost swallowed up by unlovely Braintree. Ray's grave, close to the church door, is a handsome monument, paid for by Bishop Compton and other rich friends. Drawn to it by its crowning obelisk of stone, I peer at the panels underneath lettered in a close Latin script. They are almost illegible now. It doesn't matter. He is commemorated for ever in horehound and woundwort, purple-crested cow wheat, henbane and hemp agrimony, the native flowers that first awoke in him his lifelong passion for plants. And fittingly, it was he who first used the word which described the subject of his life's work.

The *Philosophical Transactions* in 1691 had described Ray as an 'incomparable botanist',[29] a newly coined term in England in the late seventeenth century. But it was John Ray himself, writing in 1696, who first used the word 'botany'.[30] Here it was at last, riding in on its Greek root, the word to describe the labours of almost 2,000 years, to supplant the *stirpium*, the *planta*, the *res herbaria*, the simpling, the herborising and all the other terms by which generations of earlier plantsmen had tried to describe the substance and focus of their work. The long, careful, patient study undertaken by my heroes Theophrastus, Ghini, Cesalpino, Turner, Gesner and Johnson, to organise and disseminate the naming of plant names, now had its own name. And armed with this name, it crossed into a different world. It left the philosophers behind and instead engaged wholeheartedly with a new breed, the scientists of the Enlightenment. Ray, finally, had worked out the rules that could clarify nature's game. He had provided a more solid foundation for future scholars to build on than anyone else before him. There was still much more to do and he understood that, as well as recognising how his achievements might seem to those looking back over another 300 years of progress. 'I predict that our descendants will reach such heights in the sciences that our proudest discoveries will seem slight, obvious, almost worthless,' he wrote. 'They will be tempted to pity our ignorance and to wonder that truths easy and manifest were for so long hidden and were so esteemed by us, unless they are generous enough to remember that we broke the ice for them, and smoothed the first approach to the heights.'[31]

EPILOGUE

OF COURSE, THE story does not end with Ray. He forges the rules that will steer his successors through the complex maze of nomenclature that lies ahead. He establishes the study of plants as a scientific discipline. He gives this study a new name – botany.[1] Ray is the last of the heroes whose work gradually shifted the study of plants away from superstition and towards science. But this particular story cannot have an end: as ways of seeing change, new things are seen. New relationships are revealed. New ways of sorting plants become possible – inevitable even. Spectacles had helped Fuchs. He's wearing them in the portrait that his artist, Albrecht Meyer, prepared for *De historia stirpium* (1542). The first microscope, invented towards the end of the sixteenth century, showed Ray and his contemporary Nehemiah Grew complexities in the structure of plants that previous scholars could never have dreamed of. But ahead of Ray lay electron microscopes, Watson and Crick, the double helix, DNA. The task of defining and categorising the natural world, previously the domain of philosophers and naturalists, has now, in the twenty-first century, been taken over by physicists, phytochemists, molecular systematicists who are just as driven by the need to sort and order, to find perfection in hierarchy and classification, as Cesalpino ever was.

And somewhere we have to nod, however grudgingly, to Carl Linnaeus (1707–1778), the Swedish botanist who described his own book, *Species plantarum*, published in 1753, as 'the greatest achievement in the realm of science'. Enthroned as professor of medicine at the University of Uppsala, he called his students 'apostles'. Like Mattioli, he had the good fortune to publish the right book at the right time. He captured the *zeitgeist*, understood what was required and, with the ruthless efficiency of a computer programme, imposed brisk two-module name tags on nearly 6,000 plants. Since 1725, the Society of Gardeners had been meeting regularly in London to look at plants, especially those then pouring in from the Cape and the East Indies, in the hope of bringing some order to their naming. Novelties commanded high prices. Nurseries competed savagely for new plants and sent them out to rich customers under whatever name they fancied. The brilliant glory lily, which created a sensation when it was first brought into Europe from the tropics, had been 'Methonica' to one nursery, 'Lilium zeylanicum superbum' to another, 'Mendoni' to a third. Linnaeus decreed that it should henceforth be called *Gloriosa superba*, one of its earliest names. And, surprisingly, the rest of the world eventually agreed. Just in time, order had been wrested from chaos. Between 1730 and 1760, the number and variety of plants being grown in England increased fivefold.

The binomial naming system that Linnaeus used was not his invention. In a haphazard way, it had been around since the beginning: speaking for instance of poppies, Theophrastus had distinguished different kinds as 'mekon e melaina', 'mekon e keratitis', 'mekon e rhoias'. Brunfels and Fuchs had both used two-part names, but randomly, not as part of a rational plan. Andrea Cesalpino and Gaspard Bauhin[2] had both seen the advantages of the brief surname/Christian name system being applied to plants as well as people. It is a logical way of showing which group a plant belongs to and pinpointing its particular place in that group. But Linnaeus recognised more clearly than anyone else before him that all a name had to do was designate. It did not have to describe. Scholars of the seventeenth and early eighteenth centuries had drifted away from the short, sharp binomial towards much longer polynomial tags that tried to pin down the exact, distinguishing characteristics of the plant in question. In one way that was useful. A name such as 'Plantago foliis ovato-lanceolatis pubescentibus, spica cylindrica, scapo tereti' tells you that this is a plantain with ovate lanceolate leaves becoming softly hairy, a cylindrical head and a smooth stem. But it doesn't fit the mouth as comfortably as *Plantago media*, our hoary plantain. Nor is it as easy to remember.

The binomial system worked too, because it mirrored the way that common names had evolved. Hoary plantain is, in effect, a binomial tag. The collective name is plantain, the distinguishing name hoary, which differentiates this kind of plantain from the ribwort plantain (*Plantago lanceolata*), the greater plantain (*Plantago major*) or the sea plantain (*Plantago maritima*). In the English language the describing word comes before the generic one. In Latin it's the other way around. There will always be a place for common names – they are both vivid and familiar. But they are not universal. When, in 1892, Nathaniel Colgan of Dublin tried to establish the true identity of the shamrock, patriotic Irishmen from twenty different counties inundated him with plants. Some sent white clover, some red, some sent lesser yellow trefoil, some spotted medick. No one sent wood sorrel, which in England is sometimes called shamrock.[3] A widespread flower such as the marsh marigold (*Caltha palustris*) has about sixty common names in France, another eighty in Britain, and at least 140 in Germany, Austria and Switzerland.[4]

But taxonomy, which distinguishes, names and groups plants in a systematic way to create, in effect, a register of biodiversity, has to operate in a universal language. For centuries scholars had used Latin as the common denominator and, as Mark Griffiths points out, without that 'single accessible text of living things, without a *lingua franca* governed by universal rules, that one "language" would become many tongues, vernaculars, many argots and slangs: biodiversity would be Babel, and then fall silent'.[5] Standardisation was Linnaeus's gift to those still desperately searching for a unifying scheme.

Born in Småland, a province in southern Sweden, two years after John Ray's death, Linnaeus goes on to study medicine at Uppsala. His mentor and benefactor is Olaf Rudbeck, a tutor at the university. In gratitude, Linnaeus later names the daisy-flow-ered rudbeckia after him (Johann Siegesbeck, who had dared to criticise the great man, gets a small weed, *Siegesbeckia orientalis*). In 1732 he begins a 3,000-mile journey through Lapland and in his *Flora Lapponica* (1737) records the plants he found there. He goes to Hamburg, Amsterdam and London, where he meets Sir Hans Sloane, President of the Royal Society. He is employed by George Clifford, a wealthy merchant banker, to classify and describe all the plants in the garden and herbarium at Clifford's estate, the Hartekamp, near Haarlem. In his spare time, Linnaeus classifies his benefactor's library: I, Patres: Graeci, Romani; II, Comment-atores: Theophrasti, Dioscoridis . . . Returning to Sweden, he practises as a doctor, specialising in gonorrhoea. In 1741, he is offered a professorship at Uppsala and devotes himself to his *Species plantarum*, which builds on the *Genera plantarum* he had published in Leiden in 1737. As well as standardising plant names, abolishing the synonyms which since the beginning had been a muddlesome problem for scholars such as Turner and Johnson, he introduces the concept of precedence. The earliest published name of a plant is the one to be preferred. He adopts sixty of the names that Otto Brunfels had used for the plants in his *Herbarum vivae eicones* (1530–36) and eighty of those included by Leonhart Fuchs in *De historia stirpium* (1542). Though some complained that 'he seems so vain as to imagine he can prescribe to all the world', his system of naming plants prevails. The *Species plantarum* is now accepted as the starting point of our present system of naming plant names.

While his system succeeds (the Lee and Kennedy nursery is using it by 1760), his method does not. Linnaeus has proposed a new way of grouping plants based on the number and arrangement of the stamens and carpels within a flower. 'The actual petals of a flower contribute nothing to generation,' he wrote, 'serving only as the bridal bed which the great Creator has so gloriously prepared, adorned with such precious bedcurtains, and perfumed with so many sweet scents, in order that the bridegroom and bride may therein celebrate their nuptials with the greater solemnity.' Tournefort, whose system had been based on the arrangement of petals, is neatly demolished. The method of classifying plants Linnaeus was taught at high school is replaced by one of his own, which he has been developing since the 1730s and which he calls a 'systema sexuale'. It is considered deeply shocking. The Bishop of Carlisle rails against the 'gross prurience' of Linnaeus's mind. He fears that the book will 'shock female modesty', at the same time doubting whether many 'virtuous students' would be able to follow Linnaeus's analogies. In St Petersburg, Johann Siegesbeck condemns the 'loathsome harlotry' of Linnaeus's method. 'Who would have thought that bluebells, lilies and onions could be up to such immorality?' he asks. In Oxford, Johann Jacob Dillenius, the Sherardian Professor of Botany, writes to a fellow botanist, Richard Richardson, that although Linnaeus has 'a thorough insight and knowledge of Botany' he is afraid his method will not hold. And it does not. Linnaeus's method of classifying plants, the 'systema sexuale' scarcely outlives him.

Since 1867, the actual names that plants bear have been regulated by an International Code of Botanical Nomenclature,[6] which establishes the basic hierarchy of the plant world. At the bottom, in the lowest rank, is the *species* name which distinguishes between plants that are closely related (like our creeping and meadow buttercups, *Ranunculus repens* and *R. acris*). Sometimes the specific names are descriptive, as in *repens* (creeping); sometimes they indicate the country of origin: *sinensis* (Chinese); sometimes they encapsulate a plant's history: *officinalis* (of apothecaries' shops. 'Opificina' – later corrupted to 'officina' – was the original Latin term for a pharmacy).

Above the species is the *genus*, the bigger group in which all the species are combined – the buttercups, which are all *Ranunculus*, the forget-me-nots which are all *Myosotis*, the plantains which are all *Plantago*. Genera vary greatly in their size and distinctiveness. Some, such as the *Ginkgo*, have only one ancient representative. Others, such as *Euphorbia*, have more than 2,000 members, some annuals, some perennials, some succulents, some shrubs, some trees. Theophrastus was right in thinking the simple division of plants he proposed – herbs, sub-shrubs, shrubs and trees – was a device that might not prove tenable. Above the genus is the *family*, which collects related genera together: columbines, monkshoods, spring aconites, hellebores and meadow rues are gathered with buttercups in the family of Ranunculaceae; tulips, fritillaries and erythroniums join lilies in the Liliaceae. Like genera, families vary enormously in size. The family of Orchidaceae accommodates

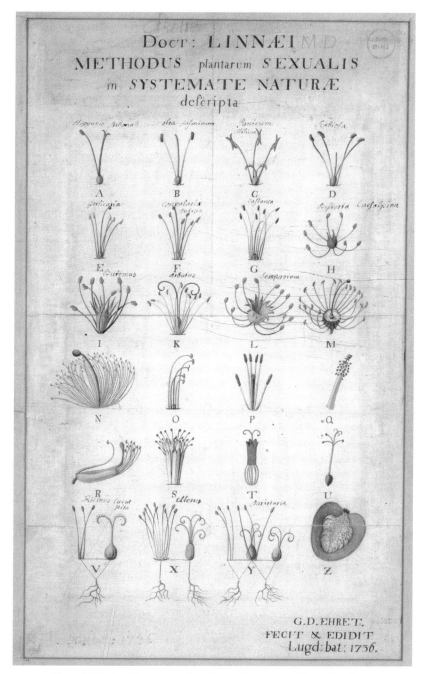

Plate 156: An illustration by Georg Dionysius Ehret for the Hortus Cliffortianus (1735–48) in which the Swedish plantsman, Carl Linnaeus, first began to work out his 'methodus plantarum sexualis', grouping plants according to the number and arrangement of their stamens

around 800 genera, at least 20,000 species. Families, though, shrink and grow as each generation of botanists proposes a new set of defining characteristics. So do the *orders*, which stand above them and which pull various families into cryptic proximity: the barberry family (Berberidaceae) and the akebia family (Lardizabalaceae), for instance, sit with the buttercup family, Ranunculaceae, in an order called the Ranunculales. Finally there are the *divisions*, vast overarching categories, which separate flowering plants from other types of plants such as ferns or mosses.

Ray's Six Rules had provided the conceptual framework for a future system. And the idea of a hierarchy was generally accepted, as was Linnaeus's useful shorthand, the two-name tag. But the classification of plants remained as fluid as ever because nobody could agree on the most convincing indicator of their similarities and differences. Some botanists returned to Lobelius's method and used the leaf as the defining characteristic. Others stuck with the flower. But the form and structure of plants – their morphology – could be influenced to a troubling degree by the environment in which they grew. Theophrastus recognised this: the plane tree by the stream in the Lyceum 'sent its roots a distance of 33 cubits, having both room and nourishment'. The particular silver firs that grew in a sheltered valley in Arcadia, 'excelled greatly in height and stoutness'. Perhaps other characteristics would be more stable? When the delicate, intricate structure of pollen grains was revealed in the vacuum chamber of the electron microscope, some thought that here was a secure indicator of differences. More recently, phytochemical properties have been proposed as the key. By bringing together nasturtium and oil-seed rape (both contain mustard oil), taxonomists have returned to the method of the earliest herbals: grouping by use. So, species have continued to shift from one genus to another. Genera have split and merged as different botanists used different criteria to create different groupings. Some are inclined to be 'lumpers', wanting to create big, baggy, loosely connected genera. Others are 'splitters', seeing each tiny morphological difference as a justification for creating a new species with its own specific name.

Some families such as the Liliaceae became very baggy indeed. While the American taxonomist Arthur Cronquist (1919–1992), by nature a lumper, could always find reasons to maintain families in fairly large gatherings of different genera, Rolf Dahlgren (1932–1987) argued for more and smaller families with more uniform characteristics. Sitting in judgment at Kew, the Family Planning Committee (it really exists) discusses the arguments for and against. How are we to make sense of it all, when the taxonomists themselves so often disagree? From Bentham and Hooker in 1862–83, to Cronquist in 1988, eight major systems of plant classification have been proposed in the last hundred years alone.[7] But do we now, at last, have incontrovertible proof about the ways that plants relate to one another? Have the complex

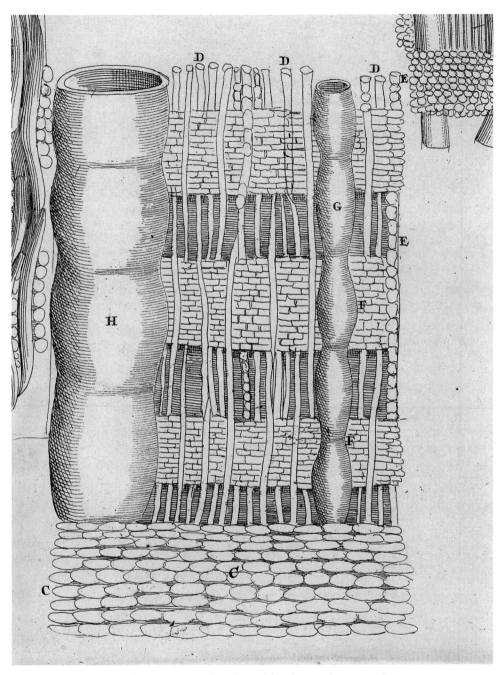

Plate 157: Hugely enlarged by the newly invented microscope, this is the xylem (the tissue that carries water from the roots to other parts of the plant) of an oak, drawn by the Italian plantsman, Marcello Malpighi for his Anatome plantarum *(1679)*

inter-relationships of the natural world finally been decoded, the clues unravelled? Has the essential *psyche* of a plant, the concept that Aristotle and Theophrastus worried away at so long, finally been pinned down?

On a gorgeous May morning in 2005, with great candles of blossom lighting up the horse chestnuts that the Flemish ambassador Ogier Ghiselin de Busbecq introduced so long ago that we've forgotten they were ever strangers, my final pilgrimage takes me to the Royal Botanic Gardens, Kew, where Professor Mark Chase heads the Molecular Systematics Section. The big money that went into the human genome project generated techniques which quickly filtered into other disciplines. By analysing the DNA of plants, scientists can now work out a kind of evolutionary tree, and make clear relationships that no outward character could ever suggest. Flowering plants evolved more than 150 million years ago (inexplicably, I suddenly see a great brontosaurus foot crushing a marestail, as the hoof of my horse had crushed the tulips and Juno irises in the Tien Shan mountains of Kazakhstan); in 150 million years, plants that were once closely related can take completely separate evolutionary paths and end up looking as different as, say, roses and nettles. But the DNA of those two plants, the code that's been hidden within them for millions of years, shows that they actually belong to the same big order, the fabids (it also takes in cannabis, cucumber, pear, strawberry and many other seemingly disparate families of plants). Starting in the 1980s, Chase and his colleagues gathered 500 sequences of one gene to analyse. Their computers weren't up to the task and crashed. By 1993, they'd overcome that problem and it took the newly named Angiosperm Phylogeny Group just two years to amass a second set of data, which gave the same sometimes surprising results. The lotus should not be sitting with the water lily, which it seems so closely to resemble, but with plane trees and South African proteas. Bravely, the group began a major re-structuring of the hierarchy. Cesalpino's umbellifers have a new name, and his pea group is split up. But he himself is honoured at the head of a new family, the Cesalpiniaceae, close to the sweet pea and mimosa. Dioscorides has an order named after him, the Dioscoreales, even further up in the hierarchy. Theophrastus gets nothing.

It is a monumental shift. But Professor Chase argues it is based on incontrovertible evidence. You can't reject it just because it's not what you expect. So, in Leiden, where in 1593 Clusius went to set up a botanic garden, the old order beds are being remade to reflect the new classification. At the university in Oxford, students of systematics and taxonomy are now taught according to the new system. In the Oxford Botanic Garden, founded in 1621 so that 'learning may be improved', the order beds, last remade in 1884 according to Bentham and Hooker's rules, are once again being dug up and rearranged. A new order has begun.

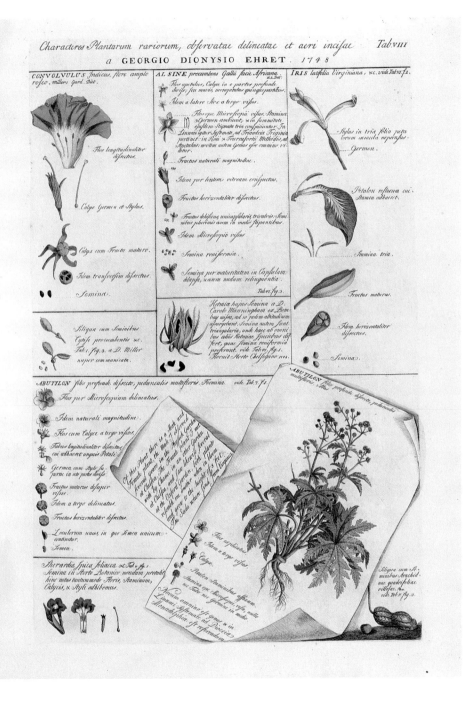

Plate 158: 'Characters of flowers', one of the plates engraved by
the German artist, Georg Dionysius Ehret for his Plantae et
papiliones rariores (1748)

CHRONOLOGY

387 BC	Plato founds the Academy
384 BC	Aristotle born
*c.*372 BC	Theophrastus born
368 BC	Plato finishes his *Republic*
347 BC	Plato dies. Speusippus heads Academy. Aristotle leaves Athens for Atarneus, Assos, Lesbos
343 BC	Aristotle goes to Macedon as tutor to Alexander
336 BC	Alexander succeeds to throne of Macedon
335 BC	Aristotle returns to Athens, founds Peripatetic School at the Lyceum in Athens
331 BC	Alexander the Great's expedition to Egypt
330 BC	Alexander destroys Darius's Persepolis, bringing Greek culture to Western Asia, and Asian plants into Greek pantheon
327 BC	Alexander sets out on Indian expedition
322 BC	Aristotle dies. Theophrastus heads Peripatetic School
307 BC	Museum and Library of Alexandria begun under Ptolemy Soter
287 BC	Theophrastus dies. Strato of Lampsacus heads Peripatetic School
285 BC	Ptolemy II Philadelphus King of Egypt
280 BC	The Colossus of Rhodes, 105 ft high, is finally set in place
246 BC	Ptolemy II Philadelphus dies
218 BC	Hannibal travels over the Alps to invade Italy with 100,000 men and fifty elephants

147 BC	Greece ruled by Romans
47 BC	Caesar sacks Alexandria and the Library is destroyed by fire
46 BC	Caesar introduces the Julian calendar with 365 days in a year
AD 23/24	Pliny the Elder born at Verona
AD 40	Pedanios Dioscorides born at Anazarbus, Cilicia
AD 43	Romans invade Britain
AD 70	Jewish diaspora begins, after the sacking of Jerusalem
AD 77	Pliny's *Natural History*
c. AD 77	Dioscorides's *De materia medica*
AD 79	Pliny dies in Vesuvius eruption
AD 80	The Colosseum in Rome is finished, with seats for 87,000 spectators
c. AD 100	Papyrus produced in sheets, rather than rolls
c. AD 105	Paper of rags and hemp is made in China
AD 127	Hadrian's wall, separating England from Scotland, is virtually finished
AD 130	Galen of Pergamum born
AD 201	Galen dies
AD 330	Constantinople founded by Constantine
AD 391	Theodosius destroys Temple of Serapis at Alexandria
AD 406	Vandals overrun much of Gaul
AD 410	Sack of Rome by Alaric the Visigoth
AD 425	University founded in Constantinople
AD 452	Huns under Attila invade northern Italy
c. AD 512	Juliana Anicia's codex
AD 529	Emperor Julian closes Aristotle's School in Athens and St Benedict founds monastery at Monte Cassino
AD 622	Mohammed flees to Medina and establishes the Islamic faith
AD 650	The Anglo-Saxon epic poem *Beowulf* is written
AD 711	Spain invaded by Islamic forces
AD 785	Offa's Dyke built to keep the Welsh out of England

c. AD 800	Serapion the Younger writes his medical treatise
AD 832	The House of Wisdom founded in Baghdad
c. AD 854	First Arab translation of Dioscorides
AD 865	First major invasion of Britain by Vikings
AD 978	The twenty-four physicians at 'Adud ad-Dawla's teaching hospital in Baghdad form a medical faculty
AD 980	Avicenna born
AD 985	Medical school established at Salerno, the first in Europe
AD 995	200 British plants listed in Abbot Aelfric's *The Glossary to Grammatica Latino-Saxonica*
1037	Avicenna dies after completing a medical encyclopaedia in use until the seventeenth century
1066	Battle of Hastings where Harold, King of England, is killed by William the Conqueror
1080	Adelard of Bath born
1080	Bayeux tapestry made
1085	El Cid storms Toledo
1085	Domesday survey carried out
1087	Constantine the African translates Arab medical works into Latin
*c.*1130	Adelard of Bath begins his *Quaestiones naturales*
1140	Route opened through the St Gothard Pass in Switzerland
1145	Adelard of Bath dies
*c.*1150	Matthaeus Platearius's *Circa instans*
1163	Work begins on Notre Dame Cathedral in Paris
1170	Thomas Becket murdered in Canterbury Cathedral
*c.*1200	Albertus Magnus born
*c.*1200	Inca civilisation dominates the Cuzco Valley, Peru
1219	Genghis Khan invades Transoxiana and Persia
1222	Genghis Khan conquers Afghanistan
1224	Emperor Frederick II establishes the university at Naples
1227	Genghis Khan dies at the head of an army of 129,000 men

1231	Frederick II orders all doctors and teachers of medicine to present themselves for examination at the University of Salerno
1250	First illustration of a wheelbarrow in Europe
1254	Marco Polo born
c.1256	Albertus Magnus's *De vegetabilibus*
1258	Mongols sack Baghdad
1270	Marco Polo sets out on his historic overland journey east
1272	Manufacture of paper introduced into Italy, possibly from Muslim sources in Spain or Sicily
c.1280	*Tractatus de herbis* (the Salerno MS)
1280	Albertus Magnus dies
1284	Pisa's fleet destroyed by Genoese off the island of Meloria
1302	Bartolomeo de Varignana of Bologna conducts the first post-mortem on a human body
1306	Giotto frescoes in the Arena Chapel, Padua
1313	Spectacles are used in Europe
1324	Marco Polo dies
1340	Paper mill established at Fabriano, Italy, the first in Europe
1341	Petrarch crowned as Poet Laureate at the Capitol in Rome
1347	The Black Death breaks out in Constantinople, Naples, Genoa and southern France; over the next few years it spreads widely in Europe
1370	In Bruges, a Genoese trader takes out an insurance policy, the first in Europe
1377	Population of England (over fourteen) is 1,361,478
1380	Wycliffe's translation of the Bible into English
1387	Chaucer begins *The Canterbury Tales*
c.1390	The Carrara Herbal
c.1398	Teodoro of Gaza born
1403	Flowers bloom on the bronze doors made by Lorenzo Ghiberti for the baptistry of Florence Cathedral

1425	Masaccio frescoes in the Brancacci Chapel and at Santa Maria Novello, Florence
1426	The Ghent altarpiece painted by Hubert and Jan van Eyck
1428	Nicolò Leoniceno born
1438	Pisanello's portrait of Margherita Gonzaga
c.1445	*Liber de simplicibus* made in the Veneto
1452	Leonardo da Vinci born
1453	Constantinople falls after Mohammed II storms the city
1454	Ermolao Barbaro born
1454	Gutenberg invents the printing press; first text (an indulgence) is printed at Mainz
c.1460	Carnations first cultivated in Spain
1462	Sack of Mainz
1469	First printed edition of Pliny's *Natural History* published in Venice
1471	Albrecht Dürer born
1475	Hugo van der Goes starts painting the Portinari altarpiece
1475	Conrad von Megenberg's *Buch der natur*
1476	At Westminster, Caxton sets up the first English printing press
1477	First published account of Marco Polo's travels
1477	Botticelli's *Primavera*
c.1478	Teodoro of Gaza dies
c.1481	*Herbarius* printed in Rome by Johannes Philippus de Lignamine
1483	Teodoro of Gaza's translation of Theophrastus published at Treviso
1485	*Der Gart der Gesundheit* published in Mainz
1486	Euricius Cordus (German botanist) born
1488	Otto Brunfels born
1490	Aldine Press founded in Venice by Aldus Manutius
c.1490	Luca Ghini born
1492	Christopher Columbus's voyage to America
1492	Leoniceno's *Indication of Errors in Pliny*
1492	Spanish troops complete the conquest of Granada

1493	Ermolao Barbaro dies
1493	The Pope divides the territories of the New World between Spain and Portugal
1497	Vasco da Gama leaves Lisbon on the voyage that takes him to India
1498	Vasco da Gama reaches Calicut on the Malabar coast
1498	Earliest known case of syphilis in Europe
c.1500	Pier Andrea Mattioli born
1501	Leonhart Fuchs born
1501	Michelangelo begins his statue of David in Florence
1502	Vasco da Gama establishes Portuguese colony at Cochin
1503	Trade opens up with West Indies
c.1503	Dürer's famous painting of a piece of turf
1505	Mail service established between Brussels and Vienna
1507	Guillaume Rondelet born
1508	William Turner born
1508	Michelangelo begins work on the ceiling of the Sistine Chapel in Rome
1510	Portugal acquires Goa
1515	Valerius Cordus (German botanist) born
1517	Pierre Belon born
1517	Martin Luther denounces the sale of Papal indulgences
1518	Rembert Dodoens (Netherlands physician and botanist) born
1519	Leonardo da Vinci dies
1524	Nicolò Leoniceno dies
1526	Carolus Clusius (Netherlands botanist Charles de l'Écluse) born
1526	Portuguese ships visit New Guinea
1526	*The Grete Herball* published
1528	Albrecht Dürer dies
1530	Brunfels's *Herbarum vivae eicones*
1532	Sulaymān I invades Hungary and advances towards Vienna

1533	At Padua, Francesco Buonafede is appointed first professor of *simplicia medicamenta* (plants for medicine)
1534	Otto Brunfels dies
1535	Fuchs starts his teaching career at the University of Tübingen
1535	Euricius Cordus dies
1535	Sir Thomas More executed for refusing the oath of Supremacy
1535	Pierre Pena born
1536	John Calvin settles in Geneva
1538	Turner's *Libellus de re herbaria novus*
1538	Flemish botanist Lobelius (Matthias de l'Obel) born
1540	Turner flees to France to escape religious persecution
1541	Spaniards begin the conquest of Peru
1541	Hernando de Soto crosses Arkansas and Oklahoma
1542	Seafarers reach Japan
1542	Fuchs's *De historia stirpium*
1543	The first Protestant is burned in Spain
1544	Botanic garden established at Pisa (first in Europe)
1544	Valerius Cordus dies
1544	Mattioli's *Commentarii* first published
1545	Botanic garden established in Padua
1545	British physician John Gerard born
1545	The British warship, the *Mary Rose*, sinks in Portsmouth harbour
1546	Pierre Belon travels in the Levant
1546	Turner's books banned by decree of Henry VIII
1548	Turner's *Names of Herbes*
1550	Botanic garden established in Florence
1550	The first tomatoes are grown in Europe
*c.*1550	UK population *c.*3 million
1552	Felix Platter starts his studies at Montpellier
1553	Belon's *Les Observations de plusieurs singularités*
1554	Luca Ghini retires from his post in Pisa

1554	Dodoens *Cruydeboeck*
1554	Mattioli's Italian edition of Dioscorides published in Venice
1555	Tobacco from the New World is brought into Spain
1555	Turner's books banned by decree of Queen Mary
1555	Bishops Latimer and Ridley are burned at the stake
1556	Luca Ghini dies
1557	Ulysse Aldrovandi's expedition to the Sibylline mountains
1558	Snuff-taking is introduced by the Portuguese
1559	Jean Nicot sends seeds of tobacco to François II and other members of the French court
*c.*1560	First wave of plant introductions from Turkish Empire
1561	Cordus's *Annotationes in Pedacii Dioscoridis* published posthumously, edited by Gesner
1561	Calvinist refugees from Flanders settle in England
1563	Cesalpino's herbarium completed
1563	A further outbreak of plague in Europe
1564	Turner's *A new herball*
1564	Pierre Belon dies
1565	Lobelius at Montpellier (until 1566) with Rondelet
1566	Lobelius in England (until 1572)
1566	Leonhart Fuchs dies
1566	Guillaume Rondelet dies
1567	Botanic garden established at Bologna
1567	The Duke of Alva arrives in the Netherlands with 10,000 troops and begins a reign of terror
1568	William Turner dies
1568	Dodoens's *Florum* with seven woodcuts by Pieter van der Borcht
1569	Dodoens's *Florum* (second edition)
1570	First printed illustration of tobacco
1570	Nicholas Hilliard's portrait of Queen Elizabeth I
1570s	Crown imperial (*Fritillaria imperialis*) introduced to Vienna from Turkey

1571	Lobelius's *Stirpium adversaria nova* (with Pierre Pena)
1572	Lobelius in the Netherlands (until 1584)
1574	Dodoens's *Purgantium*
1575	Financial crisis in Spain: Philip II cannot pay his bills
1576	Plantin establishes printing press in Antwerp
1576	Clusius's *Rariorum aliquot stirpium*
1576	Lobelius's *Plantarum seu stirpium historia*
1576	Spanish armies sack Antwerp
1577	Mattioli dies
1577	Francis Drake leaves on his voyage round the world
1577	Frampton's *Joyfull newes out of the newe founde worlde*
1578	Dodoens's *A Niewe Herball* (translated by Henry Lyte)
1581	Lobelius's *Kruydtboeck*
1581	Galileo discovers the principle of the pendulum
1583	Clusius's *Rariorum aliquot stirpium*
1583	Clusius's *Stirpium nomenclator*
1583	Dodoens's *Stirpium historiae*
1583	Cesalpino's *De plantis*
1583	An agave from the New World flowers in the Pisa botanic garden
1584	Lobelius in England as botanist to King James
1585	New World peppers fruit in Italy, Spain and Czechoslovakia
1585	Dodoens dies
1585	Elizabeth sends 7,000 English troops to the Netherlands to help Dutch and Flemish rebels in their struggle against Hapsburg rule
1585	An English expedition lands at Roanoke, Virginia
1586	William Camden's *Britannia*
1586	An aloe from the New World flowers in the garden of Joseph de Casabona, Duke of Tuscany
1588	Philip II attempts to conquer 'heretical' England with a Spanish Armada
1589	Richard Hakluyt publishes his *Principal Navigations*

1590	Spenser's *Faerie Queene*
1592	Clusius appointed director of new botanic garden at Leiden
1592	Fabio Colonna's *Phytobasanos* is the first plant book to be illustrated with copper plate engravings rather than woodcuts
1592	The plague kills 15,000 people in London
1596	Philip Symonson's first map of the Kentish coast
1597	Gerard's *Herball*
1597	Shakespeare's *Romeo and Juliet*
1599	Gerard's *Catalogus arborum*
1599	The Globe theatre built at Southwark, London
1600	Pierre Pena dies
1600	Population of France *c.*16 million, of Portugal *c.*2 million
1601	Clusius's *Rariorum plantarum historia*
1602	Dutch East India Company founded
1603	Accademia dei Lincei founded in Italy, the first scientific society in Europe
1605	Guy Fawkes's Gunpowder Plot to blow up the Houses of Parliament
1608	Gerard elected Master of the Barber-Surgeons' Company
1608	Galileo refines the microscope, proposed in 1590 by Zacharias Jensen
1609	Carolus Clusius dies
1609	Tea shipped from China to Europe by the Dutch East India Company
1612	John Gerard dies
1612	Tobacco first planted in Virginia
1613	Jean Bauhin describes *c.*4,000 plants in his *Historia universalis plantarum* (not published until 1650–51)
1616	Lobelius dies
1619	William Harvey's discovery of the circulation of the blood
1620	Pilgrim Fathers sail from Plymouth in the *Mayflower*
1621	Oxford Botanic garden established (first in England)

1620s	Flood of New World plants into Europe
1623	Gaspard Bauhin's *Pinax theatri botanici* describes *c*.6,000 plants
1624	Dutch settle in New Amsterdam
1626	Jardin des Plantes established in Paris
1627	John Ray born
1629	Thomas Johnson sets out on first plant-hunting trip to Kent
1629	John Parkinson's *Paradisi in sole paradisus terrestris*
1630	John Winthrop sails with the Plymouth Company and founds a settlement in Massachusetts Bay
1632	Galileo's *Dialogo sopra*
1633	Johnson's edition of Gerard's *Herball* with descriptions of *c*.2,850 plants
1633	A bunch of bananas, the first seen in Britain, hangs outside Thomas Johnson's apothecary shop
1635	Academie Française established
1636	Harvard College established at Newe Towne, Cambridge, Massachusetts
1638	First printing press in America operates at Cambridge, Massachussetts
1640	Parkinson's *Theatrum botanicum* with descriptions of *c*.3800 plants
c.1641	Jacob Bobart appointed gardener at Oxford Botanic Garden
1642	Civil War breaks out in England
1644	Thomas Johnson dies of wounds received at the Siege of Basing House
1648	George Fox sets up his Society of Friends (the Quakers)
1651	UK population *c*.5 million
1652	Dutch East India Company sets up first colony in the Cape
1652	London's first coffee house opens in Cornhill
1654	Portuguese drive Dutch out of Brazil
1655	Sir Hugh Platt's *The Garden of Eden* (fourth edition published London)
1660	Pepys begins his *Diary*

1660	Royal Society established (28 November)
1665	Robert Hooke's *Micrographia* describes early experiments with a microscope
1666	Plague and Great Fire in London
1668	Isaac Newton constructs the first reflecting telescope
1669	Robert Morison appointed Professor of *res herbaria* at Oxford
1670	Ray publishes his *Catalogus plantarum Angliae*
1675	Observatory established at Greenwich
1678	Bunyan's *Pilgrim's Progress*
1682	Nehemiah Grew describes the function of stamens in flowers (written 1676)
1683	William Penn's *A General Description of Pennsylvania*
1683	Dampier begins his voyage round the world
1687	Isaac Newton's *Principia mathematica*
1688	London underwriters meet in Lloyd's coffee house
1690	Ray publishes his *Synopsis methodica*
1692	Witch hunt in Salem, Massachusetts
1698	Peter the Great of Russia imposes a tax on beards
1700	Population of France *c.*19 million, of Britain and Ireland *c.*7.5 million
1703	Ray's *Methodus emendata*
1704	J. S. Bach writes his first cantata
1705	John Ray dies
1707	Carl Linnaeus (Swedish botanist and physician) born
1735	Linnaeus's *Systema Naturae*
1753	Linnaeus's *Species plantarum*

CAST LIST

ALBERTUS MAGNUS *c*.1200–1280
Dominican monk and writer who *c*.1256 produced *De vegetabilibus*. Like Aristotle, concerned about the notion of a soul, or psyche in living things. The first writer since Theophrastus to enquire into the nature of plants.

ALDROVANDI, ULYSSE 1522–1605
Italian plantsman, who studied under Luca Ghini. In 1550 founded a natural history museum in Bologna. In 1557, made a historic journey to the Sibylline mountains, the first expedition ever arranged with the specific purpose of collecting and recording the plants of a particular area. Curator of the botanic garden at Bologna and centre of a wide network of contacts, which included the Papal envoy, Bishop Rossano in Madrid. His letters to his contemporary, Mattioli, cover a span of twenty-two years.

ALPINO, PROSPERO 1553–1617
Italian doctor who accompanied Venetian consul to Egypt. First European to write of the coffee plant, which he had seen growing in Cairo. His *De plantis Aegypti* published 1592. Succeeded to chair of botany at Padua, created by Venetian republic in 1533. Introduced the fan palm (*Chamaerops humilis*) at Padua.

ANGUILLARA, LUIGI *c*.1512–1570
Studied under Luca Ghini. Travelled widely in the Levant, the Aegean and Crete. Custodian of the botanic garden in Padua. Subject of fierce attack by Mattioli, after he (Anguillara) had presumed to question some of his fellow Italian's attributions. Eventually forced to resign his post at Padua and retreat to Ferrara.

ARISTOTLE 384 BC–322 BC
Greek philosopher who studied under Plato at the Academy. In 342 BC summoned to Macedonia to act as tutor to Alexander, later the Great. After Plato's death, founded his own school in Athens, the Lyceum. Wrote the book on animals (*Historia animalium*) that inspired Theophrastus, his pupil, to produce a similar work on plants.

AVICENNA AD 980–1037
Personal physician to many rulers in the East. His *Qanun*, translated into Latin by Gerard of Cremona in the twelfth century, remained a standard medical textbook for 500 years after his death. It contained details of *c*.650 plants.

BARBARO, ERMOLAO 1453/4–1493

Teacher of rhetoric and poetics at Padua and Venice. Venetian ambassador to the Holy See. One of the first scholars to question the absolute authority of the classical authors such as Pliny and Dioscorides. His *Castigationes Plinianae* was published in 1492–3 and his *Corollarium Dioscorides* in 1516.

BAUHIN, GASPARD 1560–1624

The younger of the Swiss Bauhin brothers whose work gave Protestant Europe an overall view of the flora of Europe and the means to accurately identify plants. Gaspard, who studied medicine at Basel and Padua, was later appointed professor of medicine at the University of Basel. Described *c.*6,000 plants in his *Pinax theatri botanici* (1623).

BAUHIN, JEAN 1541–1613

Studied under Fuchs at Tübingen and Rondelet at Montpellier before becoming private physician to the Duke of Wurtemberg at Montbelliard. His *Historia universalis plantarum* (finished by 1613 but published posthumously in 1650–51) contained descrptions of *c.*5,000 plants but failed to build on Cesalpino's profound thinking.

BELON, PIERRE 1517–1564

French nurseryman and traveller whose garden at Touvoie, near Le Mans, contained an important collection of foreign trees and shrubs, including the cedar of Lebanon and the first tobacco plants that anyone in France had ever seen. In 1546 he began a three-year journey through the Levant; his account *Les Observations de Plusieurs Singularités* (1553) provided a vivid first-hand account of his experiences.

BOBART, JACOB *c.*1599–1680

Gardener, then director (*horti praefectus*) of the botanic garden set up in Oxford in 1621. In 1648 he issued an important *Catalogus plantarum* listing the plants that grew in the garden, modelled on one that Jean Robin had prepared for Louis XIII.

BRASAVOLA, ANTONIO MUSA 1500–1555

Pioneering Italian scholar and plantsman whom William Turner acknowledged as 'som tyme my master in Ferraria'. Personal physician to Duke Hercules II of Ferrara. His *Examen omnium simplicium medicamentorum* (1536) a discourse on the identity of Dioscorides's plants, is cast as a conversation between the author and two characters, whom he calls Senex and Herbarius. It was one of the most popular tracts of its day.

BRUNFELS, OTTO 1488–1534

Carthusian monk who converted to the Lutheran cause. Studied at University of Basel and practised as a doctor in Strasbourg. Author of *Herbarum vivae eicones* published 1530–36, but outshone by his illustrator, Hans Weiditz (q.v.).

BUSBECQ, OGIER GHISELIN DE 1521–1592

Ambassador sent by the Holy Roman Empire to Constantinople. Avid collector of precious artefacts and plants, which he sent back to Europe. It was possibly he who brought Juliana'a precious book for the Imperial Library in Vienna. He was responsible, too, for introducing the tulip into Western Europe.

CAMERARIUS, JOACHIM 1500–1574

Taught at the University of Leipzig. One of the few people Leonhart Fuchs admired and trusted. 'Would that such an adversary were my lot more often,' he wrote to Camerarius in 1541–2, 'one with whom I can argue about truth in a friendly and brotherly way.'

CESALPINO, ANDREA 1519–1603

Brilliant Italian plantsman who studied under Luca Ghini at Bologna and later succeeded him as curator of the botanic garden at Pisa. Made a fine herbarium (1563) in which plants are laid out according to similarities in fruit and seed. His book *De plantis libri xvi* (1583) is the first serious attempt since Theophrastus to find a system of sorting and ordering plants in meaningful groups.

CLUSIUS, CAROLUS (Charles de l'Écluse) 1526–1609

Studied briefly under Rondelet at Montpellier. Travelled widely in Spain and Portugal, describing the plants he had seen in his *Rariorum aliquot stirpium per Hispanias observatorum historia* (1576). Later travels took him to Germany, Austria and Hungary (1580). Professor of botany at University of Leiden (1593), where he brought his famed collection of plants and established a botanic garden.

CORDUS, EURICIUS 1486–1535

Born at Siemershausen, Hesse, the thirteenth child of a family of peasants. In 1521 studied medicine at Ferrara in Italy. From his base at the newly founded Lutheran university of Marburg, published a reforming *Botanologicon* (1534), prompted by his concern that ingredients in apothecaries' shops, the raw materials of their medicines, were often wrongly labelled.

CORDUS, VALERIUS 1515–1544

Son of Euricius who 'had reared the child even from the cradle in the midst of herbs and flowers'. Studied at Padua, Ferrara and Bologna where he met Luca Ghini. 'While still a youth, explained to men the working of Nature and the powers of plants.' Highly regarded by his contemporaries but was kicked by his horse and died of a fever in Rome before his potential could be realised. His *Annotationes in pedacii Dioscoridis* (1561) contained an account of *c.*500 plants.

COYS, WILLIAM *c.*1560–1627

Had a well-known garden with 342 different kinds of plant at Stubbers, North Ockendon, Essex, where in 1604 the yucca bloomed for the first time in England. Firmly stitched into the sixteenth-century network of plant enthusiasts, a correspondant of Goodyer and Lobelius. Had fruitful relationship with the plant collector William Boel who passed on specimens that he had found in Spain.

DIOSCORIDES, PEDANIOS AD 40–??

Greek physician and author, who studied in Alexandria before joining the Roman army as a doctor. Compiled medical treatise *De materia medica* (*c.* AD 77) which drew widely on local knowledge and traditions. For the next 1,500 years, widely regarded (with Pliny) as the ultimate authority on medicinal plants.

DODOENS, REMBERT 1517–1585

French physician and author. Studied medicine at Louvain, before visiting universities in Italy and Germany. Court physician to the Emperor Maximilian II at Vienna. Appointed to chair of medicine at Leiden (1582). His *Cruydeboeck* (1554) with 715 illustrations, was published in Flemish by Jan van der Loe of Antwerp.

DÜRER, ALBRECHT 1471–1528

Painter and master engraver of the German Renaissance. 'Be guided by nature,' he wrote. 'Do not depart from it, thinking that you can do better yourself.' His piece of turf painted *c.*1503, was the most extraordinary mirror of the natural world that any artist had ever produced.

FUCHS, LEONHART 1501–1566

Professor of medicine at the Protestant University at Tübingen, Germany. Author of *De historia stirpium* (1542), better written, but not so well illustrated as Brunfels's *Herbarum vivae eicones* published twelve years earlier. Splenetic, opinionated, he died before publishing the mammoth encyclopaedia that occupied the last twenty-four years of his life.

GALEN CLAUDIUS, AD 130–*c*.200
Greek author and physician, who studied at Alexandria and travelled in Asia Minor. Became personal physician to the emperor, Marcus Aurelius. The first man to arrange his written material in alphabetical order. But he made drugs, not plants, his starting point, so the order related to medicines, not the plants from which they were made.

GARRETT, JAMES *fl.* 1590s–1610
Apothecary and plantsman, one of the clever group of Flemish Huguenots who 'came for reli-gion' and settled permanently in London. In his garden at London Wall, Garrett grew the first tulips seen in England. Warned printer John Norton of the many failings of Gerard's *Herball*.

GERARD, JOHN 1545–1612
Describes himself as 'master of Chirurgerie'; Warden of Company of Barber-Surgeons (1597) becoming Master in 1608. Had a garden in Holborn, London, 'the little plot of myne own espe-ciall care and husbandry'; supervised Lord Burghley's gardens in the Strand and was curator of the College of Physicians' garden. Author of the famous, but flawed *Herball* (1597).

GESNER, CONRAD 1516–1565
Brilliant young Swiss scholar and encyclopaedist who was almost as familiar with Germany, France and Italy as with his homeland. Died before he could publish the monumental *Historia plantarum* which occupied the last ten years of his life. Amassed a collection of *c*.1,500 illustrations of plants, some executed by himself, all heavily annotated with habitats, synonyms and detailed description. The greatest might-have-been of the naming of names.

GHINI, LUCA 1490–1556
Gifted teacher who inspired an entire generation of plantsmen. In 1544, moved from the univer-sity at Bologna to Pisa where he set up a botanic garden, a resource centre for the medical students of the Medici's new university. Pioneered the preparation and use of the *hortus siccus* or herbarium as a tool for the better study of plants. Universally admired in the plant world – a rare trait.

GOODYER, JOHN 1592–1664
Fellow of Magdalen College, Oxford and fine plantsman with a garden in Hampshire where he grew many exotics. Helped Johnson with a new edition of Gerard's *Herball*. Made a painstaking interlinear translation of Dioscorides, the first version in English.

GREW, NEHEMIAH 1641–1712
A pioneer in the anatomy of plants and Secretary of the Royal Society 1677–9. Slightly younger than John Ray but equally committed to the idea of turning the study of plants into a scientific discipline. His seminal work *Anatomy of Plants* was published in 1682.

JOHNSON, THOMAS *c*.1600–1644
Pioneering apothecary with a shop on Snow Hill in the City of London. Arranged the earliest plant-hunting excursions ever made in England, a first step towards compiling a British flora. Edited a new edition of John Gerard's flawed *Herball*. Died in the Civil War, fighting for the king.

JOSSELYN, JOHN *fl.* 1630s–1670s
An early emigrant from England to Massachussetts, arriving first in July 1638. His *New England's Rarities Discovered* (1672) described the natural wonders of the New World for English readers.

LATIMER, HUGH *c.*1485–1555

English reformer and priest, whose sermons made Cambridge a pioneering centre of the Reformation in England. Twice sent to the Tower during Henry VIII's reign and twice reprieved. Condemned as a heretic by Queen Mary and burned at the stake together with the Bishops Ridley and Cranmer.

LEONARDO DA VINCI 1452–1519

Italian painter, sculptor, engineer and architect, enrolled in the Florence painters' guild by the time he was twenty. Made some of the earliest physiotypes, coating the leaves of plants with the soot produced by a candle flame. Pressed on sheets of paper, they showed the leaf's intricate structure of veins and supporting ribs.

LEONICENO, NICOLÒ 1428–1524

Professor of medicine at the University of Ferrara. In 1492, published *Indications of Errors in Pliny and in Several other Authors who have Written on Medicinal Simples* and so became the first man to cast doubt on the veracity of the classical canon.

LINNAEUS, CARL VON LINNÉ 1707–1778

Swedish naturalist and taxonomist, who successfully imposed a universal system on the nomenclature of plants, using a binomial system of *genus* followed by the *species*. Evidently unaware of the fact that, in the famous portrait of him in Lapland costume, he is wearing a woman's dress.

LOBELIUS (MATTHIAS DE L'OBEL) 1538–1616

Flemish scholar and plantsman who, after studying under Rondelet at Montpellier, travelled in Europe with his friend Pierre Pena. Finally settled permanently in England, dedicating his *Stirpium adversaria nova* (1570) to Elizabeth I. Appointed superintendent of Edward Zouche's garden in Hackney, then (in 1607) herbalist to James I.

LYTE, HENRY 1529–1607

English landowner (he lived at Lyte's Cary, Somerset) and plantsman, one of a long line of British amateur botanists. Travelled on the continent and translated into English the French edition of Dodoens's herbal. It appeared in 1578 as the *Niewe Herball or Historie of Plantes*.

MATTIOLI, PIER ANDREA 1501–1577

Unlike most other Italian scholars of the age, he never taught, but made the most of his prestigious position as personal physician to Emperor Ferdinand I. By nature a compiler, a recorder, not an original thinker. Nevertheless, his famous book, *Commentarii in VI Libros Pedacii Dioscoridis* was a wildly successful bestseller, appearing in sixty-one different editions.

MONARDES, NICOLAS 1493–1588

Spanish physician who, in his *Dos libros* (1569), provided the first detailed description of New World plants, including tobacco and coca. His work was translated into English by John Frampton as *Joyfull news out of the newe founde worlde* (1577).

MORGAN, HUGH *fl.* 1540s–1613

Queen Elizabeth's personal apothecary who between 1569 and 1587 had a well-known garden at Coleman Street in the City of London. 'A curious conserver of simples' wrote his contemporary, John Gerard. Kept in touch with the sea captains who brought their ships into the Port of London. Through them, he became better acquainted with plants of the West Indies than anyone else in Britain. Friend of Turner's whose first sight of mistletoe was in Morgan's shop.

MORGUES, JACQUES LE MOYNE DE c.1533–1588

Flemish Huguenot painter with a particular interest in plants. In 1564, as cartographer and artist-recorder, joined exploratory expedition to Florida. When Spaniards attacked the Huguenot colony there, de Morgues escaped and returned to France. Later settled in London, part of the large Huguenot influx.

MORISON, ROBERT 1620–1683

First professor of *res herbaria* at Oxford (1669) having previously gardened for Gaston d'Orleans at Blois (1650–60). His *Plantarum umbelliferarum* (1672), planned as the first monograph on a specific group of plants, failed to find sufficient subscribers and was never completed. Knocked down by a coach in the Strand, London and died of his wounds.

ORTA, GARCIA DE c.1490–1570

Portuguese physician who in 1534 sailed for Goa, where he stayed for more than thirty years. His *Coloquios dos simples, e drogas he cousas medicinais da India* (1563) is an account of the plants and medicines he discovered there. Translated by Clusius fom Portuguese into Latin (1567).

PARKINSON, JOHN 1567–1650

Apothecary to James I, with a garden in Long Acre, London. His *Paradisi in sole paradisus terrestris* (1629) with its punning Park-in-sun title, was followed by the *Theatrum botanicum* (1640). This 'Theater of Plants . . . distributed into sundry classes or Tribes' contained descriptions of 3,800 plants, twice as many as Gerard had included in his *Herball*. Parkinson's book marked the end of the herbal tradition.

PLANTIN, CHRISTOPHE c.1520–1589

Emigrated from Touraine to Antwerp, where he established himself as the most successful printer of the age. Amassed vast collection of woodblock illustrations of plants. Published many of the important plant books produced in the second half of the sixteenth century, written by French and Flemish authors such as Dodoens, Clusius, and Lobelius.

PLATTER, FELIX 1536–1614

Left a vivid account of his years as a medical student at Montpellier, at a time of religious upheaval in the Languedoc. Studied under Rondelet and became a renowned physician in his home town, Basel. In later life, acquired the drawings that Hans Weiditz had made for Brunfels's *Herbarum vivae eicones*.

PLINY THE ELDER AD 23–79

Roman soldier, cavalry commander and author (*c.* AD 77) of a *Historia naturalis*, an encyclopaedic ragbag of information about science, art, plants, animals with digressions on human inventions and institutions. Throughout the Middle Ages it remained an important, over-valued source. Pliny died investigating the eruption of Vesuvius at Pompeii.

RAY, JOHN 1627–1705

Produced a British flora, published finally in 1670 as *Catalogus plantarum Angliae*. Studies in the field encouraged by Royal Society, newly set up in 1660. Made several long trips to Europe with his friend Sir Francis Willughby. Strove (in parallel with Tournefort in France) to create a water-tight system of nomenclature for plants. His *Synopsis methodica* of 1690 was the distillation of a lifetime's search for order in the natural world.

RIDLEY, NICHOLAS c.1500–1555

Bishop of London and martyr, an important member of the group of Cambridge reformers who met regularly at the White Horse Inn to argue about religion. Tutor to William Turner to whom he taught Greek, tennis and archery. Believed in justice, reason and the church's duty to defend the oppressed. Argued against the superstition and nepotism of the Catholic Church. Burned at the stake by order of Mary, Queen of Scots.

ROBIN, JEAN 1550–1629

Arboriste et simpliciste to Henri III of France. Directed gardens at the Louvre and established network of useful contacts in England, Italy, the Netherlands and Switzerland. Established a fine collection of plants in his garden on the Île de la Cité, 'at the signe of the blacke head in the street called Du Bout du Monde'.

RONDELET, GUILLAUME 1507–1566

Practised as a doctor in the Auvergne before his appointment to the medical faculty at the University of Montpellier in the Languedoc. Like Ghini, a charismatic teacher, gathering around him a clutch of brilliant students. Many of them were Protestants, unable to study in Paris or at other Catholic-controlled universities.

TEODORO OF GAZA *c*.1398–*c*.1478

A native of Thessalonica who opened a school in Constantinople *c*.1422. Fled to Italy as Sultan Murad II laid siege to the city. Called to Rome to assist in the translation of ancient texts in the Vatican Library. Spent five years working on Aristotle's treatise on animals and Theophrastus's on plants. The translation was finally published in Treviso in 1483.

THEOPHRASTUS *c*.372 BC–287 BC

Greek philosopher, who studied under Aristotle. After Aristotle's death he took over as head of the Peripatetic School at the Lyceum in Athens. The first person to write down descriptions of plants in terms of their similarities and differences. His *Historia plantarum* and *Causae plantarum* were translated in 1916 by Sir Arthur Hort as *Enquiry into Plants*.

TOURNEFORT, JOSEPH PITTON DE 1656–1708

Studied at Montpellier under Pierre Magnol and then travelled widely in Spain and the Pyrenees. Professor of *res herbaria* in Paris by 1683. His *Élémens de botanique* (1694) classifies plants according to the form of the corolla. The system prevailed, until superceded by Linnaeus's arrangement.

TURNER, WILLIAM *c*.1508–1568

Cleric and plantsman, called 'the father of English botany' because he was the first Englishman to write (in English) a decent book on plants. His *Names of Herbes* (1548) was followed by a *New Herball* (1551–64). Fiercely Protestant and twice forced to flee England on account of his religious views, always trenchantly expressed.

WEIDITZ, HANS *before* 1500–*c*.1536

Draughtsman and engraver. Studied under Albrecht Dürer and, with his illustrations for Otto Brunfels's *Herbarum vivae eicones*, produced the first lifelike portraits of plants to appear in a printed book.

NOTES

Introduction

1   From the Introduction to 'A Description of a Journey Undertaken for the Discovery of Plants into the County of Kent' (1632) in *Thomas Johnson: Journeys in Kent and Hampstead*, edited by J. S. L. Gilmour (Pittsburgh, PA, 1972). All the quotations in this chapter are taken from this translation (pp. 101–126) of Johnson's *Descriptio itineris plantarum* of 1632.

2   On the matter of the cannon at least, Johnson exaggerated. The *Britannia* carried fifty-five not sixty-six.

3   Cannabis was widely cultivated for its fibres, which were made into hemp. An Act of Henry VIII's required all landowners with more than sixty acres of arable land to grow cannabis to make ropes for his navy. See H. Godwin, 'The Ancient Cultivation of Hemp', *Antiquity*, 41, 1967, pp. 42–50.

I In the Beginning 370 BC–290 BC

1   R. D. Hicks (ed.), *Diogenes Laertius Lives of Eminent Philosophers* (London, 1925), vol. I, Book 5, ch. 2. Diogenes was probably writing in the third century BC.

2   Professor Bob Sharples notes that Theophrastus often uses 'male' and 'female' of what are not in fact different sexes of the same plant, but of different species that seemed to him as it were more or less 'manly'.

3   *Theophrastus Enquiry into Plants*, Book I, iii, 5, p. 191. All quotations from Theophrastus's *Enquiry into Plants* are taken from Sir Arthur Hort's translation for the Loeb Classical Library series, published by William Heinemann in 1916. References have been given for the longer quotations only.

4   Hort, *Enquiry into Plants*, Book III, x, 3–4, p. 225.

5   The difference between the two was not resolved until the late eighteenth century, much of the work being done by Johann Heinrich Troll (1756–1824).

6   Hort, *Enquiry into Plants*, Book IV, vii, 3–5, p. 341.

7   The word was introduced by the German biologist Ernst Haeckel in 1866.

8   Hort, *Enquiry into Plants*, Book IV, i, 1–2, p. 287.

9   Ibid., Book VIII, iv, 4–6, p. 171.

10   Ibid., Book IX, v, 1–3, p. 243.

11   Ibid., Book IX, viii, 7–8, p. 259.

[12] Ibid., Book IX, xvi, 6–8, p. 303.

[13] Ibid., Book IX, xvi, 9, p. 305.

[14] Ibid, Book IX, xvi, 3–5, p. 299.

[15] Ibid., Book IV, viii, 1–3, p. 347.

[16] Ibid., Book IV, iii, 1–3, p. 305.

[17] Ibid., Book VI, vi, 3–5, p. 39.

[18] Ibid., Book I, xiv, 3–5, p. 101.

[19] Cato the Elder, *De re rustica*, Book LVI. Quoted from *On Agriculture*, W. D. Hooper's translation for the Loeb Classical Library series, revised by H. B. Ash (London, 1934).

[20] Hort, *Enquiry into Plants*, Book II, ii, 9–11, p. 117.

[21] A. L. Peck (ed.), *Aristotle's Parts of Animals* (London, 1937) I, 5, 645a, 10.

[22] It was normal in ancient Greece to call slaves of any age 'boys'; the point was that they did not have the legal rights of adults.

[23] Hicks, *Diogenes Laertius Lives*, vol. I, Book 5, ch. 2.

II All Men by Nature Desire to Know 600 BC–60 BC

[1] See B. Ebell, *The Papyrus Ebers* (Copenhagen and London, 1937).

[2] Akkadian was the language spoken in Babylonia and Assyria. See R. Campbell-Thompson, *The Assyrian Herbal* (London, 1924).

[3] Sir Arthur Hort, *Theophrastus Enquiry into Plants* (London, 1916), Book IX, viii, 7–8, p. 259.

[4] Aristotle, *Historia animalium*, I, 491a, 9. All quotations are taken from *Aristotle's Parts of Animals*, A. L. Peck's translation for the Loeb Classical Library series, published by William Heinemann in 1937.

[5] Aristotle, *Historia animalium*, I, 409a, 5–8.

[6] For a full analysis of Aristotle's method, see James G. Lennox, *Aristotle's Philosophy of Biology* (Cambridge, 2001), and D. W. Thompson, On *Growth and Form* (abridged edn, Cambridge 1971).

[7] Aristotle, *De generatione animalium*, IV, 12, 694b, 12–15.

[8] For a full account, see John Patrick Lynch, *Aristotle's School* (Berkeley, CA, 1972).

[9] R. D. Hicks (ed.), *Diogenes Laertius Lives of Eminent Philosophers* (London, 1925), vol. V, Book 1.

[10] Cicero, *Academia*, I, 9.34, quoted in Lynch, *Aristotle's School*.

[11] R. W. Sharples in D. J. Furley (ed.), *From Aristotle to Augustine: Routledge History of Philosophy*, vol. I (London, 1999).

[12] Bob Sharples questions whether either the Lyceum or the Academy survived Sulla's sack of Athens in 86 BC. There were certainly state-funded teachers of these philosophies in Athens at the end of the second century AD and there was a neo-Platonic school until AD 529, but it's not clear whether the same specific titles were used.

[13] Strabo XIII, 1.54, quoted in Lynch, *Aristotle's School*.

[14] Athenaeus I, 3a–b.

III The Alexandrian Library 300 BC–40 BC

[1] Quoted in Edward Alexander Parsons, *The Alexandrian Library* (New York, 1952).

[2] For the hieroglyphics for these plants and many others, see Victor Loret, *La Flore pharaonique* (Paris, 1887).

[3] Sir Arthur Hort, *Theophrastus Enquiry into Plants* (London, 1916), Book IV, viii, 3–4, p. 345.

[4] For a full account, see R. W. Sharples in D. J. Furley (ed.), *From Aristotle to Augustine: Routledge History of Philosophy*, vol. I (London, 1999).

5   See Edward Gibbon, *The History of the Decline and Fall of the Roman Empire* (London, 1776–88), Ch. LI.

6   The full story is told in M. Casanova, *L'incendie de la Bibliothèque d'Alexandrie par les Arabes* (Paris, 1923).

IV   Pliny the Plagiarist AD 20–AD 80

1   Though he is not in any way pushing forward the debate on plants, there is a view that Pliny used his *Natural History* to celebrate the Roman Empire and its resources.

2   See Pliny, *Letters* (London, 1915), III, epistle 5.

3   Pliny, *Natural History* (London, 1952), XXIII, 112. Translated by H. Rackham for the Loeb Classical Library series (London, 1952).

4   See Pliny, *Letters*, V, epistle 6, p. 32ff.

5   Pliny, *Natural History*, XVI, 60, 140. He says the art of topiary was introduced by Gaius Matius.

6   M. Launey, 'Le verger d'Heracles à Thasos', *Bulletin de correspondance hellenique*, 61, 1937, pp. 380–409.

7   Pliny, *Natural History*, XXI, 8.

8   Ibid., XXV, 16.

9   For the full account, see Pliny the Younger, *Letters*, VI, epistle 16.

V   The Medicine Men AD 40–AD 400

1   From the Preface of Dioscorides's *De materia medica*. See R. T. Gunther (ed.), *Dioscorides de Materia Medica: The Greek Herbal of Dioscorides* (Oxford, 1934).

2   From Goodyer's interlinear translation of Dioscorides, quoted in Gunther, *Dioscorides*.

3   Pliny, *Natural History*, XXV, 4. Translated by H. Rackham for the Loeb Classical Library series (London, 1952).

4   Biblioteca Nazionale, Naples, MS gr.1, fol. 148.

5   Wellcome Institute Library, London, MS 5753.

6   Claudius Galenus, *Opera omnia* (Leipzig, 1821–33), vol. 14, pp. 30–31.

7   See Charles Singer, 'The herbal in Antiquity and its transmission to Later Ages', *Journal of Hellenic Studies*, vol. 47 (1927), pp. 1–52.

VI   Juliana's Book AD 500–AD 600

1   For a full description, see *Medieval Herbals: The Illustrative Traditions* (London, 2000) by Minta Collins, whose lucid text first introduced me to Juliana. Her book has been an important source and I am grateful for her generosity in allowing me to quote from it.

2   Österreichische Nationalbibliothek, Vienna, MS med. gr. 1. A colour facsimile with commentary by H. Gerstinger was published in Graz in 1970.

3   See Collins, *Medieval Herbals*, p. 44.

4   Bibliothèque Nationale, Paris, MS gr. 2286.

5   See Collins, *Medieval Herbals*, p. 42.

6   See E. S. Forster (trs.), *The Turkish Letters of Ogier Ghiselin de Busbecq* (Oxford, 1927).

7   The manuscript is now in the library of Magdalen College, Oxford.

8   Biblioteca Nazionale, Naples, MS Ex Vindob. Gr 1.

VII The Arab Influence AD 600–1200

1 Syriac was a dialect of Aramaic, the ancient language of the Middle East, still spoken in parts of Syria and the Lebanon. It originated in Aram and by the fifth century bc had spread to become the *lingua franca* of the whole Persian Empire. It is the language of the later Books of the Old Testament. Syriac was spoken in Syria until the thirteenth century and is still used in the liturgies of some Eastern churches.

2 They were followers of Nestorius, patriarch of Constantinople (AD 428–431), who believed that Christ was two distinct persons, one human, one divine.

3 Son of and co-ruler with Constantine VII Porphyrogenitus.

4 Cordoba was the centre of Moorish Spain between 711 and 1236.

5 See Minta Collins, *Medieval Herbals: The Illustrative Traditions* (London, 2000), for a detailed analysis of this often quoted account.

6 Dioscorides, *De materia medica*, Book II, ch 167. See R. T. Gunther (ed.), *Dioscorides de Materia Medica: The Greek Herbal of Dioscorides* (Oxford, 1934).

7 Bibliotheek der Rijksuniversiteit, Leiden, MS.or.289.

8 For a full description see Collins, *Medieval Herbals*, pp. 118–124.

9 Süleymaniye Mosque Library, Istanbul, MS Ayasofia 3703, reproduced in facsimile as *Farmacopea Araba Medievale*, edited by Alain Touwaide (Milan, 1992–3).

10 It was given to the library by Sir Thomas Adams, 'Militis & Baronetti' as the handwritten frontispiece describes him.

11 See Charles Raven, *English Naturalists from Neckham to Ray* (Cambridge, 1947).

VIII Out of the Black Hole 1100–1300

1 Süleymaniye Mosque Library, Istanbul, MS Ayasofia 3703, reproduced in facsimile as *Farmacopea Araba Medievale*, edited by Alain Touwaide (Milan, 1992–3).

2 MS Ayasofia 3703, *Rubus fruticosus*, fol. 17v.

3 MS Ayasofia 3703, *Physalis alkekengi*, fol. 35v.

4 *Tractatus de herbis*, British Library, London, MS Egerton 747.

5 Otto Pächt, 'Early Italian Nature Studies and the Early Calendar Landscape', *Journal of the Warburg and Courtauld Institutes*, XIII (1950), pp. 13–47.

6 Ibid.

7 Bartholomew of England, *De proprietatibus rerum*, ch. 196. See Bateman, *Batman uppon Bartholome his Booke De proprietatibus rerum* (London, 1582).

8 *The Lay of the Nine Healing Herbs*, British Library, London, MS Harley 585, fol. 174v.

9 Bibliotheek der Rijksuniversiteit, Leiden, MS Voss.lat.Q.9.

10 O. Cockagne in *Leechdoms, Wort-Cunning and Starcraft of Early England* (London, 1864–6), a translation of MS Cotton Vitellius C III in the British Library, London.

11 Ibid.

12 The first manuscript once belonged to William Harvey (1578–1657), the physician who published the treatise on the circulation of blood.

13 See Charles Singer, *From Magic to Science: Essays on the Scientific Twilight* (London, 1928).

14 Spare pages at the back of the manuscript are scribbled over with prescriptions of the late sixteenth and early seventeenth century: pains in the head caused by 'fumes from the stomach' can be cured by a concoction of coriander, cinnamon, cloves, mace, nutmeg and leaves of red rose. The English practitioner who wrote these notes made much use of guaiacum, newly arrived as a wonder drug of the tropics and thought to be especially effective against syphilis.

15 See, for instance, MS Ashmole 1462 in the Bodleian Library, Oxford, which was made *c.*1190–1200.

16 British Library, London, MS Sloane 1975.

IX The Image Makers 1300–1500

1 Francesco Petrarch, *De rebus memorandis* (Book of Memorable Things) (Basel, 1563).

2 Printing with moveable metal type was invented by the Chinese in the eleventh century and had been used in Korea since the fourteenth century.

3 Bibliothèque Nationale, Paris, MS Lat. 6823.

4 Bibliothèque de l'École des Beaux Arts, Paris, MS Masson 116.

5 Carrara Herbal, British Library, London, Sloane MS 2020.

6 Otto Pächt, 'Early Italian Nature Studies and the Early Calendar Landscape', *Journal of the Warburg and Courtauld Institutes*, vol. XIII (1950), pp. 13–47.

7 *Liber de simplicibus*, Biblioteca Marciana, Venice, MS Lat. VI 59.

8 The English art critic John Ruskin (1819–1900), mad about Venice, champion of all things Venetian, employed an artist, Antonio Caldara, to make copies of Amadio's illustrations.

9 Bibliothèque Nationale, Paris, MS nouv.acq.Lat.1673, fol. 28v.

10 Biblioteca Casanatense, Rome, MS 4182.

11 Petrarch and his fellow humanists of the fourteenth century had encouraged a similar shift in script which gradually changed from Gothic to a more legible Renaissance hand, the *litera fere-humanistica.*

12 See especially the Medicina antiqua, Österreichische Nationalbibliothek, Vienna, MS Vindobonensis 93.

13 See, for instance, the tapestries made in Brussels 1466 at the Musée d'histoire de Bern and the Unicorn tapestries at the Metropolitan Museum, New York.

14 Musée du Louvre, Paris.

15 Antonio Pisanello, *Study of Plants*, *c.*1438–42, pen and ink, brown wash and white heightening on red prepared paper, Musée Ingres, Montauban.

16 For a full account, see Thomas Kren and Scott McKendrick, *Illuminating the Renaissance*, the catalogue of an exhibition held at the Paul Getty Museum, Los Angeles, in 2003 and at the Royal Academy, London, in 2004.

17 See, for instance, the fat caterpillar, dragonfly, peacock butterfly, wasps, flies and hoverfly on the borders of the Cocharelli Treatise, British Library, London, Add.MS 28841, fol. iv.

18 But see the Book of Hours made by Jean Bourdichon for Anne of Brittany where 340 plants, named in French and Latin, are displayed in the borders.

19 Albrecht Dürer, *Iris*, watercolour and body colour, brush, pen, on two sheets stuck together, Bremen, Kunsthalle, Kupferstichkabinett Inv. 35.

20 Under the plan is a note: 'Let us have fountains on every piazza.'

21 Leonardo da Vinci, *A Treatise on Painting*, translated by John Francis Rigaud (London, 1877), ch. 334.

22 Albrecht Dürer, *Vier bucher von menschlicher proportion* (Nuremberg, 1528).

23 Graphische Sammlung Albertina, Vienna.

24 See, for example, the exotic date palm, Italian cypress and umbrella pine in Van Eyck's famous Ghent altarpiece made in 1432, or the plantain, dandelion, buttercup, wild strawberry, primrose, violets and ferns in the turf of *St John Writing the Gospel* by Dirk Bouts (*c.*1420–*c.*1475). When Bouts died, Dürer was still only four years old. In the centre panel of Hans Memling's triptych of 1484, St Christopher carries the Christ child through grass spangled with dandelion, mallow, campanula, martagon lilies. Memling's flowers include a large clump of creamy narcissus.

X Theophrastus Reborn 1250–1500

1 *'In hoc sexto libro vegetabilium nostrorum magis satisfacimus curiositati studentium quam philosophiae. De particularibus enim philosophia esse non poterit.'*

2 The *Herbarius* of Apuleius Platonicus was printed in Rome *c.*1481 by Johannes Philippus de Lignamine.

3 For a full account of the effect of printing on fifteenth- and sixteenth-century Europe, see E. L. Eisenstein, *The Printing Press as an Agent of Change* (Cambridge, 1979).

4 Marie Boas, *The Scientific Renaissance* 1450–1630 (London, 1962).

5 Preface to the *De Gart der Gesundheit* (Mainz, 1485), quoted in A. Arber, *Herbals, their origin and evolution 1470–1670* (Cambridge, 1912), pp. 24–6.

XI Brunfels's Book 1500–1550

1 Otto Brunfels, *Herbarum vivae eicones*, (Strasbourg, 1532), Dedication.

2 '. . . which has been learned not from books but from experience'.

3 'I've accepted the name given by the artists who painted this flower'.

4 'They persuaded me to include a picture of the herb which is commonly called Good Henry, or Schwerbel. The herb women told me that.'

5 Brunfels, *Herbarum vivae eicones*, as quoted in T. A. Sprague, 'The Herbal of Otto Brunfels' in *Journal of the Linnaean Society*, Botany vol. 48 (London, 1928), pp. 79–124, read to the society on 3 November 1927.

6 Ibid.

XII The Irascible Fuchs 1500–1570

1 From the Dedicatory Epistle of Leonhart Fuchs, *De historia stirpium* (Basel, 1542), translated by Elaine Mathers and John Heller in the facsimile edition and commentary published by Stanford University Press in 1999. All quotations from *De historia stirpium* are from this edition and are reprinted by kind permission of the publisher.

2 Ibid.

3 Meyer's original drawings are now at the Österreichische Nationalbibliothek, Vienna.

4 Fuchs, *De historia stirpium*, Cap CXLVII, p. 392.

5 Ibid., Dedicatory Epistle.

6 George Hizler, *Oratio de vita et morte ... Leonharti Fuchsii* (Tübingen, 1566), translated by Elaine Mathers and quoted in the Fuchs facsimile published by Stanford University Press.

7 'On August 14, 1535, the honourable Leonhart Fuchs, doctor of medicine, summoned and sent by our illustrious prince, was admitted to the council of the academy to teach medicine at an annual salary of 160 florins, and has sworn to his hiring and ... to contribute to the university articles for publishing, and the university agrees to pay 15 florins for him to publish his own Books himself.' Translated from the Latin original at Universitätsarchiv, Tübingen, fol. 66v, and quoted in the Fuchs facsimile published by Stanford University Press.

8 See the *Dienerbuch* – a record of people, events, activities for the town – for 1549. 'Doctor Leonhart Fuchs occupies the nunnery at Tübingen, wherein much construction has been done for him. He uses the garden by the house and expects that he might realise 20 pounds from it ... the house is being improved and rebuilt, which he deserves, with window, stove and all other things. The university has so much income that it can well support the doctor.' From Klaus Dobat and Karl Mägdefrau, '300 Jahre Botanik in Tübingen', *Attempto* 55–56 (Tübingen, 1975), pp. 8–27.

9   Ibid.

10   Original letter, written in German, in the Old Royal Collection, Royal Library, Copenhagen, quoted in the commentary to the Fuchs facsimile published by Stanford University Press.

11   Title page, originally in Latin, of *De historia stirpium*, published by Isingrin, Basel, 1542.

12   Letter from Fuchs to Camerarius, dated 23 November 1542, in the Trew Collection, Universitätsbibliothek, Erlangen. Twenty-six of these letters came into the possession of Christoph Jacob Trew (1694–1769), a physician and a wealthy patron of botany.

13   Letter from Fuchs to Camerarius, undated but probably written end 1541, or early 1542.

14   See Marcel de Cleene and Marie Claire Lejeune, *Compendium of Symbolic and Ritual Plants in Europe* (Ghent, 2003), p. 370.

15   Fuchs gave the foxglove its Latin name, a translation of the German common name, 'fingerhut'. Meyer's illustration (see plate 72), an afterthought on p. 893 of the *Historia*, is the first published picture of the flower, which for centuries had been used by country people as a medicine. (Its power was confirmed by William Withering in *An Account of the Foxglove, and Some of its Medicinal Uses, with Practical Remarks on Dropsy, and Other Diseases* (Birmingham, 1785).)

16   Fuchs, *De historia stirpium*, p. 228, as translated in the Fuchs facsimile published by Stanford University Press, p. 368.

17   T. A. Sprague and E. Nelmes, 'The Herbal of Leonhart Fuchs', *Journal of the Linnaean Society*, Botany vol. 48 (London, 1928), p. 553, read on 29 November 1928.

18   Fuchs's *De historia stirpium* was also a beautifully made book, which is perhaps why the pre-Raphaelite William Morris and the Victorian art critic John Ruskin both bought copies from the London shop of the antiquarian Bookseller, Bernard Quaritch.

19   Fuchs, *De historia stirpium*, Dedicatory Epistle.

20   From the Fuchs–Camerarius correspondence in the Trew Collection, Universitätsbibliothek, Erlangen, translated by Elaine Mathers.

21   The manuscript, bound in nine folio volumes and including 1,529 hand-coloured pictures of plants, is in the Österreichische Nationalbibliothek, Vienna.

22   Conrad Gesner, *Bibliotheca universalis* (Tiguri, 1545).

23   Letter, written by an amanuensis, from Gesner to Fuchs, 18 October 1556, translated by John Heller from the original in the Bibliothek Zentrum, Zurich, MS C50a no.20.

24   Letter from Fuchs to Camerarius, 24 November 1565, in the Trew Collection, Universitätsbibliothek, Erlangen, translated by Elaine Mathers.

25   Rauwolf's collection is now in the Rijksherbarium, Leiden.

26   Letter from Fuchs at Tübingen to Rondelet at Montpellier, 10 December 1556, Universitätsarchiv, Basel, Fr Gr II 5a, no. 44, translated from the Latin by Karen Meier Reeds and quoted in her Book, *Botany in Medieval and Renaissance Universities* (New York and London, 1991).

27   Letter from Fuchs to Camerarius, 24 November 1565, in the Trew Collection, Universitätsbibliothek, Erlangen, translated by Elaine Mathers.

28   Ch. XLI, p. 256 from Fuchs's original manuscript in the Österreichische Nationalbibliothek, Vienna.

29   Letter from Fuchs to Camerarius, 3 April 1563, in the Trew Collection, Universitätsbibliothek, Erlangen, translated by Elaine Mathers.

XIII In Italy 1500–1550

1   The Latin name for the Volga was the *flumen Rha* from which rhubarb, *Rheum rhaponticum*, gets its name.

2   See David Abulafia (ed.), *The Mediterranean in History* (London, 2003).

3   Biblioteca Nazionale Marciana, Venice, MS Ital. II XXVI 4860. See also Mauro Ambrosoli, *The Wild and the Sown* (Cambridge, 1997).

4   Nicolò Leoniceno, Introduction to *Plinii ac plurinum aliorum auctorum . . .* (Indication of Errors in Pliny) (Ferrara, 1492).

5   Marcello Virgilio Adriani, Preface to *Dioscorides Materia Medica* (Florence, 1518).

6   Antonio Musa Brasavola, *Examen omnium simplicium medicamentorum . . .* (Rome, 1536).

7   Ibid.

8   Ibid.

9   Sir Walter Raleigh, *The History of the World* (London, 1614).

XIV The First Botanic Gardens 1540–1600

1   For a full account of the botanic garden at Pisa, see Fabio Garbari, Lucia Tongiorgi Tomasi and Alessandro Tosi, *Giardino dei Semplici* (Pisa, 2002).

2   See Emilio Tolaini, *Forma Pisarum. Storia urbanistica della città di Pisa* (Pisa, 1979).

3   Archivio di Stato di Firenze, Mediceo 1171, cc256–7, quoted in Garbari et al, *Giardino*.

4   Biblioteca Universitaria di Bologna, MS Aldrovandi 136, *Observationes variae* XIX.

5   Giovanni Battista de Toni, *I placiti di Luca Ghini* (Venice, 1907), p. 29.

6   Ibid., pp. 24–25.

7   See S. Seybold, 'Luca Ghini, Leonhart Rauwolf und Leonhart Fuchs', *Jh. Ges. Naturkunde*, 145 (1990).

8   Letter to George Marius, dated 12 December 1558, in Pier Andrea Mattioli, *Epistolarum medicinalium* (1561) in *Opera* (Frankfurt, 1598), Book 3, p. 118.

9   See Bartolomeo Taegio, *La villa* (Milan, 1559).

10 The site of this second garden is commemorated in the street name Via del Giardino in Pisa.

11 Andrea Cesalpino, *De plantis libri* XVI (Florence, 1583), translated from the Dedication.

12 Ibid., Lib. I, cap. XIII.

13 M. Lobelius and Pierre Pena, *Stirpium adversaria nova* (London, 1570), p. 161.

14 Letter, dated 26 September 1592, quoted in G. Calvi, *Commentarium inserviturum historiae Pisani vireti Botanici Accademici* (Pisa, 1777).

15 Al-Ghassani was physician to Sultan Ahmad al-Mansur and his book, dealing with 379 Moroccan plants and drugs, was called *Hadiquat al-azhar fi sarh mahiyat al-ushb wa al-aggar*.

16 Cesalpino, *De plantis*, translated from the Dedication.

XV The Long-nosed Nitpicker 1540–1600

1   Pierre Belon, *Les Observations de plusieurs singularités* (Paris, 1555).

2   Giovanni Battista de Toni, *I placiti di Luca Ghini* (Venice, 1907), p. 23.

3   See letter to George Marius, dated 12 December 1558, in Pier Andrea Mattioli, *Epistolarum medicinalium* (1561) in *Opera* (Frankfurt, 1598), Book 3, p. 118.

4   Ibid., Book 3, p. 171.

5   Pier Andrea Mattioli, *Commentarii in libros sex Pedacii Dioscoridis Anazarbei* (1565 edition), Book 2, ch. 139, pp. 544–5.

XVI Weaving the Web 1500–1580

1   The first scientific society in Europe, the Accademia dei Lincei, was founded by a Roman nobleman, Federico Cesi, in 1603. The name 'lynx-eyed' was suggested by Galileo, a founder member.

2   Amatus Lusitanus, *In Dioscoridis … de medica materia libros quinque enarrationes* (Venice, 1553).

3   From William Turner's *A new herball* (London and Cologne, 1551–1568).

4   Pieter Coudenberg in a letter to Conrad Gesner, quoted in Gesner's *De hortis Germaniae* (Tiguri, 1561), p. 244.

5   Preface to Turner, *A new herball*, 1568 edition.

6   Turner, *A new herball*, 1551 edition.

7   Marjorie Blamey and Richard Fitter, *Wild Flowers* (London and Glasgow, 1980).

8   Public Record Office, Edw. VI Dom vii, no. 32, quoted in W. R. D. Jones, *William Turner* (London, 1988).

9   Public Record Office, Edw. VI Dom xi., no. 14, fol. 24.

10 British Museum, London, Lansdowne MS 2, no. 63, ff. 139–40.

11 Public Record Office, Edw. VI Dom xiii, no. 19.

12 Quoted in Blanche Henrey, *British Botanical and Horticultural Literature Before 1800* (London, 1975).

13 British Library, London, Lansdowne MS VIII, no. 3.

14 W. Pierce, *The Marprelate Tracts*, 1588, 1589 (London, 1911).

15 See B. Dietz, *The Port and Trade of Early Elizabethan London*, Documents, London Record Society (London, 1972), pp. 63, 78, 138ff.

16 Turner, *A new herball* (1568 edition), part II, p. 27.

17 Ibid., part III, p. 80.

18 He included, for example, the foxglove, which he said, 'groweth very much in Englande, and specially in Norfolke about ye cony holes in sandy ground'.

XVII Protestants Prevail 1530–1580

1   Writing in *De naturis rerum* in praise of the weasel, the medieval author Alexander Neckham noted how 'educated by nature, it knows the virtues of the herbs, although it has neither studied medicine at Salerno nor been drilled in the schools at Montpellier'.

2   For a full account of the university at Montpellier, see Karen Meier Reeds, *Botany in Medieval and Renaissance Universities* (New York and London, 1991).

3   Before it ever became established as a centre for the wine trade, Montpellier's wealth was founded on spice.

4   Seán Jennett (trs.), *Beloved Son Felix: The Journal of Felix Platter, a medical student in Montpellier in the sixteenth century* (London, 1961). All subsequent quotations from Platter are taken from this source and are reproduced here by permission.

5   Laurentius Joubertus, *Gulmielmi Rondeletii Vita in Operum Latinorum* (Frankfurt, 1599).

6   The Place des Cénevols no longer exists; it was swept away during the construction of the Rue Nationale, now the Rue Foch. Catalan's own sons had been lodging in Strasbourg until they went on to stay with Platter's father in Basel. This system of exchange was common at the time and cut down on the cost of a university education.

7   In Platter's day it stood on the Rue de l'Université, now renamed the Rue de l'École de Pharmacie.

8   W. G. Waters (trs.), *Journal of Montaigne's Travels* (London, 1903).

XVIII Gesner's Masterpiece 1530–1580

1   The final volume of Gesner's *Historia animalium* did not come out until 1587, twenty-two years after Gesner's death.

2   Heinrich Zoller, Martin Steinmann, Karl Schmidt (eds), *Conradi Gesneri Historia Plantarum*, 3 vols (Zurich, 1972–4).

3   For a full account of Gesner's *Bibliotheca universalis*, see Hans Fischer, 'Conrad Gesner (1516–1565) as Bibliographer and Encyclopedist', *The Library*, Fifth Series, vol. XXI, no. 4, December 1966, pp. 269–81.

4   E. L. Greene, *Landmarks of Botanical History* (Stanford, CA, 1983), p. 797.

5   From the Preface of Conrad Gesner, *De hortis Germaniae* (Tiguri, 1561).

6   The long correspondence between Gesner and Jean Bauhin was published in 1591.

7   Universitätsbibliothek, Erlangen Inv. MS 2386, fol. 273v.

8   Conrad Gesner, in a letter dated 26 November 1565, collected in *Epistolarum medicinalium* (Tiguri, 1577). Twenty of the letters in this volume are addressed to Zwinger (1533–88), who was born in the year that Gesner first went to study in Paris.

9   Universitätsarchiv, Basel, UAB Fr Gr I 12 #203 (1596).

XIX New Pastures 1550–1580

1   Seán Jennett (trs.), *Journal of a Younger Brother, The Life of Thomas Platter* . . . (London, 1963), p. 165–6.

2   Michault had studied with Busbecq in Italy and subsequently became Imperial Ambassador at the Portuguese Court.

3   From the first letter, dated Vienna, 1 September 1555, and reprinted in Edward Seymour Forster (trs.), *The Turkish Letters of Ogier Ghiselin de Busbecq* (Oxford, 1927).

4   Sir John Chardin, *Travels in Persia*, trs. E. Lloyd (London, 1927).

5   John Gerard, *The Herball or Generall historie of plantes* (London, 1597), p. 153.

6   John Parkinson, *Paradisi in sole paradisus terrestris* (London, 1629).

7   John Frampton, *Joyfull newes out of the newe founde worlde* (London, 1662), fol. 1.

8   A particularly virulent form of syphilis had come to Europe when trade with the New World opened up in the decade after 1490.

9   Frampton, *Joyfull newes*, fol. 40.

10 Ibid., fol. 102.

11 Ibid., fol. 103.

12 Codex Barberini, Lat. 241, Biblioteca Apostolica Vaticana, Rome.

XX Plantin's Team 1560–1620

1   Ludovico Guicciardini, *Descrittione di tutti i Paesi Bassi* (Antwerp, 1567).

2   The business remained here until the middle of the nineteenth century. The building is now a museum with the presses, woodblocks (3,874 of them), page proofs, cases of fonts and furnaces to cast the type still as they were in Plantin's time.

3   Translation from Colin Clair, *Christopher Plantin* (London, 1960).

4   When Rondelet died, he left Lobelius all his manuscripts.

5   It was published by Plantin in 1567, in an edition of 1,250 copies. The paper cost about forty-seven florins, the printing a little over twenty-nine florins and the illustrations ten florins. His total investment in the book amounted to about ninety-one florins and delivered a profit of 150 per cent.

6 The link with Pisa continued when Francesco Malocchi (*prefetto* from 1596 to 1613) took over from Casabona. Pigments were ordered from Guido Marucelli's shop on the Ponte della Carraia in Florence 'to paint certain plants to be sent abroad to Carolus Clusius' (Archivio di Stato di Pisa 518, payment no. 69, dated 10 June 1606, quoted in Garbari et al, *Giardino dei Semplici*).

7 De Morgues was born in Dieppe, a centre renowned for its cartographers and illuminators.

8 See M. Lobelius, *Plantarum seu stirpium historia* (Antwerp, 1576), p. 14.

9 In April 1605 this same fritillary flowers in the London garden of James Nasmyth, surgeon to King James I, the first time it has been seen in England.

10 M. Lobelius, *Stirpium adversaria nova*, with Pierre Pena (London, 1570), p. 312.

XXI The Last of the Herbals 1560–1640

1 Testimony by George Baker printed in the preliminary pages of the first edition of John Gerard, *The Herball or Generall historie of plantes* (London, 1597).

2 Ben Jonson wrote his epitaph.

3 The story is told by William How in his *Stirpium illustrationes* of 1655.

4 He later retracted it, perhaps as a result of his dealings with Gerard over the *Herball*. The Natural History Museum in London has a copy of the catalogue in Lobelius's own hand with a cross note: 'haec esse falsissima M. Lobel' (This is most false, M. Lobel).

5 Gerard, *Herball*, p. 1,391.

6 Ibid., Dedicatory Letter.

7 Ibid., p. 275.

8 In the parsonage lived George Fuller, rector of Hildersham 1561–91, 'a very kinde and loving man, and willing to shew unto any man the saide close, who desired the same'.

9 Gerard, *Herball*, 1633 edition edited by Thomas Johnson, Johnson's address 'to the reader'.

10 Ibid., p. 1,516.

XXII English Achievements 1629–1664

1 Edward, Lord Herbert of Cherbury, *Autobiography*, 1599, edited by S. L. Lee (London, 1886), pp. 57–9.

2 Sir Henry Wotton, letter to Thomas Johnson, 2 July 1637, quoted in A. Arber, *Herbals, their origin and evolution 1470–1670* (Cambridge, 1912).

3 Translation of Johnson's *Descriptio itineris plantarum* (1632) taken from J.S.L. Gilmour (ed.), *Thomas Johnson: Journeys in Kent and Hampstead* (Pittsburgh, PA, 1972). All subsequent quotations from Johnson are taken from this source.

4 The shrine had been destroyed by Thomas Cromwell scarcely a hundred years earlier.

5 For a full account of the journey, see W. J. Thomas, *The Itinerary of a Botanist through North Wales in the Year 1639* (Bangor, 1908).

6 All Goodyer's papers are deposited in the library of Magdalen College, Oxford. For a full account of Goodyer's life, see R. T. Gunther, *Early British Botanists and their Gardens* (Oxford, 1922).

7 His translation, a full year's work, was the only version of Theophrastus in English until Sir Arthur Hort provided one for the Loeb Classical Library in 1916.

8 Those three volumes comprised Jean Bauhin's *Historia plantarum universalis*, published posthumously in 1650.

XXIII The American Connection 1620–1675

1 Hieronymus Bock in the Preface to the *Kreuter Buch* (Strasbourg, 1551 edition).
2 Conrad Gesner, *Correspondence*, edited by Jean Bauhin (1591).
3 List bound among the Goodyer papers, Magdalen College, Oxford, Goodyer MS 11, fol. 21.
4 Roger Williams, *Key into the Language of … the natives in that part of America called New England* (London, 1643), p. 98
5 The Royal Society's *Philosophical Transactions* (1668).
6 Francis Higginson, *New England's Plantation, or a Short and True Description of the Commodities and Discommodities of that Countrye, Written by a reverend divine now there resident* (London, 1630).
7 John Josselyn, *New England's Rarities Discovered* (London, 1672). Josselyn's first visit to the New World started in Boston in July 1638. From there he sailed up the coast to Scarborough, where he stayed for the next eighteen months.
8 Ibid.
9 Salem was established by Puritan settlers who set up the Massachusetts Bay Colony there in 1628. Winthrop became its first governor and planted a garden on Conant's Island in Boston harbour.
10 Massachusetts Historical Society, Winthrop Papers, vol. III.
11 John Ray, *Synopsis methodica stirpium Britannicarum* (London, 1690).

XXIV The Beginning of the End 1650–1705

1 See John Ray, *Methodus plantarum emendata*, published in Amsterdam in 1703.
2 It still goes on, even if twenty-first-century scientists analysing DNA to demonstrate kinship between plants have moved far beyond Ray's sensible third rule, that the characteristics used to group plants should be obvious and easy to grasp.
3 John Ray, *Methodus plantarum nova* (London, 1682).
4 Taken from the English version of the Preface in *Ray's Flora of Cambridgeshire*, translated and edited by A. H. Ewen and C. T. Prime (Hitchin, 1975).
5 Ibid.
6 R. T. Gunther (ed.), *Further Correspondence of John Ray* (London, 1928), p. 25.
7 Ibid., p. 68.
8 Preface to John Ray, *Observations* (London, 1673).
9 Ray's herbarium is in the Natural History Museum, London.
10 Letter to Lister dated 18 June 1667, *Correspondence of John Ray*, Ray Society (London, 1848), pp. 13–14.
11 John Ray, Preface to *Methodus plantarum nova* (London, 1682), translated in C. E. Raven, *John Ray Naturalist, His Life and Works* (Cambridge, 1942).
12 The first road maps of Britain had only recently been published. They were prepared by Scotsman James Ogilby (1605–1676) who, by order of Charles II, brought out *Britannica . . . the Principal Roads Thereof* in 1675, illustrated with a hundred copperplate engravings.
13 Gunther, *Further Correspondence*, p. 181.
14 Willughby, whom he had taught at Cambridge and who had been his companion on nearly all the journeys he had made in Britain and abroad, had died in 1672.
15 Letter to Tancred Robinson, 1684, *Correspondence of John Ray*, p. 146.
16 The volumes were illustrated by engravings taken from original work done in Brazil by the artists Frans Post and Albert Eckhout. The portfolio of their work, containing more than 1,500 sketches, is in the Jagiellonian Library in Krakow.

[17] The wood engravings which had illustrated the early plant books were now obsolete. Copperplate engravings allowed artists to show the parts of plants in much greater detail. The earliest botanical book to use copperplate etchings had been Fabio Colonna's *Phytobasanos* of 1592.

[18] Gunther, *Further Correspondence*, p. 146. On 21 May 1685 Francis Aston, Secretary of the Royal Society, had written to the former Secretary, William Musgrave: 'Mr Ray's *History of Plants* being designed to be printed with old figures, we have prevailed that it may be printed without figures ... I believe it will be an incomparable book.' Quoted in R. T. Gunther, *Early Science in Oxford* (Oxford, 1945).

[19] Preface to John Ray, *Historia plantarum*, vol. I (London, 1686).

[20] The Oxford Botanic Garden was founded in 1621 near the River Cherwell, on a site outside the east gate of the city. The fine gateway was designed by Inigo Jones. Though Robert Morison did not take up his chair until 1669, Jacob Bobart had been appointed gardener *c.*1641. In his account of Oxford *c.*1670–1700, Thomas Baskerville wrote, 'After the walls & gates of this famous garden were built, old Jacob Bobert father to this present Jacob may be said to be ye man yt first gave life & beauty to this famous place, who by his care & industry replenish'd the walls, with all manner of good fruits our clime would ripen, & and bedeck the earth wth great variety of trees plants and exotick flowers, dayly augmented by the botanists, who bring them hither from ye remote quarters of ye world.'

[21] Ray, *Historia plantarum*, pp. 183, 363.

[22] Ibid., pp. 278–9.

[23] Rudolph Jakob Camerarius, a pioneer in the study of sexual reproduction in plants, did not publish his *De sexu plantarum* until 1694. It was followed in 1718 by Sebastien Vaillant's *Sermo de natura florum*.

[24] Preface to Ray's *Historia plantarum*, vol. II (London, 1688).

[25] Courten was the grandson of Sir William Courten, silk merchant and coloniser of Barbados. The younger Courten's collection was later acquired by Sir Hans Sloane and became one of the foundations of the British Museum.

[26] Ray was, however, avidly read by the Italian scholar Marcello Malpighi and by the Frenchman Joseph Pitton de Tournefort, whose own book, *Élémens de botanique* was published in 1694.

[27] Gunther, *Further Correspondence*, p. 191.

[28] In *Institutiones rei herbariae* (1700), Tournefort described a system of assigning species to *classis* according to the form of their flowers. Plant genera were organised and described in a lucid, straightforward fashion that made them easy to identify. For a while, Tournefort's system was widely adopted in Europe.

[29] *Philosophical Transactions*, XVII, no. 193, p. 528.

[30] 'The great difficulties the lovers of Botanie are forced to encounter . . .' in *Philosophical Letters*, 1718, p. 290.

[31] From the Preface to the second edition of John Ray, *Synopsis methodica stirpium Britannicarum* (London, 1696).

Epilogue

[1] Renaissance scholars had used the terms *herbae* and *plantae*, though in his translation of Theophrastus, Teodoro of Gaza had preferred *stirpes*. This was the word enthusiastically taken up in book titles by later authors such as Fuchs, Lobelius and Clusius. With his *Botanologicon* of 1534, Euricius Cordus had favoured Greek words over Latin ones, but it was not a popular move. In giving a new, specific name to the study of plants, Ray returned to the Greek *botan-* root.

2   See Gaspard Bauhin's *Pinax theatri botanici*, published in Basel in 1623, the year before he died.

3   The full story is told in the *Journal of the Royal Society of Antiquaries of Ireland*, 26, 1896, pp. 211–226, 349–361.

4   See William Stearn, *Dictionary of Plant Names for Gardeners* (London, 1996).

5   Mark Griffiths (ed.), *Index of Garden Plants* (London, 1994).

6   The first code was drawn up by the Swiss botanist Alphonse de Candolle and confirmed the concept of precedence in choosing plant names.

7   See R. K. Brummitt, *Vascular Plant Families and Genera* (London, 1992).

BIBLIOGRAPHY

Abulafia, David (ed.) *The Mediterranean in History* (London, 2003)

Acosta, Christobal *Tractado de las drogas y medicinas . . .* (Burgos, 1578)

Acton, William *Journal of Italy* (London, 1691)

Agnew, D. C. A. *Protestant Exiles from France in the reign of Louis XIV* (London, 1871–4)

Allen, D. A. *The Naturalist in Britain: A Social History* (London, 1976)

Allen, Mea *The Tradescants, their Plants, Gardens and Museums 1570–1662* (London, 1964)

Alpino, Prospero *De plantis Aegypti* (Venice, 1592)

Ambrosoli, Mauro *The Wild and the Sown* (Cambridge, 1997)

Ancona, M. Levi d' *Botticelli's Primavera: A botanical interpretation including astrology, alchemy and the Medici* (Florence, 1983)

Ancona, M. Levi d' *The garden of the Renaissance: botanical symbolism in Italian painting* (Florence, 1977)

Anderson, Alexander *The Coming of the Flowers* (London, 1932)

Anderson, Frank *An Illustrated History of the Herbals* (Columbia, NY, 1977)

Arber, A. *Herbals, their origin and evolution 1470–1670* (Cambridge, 1912)

Arber, A. *The Natural Philosophy of Plant Form* (Cambridge, 1950)

Arber, A. 'From Medieval Herbalism to the Birth of Modern Botany' in *Science, Medicine and History: Essays written in honour of Charles Singer*, edited by E. Ashworth Underwood, vol. I, pp. 317–36 (London, 1953)

Aristotle *Parts of Animals, see* Peck, A. L.

Backer, W. D., et al *Botany in the Low Countries*, Plantin-Moretus Museum catalogue (Antwerp, 1993)

Backlund, Anders, and Kate Bremer 'To be or not to be', *Taxon*, vol. 47, pp.391–400

Balme, D. M. 'Development of Biology in Aristotle and Theophrastus', in *Phronesis* 7 (1962), pp. 91–104

Barlow, H. M. *Old English Herbals 1525–1640*, from Proceedings of the Royal Society of Medicine, 6 (London, 1913), pp. 108–49

Barnes, J. (ed.) *Cambridge Companion to Aristotle* (Cambridge, 1995)

Barrelier, Jacques de *Plantae per Galliam et Italiam observatae* (Paris, 1714)

Barrett, C. R. B. *History of Apothecaries* (London, 1905)

Bartholomew of England *De proprietatibus rerum, see* Bateman

Bateman, *Batman uppon Bartholome his booke De proprietatibus rerum* (London, 1582)

Bauhin, Gaspard *Pinax theatri botanici* (Basel, 1623 and 1658)

Bauhin, Jean *Historia plantarum universalis* (Yverdon, 1650)

Baumann, Felix *Erbario Carrarese* (Bern, 1974)

Bayon, H. P. *Masters of Salerno* (London and New York, 1953)

Beer, G. R. de *Early Travellers in the Alps* (esp. for Gilbert Burnet's journey in 1685: Zurich–Chur–Chiavenna, which mirrors William Turner's) (London, 1966)

Belon, Pierre *Les Observations de plusieurs singularités* (Paris, 1555)

Birch, Thomas *History of the Royal Society* (London, 1756–7)

Blamey, Marjorie and Richard Fitter *Wild Flowers* (London, 1980)

Blunt, W. *The Art of Botanical Illustration* (London, 1950)

Blunt, W., and S. Raphael *The Illustrated Herbal* (London, 1979)

Boas, F. S. (ed.) *The Diary of Thomas Crosfield* (London, 1935)

Boas, Marie *The Scientific Renaissance 1450–1630* (London, 1962)

Bock, Hieronymus *Kreuter Buch* (Strasbourg, 1539)

Bodleian Library 'Duke Humphrey and English Humanism in 15thC', Bodleian Library exhibition catalogue (Oxford, 1970)

Bollea, L. C. 'British Professors and Students at the University of Pavia', *Modern Philology*, 23 (1925), 2, pp. 236ff

Bosse, Abraham, L. de Chastillon, N. Robert, *Recueil des plantes gravées par ordre du Roi Louis XIV* (Paris, n.d.)

Bostock, John (trs.) *The Natural History of Pliny* (London, 1855–7)

Boulger, G. S. 'A Seventeenth-Century Botanist Friendship', *Journal of Botany* (1918), p. 197ff

Britten, James, and Robert Holland *Dictionary of Plant Names* (London, 1886)

Brown, Robert *Prodromus florae Novae-Hollandiae* (London, 1810)

Brunfels, Otto *Herbarum vivae eicones* (Strasbourg, 1530–36)

Bry, Theodor de *Anthologia Magna* (Frankfurt, 1626)

Bullein, William *The booke of simples*, Part I of *Bullein's bulwarke of defence againste all sicknes* (London, 1562)

Calvi, G. *Commentarium inserviturum historiae Pisani vireti Botanici Accademici* (Pisa, 1777)

Camden, William *Britannia* (London, 1586)

Campbell-Thompson *The Assyrian Herbal* (London, 1924)

Casanova, M. *L'incendie de la Bibliothèque d'Alexandrie par les Arabes* (Paris, 1923)

Cecil, Alicia *A History of Gardening in England* (London, 1895)

Cesalpino, Andrea *De plantis libri XVI* (Florence, 1583)

Cesalpino, Andrea, and Silvio Boccone *Museo di piante rare della Sicilia, Malta, Corsica, Italia, Piemonte e Germania con l'appendix ad libros de plantis A Caesalpini* (Venice, 1697)

Chardin, Sir John *Travels in Persia*, translated by E. Lloyd (London, 1927)

Childe, Vere Gordon *Man Makes Himself* (London, 1951)

Choate, Helen A. 'The Origin and Development of the Binomial System of Nomenclature', *The Plant World* 15:257–263 (1912)

Chroust, A. H. 'The miraculous disappearance and recovery of the Corpus Aristotelicum', *Classica et Mediaevalia*, XXIII (1962), pp. 50–67

Clair, Colin *Christopher Plantin* (London, 1960)

Clair, Colin 'Refugee Printers and Publishers in Britain during the Tudor period', *Proceedings of the Huguenot Society of London*, XXII (1976)

Clarke, W. A. *First Records of British Flowering Plants* (London, 1900)

Cleene, Marcel de, and Marie Claire Lejeune *Compendium of Symbolic and Ritual Plants in Europe* (Ghent, 2003)

Clusius, Carolus *Rariorum aliquot stirpium per Hispanias . . .* (Antwerp, 1576)

Clusius, Carolus *Rariorum aliquot stirpium, per Pannoniam . . .* (Antwerp, 1583)

Clusius, Carolus *Rariorum plantarum historia* (Antwerp, 1601)

Coats, Alice M. *Flowers and their Histories* (London, 1956)

Cockagne, Oswald *Leechdoms, Wort-Cunning and Starcraft of Early England*, 3 vols (London, 1864–6)

Coles, William *Adam in Eden* (London, 1657)

Coles, William *The Art of Simpling* (London, 1656)

Colin, D. *Gardens and Gardening in Papal Rome* (Princeton, NJ, 1991)

Collins, Minta *Medieval Herbals: The Illustrative Traditions*, British Library Studies in Medieval Culture (London, 2000)

Colonna, Fabio *Phytobasanos* (Naples, 1592)

Cordus, Euricius *Botanologicon* (Cologne, 1534)

Cordus, Valerius *Annotationes in pedacii Dioscoridis* (Strasbourg, 1561)

Cornut, Jacques Philippe *Canadensium plantarum, aliarumque nondum editorum historia* (Paris, 1635; reprinted New York, 1966)

Dalechampius, Jacobus *Histoire generale des plantes* (Lyons, 1653; the French translation by Jean de Moulins of the Latin original was published in Lyons, 1587–8)

Dandy, J. E. *The Sloane Herbarium* (London, 1958)

Dannenfeldt, K. H. *Leonhard Rauwolf: sixteenth-century physician, botanist and traveler* (Cambridge, MA, 1968)

D'Aronco, M. A., and M. L. Cameron (eds) *The Old English Illustrated Pharmacopoeia* (Copenhagen, 1998)

Dietz, B. *The Port and Trade of Early Elizabethan London*, Documents, London Record Society (London, 1972)

Diogenes Laertius *Lives of the Philosophers, see* Hicks, R. D.

Dioscorides *De materia medica, see* Gunther, R. W. T.

Dodoens, Rembert *Cruydeboeck* (Antwerp, 1554)

Dodoens, Rembert *Florum et coronarium odoratarumque* (Antwerp, 1568)

Dodoens, Rembert *Histoire des plantes* (Antwerp, 1557)

Dodoens, Rembert *Stirpium historiae pemptades sex* (Antwerp, 1583)

Duff, E. G. *A Century of the English Book Trade 1457–1557* (London, 1905)

Dürer, Albrecht *Vier bucher von menschlicher proportion* (Nuremberg, 1528)

Earle, John *English Plant Names from the Tenth to the Fifteenth Century* (Oxford, 1880)

Ebell, B. *The Papyrus Ebers* (Copenhagen and London, 1937)

Einstein, L. *The Italian Renaissance in England* (New York, 1902)

Eisenstein, E. L. *The Printing Press as an Agent of Change* (Cambridge, 1979)

Emery, F. *Edward Lhwyd* (Cardiff, 1971)

Emmart, E. W. (ed.) *The Badianus Manuscript*, a facsimile of the Codex Barberini Latin 241 Vatican Library, Rome (Baltimore, MD, 1940)

Evelyn, John *The Diary* (Oxford, 1955)

Ewan, Joseph *A Flora of North America* (New York, 1969)

Farrar, Linda *Ancient Roman Gardens* (Stroud, 2000)

Farrington, Benjamin *Greek Science* (Harmondsworth, 1961)

Farrington, Benjamin *Science in Antiquity* (London, 1969)

Ferri, Sara, and Francesca Vannozzi *I Giardini dei Semplici e gli orti botanici della Toscana* (Perugia, 1993)

Fischer, Hans 'Conrad Gesner (1516–1565) as Bibliographer and Encyclopedist', *The Library*, Fifth Series, vol. XXI, no. 4, December 1966, pp. 269–81

Fisher, Celia *Flowers in Medieval Manuscripts* (London, 2004)

Fletcher, Richard *The Cross and the Crescent: Christianity and Islam from Mohammad to the Reformation* (Harmondsworth, 2003)

Forster, E. S. (trs.) *The Turkish Letters of Ogier Ghiselin de Busbecq* (Oxford, 1927)

Frampton, John *Joyfull newes out of the newe founde worlde* (London, 1577)

Fuchs, Leonhart *De historia stirpium* (Basel, 1542), read in the facsimile reprint, edited by Frederick Meyer, Emily Emmart Trueblood and John L. Heller (Stanford, CA, 1999)

Fuller, Thomas *The history of the worthies of England* (London, 1662)

Furley, D. J. (ed.) *From Aristotle to Augustine: Routledge History of Philosophy*, vol. I (London, 1999)

Galenus, Claudius *Opera omnia* (Leipzig, 1821–33; originally printed Geneva, 1579)

Garbari, Fabio, Lucia Tongiorgi Tomasi and Alessandro Tosi *Giardino dei Semplici* (Pisa, 2002)

Gerard, John *The Herball or Generall historie of plantes* (London, 1597; Johnson edition, 1633)

Gerstenberg, Kurt *The Art of Albrecht Dürer* (London, 1971)

Gerstinger, H. (ed.) *Dioskurides: Codex Vindobonensis*, facsimile edition of the Juliana Anicia codex MS med. gr. 1 (Graz, 1970)

Gesner, Conrad *De hortis Germaniae* (Tiguri, 1561)

Gesner, Conrad *Epistolarum medicinalium* (Tiguri, 1577)

Gesner, Conrad *Historia Plantarum* (Basel, 1541), read in the facsimile edited by Heinrich Zoller et al. (Zurich, 1972)

Gibbon, Edward *The History of the Decline and Fall of the Roman Empire* (London, 1776–88)

Gillispie, C. C. (ed.) *Dictionary of Scientific Biography* (New York, 1970–80)

Gilmour, J. S. L. *British Botanists* (London, 1944)

Gilmour, J. S. L. (ed.) *Thomas Johnson: Journeys in Kent and Hampstead*, (Pittsburgh, PA, 1972)

Godwin, Sir H. *The History of the British Flora* (Cambridge, 1975)

Godwin, Dr H. 'The Ancient Cultivation of Hemp' in *Antiquity* 41 (1967), pp. 42–50

Goldthwaite, R. *Private Wealth in Renaissance Florence: A Study of Four Families* (Princeton, NJ, 1968)

Gotthelf, Allan and James G. Lennox, *Philosophical Issues in Aristotle's Biology* (Cambridge, 1987)

Green, J. R. *A History of Botany in the United Kingdom* (London, 1914)

Green, M. L. 'History of Plant Nomenclature' in *Kew Bulletin* 1927, pp. 403–14

Greene, E. L. *Landmarks of Botanical History* (Stanford, CA, 1983)

Grew, Nehemiah *The Anatomy of Plants* (London, 1682)

Griffiths, Mark (ed.) *Index of Garden Plants* (London, 1994)

Gudger, E. W. 'Pliny's *Historia Naturalis*: the most popular natural history ever published', *Isis* 6 (1924), pp. 269–81

Gunther, R. T. (ed.) *Dioscorides de Materia Medica: The Greek Herbal of Dioscorides* (Oxford, 1934)

Gunther, R. T. *Early British Botanists and their Gardens* (Oxford, 1922)

Gunther, R. T. *Early Science in Cambridge* (Oxford, 1937)

Gunther, R. T. *Early Science in Oxford* (Oxford, 1945)

Gunther, R. T. *Further Correspondence of John Ray*, published by the Ray Society (London, 1928)

Gunther, R. T. *The Herbal of Apuleius Barbarus*, facsimile of MS Bodley 130 (Oxford, 1925)

Gwyn, R. D. *Huguenot Heritage: The History and Contribution of the Huguenots in Britain* (London, 1985)

Hakluyt, Richard *The Principal Voyages and Discoveries of the English Nation* (Glasgow, 1904)

Hakluyt Society, *The Travels of John Sanderson in the Levant (1584–1602)* (London, 1931)

Hale, J. R. *England and the Italian Renaissance* (London, 1954)

Hall, A. R. *The Scientific Revolution 1500–1800* (Cambridge, 1962)

Hallam, H. E. *Rural England 1066–1348* (Glasgow, 1981)

Hanmer, Sir Thomas *The Garden Book of Sir Thomas Hanmer* (London, 1933)

Hedrick, Ulysses P. *A History of Horticulture in America to 1860* (New York, 1950; reprinted Portland, OR, 1988)

Henrey, Blanche *British Botanical and Horticultural Literature Before 1800* (London, 1975)

Herbert, Edward, Lord *Autobiography* (1599), edited by S. L. Lee (London, 1886)

Hicks, R. D. (ed.) *Diogenes Laertius Lives of Eminent Philosophers*, Loeb Classical Library series, (London, 1925)

Higginson, Francis *New England's Plantation . . .* (London, 1630)

Hirsch, R. *Printing, selling and reading 1450–1550* (Wiesbaden, 1967)

Hoeniger, F. D. and J. F. M. *The Development of Natural History in Tudor England* (Charlottesville, VA, 1969)

Holland, Dr Philemon *The Historie of the World. Commonly called, the Naturall Historie of C. Plinius Secundus* (London, 1601)

Hort, Sir Arthur (ed.) *Theophrastus Enquiry into Plants*, 2 vols, Loeb Classical Library series (London, 1916)

How, W. *Phytologia Britannica* (London, 1650)

Hubert, Robert *A catalogue of many natural rarities* (London, 1665)

Hunger, F. W. T. *The Herbal of Pseudo-Apuleius* (Leiden, 1935)

Hunger, F. W. T. *Charles de l'Écluse* ('s-Gravenhage, 1927–43)

Jackson, B. D. *A Catalogue of plants cultivated in the garden of John Gerard 1596–1599* (London, 1876)

Jashemski, Wilhelmina Feemster *A Pompeian Herbal* (Austin, TX, 1999)

Jeffers, R. H. *The Friends of John Gerard* (Falls Village, CT, 1967–9)

Jennett, Seán (trs.) *Beloved Son Felix: the Journal of Felix Platter, a medical student in Montpellier in the Sixteenth Century* (London, 1961)

Jennett, Seán (trs.) *Journal of a Younger Brother, The Life of Thomas Platter . . .* (London, 1963)

Johnson, Francis R. 'Latin versus English: the sixteenth-century debate over scientific terminology', *Studies in Philology*, 41, pp. 109–135

Johnson, F. R. *Astronomical Thought in Renaissance England: A Study of the English Scientific Writings from 1500–1645* (Baltimore, MD, 1937)

Johnson, George W. *A History of English Gardening* (London, 1829)

Johnson, T. *Descriptio itineris plantarum* (London, 1632)

Johnson, T. *Iter plantarum investigationis* (London, 1629)

Johnson, T. *Mercurius botanicus* (London, 1634 and 1641)

Jones, W. R. D. *William Turner, Tudor Naturalist, Physician and Divine* (London, 1988)

Josselyn, John *New England's Rarities Discovered* (London, 1672)

Joubertus, Laurentius *Operum Latinorum* (Frankfurt, 1599)

Kessler, H. L. (ed.) *Studies in Classical and Byzantine Manuscript Illumination* (London and Chicago, 1971)

Kew, H. Wallis, and H. E. Powell *Thomas Johnson: Botanist and Royalist* (London, 1932)

Koreny, Fritz *Albrecht Dürer and the Animal and Plant Studies of the Renaissance* (Boston, 1985)

Kren, Thomas, and Scott McKendrick *Illuminating the Renaissance* (Los Angeles and London, 2003)

Lambarde, W. *A perambulation of Kent, containing the description, Historye and Customes of the Shyre* (London, 1576)

Launey, M. 'Le verger d'Heracles à Thasos', *Bulletin de correspondance hellenique*, 61 (1937)

Legre, L. *La Botanique en Provence au xvième siècle*, vols I–V (Marseille, 1899–1904)

Leighton, Ann *Early English Gardens in New England* (London, 1970)

Lennox, James G. *Aristotle's Philosophy of Biology* (Cambridge, 2001)

Leoniceno, Nicolò, *Plinii ac plurinum aliorum auctorum . . .* (Ferrara, 1492)

Linnaeus, C. *Genera plantarum* (Leiden, 1737)

Linnaeus, C. *Species plantarum* (Stockholm, 1753)

Lisle, Edward *Observations in Husbandry* (London, 1757)

Lobelius, M. *Kruydtboeck* (Antwerp, 1581)

Lobelius, M. *Plantarum seu stirpium historia* (Antwerp, 1576)

Lobelius, M. *Plantarum seu stirpium icones* (Antwerp, 1581)

Lobelius, M. *Stirpium illustrationes* (London, 1655)

Lobelius, M., and Pierre Pena *Stirpium adversaria nova* (London, 1570)

Loret, Victor *La Flore pharaonique* (Paris, 1887)

Lowry, M. *The World of Aldus Manutius. Business and scholarship in Renaissance Venice* (Oxford, 1979)

Lusitanus, Amatus *In Dioscoridis . . . de medica materia libros quinque enarrationes* (Venice, 1553)

Lynch, John Patrick *Aristotle's School* (Berkeley, CA, 1972)

Lyte, Henry *A Niewe Herball, or Historie of Plantes* (London, 1578)

MacCulloch, Diarmuid *Reformation: Europe's House Divided 1490–1700* (London, 2003)

MacDougall, Elisabeth Blair *Fountains, Statues and Flowers: Studies in Italian Gardens of the Sixteenth and Seventeenth Century* (Dumbarton Oaks, Washington, DC, 1994)

MacDougall, Elisabeth Blair, and Jashemski, Wilhelmina F. (eds) *Ancient Roman Gardens*, Dumbarton Oaks Colloquium (Washington, DC, 1981)

Magnol, Pierre *Botanicon monspeliense* (Montpellier, 1686)

Magnol, Pierre *Hortus regius monspeliensis* (Montpellier, 1697)

Malpighi, Marcello *Anatome plantarum* (London 1675, 1679)

Markham, Sir Clements (trs.) *Colloquies on the Simples and Drugs of India* (London, 1913); *see also* Orta, Garcia de

Marshall, W. *The Rural Economy of the West of England* (London, 1796)

Matthews, L. G. *The Royal Apothecaries* (London, 1967)

Mattioli, Pier Andrea *Commentarii in libros sex Pedacii Dioscoridis Anazarbei* (Venice, 1554)

Mattioli, Pier Andrea *Opera* (Frankfurt, 1598)

McLean, Antonia *Humanism and the Rise of Science in Tudor England* (London, 1972)

Merret, Christopher *Pinax rerum naturalium britannicarum* (London, 1666)

Moir, E. *The Discovery of Britain: The English Tourist 1540–1840* (London, 1964).

Monardes, Nicolas *Dos Libros* (Seville, 1569–71)

Morison, Robert (ed.) *Icones et descriptiones rariorum plantarum Siciliae, Melitae, Galliae et Italiae* (Oxford, 1674)

Morison, Robert *Plantarum umbelliferarum distributio nova* (Oxford, 1672)

Morton, A. G. *History of Botanical Science* (London, New York, 1981)

Nasr, Seyyed Hossein *Islamic Science* (n.p., 1976)

Nissen, Claus *Herbals of Five Centuries* (Zurich, 1958)

Noltie, Henry (ed.) *The Long Tradition*, Botanical Society of the British Isles conference report no. 20 (1986)

North, F. J. *Humphrey Lluyd's map of England and Wales* (Cardiff, 1937)

Ogilby, J. *Britannia . . . or an illustration of the Kingdom of England and Dominion of Wales* (London, 1675)

Oliver, Francis Wall *Makers of British Botany* (Cambridge, 1913)

Orta, Garcia de *Coloquios dos simples* (Goa, 1563); *see also* Markham, Sir Clements

Oviedo, Gonzalo Fernandez de *Dela natural historia de las Indias* (Toledo, 1526), edited and translated by S. A. Stoudemire as *Natural History of the West Indies* (Chapel Hill, NC, 1959)

Pächt, Otto 'Early Italian Nature Studies and the Early Calendar Landscape', *Journal of the Warburg and Courtauld Institutes*, XIII (1950) pp. 13–47

Panofsky, Erwin *The Life and Art of Albrecht Dürer* (1955; reprinted Princeton, NJ, 1971)

Panofsky, Erwin *Renaissance and Renascences in Western Art* (New York, 1972)

Parkinson, John *Paradisi in sole paradisus terrestris* (London, 1629)

Parkinson, John *Theatrum botanicum* (London, 1640)

Parsons, Edward Alexander *The Alexandrian Library* (New York, 1952)

Passe, Crispin de *Hortus Floridus* (Utrecht, 1614)

Peck, A. L. (ed.) *Aristotle's Parts of Animals*, Loeb Classical Library series (London, 1937)

Petrarch, Francesco *De rebus memorandis* (Basel, 1563)

Pierce, W. *The Marprelate Tracts 1588, 1589* (London, 1911)

Plat, Sir Hugh *Garden of Eden* (London, 1654)

Plat, Sir Hugh *The Jewell House of Art and Nature* (London, 1594/1653)

Platter, Felix *Beloved Son Felix: the Journal of Felix Platter, a medical student in Montpellier in the Sixteenth Century*, see Jennett, Seán

Pliny the Elder *Natural History*, Loeb Classical Library series (Cambridge, MA, 1980)

Pliny *Letters*, translation by William Melmoth for the Loeb Classical Library series (London, 1915)

Prest, John *The Garden of Eden: The Botanic Garden and the Re-Creation of Eden* (London, 1981)

Pulteney, R. *Historical and Biographical Sketches of the Progress of Botany in England* (London, 1790)

Raleigh, Sir Walter *The History of the World* (London, 1614)

Rashed, Roshdi (ed.) *Encyclopaedia of the History of Arabic Science* (London and New York, 1996)

Raven, C. E. *English Naturalists From Neckham to Ray* (Cambridge, 1947)

Raven, C. E. *John Ray Naturalist, His Life and Works* (Cambridge, 1942)

Raven, John *Plants and Plant Lore in Ancient Greece* (Oxford, 2000)

Ray, John *Catalogus plantarum Angliae* (London, 1670)

Ray, John *Catalogus plantarum circa Cantabrigiam nascentium* (1660), translated and edited by A. H. Ewen and O. T. Prime (Hitchin, 1975)

Ray, John *Dictionariolum trilingue*, reprint of the 1675 original by the Ray Society (London, 1981)

Ray, John *Historia plantarum*, 3 vols, (London, 1686–1704)

Ray, John *Methodus plantarum emendata* (London and Amsterdam, 1703)

Ray, John *Methodus plantarum nova* (London, 1682)

Ray, John *Synopsis methodica stirpium Britannicarum* (London, 1690)

Raymond, J. *Itinerary containing a Voyage, made through Italy in the yeare 1646 and 1647* (London, 1648)

Rea, John *Flora, seu de florum cultura* (London, 1665)

Reeds, Karen Meier *Botany in Medieval and Renaissance Universities* (New York and London, 1991)

Riddle, John *Dioscorides on Pharmacy and Medicine* (Austin, TX, 1986)

Rohde, E. S. *The Old English Herbals* (London, 1922)

Ruel, J. *De natura stirpium libri tres* (Paris, 1536)

Sachs, Julius von *History of Botany 1530–1860* (Oxford, 1890)

Sadek, M. M. *The Arabic Materia Medica of Dioscorides* (Quebec, 1983)

Sarton, George *Introduction to the History of Science* (Baltimore, 1927–48; reprinted 1962)

Sarton, George *Six Wings* (Bloomington, IN, 1957)

Seward, A. C. 'The Foliage, Flowers and Fruit of Southwell Chapter House', *Cambridge Antiquarian Soc. Comm.*, XXXV, pp. 1–32

Seybold, S. 'Luca Ghini, Leonhart Rauwolf und Leonhart Fuchs', *Jh. Ges. Naturkunde*, 145 (1990)

Singer, Charles *From Magic to Science: Essays on the Scientific Twilight* (London, 1928)

Singer, Charles *Greek Biology and Greek Medicine* (Oxford, 1920)

Singer, Charles 'Early English Magic and Medicine', *Proc. British Academy*, read 28 January 1920 (London, 1920)

Singer, Charles 'Greek science and modern science', inaugural lecture, University College, London, 12 May 1920 (London, 1920)

Singer, Charles 'The herbal in Antiquity and its transmission to later ages' *Journal of Hellenic Studies*, vol. 47 (1927), pp. 1–52

Singer, Charles 'Herbals', *Edinburgh Review*, 237, January 1923, pp. 95–102

Southwell, T. *Notes and Letters on the Natural History of Norfolk* (London, 1902)

Sprague, T. A. 'The Herbal of Otto Brunfels', *Journal of the Linnaean Society*, Botany vol. 48, (London, 1928) pp. 79–124

Sprague, T. A. 'Plant Morphology in Albertus Magnus', *Kew Bulletin* (1933), pp. 431–440

Sprague, T. A. and Nelmes, E. 'The Herbal of Leonhart Fuchs' in *Journal of the Linnaean Society*, Botany vol. 48 (London, 1931), pp. 545–642

Stafleu, Frans A. *Taxonomic literature* (Utrecht, 1976)

Stafleu, Frans A. et al *International code of botanical nomenclature* (Utrecht, 1978)

Stannard, Jerry 'A fifteenth century botanical glossary', *Isis* 55, pp. 353–67

Stannard, Jerry 'Pliny and Roman Botany', *Isis*, 56 (1965), pp. 420–25

Stearn, W. *Botanical Latin* (Newton Abbott, 1992)

Stearn, W. T. (ed.) *Turner's Libellus and Names of Herbes*, fascimile edition published by the Ray Society (London, 1965)

Stearn, William T. *Dictionary of Plant Names for Gardeners* (London, 1996)

Stearn, William T. 'The background of Linnaeus's contributions to the nomenclature and methods of systematic biology', *Systematic Zoology*, 7: 4–22

Stearn, William T. 'From Theophrastus and Dioscorides to Sibthorp and Smith', *Journal of the Linnaean Society*, London 8: 285–298

Stearn, William T. 'The origin and later development of cultivated plants', *JRHS*, 110, (1965), pp. 279–290 and 322–340

Stoye, J. W. *English Travellers Abroad 1604–1667: Their Influence in English Society and Politics* (London, 1952)

Strabo, Walahfrid *Hortulus* (Vienna, 1510)

Stroup, Alice *A Company of Scientists* (Berkeley and Los Angeles, 1990)

Sweerts, Emmanuel *Florilegium* (Frankfurt, 1612)

Szafer, Wladyslaw *Zarys historii botaniki w Krakowie* (History of Botany in Cracow) (Krakow, 1964)

Thacker, C. 'Huguenot Gardeners in the Age of Gardens', *Proceedings of the Huguenot Society of London*, 24 (1912), pp. 60–65

Theophrastus *De causis plantarum* and *Historiae plantarum*, see Hort, Sir Arthur

Thomas, Hugh *Rivers of Gold: The Rise of the Spanish Empire* (London, 2003)

Thomas, K. *Religion and the Decline of Magic* (London, 1971)

Thomas, Keith *Man and the Natural World* (London, 1983)

Thomas, W. J. *The Itinerary of a Botanist through North Wales in the Year 1639* (Bangor, 1908)

Thompson, D. W. *On Growth and Form*, abridged edition (Cambridge, 1971)

Thorndike, L. *The Herbal of Rufinus* (Chicago, 1946)

Thorndike, L. *A History of Magic and Experimental Science* (vol. VI covers the sixteenth century) (New York, 1941)

Tolaini, Emilio *Forma Pisarum. Storia urbanistica della città di Pisa* (Pisa, 1979)

Tomasi, Lucia Tongiorgi, and Gretchen A. Hirschauer *The Flowering of Florence*, exhibition catalogue (Washington, DC, 2002)

Toni, Giovanni Battista de *I placiti di Luca Ghini* (Venice, 1907)

Tooley, R. V. *Maps and Map Makers* (London 1949; new ed., 1978)

Tosi, Alessandro *Ulisse Aldrovandi e la Toscana* (Florence, 1989)

Tournefort, J. Pitton de *Élémens de botanique* (Paris, 1694)

Tournefort, J. Pitton de *Histoire des plantes qui naissent aux environs de Paris avec leur usage dans la medicine* (Paris, 1698)

Touwaide, Alain (ed.) *Farmacopea Araba Medievale*, facsimile of MS Ayasofia 3703 (Milan, 1992–3)

Turner, William *Libellus de re herbaria* (London, 1538)

Turner, William *The Names of Herbes*, a facsimile of the 1548 edition published by the Ray Society (London, 1965)

Turner, William *A new herball* (London and Cologne, 1551–1568)

Underwood, E. Ashworth *A History of the Worshipful Society of Apothecaries* (London, 1963)

Vinci, Leonardo da *A Treatise on Painting*, translated by John Francis Rigaud (London, 1877)

Walters, S. M. and C. J. King, *European Floristic and Taxonomic Studies* (Faringdon, 1975)

Waters, W. G. (trs.) *Journal of Montaigne's Travels* (London, 1903)

Webster, Charles *The Great Instauration: Science, Medicine and Reform, 1626–1660* (London, 1975)

Weitzmann, Kurt 'Greek Sources of Islamic Scientific Illustrations' and other contributions in *Studies in Classical and Byzantine Manuscript Illumination, see* Kessler, H. L.

Wheeler, Rev. Sir George *A Journey into Greece* (London, 1682)

Williams, Roger *Key into the Language of . . . the natives in that part of America called New England* (London, 1643)

Wilson, N. G. *Books and Readers in Byzantium*, Dumbarton Oaks Papers (Washington, DC, 1975)

Withering, William *An Account of the Foxglove* (Birmingham, 1785)

Zoller, Heinrich, Martin Steinmann, Karl Schmidt (eds) *Conradi Gesneri Historia Plantarum*, 3 vols, (Zurich, 1972–4)

Manuscripts

CAMBRIDGE

University Library: MS Ee.5.7

FLORENCE

Biblioteca Nazionale: MS Pal.586

ISTANBUL

Süleymaniye Mosque Library: MS Ayasofia 3703 (available in facsimile as *Farmacopea Araba Medievale*, edited by Alain Touwaide, Milan, 1992–3)

Topkapi Library: MS 2127

LEIDEN

Bibliotheek der Rijksuniversiteit: MS Voss.lat.Q.9; MS.or.289

LONDON

British Library: MS Cotton Vitellius C III; MS Egerton 747 (available in facsimile as *A Medieval Herbal* with commentary by Minta Collins and plant list by Sandra Raphael, British Library, London, 2003); MS Egerton 2020 (The Carrara Herbal); MS Harley 585; MS Sloane 1975; MS Sloane 4016; Add.MS 28841 (The Cocharelli Treatise); Add.MS 41623

Wellcome Institute: MS 5753 (The Johnson Papyrus)

NAPLES

Biblioteca Nazionale: MS gr.1 (available in facsimile as the *Codex Neapolitanus*, Graz, 1992)

OXFORD

Bodleian Library: MS Bodley 130; MS Ashmole 1462

PARIS

Bibliothèque Nationale de France: MS gr.2286; MS Lat. 6823; MS nouv.acq.Lat.1673

Bibliothèque de l'École des Beaux Arts: MS Masson 116

ROME

Biblioteca Casanatense: MS 4182

VATICAN

Biblioteca Apostolica Vaticana: MS Barberini Lat. 241 (available in facsimile as *The Badianus Manuscript*, edited by E. W. Emmart, Baltimore, MD, 1940)

VENICE

Biblioteca Nazionale Marciana: MS Lat. VI; MS Ital. II XXVI 4860

VIENNA

Österreichische Nationalbibliothek: MS med. gr. 1 (Juliana Anicia codex, available in facsimile as *Dioskurides: Codex Vindobonensis* with a commentary by H. Gerstinger, Graz, 1970); MS Vindobonensis 93 (Medicina antiqua, available in facsimile with introduction by Peter Murray-Jones, London, 1999)

ACKNOWLEDGEMENTS

My first thanks must go to the people who spared time from their own work to help me with mine. Minta Collins allowed me to draw on the extensive research contained in her *Medieval Herbals*, and also with great care read the four chapters of my own book covering the medieval period. They have been greatly improved by her attention. Professor Bob Sharples, of the Department of Greek and Latin at University College London kindly shared his unequalled knowledge of Theophrastus and commented, to great effect, on the four chapters relating to the classical world. Dr Brent Elliott, Librarian of the Lindley Library in London reviewed the early chapters on Brunfels and Fuchs and made, as always, pertinent and useful suggestions. At the Royal Botanic Gardens, Kew, Professor Mark Chase, head of the Molecular Systematics Section, spent a great deal of time explaining the work of the Angiosperm Phylogeny Group. He also agreed to read and comment on the Epilogue as well as the chapter dealing with John Ray. Caryl Hubbard was the first person to read the manuscript in its entirety and her comments, as well as her support and encouragement, were given at the time when I needed them most. All these people know how much I am indebted to them. Any inaccuracies that remain are, of course, entirely my own.

In Italy, my work was eased by the kind encouragement given by Dr Chiara Nepi in the Natural History Museum at Florence University. She made it possible for me to see Cesalpino's herbarium, arranged to copy various sections so that I could translate them into English, and later was invaluable in supplying photographs. In Pisa, Professor Fabio Garbari in the university's Department of Botany, generously allowed me to quote from *Giardino dei Semplici* which he wrote with Lucia Tongiorgi Tomasi and Alessandro Tosi. He also made available copies of several important portraits which belong to the university. I am much in their debt. I would also like to thank Beatrice Monti della Corte for offering me a place at Santa Maddalena, a writers' retreat ideally placed for the research I needed to do in Florence. I had a memorable six weeks there.

The staff in the Rare Books Room at Cambridge University Library have been untiringly efficient at producing the often obscure books I needed to see. I appreciate their help and advice very much indeed. Nor could I have survived without the staff at the London Library who regularly sent parcels of books to me in the country. That is an unbelievable luxury. I am grateful too, to the British Library and the Wellcome Library for allowing me to consult manuscripts in their collections.

My agent, Caradoc King at A. P. Watt, has, as always, given great support. At Bloomsbury, I would like to thank Liz Calder who commissioned this project and the tenacious band who turned it into a book: the design director, Will Webb, and the production director, Penny Edwards. Victoria Millar was a brilliant editor, as tireless in pursuit of a footnote as she was in tightening up wobbles in the narrative. I respect her dedication and owe her a great deal. Heather Vickers handled the complicated picture research and Douglas Matthews provided the index.

Finally, I would like to thank my husband, Trevor Ware, who came to Kazakhstan, Guyana, Athens, Florence, Amsterdam, Bruges, Antwerp and all the other places this book has taken me to. Faced with the prospect of yet another museum, yet another library, his good humour rarely wavered.

Quotations from *Thomas Johnson: Botanical Journeys in Kent and Hampstead* edited by J. S. L. Gilmour (1972) are reproduced by courtesy of the Hunt Institute for Botanical Documentation, Carnegie Mellon University, Pittsburgh, PA; the quotations from *John Ray Naturalist, His Life and Works* (1942) and *English Naturalists from Neckham to Ray* (1947) both by Charles Raven, are reproduced by kind permission of the Cambridge University Press; material from *Medieval Herbals: The Illustrative Tradition* (2000) by Minta Collins is reproduced by kind permission of the author and the British Library; quotations from Otto Pächt's article in Volume 13 of the *Journal of the Warburg and Courtauld Institutes* are reproduced by permission of the Editors of the *Journal*; the quotation from *The Scientific Renaissance* (1962) by Marie Boas is reproduced courtesy of the author; translations from the commentary to and facsimile edition (1999) of Fuchs's *De historia stirpium* are reproduced thanks to the generosity of Stanford University Press; the quotation from *Collins Gem Guide: Wild Flowers* is reprinted by permission of HarperCollins Publishers Ltd, copyright © Marjorie Blamey and Richard Fitter (1980); quotations from *British Botanical and Horticultural Literature before 1800* (1975) by Blanche Henrey and *Early Science in Oxford* (1945) by R. T. Gunther are reproduced by permission of Oxford University Press; translations by Seán Jennet from *Beloved Son Felix* (1961) and *Journal of a Younger Brother* (1963) are reproduced by permission of Pollinger Ltd and the proprietor; the quotation from the *Index of Garden Plants*, edited by Mark Griffiths (© Mark Griffiths; first published in by Pan Macmillan in 1993) is included courtesy of Pan Macmillan Ltd. It has not been possible to trace the copyright holders of *Christopher Plantin* (1960) by Colin Clair, published by Cassell, an imprint of the Orion Publishing Group, or of *Ray's Flora of Cambridgeshire* (1975), translated and edited by A. H. Ewen and C. T. Prime from which material has also been quoted.

Every reasonable effort has been made to contact copyright holders of material reproduced in this book. If any have been inadvertently overlooked, the publishers would be glad to hear from them and to make good in future editions any errors or omissions brought to their attention.

LIST OF ILLUSTRATIONS

20 Dedication, Juliana Anicia codex, MS med. gr. 1, fol. 26r. Österreichische Nationalbibliothek, Vienna, Picture Archive

21 Asphodel, Juliana Anicia codex, MS med. gr. 1, fol. 26v. Österreichische Nationalbibliothek, Vienna, Picture Archive

22 Bramble (*Rubus fruticosus*), Juliana Anicia codex, MS. med. gr. 1, fol. 83v. Österreichische Nationalbibliothek, Vienna, Picture Archive

23 Spurge, *Codex Neapolitanus*, MS gr. 1, fol. 142r. Courtesy of the Biblioteca Nazionale, Naples

24 Adianton, *Codex Neapolitanus*, MS gr. 1, fol. 14v. Courtesy of the Biblioteca Nazionale, Naples

25 Arabian pharmacy, MS Ayasofia 3703, fol. 2r. Courtesy of the Süleymaniye Mosque Library, Istanbul

26 Voss.lat.Q.9, fol. 38v, sixth century, second half. Bibliotheek der Rijksuniversiteit, Leiden

27 Al-nilufar (*Nymphaea alba*, L., Waterlily), MS.or.289, fol. 33v, AD 1083. Bibliotheek der Rijksuniversiteit, Leiden

28 Vine, Keir Collection 2, 11:63 Courtesy of the Keir Collection, London

29 Bantafullun, MS Ayasofia 3703, fol. 21. Courtesy of the Süleymaniye Mosque Library, Istanbul

30 Bird and grasshopper, MS Ayasofia 3703, fol. 3v. Courtesy of the Süleymaniye Mosque Library, Istanbul

31 Bramble (*Rubus fruticosus*), MS Ayasofia 3703, fol. 17v. Courtsey of the Süleymaniye Mosque Library, Istanbul

32 *Gladiolus italicus*, MS Ayasofia 3703. Courtesy of the Süleymaniye Mosque Library, Istanbul

33 'Alleluia', MS Egerton 747, fol. 12. By permission of the British Library, London

34 'Spargula', MS Egerton 747, fol. 98. By permission of the British Library, London

35 'Henne belle', MS Cotton Vitellius C III, fol. 23v. By permission of the British Library, London

36 Mugwort, MS Cotton Vitellius C III. By permission of the British Library, London

37 Asphodel, MS Ashmole 1462, fol. 23r. Bodleian Library, University of Oxford

38 Artemisias, MS Sloane 1975, fol. 16v. By permission of the British Library, London

39 Madonna lily, MS Masson 116, fol. 206. Bibliothèque de l'École des Beaux Arts, Paris

40 Pine, MS Egerton 2020, fol. 46r. By permission of the British Library, London

41 Vines (*Vitis vinifera*), MS Egerton 2020, fol. 27v. By permission of the British Library, London

42 'Botracion statice', Codex Vindobonensis 93, fol. 29r. Österreichische Nationalbibliothek, Vienna, Picture Archive

43 Martagon lily, Add.MS 41623. By permission of the British Library, London

44 Waterlilies, Add. MS 35214, fol. 95. By permission of the British Library, London

45 Portrait of Margherita Gonzaga, *c*.1438–1440 (wood panel) by Antonio Pisanello (1395–1455). Musée du Louvre, Paris, France / Bridgeman Art Library

46 *Study of Flowers* (pen and ink over metalpoint) by Leonardo da Vinci (1452–1519). Galleria dell'Accademia, Venice, Italy / Bridgeman Art Library

47 *Great piece of turf – study of weeds*, 1503 (watercolour and body colour on vellum) by Albrecht Dürer (1471–1528). Graphische Sammlung Albertina, Vienna, Austria / Bridgeman Art Library

48 'Hyppuris', MS Sloane 4016, fol. 44v. By permission of the British Library, London

49 Mandrakes, MS Chigi. F. VII. 159, fol. 195v. By permission of the Biblioteca Apostolica Vaticana, Rome

50 Portrait of Teodoro of Gaza. Hunt Institute for Botanical Documentation, Carnegie Mellon University, Pittsburgh, Pennsylvania

51 Madonna and Child by Domenico Veneziano, *c*.1445, Samuel H. Kress Collection. Image © 2005 Board of Trustees, National Gallery of Art, Washington

52 Garden, illustration from Conrad von Megenberg's *Buch der Natur*, 1478. Private Collection / Bridgeman Art Library

Österreichische Nationalbibliothek, Vienna, Picture Archive

[79] Portrait of Luca Ghini. Courtesy of Botanical Museum, University of Pisa

[80] *Visitation of the Blessed Virgin Mary to Saint Elizabeth* by Domenico Ghirlandaio, 1485. © Photo Scala, Florence / Basilica Santa Maria Novella

[81] John VII Palaeologus (1391–1448), Eastern Roman Emperor, as one of the Three Kings, detail from the *Journey of the Magi* cycle by Benozzo di Lese di Sandro Gozzoli (1420–1497). Palazzo Medici-Riccardi, Florence, Italy / Bridgeman Fine Art Library

[82] Map of Venice, MS Ayasofia 2612. Courtesy of the Süleymaniye Mosque Library, Istanbul

[83] 'Oculis Bovis', Add.MS 41623, fol. 97v. By permission of the British Library, London

[84] Agave by Jacopo Ligozzi (*c*.1547–1632). Florence, Gabinetto dei Disegni e delle Stampe degli Uffizi © 1990, Photo Scala, Florence

[85] Iris Susiana, Iris hyphium no. 1891 by Jacopo Ligozzi. Florence, Gabinetto dei Disegni e delle Stampe degli Uffizi © 1990, Scala, Florence

[86] Padua Botanic Garden from P. Tomasini, *Gymnasium Patavinum*, 1654. By permission of the British Library, London

[87] Pisa Botanic Garden from M. Tilli, *Catalogus plantarum horti Pisani*, 1723. © Royal Horticultural Society, Lindley Library

[88] Coffee from M. Tilli, *Catalogus plantarum horti Pisani*, 1723. © Royal Horticultural Society, Lindley Library

[89] Portrait of Andrea Cesalpino. Courtesy of the University of Pisa

[90] Index, Andrea Cesalpino's herbarium. Courtesy of Sezione Botanica del Museo di Storia Naturale dell'Università di Firenze

[91] Andrea Cesalpino's herbarium, fol. 120. Courtesy of Sezione Botanica del Museo di Storia Naturale dell'Università di Firenze

[92] Villa di Pratolino by Joost Utens (sixteenth century). Florence, Museo di Firenze com'era © 1990, Photo Scala, Florence

[93] Title page, Andrea Cesalpino, *De plantis libri XVI*, 1583. © Natural History Museum, London

[94] Cypress vine (*Ipomoea quamoclit*) by Jacopo Ligozzi. Florence, Gabinetto dei Disegni e delle Stampe degli Uffizi © 1990, Photo Scala, Florence

[95] Portrait of Pier Andrea Mattioli. Courtesy of the Botanical Museum, University of Pisa

[96] Manuscript page from an Italian edition of Mattioli's *Commentarii in libros sex Pedacii Dioscoridis Anazarbei*. Author's own collection

[97] Yew from Mattioli's *Commentarii in libros sex Pedacii Dioscoridis Anazarbei*, 1554. Courtesy of the Wellcome Library, London

[98] Woodblock of sea lavender (*Limonium*), page 980, Pier Andrea Mattioli, *Commentarii . . . Pedacii Dioscoridis de materia medica*, Venice, Valgrisi, 1562–1565. Collection of Rachel Lambert Mellon, Oak Spring Garden Library, Upperville, Virginia

[99] Iris tuberosa by Jacopo Ligozzi. Florence, Gabinetto dei Disegni e delle Stampe degli Uffizi © 2005, Photo Scala, Florence. Courtesy of the Ministero Beni e Att. Culturali.

[100] Title page, *The grete herball*, 1526. © Royal Horticultural Society, Lindley Library

[101] Title page, William Turner, *Libellus de re herbaria*, 1538

[102] Title page, William Turner, *The names of herbes*, 1548. © The Natural History Museum, London

[103] Title page, William Turner, *A new herball*, 1551. © The Natural History Museum, London

[104] Root, seeds and leaves of cuckoo pint from William Turner, *A new herball*, 1551. © The Natural History Museum, London

[105] Anagyris from William Turner, *A new herbal*, 1551. © Royal Horticultural Society, Lindley Library

INDEX

Plate 159 (overleaf): Houseleek from Luigi Anguillara's Semplici *(1561)*

A NOTE ON THE AUTHOR

Anna Pavord is the gardening correspondent for the *Independent* and the author of eight previous books, including the bestselling *The Tulip*. She contributes to a number of magazines, both in the US and the UK, and regularly fronts programmes for BBC Radio 3 and 4. She chairs the Gardens Panel of the National Trust and sits on the Parks and Gardens Panel of English Heritage. She lives in Dorset, England, where she spent thirty years restoring the garden of an old rectory. She has recently moved to a new house and started another garden. She is married and has three daughters.